Undisputed

Also by Chris Jericho and
Peter Thomas Fornatale:

A Lion's Tale: Around the World in Spandex

Undisputed

How to Become the World Champion in 1,372 Easy Steps

BY CHRIS JERICHO

with Peter Thomas Fornatale

GRAND CENTRAL
PUBLISHING

NEW YORK   BOSTON

This book is a work of fiction. Names, characters, places, and incidents are the product of the author's imagination or are used fictitiously. Any resemblance to actual events, locales, or persons, living or dead, is coincidental.

Grand Central Publishing
Hachette Book Group
1290 Avenue of the Americas
New York, NY 10104

www.HachetteBookGroup.com

Grand Central Publishing is a division of Hachette Book Group, Inc. The Grand Central Publishing name and logo is a trademark of Hachette Book Group, Inc.

The publisher is not responsible for websites (or their content) that are not owned by the publisher.

Printed in the United States of America

Originally published in hardcover by Hachette Book Group
First mass market edition: February 2012

10 9 8 7

This book is dedicated to Sweet Loretta Modern.
It's also dedicated to all of the Jerichoholics
who have stood behind me through all
of the trials and tribulations
over the last twenty years.
If I were wearing a hat, I would tip it
to all of you.

CJ

Foreword

Wow, what an honor to write the foreword to Chris Jericho's new book! To be asked by Chris himself, no less. Yes, it's an honor—the same way it's an honor for an old, broken-down ballplayer to attend the game where his long-standing record is shattered. Yes, that's me, the old ballplayer, hobbling out onto the field, waving to the fans, doing my best to look happy when the thing that was most important to me, the thing that kept me going when the going got rough, the very thing that defined who I was and how I felt about myself has been stripped away from me.

You see, back some time ago, in another decade, in fact (I believe the year was 1999), I wrote a little something called *Have a Nice Day*, which shocked the world by being not only commercially successful but surprisingly readable as well. Possessing an underlying warmth to complement the sophomoric humor and wince-inducing stories, my book was like the literary equivalent to the early-'90s Lex Luger; it was indeed the "Total Package." It was also responsible for letting loose a flood of other wrestling books—some good, some bad, others downright ugly. But I was always confident that when that flood eventually subsided, there would be one book standing tall, refusing to be swept away with the rest of the wrestling refuse. Then Jericho had to send me his first book.

I must say, I really enjoyed an early, incomplete manuscript of *A Lion's Tale: Around the World in Spandex*— at first. I found myself rooting for Chris as he forged his way through the rough-and-tumble Canadian independent wrestling scene and feeling his pain as he attempted to clear hurdles both physical and psychological in wrestling meccas around the world—Mexico; Germany; Japan; Pikeville, Kentucky. But somewhere around Kentucky and Tennessee, in the middle of Bruiser Bedlam, Corny, Ricky, and Robert, I sat bolt upright in bed, my genuine enjoyment and hearty out-loud laughter turned to sheer terror in a heartbeat. "Oh no," I vividly remember thinking. "What if this book is better than mine?"

The wrestling world is full of unique characters, all of them with unique tales worth telling. Anyone who has spent any time on the road is sure to have a number of stories likely to fall under the "truth is stranger than fiction" category, and given the proper time and dedication to the craft of writing, many wrestlers might be capable of turning their true-life tales into first-rate tomes. Which meant my book would be safely ensconced at that number one spot in readers' hearts and minds pretty much forever. Quite simply, no pro wrestler was going to dedicate enough time and energy to producing a book that could ever do the subject true justice. Most wrestlers were going to tell their story to a hired hand for a given period of time and hope for the best. Sometimes the results were very good—and sometimes they weren't. Most of them just lacked that certain *something*, that authenticity that rings true only when a wrestler has spent hundreds of hours in solitude—thinking, being, and willing the words onto the written page. Yes, my spot was indeed safe—until Jericho came around.

All right, all right, Bret Hart's book is another notable exception, and is a tremendous read. But I think I identified with Chris's book more, with his ability to take both himself and his subject seriously while simultaneously giving a nod and a wink to the utter absurdity of so much that was going on around him. I identified so much that I spent many hours on the phone with Chris, giving him tips, offering advice—an adjective here, a little more emphasis there. Kind of like an all-star pitcher teaching a formidable opponent how to identify the spin on his curveball—so he can more easily crush it when next they meet.

And now Chris Jericho has written another book. Not only has he learned all the tricks of the trade, but he'll be directing his powerful prose and award-winning wit at subjects that *A Lion's Tale* left untouched: his incredible run in the WWE, his band Fozzy, the joys of fatherhood, and his memorable tenure on that *Duets* reality show. Along the way, he'll shed light and share perspectives on top WWE stars, and, best of all, will chart a memorable course into the mind of Vince McMahon.

Chris will remind readers on more than one occasion that a certain best-selling author/hardcore legend never defeated him in the ring. For that reason alone, I will never admit defeat on the literary battlefield, will never wave the white flag of surrender in the Foley-Jericho war of words. But if a reader happens to laugh a little louder

at his words than mine, or finds that his pages turn a little
faster and keep them awake a little longer, I'll try not to
protest too much. Because I know Chris Jericho is going
to crush this thing. Have fun, enjoy the book, feel free to
laugh out loud. I'll be over here, waving, pretending to be
happy, as I think back to the good old days of 1999.

Mick Foley

Bonus Foreword

I was talking about the new book while on a WWE tour of Puerto Rico in September of 2010, when Zack Ryder inquired why I hadn't asked him to write the foreword. When I replied that (a) I had already received a great one from Mick Foley and (b) Zack hadn't offered, he vowed that he would write one anyway and post it on Twitter for all the world to see.

Funny thing is, when he did, I really liked it, so I decided to include it in this book, unbeknownst to him.

WWWYKI.

CJ

When Chris asked that I write the foreword for his new book, I was thrilled. I could write about all the classic matches Chris has had or about all of the championships that he has won, but you're going to read about that in this book. I'm going to make this foreword a little more personal.

Like yours truly, Chris is a bro from Long Island. Maybe that's why I instantly became a Jerichoholic in the mid-1990s when he entered my living room via a television screen. I'll never forget searching for weeks for his WCW action figure; he was the hardest one to find in the set. When I was in ninth grade, I celebrated my birthday at the WWE's New York restaurant. Who did I pick to be on my cake? You guessed it: Y2J!

When I first started wrestling, I didn't shave my forearms because Chris didn't either. (Now I have to shave them because my lady likes me nice and smooth.) Speaking of body hair, Chris Naired my back once after a show. He confessed that it was one of the greatest moments of his career. In closing, whether you like him or not, Chris Jericho is the best in the world at what he does.

Woo Woo Woo. You Know It!

Zack Ryder

Contents

Contents

Undisputed

Introduction

The two dark shapes stared menacingly at me from the shadows of my closet.

I stared back at them the way a recovering amnesiac might look at himself in the mirror. I vaguely recognized what I was seeing but couldn't quite put a finger on it.

I knew I had seen them before; at one point they were my closest friends. I had been through wars, suffered my greatest losses, and enjoyed my biggest successes with them by my side.

But I hadn't seen them in over two years and wasn't quite sure what to say.

From the looks of them, they had seen better days. They were covered in dust, their once shiny exteriors reduced to a lackluster hue. Their eyeholes were coated thinly with rust just like I was, which was the reason I had traveled to the wilds of the back of my closet to rescue them.

I was going back to war and needed my closest companions by my side. I couldn't trust any others to do the job they could do. They were the best in the business at what they did, and I couldn't return without them.

I reached up and slowly grabbed my black patent leather wrestling boots off the shelf.

As I packed them in my bag, along with a pair of knee pads and some workout clothes, I wondered what it would be like to lace them up again. I would find out soon enough, as I was flying out later that day to Lance Storm's wrestling school in Calgary to get reacquainted with another old friend of mine—the ring.

I had been preparing for my return to the WWE for three months and it didn't seem like it had been two years since I'd been gone. It didn't seem like eight years since I'd debuted there either. It felt like only yesterday that I was standing in the Gorilla position at the Allstate Arena in Chicago, as the clock ticked down to zero...

CHAPTER 1

Petulant Pansy

When I stepped out into the bright arena light from the darkness of the Gorilla position, I had only two things on my mind: Judy Garland and my promo segment.

I now knew how Dorothy felt when she escaped out of the black-and-white monotony of Kansas into the garish colorful wonderland of Oz. I could relate because I was also escaping, from the bland world of WCW into the glimmering land of opportunity that was the WWE.

As soon as I breached the curtain and interrupted The Rock mid-promo, the crowd response was unbelievable. JERICHO signs were everywhere and people were jumping up and down with huge smiles on their faces, ecstatic that it was me that was the big surprise at the end of the countdown and not the return of the Gobbledy Gooker.

It seemed that half of the arena had been sent personal invitations from Vince McMahon himself alerting them to the fact that Jericho was appearing tonight. I hadn't really known what to expect from the crowd, but the moment I heard their reaction I knew that I had made the right decision in leaving WCW. Due to the buildup of my debut, I was already a bigger star in WWE after thirty seconds than I had been in WCW after three years.

I had been planning this moment for months and knew exactly what I wanted to do. I had seen Michael Jackson in concert in 1993 in Mexico City and had never forgotten the monumental entrance he made. He propelled up from underneath the stage and froze with his back to the crowd and his arms in a crucifix position for what seemed for hours as the crowd went nuts with anticipation. He didn't rush the moment or move a muscle. He just stood as stiff as a statue and took his sweet time before turning around and revealing himself. I wanted to do the same thing for my debut. So I stood with my back to the crowd in a Jesus Christ pose and let the crowd rumble. Even though the Titantron read JERICHO in ten-foot-high letters, it wasn't until I spun around and people saw my face that they really exploded.

I turned with a Paul Stanley pout on my face, although a shit-eating grin might have been more apropos. I surveyed the crowd, lifted the mic to my mouth, and bellowed, "Welcome to *Raw* Is Jericho!" a takeoff on the Monday Night Jericho catchphrase that I had used in WCW.

The Rock was less than thrilled that this petulant pansy had interrupted him mid-speech. Unfazed, I launched into a five-minute soliloquy about how the WWE had become boring and stagnant and how both the company and the fans were in desperate need of a savior, someone who would take the company into the new millennium. Someone like me. I proclaimed myself to be *the* party host, the man who would inspire the entire world to chant, "Go Jericho Go!" whenever they saw me.

At this point The Rock cut me off and asked, "What is your name again?"

"My name is—"

"It doesn't matter what your name is!"

The fans in the arena, who didn't know who I was or what I was doing, erupted with glee that I had been shut up. The Rock continued his verbal assault by addressing my Y2J moniker.

"You talk about your Y2J plan, well, The Rock has a little plan of his own, the K-Y Jelly plan, which means The Rock is gonna lube his size 13 boot real good, turn that sumbitch sideways, *and stick it straight up your candy ass*!"

As a heel, my job was to sell his oral beatdown, and that I did. The problem was, I sold it like a scalded dog (Jim Ross™) and got this look on my face like I was about to cry. It was a trick I picked up in WCW, but I was soon to discover that the type of heel I was used to playing didn't fly in the brave new world of the WWE.

As a result, in the course of a couple of minutes within my first promo, I went from a confident, cocky Y2Jack the Lad to a whining, huffy crybaby. I was trying to go all out to be the bad guy, but in doing so I turned myself into a comedy figure—the type of heel that can't be taken too seriously. Even though it was a great entrance and a classic WWE moment, watching it now makes me cringe because I would never act that way anymore. But in 1999 I didn't know any better. Instead of keeping any badass credibility, I became a cowardly cartoon. It should have taken a lot more than one insult to turn me into a sniveling baby.

The worst part came at the end of the promo when The

Rock unleashed his patented "If you smel-l-l-l-l-l what
The Rock is cooking!" For some reason, I contorted my
face into a sulky Popeye-like grimace, as if I'd just found
Bluto snorting spinach off of Olive Oyl's naked ass.

It was the wrong card to play on my first night in the
WWE. My cowardly heel routine made it hard for the
audience to believe that I was a credible opponent for a
megastar like The Rock, even though that was the initial
plan. Because of my Popeye puss, that train was derailed
before it left the station.

However, there were a few other reasons why I didn't
get into a program with The Rock right from the get-go.
For one thing, I was coming from WCW, which, being
enemy territory, automatically put me under a giant
microscope. Another problem was that matches in the
WWE were constructed in a totally different way than
they were in WCW, a way that was completely foreign to
me. In WCW, we pretty much did whatever we wanted
in the ring, but in the WWE the style was much more
serious and structured. In WCW, I was able to keep my
head above water by acting as ridiculous as I could and
performing whatever comedy bits I could think of to get
noticed. But now that my head was above water and the
spotlight was on me, I still kept doing what I did best, and
that wasn't my role anymore. It wasn't what Vince wanted
from me, even though nobody ever really told me what it
was that he did want. On top of all that, I had this huge
buildup coming into the company that left me with a target on my back bigger than Val Venis's penis. I found out
very quickly that it didn't matter what I had accomplished
or what my reputation was outside of the WWE walls,
I had to prove myself all over again from scratch. And

I'd failed round one with my goofy reactions to Rocky's words.

I spent weeks writing my debut promo, and afterwards I kept writing my promos unassisted, only going over them briefly with head writer Vince Russo before each show. I decided it would be a good idea to go into full-on creep mode and insult the other superstars in the WWE, accusing them of being boring and only half as talented as me. I was never really given a specific directive to insult people, but I knew that my character thought the company was boring and stagnant, and I was there to shake things up. Russo listened to my ideas and told me, "Great, go with it."

After each promo I didn't get any feedback from Russo (or anybody else), so I figured that meant everything was good. I was intimidated by the aura of Vince McMahon and I never asked him what he thought I should do, even though in retrospect that would have been a good idea. Wrestling is like a giant high school clique, and if you're the new guy who comes in looking different and acting different, you're going to get blasted for it—mostly behind your back. With zero allies in my new company, I had nobody to stand up for me when my back was turned. Even worse, because I didn't really ask Vince or any of the boys for advice, I came across as an arrogant prick who thought he knew it all. Unbeknownst to me, I was stockpiling massive amounts of nuclear heat in the process.

After a few weeks in the company, I was in a difficult spot. On one hand, insulting everybody else was a great way to come in and make a name for myself, sharing screen time with the company's biggest stars and showcasing my promo skills. On the other hand, the more I verbally buried the big names, the more trouble I amassed for myself. To them I'm sure I was this little peon who'd been feuding in WCW with Prince Iaukea and was now getting this big push without the know-how to back it up.

When I first signed with the WWE, I asked Vince, "What do you want me to do?" He said, "Don't worry, I'm going to be watching you like a hawk. I'll tell you what I want you to do and what I don't want you to do. If I don't like something, I'll let you know. You are going to be one of my pet projects."

He had spent a lot of money to get me; a guaranteed contract of $450,000 was a very big deal at the time. He had heard great things about me, and seen a couple sparks that convinced him I might be the real deal; but he wasn't exactly on the Jericho Ho Train yet. I didn't suspect that something might be wrong, because if there was I figured Vince would tell me.

But he didn't and there was.

My second night in the company was at a *Raw* taping in Milwaukee. The plan was for me to interrupt The Undertaker, the most respected wrestler in the locker room and one of the biggest stars in the company. He was calling himself the Personification of Evil at the time, so I began my promo by calling him the personification of boring and proceeded to tell the crowd how bland and mediocre he was.

Maybe this wouldn't have been such a problem if Taker hadn't just cut a fifteen-minute promo about how he and Big Show were riding their motorcycles in the desert and they ran out of gas and Big Show picked up a scorpion and ate it or something...a promo that really *was* incredibly boring.

He knew it was boring, the crowd knew it was boring, Vince knew it was boring, Funaki knew it was boring. So when I came out and called him on it, I made things even worse because I was kicking him when he was down.

Taker responded to my claims by saying that he had more shower time than I had ring time. At first I thought he was bragging about his personal hygiene (maybe he was a clean and freshly scrubbed Deadman), until I figured out that he was really saying I was wet behind the ears and should know my role and shut the fuck up. Backstage afterwards, I walked past Shawn Michaels, who glared at me incredulously and offered the following advice: "The next time you cut a promo, maybe you want to avoid calling the biggest star in the company and the leader of the locker room boring." It was a friendly warning from HBK to watch my mouth.

I'd told Taker before the promo that I was gonna stick it to him and he'd told me to go for it. However, I crossed the line and insulted him by saying what I said. I can't believe the lack of respect I showed him and so many of the other guys in the locker room during my first month in the company, especially since I knew how important the hierarchy of the business was (and still is). Respect your elders. That aphorism had been drummed into my head my entire career, but I was so caught up in trying to be revolutionary and controversial that I forgot. And my absentmindedness cost me.

In just two short days I had more heat than Al Pacino and Robert De Niro combined. I was playing a character and didn't really believe the shit I was saying, but everyone thought I did and assumed I was an arrogant prick who thought his shit didn't stink (believe me, it does).

The original plan for my appearance in Milwaukee was for me to cut a promo on Steve Austin where I was going to talk about how he was a drunk who shaved his head bald in order to hide his receding hairline. In retrospect I'm glad that it changed, because Steve is a lot less diplomatic than Taker and I'm sure he would've opened a can of political and verbal whoop-ass on me. But things were bad enough as it was and my Walls were cracking.

I just had no idea how quickly they were about to come tumblin' rumblin' down.

The fact that Vince didn't give me any insight or guidance to what was expected from me or my promos is still confusing, especially since he was so hands-on regarding every other aspect of my career right down to the name of my finish.

I'd started to use the Boston Crab in WCW and dubbed it the Liontamer. But Vince didn't like the name because he thought it was too close to Ken Shamrock's Lion's Den training facility. "I've got too many lions running around here," he said.

So the edict went out to creative to come up with a new name for the move. You could hire one hundred monkeys and have them type for one hundred years and they wouldn't have come up with the shit I was presented.

I was handed a list of some of the worst names for a finish ever: the Salad Shooter (a takeoff on the Sharpshooter, named after an infomercial product), the Rock and Roll Finisher (because I was a rock and roller and this was my finisher...get it?), and the Stretch Armstrong. You read that right—the Stretch Fucking Armstrong (you want to take a crack explaining that one? Cos I got nothin'...). Someone was actually getting paid to think of this stuff. Then again, these were the same brainchildren who suggested changing Billy Gunn's name to Billy Bitchcakes.

After eating the list, pooping it out, eating it again, and vomiting it back up, I decided to take matters into my own hands. I thought about calling my hold the Vertebreaker (pre–Shane Helms), but Vince didn't like that. I asked HHH for suggestions and he came up with the STD—the Standing Torture Device. I have no idea if he was ribbing me or not, but while it wouldn't have been a bad idea if I were Val Venis rocking the pornstar gimmick, it didn't seem quite right for me. So I went back to the German power metal well and took another idea from Helloween, whose first album was called *Walls of Jericho*. I suggested that to Vince and he liked it, even though it didn't really make sense. But it was better than Billy Bitchcakes.

SEP.-14'99(TUE) 17:14   VINCENT K. MCMAHON   P. 002

cc: Chris Jericho

BETH ZAZZA

From:
Sent:
To:
Cc:
Subject: Jericho's finishing move

I did not see the first round of names that was sent to you, so I hope none of these are duplicates.

The Millenium Crash
Jericho Shutdown
Turn of the Century
The Bender
Y2Korkscrew
Ball-Dropper
Cloverleaf 2000
Back to the Future
Apocalypse
Big Finish
Y-2-3
The Whammer Jammer
The J Factor
Y2J Blitz
Jeri-KO'er
The Concluder
The Vanquisher
The Embarrasser! (that move is pretty degrading!)
Double Leg Vise of Torment
Figure Y2J Leglock
Millenium Buster
Y2J Catastrophe
Millenium Cruncher
Jerichonium of Pain
Lion Clutch Press
The Party favor
Eve of Destruction
Millenium Melt Down   CRASH COURSE
Twist of fate
The Savior Screw   SYMBOL OF SALVATION
The heroes welcome
Rock and Roller   END TIME
HUMILIATOR   END OF TIME
BUY RATE   END OF THE AGE
FINAL COUNTDOWN   DOOMSDAY DEVICE
APOCALYPSE NOW   POWER SLAVE
TIME'S UP   SAVIOUR SELF
TIME KILLER   NO ESCAPE
KILLING TIME   1   JERICOIL
WALL OF JERICHO

The second list of finishing hold names sent to me by the office.
As bad as the Salad Shooter and Rock and Roll Finisher were,
the Whammer Jammer, Y-2-3, and the Embarrasser (that move
is pretty degrading!) are much worse. My ideas are written at
the bottom.

CHAPTER 2

Prematurely Ejaculating Nightsticks

Due to a strange twist of happenstance, my debut match for the WWE happened to be in my hometown of Winnipeg.

During the first month of my arrival I didn't have any matches; I only cut promos on the fans, telling them how great I was and building up anticipation for my eventual first match. The original plan for the Peg was for me to cut a babyface promo professing my love for the prairies and how I still considered Winnipeg home. Then after I sucked them in I was going to turn the tide by saying how happy I was to have moved away from this freezing cesspool because I was embarrassed to have grown up there—a typical heel 101 promo.

But on the day of the show there was a bomb threat at Miami International Airport that prevented The Rock (and even worse, D-Lo Brown!) from flying into Winnipeg. Tears were shed over the absence of Brown, but since The Rock was in the main event of the show against

The Big Bossman in a Nightstick on a Pole match, his nonattendance was much more dire. Fearing a riot by the packed house of crazy Canadians, the office went into a panic. Who could replace The Rock? Who could fill the massive boots of The Brahma Bull? Who could save the day and electrify the fans like The Great One? Chris Effin' Jericho, that's who!!

So I was tapped to be The Rock's replacement, but unfortunately I had ignored the number one rule of wrestling—always bring your gear. So I sped thirty minutes back to my mom's house to get my tights and got back to the arena just in time to hear the announcement that The Rock was not going to be there but Chris Jericho would be wrestling instead.

Eight thousand fans farted in unison.

Actually they began cheering and throwing their panties in the air, even the dudes. They were going to get to see their hometown hero make his WWE wrestling debut in front of their very eyes!

I was pretty excited myself, as it was the first time I had wrestled in the arena where I had first seen my heroes Hulk Hogan, the High Flyers, Shawn Michaels, Ricky Steamboat, and Randy Savage in action. It was within these hallowed walls that I discovered my love for the business, and it was within this old barn I would have my debut match in the WWE.

The idea of a Nightstick on a Pole match was that you had to climb a pole sticking up out of the turnbuckle and grab the nightstick, which you could then use to brutalize your opponent in any way you saw fit. The nightstick was several feet above the turnbuckle, so you had to climb to the top rope, shimmy up the pole, and get the weapon. This allowed for plenty of drama as the two foes attempted to climb only to be knocked down just before they could grab the stick. It was a fun and easy match—under normal circumstances.

Hearing the crowd's reaction when my name was announced gave me a chubski. When I walked through the curtain, the roar I received was so loud it made the response I got in Chicago seem like the reaction for a Bullet Boys reunion. Peggers were jumping up and down, holding JERICHO signs in one hand, draft beers in the other, and giving each other high fives with both. In retrospect, I'm glad I didn't go through with the heel promo. Sometimes you have to give the people what they want.

I got in the ring and surveyed the crowd—*my* crowd—and got ready to give them exactly what they wanted: a great performance from their new hero. I had gone from sitting in that same crowd fantasizing about being in the ring, to actually being there.

My dream had come true! The circle of life had closed! I had returned to Winnipeg to entertain the fans the same way I had once been entertained, and I was going to reward them by having the greatest five-star match of all time in honor of my fans, my friends, my family, my . . .

"Knock knock."

"Who's there?"

"It's the Jericho Curse and I'm back, bitch!"

Ahhhh yes, my old nemesis was back in the hood and he was pissed. It had been a while and he was ready for more revenge than Bruce Kulick.

I'll never forget the roar of the crowd when the bell

rang to start the match. I'll also never forget the feeling I had when I gave Bossman a shoulder tackle and the nightstick hit the mat two seconds after he did.

At first I thought someone in the crowd had thrown their own nightstick into the ring, but when I glanced up at the pole I realized that it was our nightstick that was lying there. Someone had forgotten to properly tie it to the pole, which allowed it to fall off its perch as soon as Bossman shook the ring with his first bump. The weapon was a mere eight inches from where I was standing, and instead of an exciting match full of drama and suspense, we now had a game of pickup stick.

We spent the remainder of the match trying to grab the baton rolling around in the middle of the ring. We scrambled for it like a fumble and it kept slipping through our hands, as if it were a greased Steely Dan. The match absolutely sucked and the Jericho Curse—ensuring that my first match in any new company was terrible—had struck again.

Oh how I hated that inglorious bastard.

No one else really cared that the bout was bad, especially not The Bossman. He was laughing the whole time and for him it was just another match that would be forgotten the next day. But for me it was my first match in the WWE, and instead of it ending up outstanding, it ended up in the outhouse.

But there were some positives to focus on. After I won the match for the fine people of Winnipeg, I told the fans to meet me at Wise Guys, a local night club. The bar owner was so excited by my free advertisement that he gave me free lifetime drinks—the fact that it closed down about a year later is irrelevant. It was a true homecoming, as all of my friends were there congratulating me and telling me how proud of me they were. They thought the match had been great and didn't care about little details like prematurely ejaculating nightsticks. The place was packed, and as I looked around I saw a lot of the same friends who had been to see me at Georgie's eight years earlier working in front of eighty people. It was nice to know they'd stuck with me long enough to see me working in front of eight thousand people at the Arena.

When I first started wrestling, there were four places I dreamed about working: the Winnipeg Arena, Korakuen Hall in Tokyo, Arena Mexico in Mexico City, and Madison Square Garden in New York City. Within two months of joining the WWE, I finished achieving that dream when weeks after the disaster in the Peg I made my debut at the Garden. MSG is the world's most famous arena and the place where my father, Ted Irvine, a.k.a. the Baby-Faced Assassin, enjoyed his glory years in the NHL playing for the New York Rangers. I still remember sitting in the stands at the Garden as a four-year-old kid, complaining about the noise and getting mad at my dad because he never looked at me while he was playing. I thought the least he could do when he was skating down the ice on a breakaway was smile and wave.

MSG is a barometer for stardom within the business, and as the old saying goes, "If you can make it there, you can make it anywhere." If the fans responded to a performer in MSG, it went a long way with the McMahon family in determining who would get pushed as a star. Vince's father believed that and so did he. The shows at the Garden are still so important that Vince attends almost every one whether they are televised or not.

Once again I was scheduled to cut a promo about how I was going to save the WWE from its mediocre self. Vince wanted my opening line to be: "Welcome to Madison Square Jericho," after which I would insult the fans of New York City and tell them how much better I was than them.

The reaction I received as I walked to the ring was the ying to the Winnipeg yang. People were booing and calling me names—Y2Gay was a favorite—and I was drawing some good heel heat. I marched to the center of the ring and surveyed the crowd with an arrogant glare.

"Welcome to Madison Square Jericho!" I proclaimed pompously into the mic as the crowd jeered.

"I am the savior of the W—E!" Huh? Halfway through my tagline, the mic cut out momentarily, muting the second *W*.

Undeterred, I continued with my scathing promo, preparing to infuriate the NYC faithful.

"My g—tss knows n—b—dries! I—" Now the mic was stuttering worse than ECW-era Bubba Ray Dudley, rendering my scathing promo useless.

"I'm gonna do—what—Mad—n—cho!"

Apparently, the Jericho Curse had diverted from its usual habits and had decided to take charge of the MSG soundboard that night. Due to the technical difficulties, my reaction went from boos to catcalls to silence to laughter. I felt like a complete fool and threw the mic down in frustration, which only served to intensify the guffaws of the New York brethren. To make matters worse, Vince was watching the whole debacle from the wings, shaking his head in disbelief.

My night didn't get any better either. Later on, I was supposed to run in during a Steve Blackman–Ken Shamrock match, distract Shamrock, and have him chase me out of the building. Shamrock was an MMA fighter turned wrestler who wasn't quite in on our joke. In his mind, if he was supposed to chase me, he was going to chase me at full speed—and he did. I ran down the aisle and when he spotted me he charged as fast as he could. I knew if he caught me he would hurt me, so I took off down the aisle like Ben Johnson post water bottle swig.

When we raced through the curtain out of the audience's view, I slowed down but he didn't, and he tackled me as hard as he could in the hallway.

"Ken, did you really need to tackle me? Nobody can even see you!"

"I knew I could catch you," he replied laconically.

I have a feeling he would've chased me all the way to Yonkers until he did.

Next up was *SummerSlam*, and my assignment was to cut yet another promo, this time on D-Generation X member Road Dogg. Dogg hit the ring to massive cheers and did his patented introduction for himself: "I'm the R-to-the-O-to-the-A-to-the-D-to-the D-to-the-O-to-the-Double-G."

I interrupted him with my patented countdown clock (which had gone from ten seconds, to five seconds, to a much more efficient three seconds) and told him, "You think you're impressing everyone by spelling 'Road Dogg'? Big deal. If you want to impress me, spell 'lugubrious.'" The camera showed a close-up of his face as he mouthed, "I don't even know what that means."

It was one of the few good segments in my early WWE career. I was in the groove that night and Road Dogg totally sold my verbal barbs. But even at that, it was one of the biggest shows of the year and I was still only doing a promo. I was the one feeling lugubrious.

My first televised WWE match was on the very first episode of *Smackdown!* against Road Dogg. Backstage, I saw the sheet listing the matches for the night, but it looked different than what I was used to in WCW. Beside the listing of Chris Jericho vs. Road Dogg were a pair of initials. I asked what they meant and was told they were the initials of the agent who would assist us in putting together our match.

Someone to help us with our match? That was new to me.

In WCW, there were no agents. We would walk into an office in the arena that was deemed the War Room and the booker, Kevin Sullivan, would tell us who was winning, how much time we had, and that was about it. We would be expected to do the rest ourselves, with no direction from the office at all. But here in the WWE veteran former wrestlers were hired solely to work with the younger talent and help us put together the best possible match we could, using guidelines set by Vince himself.

Everybody was working together to produce the best match—what a concept.

Unfortunately, even though my agent, Blackjack Lanza, did the best he could to help us, my match with Road Dogg was mediocre at best, and afterwards Russo had a new plan for me. He decided that I needed a bodyguard, someone who could do my dirty work. What I didn't know when I agreed to the plan was that the guy they wanted to put me with was Mr. Hughes. Curtis

Hughes was a former football player who used to weigh 400 pounds, but by the time they put him with me he was down to about 250. I started calling him "Curtis Huge," but Vince didn't like the moniker because he'd lost a ton of weight and wasn't so huge anymore. As a matter of fact, he was pretty much the same size as me. But Russo thought Hughes looked great and was hell-bent on putting the two of us together.

I didn't care for him from the start. He loved to talk shit about how good he was. He constantly bragged about how his sunglasses never came off during his matches...like that was somehow the secret to becoming the next Lou Thesz. Combine that with the fact that Hughes was also narcoleptic—he could fall asleep at any time and once did in the ring mid-backdrop—and you can see I had a real dandy of a bodyguard.

Another thing that bugged me about Hughes was that our ring attire didn't match. I was wearing flashy rave shirts and leather pants, while he wore cheap black jeans and a ratty black T-shirt. So I gave him one of my blue sparkly shirts and told him to cut the sleeves off. He did and proceeded to wear it every single time he came to the ring. I thought he might get the hint and buy a new wardrobe but he didn't.

He just fell asleep.

My first official *Raw* match was against The Rock. Even though it was only a few months after one of the biggest debuts in WWE history, I'd lost so much steam in the eyes of the office at that point that our monumental first match was aired for free and Rock beat me clean. Our feud was being blown off before it ever started, which was peculiar for two reasons: (1) the match had been built from my first night in, and (2) I was the one with a bodyguard, which gave him an out if he lost, so why would he go over clean?

Jim Ross said before the match, "We've got Jericho vs. The Rock next, this should be a classic!" Good ol' JR doesn't say anything he doesn't mean, but despite his lofty expectations our match ended up being about as classic as the Gary Cherone Van Halen lineup. Rocky is one of my favorite opponents ever and we ended up having great chemistry, but in our first match together that chemistry was zilch, zippo, nada, bupkus (Thesaurus Author's Note: Insert other word of your choice for *nonexistent* here).

One of the biggest problems was that I still hadn't learned how to be a WWE-style heel, which required a serious, strong beatdown of the babyface during the heat, followed by quick bumping and feeding for said baby-face during the comeback. In WCW, you would just take a bump, stay down, and sell it. But in the WWE you had to jump up and down as fast as you could in order to constantly sell for the babyface. I didn't know that yet and looked lazy and slow throughout the match, and I could tell Rock was wondering what the hell I was doing.

Ugh. Nobody told me there'd be days like these...

The match had no flow and was totally scatterbrained. I was trying too hard instead of just letting my basic skills and instinct shine through. I had morphed back into 1996 Jericho during my first WCW match against Mr. JL. I was choppy and a complete klutz, like I'd been possessed by the spirit of Matt (not Mick) Foley and had moved into a van down by the river.

But the worst was yet to come.

When Rock threw me over the barrier and into the crowd, I spotted a soda cup on the floor and decided it would be cool to throw it into his face. So I did. Except the liquid in the cup wasn't Sprite—it was spit.

I had thrown someone's tobacco dip cup into the face of the biggest star in the WWE.

I was mortified. Rocky was disgusted. Hughes was sleeping.

Up to that point, Rocky had been one of the only guys in the company who was good to me, and I had disrespected him with a pure rookie mistake, on live television no less.

Even though I apologized a thousand times, he had every right to tear into me, but he never did. I think he felt bad for me because when he first started in the company he was in a situation similar to mine: a guy who was brought in to be a star but wasn't up for it at first and everybody hated him as a result.

But he certainly wasn't happy about being doused in winter mint saliva, and he must have showered for forty-five minutes that night.

After I had given Rock a worse facial than Erik Everhard ever could, I just wanted the match to end, and mercifully it soon did. Hughes slid a chair into the ring, but before I could use it, Rocky turned the tables and gave me his patented Rock Bottom on it. However Hughes was tired, and instead of sliding the chair into the ring with the smooth side up, Sleepy slid the chair in upside down. So when Rocky slammed me onto its raised metal edges it almost killed me—but not as badly as the match itself did.

After Rock covered me for the win, I woke Hughes up and we skulked to the back, both of us knowing that we'd just stunk up the joint. On the way to the sanctuary of the dressing room, Jeff Jarrett and Road Dogg asked me, "So how did it go?"—which is wrestler code for, "I saw your match and it sucked bagski."

A few days later I started hearing rumors that Vince and the other higher-ups within the company thought I couldn't work. Who could blame them? I hadn't shown anything since my arrival that would make them think otherwise. The combination of my thinking that I was better than I was (which wasn't arrogance so much as ignorance), my unfamiliarity with the WWE style, and my cowardly, comedic heel tendencies caused me to make a record-time plunge from Vince's penthouse to Vince's outhouse.

And I was about to get shit on.

Looking back now, I think one of the biggest problems I faced at the beginning of my WWE career stemmed from the fact that Vince Russo loved the character I played in WCW. He loved my cowardly heel comedy schtick and wanted me to continue in that vein. I played that character in WCW because I wasn't getting any attention from the office anyway and had nothing to lose. In the WWE main event world, money players couldn't be comedians or cowards all the time, and I had been brought in to be a major player. Major players have to be believable, and in Vince's mind while there can be elements of comedy to them, people have to believe they can kick somebody's ass. Russo didn't see things that way and kept booking me in all these preposterous WCW-esque situations.

As a result, I was caught in the middle, and I ain't talkin' about Ronnie James Dio.

After the Hughes experiment tanked, Curtis went into hibernation and I was instead saddled with Howard Finkel, who was earmarked to be the WWE version of Ralphus. I began a program with Ken Shamrock, which started with me being lowered into the ring inside of a shark cage, like Richard Dreyfuss in *Jaws*. I called Ken out, telling him that I wasn't in the cage to protect *me* from him; I was in the cage to protect *him* from me.

Ken pried the bars open and I freaked out and escaped. Backstage, Shamrock found Finkel in a blond wig, thinking that he was me. As he was accosting Harold (as I called him), I snuck up from behind, slammed Shamrock's head in a car door, and put him in the Walls as Harold took pictures.

The next week Russo decided he wanted me to wear a suit of armor—yes, an actual suit of armor—for a First Blood match on *Raw*, with the idea being I couldn't bleed if I was wearing it.

Let me ask you, dear reader, have you ever tried to wear a suit of armor? Great Caesar's Ghost, it's almost impossible to put on because—well, it's a suit of fucking armor! I wriggled and struggled gingerly to affix each section of the metal bodysuit to my extremities, trying not to gouge myself to death. Then, once I finally got it on, it was like being in a tin can with the top opened. There were all of these sharp edges cutting and digging into me. At one point I took a big step to the left and thought the codpiece was gonna saw my ballbag clean off. There was no way I was going to be able to work a match in this thing without slicing myself up worse than Abdullah the Butcher's forehead.

As a compromise, I came up with the idea of wearing

full hockey gear, including a helmet with a face cage. The show was in Dallas, whose team had played Buffalo in the NHL playoffs that year, so of course I wore a Sabres jersey for cheap heat. I walked down the ramp and got a great nasty reaction from the crowd, but just as I got to the ring the referee told me to go back to the Gorilla position. It turned out that Vince wanted Shamrock to go to the ring first, otherwise why would he face me if he saw me standing there wearing hockey gear? The fact that he was the world's most dangerous man was good enough reason for me. It was a taped show, so I went out to the ring again, but this time the reaction to my enemy jersey was lukewarm at best. The surprise had been ruined, and as I walked out to a chorus of crickets and tumbleweeds I couldn't help but think that, once again, I had been stricken by fate in a bad way. I was dying more deaths in the WWE than Jason Voorhees.

It was decided that Shamrock and I would have the blowoff match for our angle at the next PPV, *Unforgiven*. We were booked on a few live events beforehand to work on our chemistry, which was a good thing because we had none. In San Diego I backed him up against the ropes, bent his head back, and unleashed a wicked chop to the center of his chest.

"Haaaaaaa!!" I said in defiance. "Ahhhhhh!" I said in anguish two seconds later as Shamrock stuck my head up my ass. He took me down to the mat, snorting and grunting as he bent me into more positions than Jenna Jameson. I screamed at him, asking why he had taken such offense to my chop.

"I don't like those chops. They're bullshit and they don't hurt, and I'm not going to sell them."

Fair enough, but I kindly suggested the next time I did something he didn't like, to simply *tell* me about it instead of turning me into human origami.

For the finish, I was supposed to hit him with a steel chair, but when I went to ringside to grab one, all I saw were the red comfy padded kind. Needless to say, the viciousness of a chair shot is kind of diluted when the object in question is covered with a plush red feather pillow. I was expected to clock the World's Most Dangerous Man with a weapon that the Girls Next Door would use to arouse Hugh Hefner's horn.

But the soft satin sex toy was all that was available, so I improvised and whacked him over the head. Shamrock looked at me with disgust as the crowd went mild. Afterward I got in trouble from agent Jack Lanza for not making sure there was a proper steel chair at ringside. Since when was checking the furniture around the ring my job? I was surprised I didn't get in trouble for not checking the bathroom for extra toilet paper too.

Shamrock ended up pulling out of our PPV match on the day of the show with a neck injury and was replaced by X-Pac. I had some ideas I wanted to try with Ken that I thought would work with Pac as well, but he didn't show up until about 4:30 for the eight o'clock show. When he arrived, I told him I had some ideas for the Shamrock match that I wanted to transfer over to him. It was such a stupid concept, because Pac and Ken were total opposites in the ring, but I was convinced that the match I'd plotted out was a classic, and I wanted to stick to it.

I was really wrong.

X-Pac's signature move was the Bronco Buster, where the other guy would be lying prone in the corner and he'd stick his X-Cock into his opponent's face, and ride that shit up and down. I had to be different, so I wanted to take a Shawn Michaels turnbuckle flip upside down into the turnbuckle, and X-Pac would give me a reverse Bronco Buster. I figured the Michaels turnbuckle bump would prove my mettle and totally save my WWE career. Of course I completely botched it, flipping poorly and not making it all the way up into the corner. When X-Pac did the reverse Bronco Buster, it looked terrible. His crotch and my mouth were in the same place and he didn't have my legs to support him. The crowd didn't react at all to my impromptu blowjob and they didn't react to the horrible DQ finish either. X-Pac was a smart worker and the match should've been good, but it wasn't. I just couldn't get it together.

Later on I asked X-Pac what he thought about the bout and he said, "It was what it was."

Translation: "That sucked, my friend, and we both know it." The Jericho Curse was refusing to leave the party and was vomiting all over the furniture to boot. I began to wonder if I'd ever have a good match again.

To make matters worse, my new Chris Jericho shirt bombed. The first piece of Y2J merchandise was a black T-shirt with "Y2J" printed in electric blue on the front and a mock definition of the term on the back. It was a huge success.

For the second shirt I had the idea of doing a shiny rave shirt similar to the ones I wore, with "Y2J" on one of the breast pockets. However, instead of embroidering the name on, the production company stitched a cheesy black patch in the middle of the silver material that stuck out like a sore ass. The shirt resembled what a gas station attendant would wear to a club, looked terrible, and sold accordingly. It did about twelve units, and thousands of dollars went down the drain courtesy of Calamity Jane Jericho.

I was in over my head in the WWE and desperately needed an ally I could trust to come in and watch my back. My first choice was Lenny St. Clair, my old friend from Calgary who had finished up as Dr. Luther in Japan and was now living in Seattle. I believed in Lenny and knew he was a good worker who could play any character and personify any gimmick that was thrown at him. I went to Vince and said, "I have a friend who's a great performer and I'd like to get him a tryout."

"Is he a good human being?" Vince asked.

When I affirmed that he was, Vince sent me to Russo, who asked to see some photos and a tape. After all the years Lenny had been on the job, he'd never assembled a decent highlight video, so I took some of his matches and rented an editing suite. I put together a four-minute clip of his best stuff with "The Call of Ktulu" by Metallica in the background and handed it to Russo.

I wanted him to get the job because he deserved a break and, more important to me, I needed someone to help me combat the opposition I was facing. Unfortunately, after a few tryouts and bad breaks, Lenny didn't get the gig.

My one-man wolfpack remained intact.

CHAPTER **3**

Schizo Deluxe

I always prided myself on being a good performer who could get a decent match out of anyone, but now I had become the guy that nobody could get a good match with. It was completely unacceptable to me and I knew that time was running out. I needed to find somebody who could teach me the style and psychology I needed to get my head above water—and there was one man I knew who could do that.

Pat Patterson had wrestled around the world for years until finishing his in-ring career in the WWE, but it was as a backstage booker, advisor, and agent that he achieved his biggest success. Pat is a wrestling Jedi and the smartest man I've ever met in wrestling. He taught me 90 percent of what I know about how to put together a match, and when I first approached him I had no idea how little I really knew about the psychology of the business.

Every week I hung around Pat and picked his brain. He'd always been friendly to me, as we were both Canadian and he knew I'd trained in Calgary. His love and respect for Bret Hart led us to talk about the famous sixty-minute match Bret and Shawn Michaels had at *Wrestle-Mania XII*. Pat had been brought out of retirement at the request of the two of them to be the agent on the match, and he helped put it together. He was also the agent for all of The Rock's matches, which was one of the reasons why they were always good (my first match with Rocky notwithstanding). I told him I felt that I could be as valuable to the company as The Rock if I could only learn a few tricks and make a few changes to my work, which wasn't an egotistical statement as much as a straight-from-the-heart sentiment. I had all of these tools and experiences that so many other guys in the locker room didn't, but I had no idea how to use them. I had the magic spells but no magic wand, and Pat was the wizard who could help me find it.

Pat was from Montreal and had a thick French accent with a thick sense of humor to go with it, telling the same bad jokes over and over again:

"Hey, do you know who was asking about you the other day?"

"Who?"

"Nobody!!!"

"Hey Chris, your match was taken off the show."

"Really?"

"Yeah, it was canceled due to lack of interest!!"

After each moldy oldie, he would walk away howling at his comic genius.

Pat also had an affinity for butchering the English language with his French Canadian accent, which made him sound like Adam Sandler's talking goat.

"When the Dudleys Boy hit the ring, DVD hits JYD with the Sprog Flash."

Translation: "When the Dudley Boyz hit the ring, RVD hits Y2J with the Frog Splash."

He didn't know the meaning of *superimposed* either.

But Pat was deadly serious when it came to wrestling and he had no problem giving his opinion about the flaws in my work. His first piece of advice was to stop working like I was still in another country. He helped me to understand that every territory I worked in was different. Mexico was different from Japan, which was different from Germany, which was different from ECW, which was different from Smoky Mountain. But for some reason, I had figured that WCW and the WWE were the same style with the same requirements needed to be a main event performer. Not that I had a clue what it took to be a top guy in WCW, as I had never worked with Sting, Luger, Hall, Nash, Hogan, or Savage. All I knew was what I had learned in other countries over the years, and that wasn't enough to be a top star in the WWE.

Pat helped me realize that I wasn't as good as I thought I was—but that I could be. He saw the same thing in me that I did: the desire to be the best and the drive and talent to get there. From then on, I listened to everything he told me and tried to pattern my thought processes after his. I hung on his every word and studied each of his principles. We watched my matches together and I took notes as he critiqued my performance while I carried him on my back in a little sling through the swamps of Dagobah.

Pat explained to me that it was the little details that made a good worker into a great worker: timing, listening to the crowd, giving them what they want—or don't want. You had to have a crispness with everything you did in the ring. At the time, when I threw someone off the ropes, I wasn't following through with my arms or putting enough effort into it. Pat pulled me aside and told me that the way I was doing it looked bad and explained the right way to do it. To this day, I still see his face whenever I push a guy off the ropes.

Another agent who helped me develop into a legitimate WWE star was Blackjack Lanza, a retired wrestler in his sixties, whose autograph my dad got for me in 1978. He was very blunt in his criticisms that he delivered while chain-smoking, which meant that you usually got a lungful whenever he spoke. My matches were so bad at the time, I'm surprised I didn't get cancer from all the secondhand smoke I inhaled during the nonstop criticism he gave me.

But it was easy to wind Jack up during the shows, and the boys would always pull different tricks on him to get him going.

Once in Miami, Mick Foley (who has never beaten me in a wrestling match) walked through the curtain on his way to the ring and said, "Watch how Lanza reacts to this!" He grabbed the mic and told 15,000 fans how he was at the beach that day and a fan ran up to him with a copy of *Have a Nice Day* (available at fine bookstores near you). But before he was able to get it signed, he slipped in a puddle of suntan lotion that Mick had carelessly left on the beach. The guy fell down hard and threw his back out. As he was lying there writhing in pain, he looked up and said, "Mick, I can't make it to the show tonight." Mick was devastated and told him, "I'm so sorry you can't make it, is there anything I can do?" The guy said, "Yes, Mick—win one for the Slipper."

Seven of the 15,000 people chuckled as the rest of them sat in silent indifference. Lanza threw his cigarette

My gorgeous wife with her second favorite wrestler backstage at *Wrestlemania 2000*. By the way, Foley has never beaten her or any other member of the Jericho family in a wrestling match.

to the ground in disgust and screamed, "What the fuck is he doing??"

When Mick came through the curtain I told him about Jack's reaction, to which Mick responded with a big grin: "Yes! Victory!"

Boring and confusing 15,000 people was worth it to piss off Lanza.

Ever since Mick helped me get into ECW, he had always kept an eye on me, and during those tumultuous first months in the WWE he was one of the few guys who tried to help me. Mick and I wrestled each other in St. Louis right around the time that *Have a Nice Day* was released. The finish of the match saw me hitting him over his head with his own book, knocking him out, and allowing me to get the 1-2-3. (Yet another Jericho win over Foley.)

Afterwards he told me, "I don't mind if you kick and punch me as hard as you can, but you might not want to be that solid with the other guys, some of them might complain about getting stiffed the way you stiffed me tonight."

He was right in saying that my style was hard hitting from years of working with guys like Chris Benoit, Eddy Guerrero, Ultimo Dragon, and Rey Mysterio. That was Mick's nice way of telling me that I better lighten up a bit if I wanted to work with the big boys in the WWE. I appreciated his honesty and was able to tweak my work as a result. I paid Mick back for his kindness the next night on *Raw*, when I told him the only reason I had read his book was to see if he died at the end of it. (Did I mention I'm undefeated against Foley?)

A few weeks later on a chilly fall afternoon, I arrived at the Meadowlands Arena in New Jersey and found out that Vince Russo had quit the WWE and jumped to WCW. It seemed like a huge blow to the company at first because he took a lot of credit for being the main architect of the Attitude Era. But Vinny Mac and the rest of the front office weren't so worried because they knew that wasn't the case.

I asked Pat, "What do you think is going to happen?"

"I've seen them come and I've seen them go, it doesn't make a difference. As long as Vince McMahon is here, it's going to be okay. No big deal."

But it was a big deal to me, as Russo was the one who had brought me into the WWE and was my biggest supporter in the company. He was the middleman between Vince and me. The guy who constantly backed me up when Vince thought I wasn't good enough to cut it. Russo believed in me and treated me with the respect of a top guy.

Now he was gone.

Sure, he dug me into a bit of a hole with all of his preposterous cartoon ideas. But at least I had a story, a presence on the show and a raison d'être. Things in the WWE were already bad for me as it was, but now I was really up shit creek—and my paddle had just floated away to WCW.

Russo's leaving meant the end of whatever kind of push I was getting, and I soon became a denizen of *Sunday Night Heat*. I worked with such luminaries as Stevie Richards, Godfather, Gangrel, the Headbangers, Bull Buchanan, and Naked Mideon, losing to all of them. Only three months earlier the clock had hit zero in the middle of The Rock's promo, yet now I was washed up at at the ripe old age of twenty-nine.

My confidence was shot and I was scrambling, desperate to get some sort of recognition, some sort of credibility. I worked against Big Show on *Raw* in Greensboro, North Carolina, and had the idea to use the famous Antonio Inoki/Andre the Giant short-arm scissor spot, where I would put him into an arm lock and he would use his immense strength to lift me straight off the ground up onto his shoulders, seven feet in the air. Proud of my originality and technical prowess, I went to Vince and bragged, "I'm doing the short-arm scissors tonight," trying to impress him any way I could.

Then I fucked up the short-arm scissors and slapped Show squarely in the face to make up for it. He was furious about it and tore the dressing room wall down in a blind fury. Then he ripped the stereo out of his rental car. When he told Ron Simmons what he had done, Ron looked him in the face and deadpanned, "So you went into your own car and smashed in your own stereo?"

"Yes!!!"

"Damn, you sure showed him..."

I embarrassed myself even further when Arnold Schwarzenegger made a guest appearance on *Smackdown!* to promote his movie *End of Days*. In the film, he plays a character named Jericho Kane, and I instantly figured that because we were both Jerichos (You're a Jericho, I'm a Jericho, that's terrific) it would be obvious for us to do something together. (Keep in mind that I was losing to Headbanger Mosh that night.) So I wrote a detailed, intricate storyline for the two of us and handed it to Vince. He looked at it as if I had written it with a poop pen and told me he was looking forward to reading it. He must've perused it very quickly, because I saw it in a garbage can forty-five minutes later.

My storyline with Schwarzenegger had been terminated forever. (Cocky Author's Note: Yeah, it's clichéd, but it's my book so deal with it.)

Even though Vince had squashed my proposed angle with Arnold, I still had to meet him. He was one of my heroes growing up and I didn't know if I'd ever get another chance. The Schwarz had been sequestered in his dressing room all day long, but I was not to be deterred.

I walked over to his door, gave a terse knock, and barged inside.

Arnold was sitting there with his entourage and they all stared at me, annoyed. A nervous grin spread across my face as I said, "I'm sorry, Mr. Schwarzenegger, I hate to interrupt you, but I just wanted to say hi." He looked at me, his face chiseled out of granite, and replied stoically in his thick Aryan accent, "Absolutely."

"Are you having a good time today?"

"Absolutely."

"That's great. Are you ready to tear it up tonight?"

"Absolutely."

"Does your mother like bananas?"

"Absolutely."

"Do you mind if I take a picture with you?"

"Absolutely."

I wasn't sure if he meant absolutely yes or absolutely no, but I went ahead and took the picture anyway.

"Thank you so much, Mr. Schwarzenegger."

"Absolutely."

I lingered for a few seconds longer, waiting for Arnold to crack a smile or a frown or a grimace—anything to show me that he was human. But he didn't. He stared at me stone-faced until I skulked out of his room and out of his life forever.

I won't be back.

Even though my first idea had ended up in the bin, I kept the hits coming. I wrote up ideas and gave them to Vince on a weekly basis, some of them good, some of them bad, all of them unused. One of my favorites was a story with

Steve Austin where I would commandeer *Raw* and be in charge of everything, renaming it *Raw Is Jericho.* I would confront Austin, who would be in the ring at the beginning of the show, and shoot down the giant *Raw Is War* banner from the rafters with a bow and arrow, revealing a *Raw Is Jericho* banner instead. Later in the night I would kidnap Austin and throw him into the trunk of my car. At the end of the show he would use his own bow and arrow to pin my shirt to the wall and proceed to stomp a mudhole into me.

What? You think that sucks?

Okay, I just reread that, and you're right, it does suck. I wouldn't have used it either, but at least I was trying.

As my stock was falling faster than a Bob Barker erection, the Hardy Boys, Edge, and Christian were becoming the hottest acts in the company. They wrestled in a best-of-seven series that culminated in a Ladder match at *No Mercy* 1999 and absolutely tore the house down. They became bigger stars in one night than I was after four months. What stung even worse was that these guys had asked me years earlier to help them get jobs in Japan and Mexico and they were now stealing a show that I wasn't even booked on.

It was quite depressing, and I started to wonder if coming to the WWE hadn't been a huge mistake.

I sat in front of the monitor watching the PPV and taking notes on a legal pad, trying to figure out what I was doing wrong and why I was sitting on the sidelines. It was the same thing I did in WCW, when I watched the guys cut promos in the box so I could learn how to do them better.

After the show I made a point of approaching Vince in his office to tell him what I had been doing, how I'd been jotting down ideas while watching the show. I wasn't looking to kiss his ass; I was just letting him know that I was trying. I'd been dreaming about working for the WWE for twenty years, had designed and cultivated my entire career to make it there, and now that I had finally arrived, my dreams were turning to dust.

The best part about taking notes at the monitor that night was watching my old friend Tyler Palko of the Okotoks Palkos (see the *New York Times* best-seller *A Lion's Tale* by Chris Jericho for more info) and his seventy-five-year old Uncle Joe yelling and screaming at all of the action. Joe lived in Cleveland and Tyler had come to visit him and see me wrestle. He was just as disappointed that I wasn't on the show as I was, so afterwards we went down to the bar district called the Flats to drown our sorrows in a bucket of Crown Royal. After a drink or ten, I was feeling so awful about the way things were going for me that I decided to take out my aggressions by pissing all over a defenseless 50-inch Samsung TV in the bar, turning it into HPee.

I drove back to Uncle Joe's home totally loadski, which was totally dumbski, and I ended up knocking over his mailbox while pulling into the driveway. In the morning, Joe asked me if I knew anything about the fallen box.

"No, Uncle Joe. But there was a party going on down the street and I'll bet it was one of those punk kids."

Tyler knew how shmammered I'd been and asked, "Did you knock down the mailbox? Did you not knock down the mailbox?," like he was George Costanza: "If you took the raisins, if you didn't take the raisins..."

Okay, I admit it; I took the raisins *and* I knocked down the fucking mailbox. My job was tearing me apart at the seams and I had been reduced to taking out my aggressions on defenseless postal receptacles.

The next day, I showed up at the arena with a massive hangover and a massive chip on my shoulder. I was angry at the world, and when I heard Vince wanted to see me in his office I planned on telling him that I wanted a storyline and I didn't care what it was about or who it was with. I was furious that I had been left off the PPV and I refused to allow it to happen again.

I stormed into his office like it was the beach at Normandy, but before I could get a word out he said, "Would you have a problem working an angle with Chyna?"

Chyna was six feet tall and 220 pounds of solid muscle. Chyna was a big star in the company. Chyna was the Intercontinental Champion.

Chyna was a woman.

She was at the height of her fame in the company and was working regularly with guys. I wasn't crazy about the idea of working with her, but I wasn't going to tell Vince that, especially since I'd been desperately waiting to work an angle with anybody. I just assumed that *anybody* would have a penis.

But at that point, whether it was with a man, a woman, or a hermaphrodite, any angle was better than no angle at all so I put on my best Sunday school smile and said, "Of course not, Vince! I welcome the opportunity!"

What was the big deal anyway? James Bond had to fight Grace Jones in *A View to a Kill*. Kurt Russell had to fight Rosario Dawson in *Death Proof*. Larry David had to fight Rosie O'Donnell on *Curb Your Enthusiasm*. So who was I to complain about fighting Chyna? How hard could it be?

Little did I know...

*　　　*　　　*

The night before as I watched the PPV with my paws on my proverbial pud, Chyna won the Intercontinental Championship from Jeff Jarrett. Ever since I started wrestling in the gym of Westwood Collegiate with Wallass (see the award-winning *A Lion's Tale* for full details) I'd had one dream: to be the WWE Intercontinental Champion. So being in an angle with the IC Champion was huge for me—even if said champion didn't have a set of testicles.

Vince was very specific in his instructions about working with Chyna. "Just because she's a woman doesn't mean you have to go easy on her. Be tough and work strong with her, because that will get her over more."

And she was really over. Chyna was the first woman who had ever been promoted on the same level as the men, and she looked the part. She was huge and more muscular than I was, which gave her the credibility to beat up guys. She was very popular with the fans, but more importantly she was popular with the office. Plus she was also HHH's girlfriend, which didn't hurt her status either, as he was on his way to becoming one of the top stars in the company.

I entered into my feud with Chyna with the best of intentions. I wanted to make her look great in the ring, as I felt like Vince was issuing me a challenge to see if I could have good matches with her. I also wanted to like Chyna, but because of how she was booked and who her friends were, she had an ego and an attitude.

There were times when she was really nice and fun to be around. She had a goofy sense of humor and would do things like stick two asparaguses in the front of her mouth like fangs and talk in funny voices. But then the next day she would act weird and not say a word to me. She was hard to read—Schizo Deluxe.

I'm no doctor but it seemed to me like she was a germaphobe. She wore black leather gloves and didn't like to touch anyone or shake hands. And she always wore vanilla-scented perfume; whenever she entered the room it smelled like a bakery.

After Chyna had beaten Jarrett for the title, I told him I was about to start an angle with her. He looked at me with compassion and said, "Good luck...you're gonna need it."

He wasn't just whistling Dixie.

CHAPTER 4

Will Work for Food

Jericho vs. Chyna began on *Raw* in Dayton when I interrupted her mid-promo and said, "The Intercontinental Championship is one of the most illustrious championships in the history of the WWE. It's been held by such legendary performers as Bret Hart, Ricky Steamboat, Shawn Michaels, the Mountie, but now it's being held by a...woman! The idea of you bringing any credibility to the Intercontinental Championship is even more enhanced than your ridiculous fake breasts." I was totally blistering her while she just stood there thunderstruck without a comeback.

I continued to insult and question her estrogen levels for the next few weeks, building up to a match for the IC title at *Survivor Series* in Detroit. Doing promos with her wasn't so bad, nor was the idea of wrestling her. But when Vince told me that he wanted Chyna to go over at the PPV, I was a little taken aback.

I was going to have to lose to a *girl*? The thought of being pinned by her was revolting in every way, but that's what my boss wanted, and I was going to give it to him.

Chyna was an average worker at best, but knowing that she had so much political power while I was still under the microscope, I had no choice. Not only did I have to lose to her, I had to have a great match with her as well.

I went to WWE headquarters in Stamford, Connecticut, to work out the details of the match with her. HHH was there as her chaperone, helping us to decide what would and what wouldn't work. I was bound and determined to steal the show and wanted to do everything I could to make that happen. I thought of a plethora of false finishes, including a spot where we would give each other a belly-to-belly suplex from the ring apron through the announce table. But the coup de grâce was the idea I had for the finish. She was using HHH's Pedigree as her own and I wanted her to give it to me from the top rope. HHH nixed the majority of my ideas, saying they were unnecessary or too dangerous to try, and he was right; but the top-rope Pedigree made the cut.

HHH and I didn't have much of a relationship at that point although Simple Jack could figure out that he didn't really care for me. When I first came to the WWE, he gave me his phone number and said, "If you ever need anything, give me a call." A few days later in San Jose, I didn't know how to get to the venue, so I took him up on his offer.

"Hey man, it's Jericho here. Do you know how to get to the arena?"

"Yeah, I know. Get a map."

I heard the laughter of his DX cronies in the background as he hung up.

A few weeks later on Thanksgiving, DX did a bit where they went out on the streets to laugh at street people. They found a homeless man holding a sign that read WILL WORK FOR FOOD. HHH said, "Look at that guy. I bet he's a better worker than Jericho." The rest of DX (Road Dogg, Billy Gunn, X-Pac, and Chyna) nodded their heads and guffawed at their leader's rapist's wit. I confronted him about it later and he said with a smirk, "Yeah, I thought you'd find that funny."

I didn't. But I understood the relevance of the comment. It was a direct shot at me, and once again I realized if I didn't do something to turn the tide, I'd be sent packing.

The match with Chyna at *Survivor Series* started out good, but halfway through it, something happened. The Detroit crowd began loudly chanting my name, not caring that she was the babyface. It was like the fans were telling Vince they were sick of the Chyna experiment and didn't buy her getting the better of me physically. Even though the office and the locker room didn't seem to believe in me, the people still did. The fans in Detroit were mad as hell and weren't gonna take it anymore—but neither was Chyna.

She didn't like the crowd turning on her, and even though I was working my ass off to change that, the crowd wasn't buying her as a babyface champion. It was out of my control.

But the match *was* in my control and I was fairly happy with it. I was able to carry her to a decent showing, and it was one of the better bouts on the show. We did the top-rope Pedigree as a finish, and while it wasn't the prettiest thing, it got a great reaction and to my knowledge, it's the only time it's ever been done. So I had that going for me.

One of the other things that bothered me about Chyna

was that while she trusted me and expected me to put together a good match, she never helped me by telling anybody else that. When we came through the Gorilla position, everybody congratulated her on the match. Even though she had worked hard and done a good job, she just stood there and accepted the praise solo, smiling as if she'd just wrestled herself.

We had a rematch at *Armageddon*, the next PPV from Fort Lauderdale. During the weeks building it up, I had the idea to smash her thumb with a hammer. I wanted to do something dastardly to try to get her more sympathy as a babyface and got the idea from the gloves she wore wherever she went. So I kidnapped her, tied her up in a dark room, and brought the hammer down on a sausage that had been stuffed into one of the thumbs on her gloves. Kind of psycho psycho, I know, but Vince liked it.

Her thumb mutilated, she decided to exact her revenge by challenging me to a wrestling match instead of just having me arrested for assault. The next few weeks, I antagonized her and the fans by making a bunch of bad jokes about her smashed appendage. "Well, your dreams of being the next Fonz are over," and "Will you be hitch-hiking home after the show?" or "Thumbs up, Chyna, things are going to work out!"

Heath Ledger as the Joker had nothing on me.

At the PPV, Vince wanted me to do an impromptu promo before my match, so I went on about how I was going to become the Intercontinental Champion and ended it off by chanting the "Go Jericho Go" bit I'd used in my first promo with The Rock.

It was a big night for me because I was going to win the title from Chyna and become the Intercontinental Champion for the first time. Ever since I first saw Ricky the Dragon Steamboat holding that title when I was in high school, it was my biggest goal to one day be the champion just like him.

I spent the match using the unique modus operandi of torturing her injured thumb. I trapped her arms in the ropes and kicked and punched her exposed digit. I stepped and ground on it until she finally tapped out to the Rock and Roll Finisher. Just like that, despite all the shit I'd been through, my dream had become reality: Chris Jericho was the new Intercontinental Champion! More important, our match was better than the first one and ended up being the best on the show. I took great pride in the fact that I'd carried Chyna to one of the best performances of her career.

When it was over, I walked through the curtain but couldn't find her anywhere. It was customary after a match to wait in Gorilla for your opponent so you could congratulate each other and thank each other for the match, but she was nowhere to be found. I looked up and down the halls, checked the dressing rooms, and finally found her in Vince's office, conversing with HHH. They stopped talking as soon as I walked in and looked up guiltily as if I'd caught them doing something wrong.

I asked Chyna if everything was okay. She said, "Yeah, I'm fine."

I said, "Good match! I thought it went really well, huh?"

"Yeah, it was good," she said woodenly.

I could tell she was upset about something but I couldn't figure out what, as we had just put on a hell of a performance. Was she mad she lost the title? Did she not like the way I put together the match? Had she run out of vanilla perfume?

I noticed that she had the tiniest bit of a shiner under her eye, like she had caught a stiff shot. When I worked with her I knew there would be some live rounds thrown and I had no problem with that. Neither did she; it was the way she liked to work.

I could tell I had interrupted something, so I thanked her again and left the office. I could feel two pairs of eyes boring a hole in my back as I did.

I wasn't going to let her blasé attitude spoil the fact that my childhood dream had come true. I was on a high and felt like I was the king of the world. I wanted that feeling to last forever, and it did—for the next twenty-four hours or so.

Then the house of Jericho cards came crashing down.

CHAPTER 5

Green as Grass

The next day we were doing *Raw* in Tampa. I brought my girlfriend Jessica with me backstage for the first time and we were both a little nervous.

Even though the WWE was one of the biggest sports companies in the world, we didn't have a trainer or a team doctor. What we did have was a strange New Age shiatsu chiropractor named François. He was French with a long ponytail, and he was famous for being the guy who tended to Mick Foley (who incidentally has never bested me in a match) during the infamous Hell in a Cell against The Undertaker. François was convinced that he could heal any ailment with his magical powers.

"Okay, your ankle is hurting, but it has feelings and it's insulted right now. Apologize to it and your ankle will forgive you." Ummm, okay.

A few weeks earlier, Jessica had been hit by a car while she was out for a run and her back had been bothering her ever since. When François heard this, he insisted he could make her feel better and had her lie down on his table. Somehow she ended up getting a stinger that temporarily paralyzed her. It was terrifying because she could hardly move her legs, and all I could think of was my mom, who had become a quadriplegic nine years earlier. I was consoling her when I got a message that Vince needed to see me. Like one of Pavlov's dogs, I instantly snapped to attention.

I asked Jess if she would be okay with me leaving for a few minutes, and even though she was trying to be strong I could see the fear in her eyes, and I felt the same way.

I told her I'd be right back and rushed over to Vince's office. I wasn't sure exactly what he wanted to talk to me about, but I was pretty certain he was going to congratulate me for stealing the show with Chyna the night before. The more I thought about the match, the more I liked it, and I was excited to hear his feedback. Was I finally going to get some prizzops from my bizzoss?

I knocked on his door and walked in to find him talking to HHH. They gave me a strange look (similar to the one HHH and Chyna had given me the day before) and Vince asked me to come back in a few minutes. I checked on Jess, who thankfully had gotten her feeling back, and after a couple of minutes I went back to his office. This time HHH was gone and Vince was with Jim Ross, the head of talent relations, and Jack Lanza. He told me to shut the door and take a seat, and surprisingly, he didn't look happy. As a matter of fact, he looked downright pissed.

My expectations of praise were quickly shot down by feelings of dread—this wasn't gonna be good.

Vince looked me in the eye and said, "What is your problem?"

"Pardon me?"

"What the fuck is your problem?"

Uh-oh. My normally calm and collected boss was now swearing at me.

"I'm sorry, I don't understand."

"What did you do to Chyna yesterday, huh? You gave her a black eye. You were stiffing the shit out of her. How could you do that?"

Caught off guard, I tried to defend myself. "It wasn't intentional, Vince. It's just part of the job sometimes. You know that."

Vince's eyes bugged out and the veins in his neck pulsated as he said in a gravelly voice, "How could you do that, man? She's a *woman*!!"

I didn't think it was prudent at that juncture to remind him that he was the one who had told me to work strong and not to take it easy with her. Not that I had a chance to get a word in edgewise, as the Vin-Man was just getting started.

"You don't have a fucking clue what you're doing out there. You're as green as grass and it's embarrassing. I was sold a bill of goods in bringing you in here and you're not worth the paper your contract is printed on. Everybody is complaining about you."

Yikes! Well, that wasn't what I expected to hear when I walked into his office. I was in shock. Before this little tête-à-tête, I would've bet a thousand dollars Canadian that Vince was going to wrap me in his arms and congratulate me. Instead he was giving me a whipping worse than the one Jesus got in *The Passion of the Christ*.

I didn't know what to do or how to react, so I found a happy place and hid in the recesses of my mind. I figured if I tried to make excuses, he'd just fire me on the spot, so I morphed into Kevin Bacon in *Animal House* and kept repeating to myself, "Thank you, sir, may I have another?"

He gave me another, all right. And another. And another.

"You have no respect for anybody here. You even stole The Rock's catchphrase on the pay-per-view yesterday."

It took me a while to figure out what the hell he was talking about. "If you smell what The Rock is cooking"? No. "It doesn't matter what your name is!"? Nope, not that one either.

Did he mean "Go Jericho Go"? In his mind was that too similar to The Rock encouraging the fans to chant, "Rocky, Rocky, Rocky"?

Hardly a direct ripoff of a tried-and-true catchphrase, but it didn't matter what I thought. The tongue-o'-nine-tails lashing continued.

"The problem with you is that you're an elitist, you think you're better than everybody else. But you're not. You're the drizzling shits."

Well I never! I'd been called a lot of things during my career, but "the drizzling shits" was not one of them. I'd always prided myself on my work, and hearing him say that cut me to the bone. But not as much as his next statement.

"I want you to go and apologize to Chyna."

Exsqueeze me? Baking powder?

Apologize to Chyna? For what? Carrying her to two of the best matches she'd ever had? Putting up with her politics and making her look like a million loonies? What the fuck was I supposed to apologize to her about? I had a better poker face than Lady Gaga, but inside I was fucking furious.

In my mind's eye there were two scenarios: (1) tell Vince to buy a one-way ticket to hell and back, trash his office, and leave the WWE forever; or (2) obey his orders, swallow my pride like a shot of Crown, and apologize to Chyna.

It wasn't an easy choice, but I'd worked nine long years to get to the WWE and I wasn't going to let it slip away so easily.

"Okay, Vince, I'll apologize to her."

JR and Lanza nodded their heads in approval. I'm not sure why they were in the room, since they didn't say anything, but their presence made Vince's words even more biting and embarrassing. It was going to be hard looking any of these guys in the face from now on.

And the hits kept on coming.

"From now on, you have to go over every one of your matches with X-Pac. He knows how to work and how to put together matches; you don't. I want you to pick his brain and talk to him about every move you make in the ring."

I'd known X-Pac (a.k.a. Sean Waltman) for years, after working together in Japan and WCW. Now he was firmly entrenched in DX and one of Vince's golden boys. Pac was a very smart worker who understood the WWE way of doing things, and in the long run he did help me with my in-ring psychology. But it was a tough pill to swallow knowing that I had to approve everything with a guy who was not only younger than me with less experience, but was also part of the DX gang who clearly had issues with me.

I was scheduled to have a match with him that night on *Raw*, and Vince said, "You better show me something tonight, Chris. Because if you can't have a good match with Pac, you can't have a good match with anybody. I'm not going to take the title off you, that would be too obvious. So we'll do a DQ. But you better have a good one."

After those words his oral assault was finally finished. I skulked out of his office, with my tail between my legs and my heart between my bollocks.

I stopped in the hallway to take a breath and figure out what had just happened. Yesterday I was on the top of the world. Now less than twenty-four hours later, my girlfriend was barely able to move, and I had just been told that I wasn't worth the paper my contract was printed on. My career was hanging by a thread, totally dependent on my performance that night. Needless to say, it was the most important match of my life.

I went and told X-Pac what had just transpired, and of course he acted like he had no idea I had any heat. But I was far beyond caring about pride or bravado and asked him to put that night's entire match together, and it went well—not amazing or even all that memorable—but it was good enough for Vince to give me a thumbs-up after it was over.

I had gotten a reprieve and my career was saved from extinction for at least another day. But I was still deep in the hole and knew it was going to take a long time to pull myself out.

It was time to grab the rope and start climbing.

I searched the arena until I found Chyna standing smugly in the hallway, wearing gloves, smelling like vanilla, and sporting the smallest baby bruise under her eye.

She was the enemy and we both knew it—and I had to apologize to her.

"Hey, I just talked with Vince and I want to say that I'm ssoo...ssoooo...ssoooo..."

Like the Fonz, I was genetically unable to apologize to this woman.

So I stuck my fingers right up her nose.

I shook myself out of my dream state and continued talking.

"Hey, I just talked with Vince and I want to say that I'm ssss...sorry for giving you that shiner. It was an accident. But I still really liked the match, though. A lot of people told me that we stole the show."

Her face was Vulcan and it was clear she was expecting the apology, because she was quite short with her response.

"Yeah, yeah, it's okay, no problem."

She couldn't have been more insincere with her reply to my atonement, and it made me sick. But I had done what Vince wanted and now I needed to investigate a little more as to why I had been crucified.

I knew one Triple H would surely have some insight. I saw him a few minutes later and got right to the heart of the matter.

"Hey, I need to ask you a question...do I have heat?"

To his credit, he was totally honest with me. "Yeah, you've got a lot of heat. You've got scorching heat."

Even though it was axiomatic that I was in the doghouse, it was still a shock to hear him say it so bluntly.

"Why?"

"Why? Well, ever since you got here, all you talk about is how you did things in WCW. You act like you have all the answers and know everything, like you're a huge star, but you haven't proven shit. We have a different way of doing things here and you're not getting it."

In retrospect, he was right. Whenever I put together my matches, I *was* always talking about things I had done in WCW and how things *were* different in the WWE. I'd made the mistake of thinking that I could fit in right off the bat, instead of adapting to the new style like I had when I first went to Japan or Mexico or ECW.

I felt terrible, but I wanted to make as many amends as I could, so I went to talk to The Rock. I found him in the dressing room and told him that Vince had just torn me a new intestinal tract opening and asked whether he had complained to anyone about me stealing his catchphrase.

"I don't know what you're talking about."

"Well, yesterday I did a promo and got the crowd to chant, 'Go Jericho Go.'"

"Well, that's not even close to the same thing."

Rock could see that I was shaken up. "Chris, you've got to realize that the cream always rises to the top in this business. I've been watching you since WCW and you're good. But you have to rise above this and not get eaten by the sharks. I went through the same thing when I first started here, but I always kept my confidence and rose above it. You have to do the same thing."

I appreciated his pep talk, as it was nice to hear somebody say they thought I was good. After everything that had transpired during the day, I wasn't sure who or what the hell I was anymore. But Rock had walked in my shoes and was on my side—and that meant everything to me.

As I was leaving the arena I ran into Vince. Surprisingly, he gave me a big hug and didn't mention a word of what had happened earlier. "Give me a call tomorrow, kid, and we'll talk," he said before breaking out in his patented belly laugh.

I smiled back quizzically, even though I couldn't help but wonder what exactly it was that he found so damn funny.

The next day, Jessica was able to move, but her back was still screwed up and she couldn't get out of bed. I had to leave her to fend for herself, so I could drive to Tallahassee for *Smackdown!* I tried calling Vince a few times during the drive but he never answered. I was still bothered by what had happened and needed to vent, so I called Chris Benoit, who was still with WCW.

He listened to my story and I could tell by his voice that he was really angry. He felt somebody was out to get me for sure and called back a few hours later after asking Bret Hart for some advice on my behalf. Bret told him that I shouldn't be too worried because a similar thing had happened to him when he first started. He explained that Vince was like a drill sergeant who liked to tear people down and build them back up in his own image. Well, he had done half of that so far. I just hoped he wouldn't rebuild me with a bad pompadour and a loud suit.

That night I had a match on *Smackdown!* against The Big Bossman. As per my orders from the actual big bossman, I found X-Pac before the match and ran all of my ideas past him. He added a few ideas of his own and the match went well, enough so that Vince greeted me with a Laurel and Hardy handshake afterwards.

Thinking about it now, Vince had definitely taken a few Jericho molehills and blown them up into mountains in order to test me, to see how I'd react to his harsh words. But I survived his trial by fire by not flipping out, taking my verbal beatings like a man, and doing what he asked.

I was surfing the Web a few days later and was mortified (killer word) to see a post heralding how Vince McMahon had scolded Chris Jericho and said he wasn't worth the paper his contract was printed on, was green as grass, the drizzling shits, et cetera. It basically gave a word-for-word description of my crucifixion. It was bad enough having to deal with Vince's abuse without having to read about it online as well.

A few hours after the story went up online, I got a call from Russo.

"If the rumors I'm hearing are true, I want you to come back to WCW. You have an open door to work here whenever you want."

It was nice to hear but not an option for me. I'd been running down a dream for nine years to work for the WWE, and even though it had been a rocky start, I was still the Intercontinental Champion. Plus I was under contract and couldn't leave if I wanted to.

But even if I wasn't legally obligated to stay, I still wouldn't have left. As The Rock said, the cream always rises to the top, and I felt like I was Clapton, Baker, and Bruce rolled up into one. I knew I could make it in the WWE and do it in a way that Vince McMahon would appreciate.

Al Snow once told me that while we entertained millions of people weekly, there was only one person we had to impress and that was Vince himself. Even if the whole world loves you, if Vince doesn't you'll never truly make it in his company.

I had to change who I was as a performer, and I was ready for the challenge. After all, it wasn't the first time I had to reinvent myself. I'd had my confidence shattered many times before in Japan, ECW, and WCW and gotten back up and succeeded every time. I was too driven and had come too far to give up now.

You can't kill rock and roll and you can't kill Chris Jericho either.

CHAPTER 6

Looking California and Feeling Minnesota

As bad as things were going, I was soon given a shocking reminder that the WWE was only a job and things could be a whole lot worse.

We were doing a TV taping at the Nassau Coliseum in Long Island and I was warming up in the hallway when former NFL defensive end Darren Drozdov ran past me on his way to the ring for his match against D-Lo Brown.

"Slow down, man, you're gonna hurt yourself," I said as he almost bowled me over.

"Heads up, Canadian, I'm late," he said with a laugh as he ran up the stairs into Gorilla.

A few minutes later I heard a huge cry of "Ohhhhhh" emanate from the dressing room, the kind you only hear when something has gone wrong. I hurried over to the monitor to see Droz lying motionless in the ring with the paramedics (and François) huddled around him.

He had been dropped on his head when he slipped out of an attempted Powerbomb from D-Lo Brown. His lack of movement reminded me instantly of my mom. It had been my biggest fear since her accident that something would happen to me during a match that would leave me a quadriplegic as well. Seeing Droz lying there scared the living shit out of me and I started praying.

"Please let him move, God, please let him move...an arm, a leg, anything."

But the minutes ticked away and nothing changed.

The paramedics took about half an hour to get him onto the stretcher and out of the ring. It was a horrible feeling to see one of the brothers lying motionless in the middle of the arena.

It was an even worse feeling being thankful that it wasn't me.

The show continued, and when it ended I drove to the hospital to see him. Vince was there and everybody was sitting around glumly not knowing what to say or to do. It was a horrible scene, but the person I felt the most sorry for was D-Lo. He sat in the corner with his head buried in his hands and tears streaming down his face. He was blaming himself for what happened, and even though it was a total accident, I felt for him and the fact that he'd have to live with the knowledge that Droz would never walk again.

Droz never blamed anyone for his injury, and as far as I know he is still on the WWE payroll to this day. Sometimes when we have a show in Philadelphia, he'll show up in his pimped out wheelchair and is always friendly with a great attitude. He's a big man and looks out of place in the confines of the little chair, but he always has a smile and a compliment for everyone.

But what happened to Droz serves as a reminder of

how lucky I am that I've never been seriously injured in the ring.

It's also a reminder how terrified I am of ending up in the same situation.

The guy in charge of tracking down talent (the fancy word used for wrestlers, the same way "fuel dispensing technician" is used for gas station attendants) to do various promos for the WWE is Steve Lombardi, a.k.a. the Brooklyn Brawler. I cut my teeth doing promos in WCW when nobody else showed up to do them and I understood how important it was to practice every chance I got. But the first couple times Lombardi asked me to do promos for the WWE, I blew him off. I became one of the guys who suddenly had more important things to do than work on my verbal skills, like Lex Luger in WCW.

Finally Lombardi cornered me and said, "I'm not asking you to do these because I want you to do them for me. You're doing them for the company. When they ask me why you're not doing them, it just makes you look like an asshole. If you continue to blow them off, it's going to make you seem like you're a prima donna and it could really hurt you."

Once again, I wasn't keeping my eyes on the ball when it came to the little things.

So I revived my WCW attitude and did as many pretapes, PSAs, local advertisements, and interviews for DVDs as I could. I tried to get my face on as much material as possible. It got to the point where I would do most of the material in one take. But if there was a take that I didn't like, if I stumbled or mispronounced something, I would use a trick that Rick Rude taught me in WCW.

Swear.

"I'm the Ayatollah of Lock and Lollahh . . . Fuck! Fuck! Fuck! Fuck! Fuck!"

Voilà! A guaranteed second chance.

I had just done a promo for WWE ice cream bars when I was approached in the hallway by a kid who looked like he was twelve years old.

"Hi, how are you doing, Chris? I'm a big fan of your work."

I thanked the kid and started looking for security to help him find his parents. "How did you get backstage, buddy?"

"I work here now."

Work here? Okay, maybe he was a hot dog vendor or somebody's kid who was on the payroll as a gofer. I asked him in my most patronizing tone, "Really. So what do you do?"

"I'm the new writer for *Raw*. My name is Brian Gewirtz and I'm looking forward to working with you."

The new era of the WWE had arrived.

No longer would I be responsible for writing all of my promos, as Vince had decided to utilize scriptwriters the same way that Hollywood TV shows did. From now on every one of my promos would be written and delivered to me. I had the option to make changes, but the days of writing everything down on a legal pad in my room and bringing it to the shows were gone. Brian was in charge now—and he looked like he wasn't even old enough to drink a beer. But we had a lot in common and we got along right away. He understood my character and was a fan, so for the first time since Russo left I had an ally on the booking team.

I figured that after I beat Chyna for the title that my sentence with her was over and I'd move on to a feud with someone who had a dinky, but I was wrong. For some reason Vince liked the chemistry I had with Chyna and wanted to continue the story—and in doing so he came up with the all-time worst angle I was ever involved in.

He called us into his office, and as we sat in uncomfortable silence you could cut the aversion with a knife.

"The writers and I have been talking and we've decided that the two of you are going to be the co-holders of the Intercontinental title. For the first time ever in the WWE we are going to have co-champions. You'll both defend it and you will constantly debate with each other about who the champion really is. Quite frankly I think it will be an incredible dynamic."

I sat there looking California and feeling Minnesota. I couldn't believe that I'd have to share the title with her. I would've been happier just dropping it to her so I could wash my hands of the whole Chyna experience and move on to something (anything) else.

However I had once again been given my orders, and it was my job to make chicken shit into chicken salad.

But I had a feeling I was about to embark on Mission Impossible, and I ain't talking about Tom Cruise.

So we became co-champions after I German suplexed (whatever happened to that move?) Chyna and both of our shoulders ended up on the mat. The ref counted to three on both of us, and instead of calling it a draw, he decided that we would become the co-holders of the Intercontinental Championship.

Dumbest.

Idea.

Ever.

Vince's initial thought was that either of us could defend the title, but it usually ended up with me wrestling and her at ringside. At this point, I suddenly became a babyface. One week I was smashing thumbs with hammers and the next week I was slapping babies and kissing hands with Chyna in my corner rooting me on.

The turn started when the fans began cheering me *against* Chyna, but instead of building it up and making it mean something, the turn was never made official and the overall response was lukewarm at best.

I would be wrestling Gangrel, and when his valet Luna got involved, Chyna would hit Gangrel with the Pedigree behind the ref's back. I would then hit the Lionsault and cover him and get the tainted win, which as a babyface was brutal. The fans were starting to get sick of us as well and wanted to see me get involved in something new. Thankfully, Vince knew that his experiment wasn't working and decided to put it (and me) out of its misery. Somehow poor Bob Holly got dragged into it all and we had a three-way match for the title at the *Royal Rumble* in Madison Square Garden, with the winner becoming the undisputed IC Champ. After my anemic debut as a performer in MSG, I wanted to make my mark with my debut match in the Garden. I even flew my dad in for the show. It was his return to the building where he had won so many battles thirty years before, and I was excited to carry on the family tradition with a great match.

Unfortunately my family tradition ended up more like *Family Guy*.

When you work a match, the best way to do it is to call it on the fly. Have a set beginning, middle, and end and make up the rest as you go. But with Chyna you had to call the entire match beforehand. Every duck, every dip, every dodge. Usually both guys have a general idea of what's going on and if someone has a brain freeze the other guy can back you up. But you couldn't count on that with her. Bob Holly, on the other hand, was a seasoned vet and a good worker. With a guy like him, you didn't have to go over much. If I threw him off the ropes and bent over, it was obvious that I was going to give him a backdrop.

With Chyna it wasn't that easy.

"I'm going to give you a backdrop."

"What?"

"Backdrop."

"Huh?"

"Backdrop!"

"Is it a backdrop?"

"Yeah, a backdrop."

And so on and so forth. Three-way matches are never easy as it is, but surprisingly, this one was going pretty good until I threw Bob to the floor and turned back to Chyna. Suddenly I went blank and had absolutely no idea what I was supposed to do next. Time stood still as we both looked at each other blankly in front of 18,000 people. If I were a Shakespearean actor in Stratford-upon-Avon, I would've yelled, "Line!" and some guy in the pit would tell me what to say. But I was a Shakespearean actor in Madison Square Garden and didn't have that luxury. Finally, instead of yelling, "To be or not to be," Bob came back into the ring and yelled, "Bulldog her, dumb-ass!" and I snapped back into the groove. If Holly hadn't said anything, I'd probably still be there trying to figure out what the hell to do.

Finally I made Chyna tap out to the Salad Shooter and I was done with her forever—or was I?

Mercifully I moved into a program with Bob. I liked working with him because he was a hard-nosed guy and a skilled worker. I didn't have to worry if I gave him a shiner or if I hit him too hard, because I knew he didn't care and would give it back to me anyway. I had the same rules with him as I had with Benoit. Hit me as hard as you want—just don't break my nose or knock out any teeth. That's how we worked together, and we had some really good matches as a result.

Even though I still had heat with certain people in the locker room, I didn't have heat with Bob, and he helped me turn the corner both work-wise and politically. The boys had heard about my struggles with Vince and DX, and I'd become a little bit of a dressing room hero as a result. I was building relationships on a grassroots level and beginning to make some friends who were pulling for me and appreciated what I could do in the ring. Bob had been around, he respected what I had done and where I had been, and, most important, he respected me.

And slowly but surely, the rest of the roster started to as well.

I was happy with the work I had done with Bob and thought I was out of the Chynese prison, until Vince once again called her and I into his office.

"We're going to make you two partners!" he said with

a big smile. "We've got two good-looking people here and the both of you together will be unstoppable!"

I felt like puking all over his powder blue sports coat, but Vince could sell yellow snow to an Eskimo, and by the time I left his office I thought it was the best idea ever—for about three minutes. Then I realized I'd been hosed again.

So now we're supposed to be amigos and she's going to be my valet? As a babyface, it was brutal to have her walk to the ring with me and share my spotlight. It was even worse that we weren't the co-champions anymore and there was no reason for her to be with me.

Or was there?

Vince had issues with Chyna and her expanding ego and he had issues with me, so I wondered: did he put us together to see who would kill the other one first?

Luckily for me, the cavalry was about to arrive.

My best friends in the business followed my lead and jumped from WCW to the WWE. Chris Benoit, Eddy Guerrero, Dean Malenko, and Perry Saturn had been granted their release en masse from WCW and showed up on *Raw* in the biggest talent exodus in the history of the Monday Night Wars. I was surprised that WCW had been stupid enough to let them all go at once, but I wasn't at all surprised that they had all left. Eddy had been calling me for months asking how it was working for the WWE, and Chris constantly told me that he wanted to leave. In WCW it felt like we were in prison, and while I was the first one to escape, they all longed to join me.

Dean told me that when I made my WWE debut he, Chris, and Eddy gathered around a TV backstage at *Nitro* to watch, and just as I walked out to confront The Rock, one of the producers made them change the channel. According to WCW logic I was now the enemy and they weren't allowed to be friends with me anymore.

There was a huge buzz throughout the business when they appeared in the WWE, especially for Chris and Eddy. But in his first match in the company, Benoit, who had walked out of WCW as the World Champion, wrestled WWE Champion HHH and was pinned clean in about ten minutes. Once again, Vince didn't care what anyone had accomplished outside his walls, you had to prove yourself all over again when you came to work for him.

It was his World (Wrestling Entertainment), and we were just living in it.

CHAPTER 7

Too Esoteric for Our Demographic

Rich Ward and I originally put Fozzy Osbourne together as a fun side project, consisting of a bunch of friends playing our favorite heavy metal songs. We only played two gigs together, but because Jericho from the WWE and Rich from Stuck Mojo (who had a significant underground following, selling three-quarters of a million records worldwide) had started a band, there was a buzz about us from the start.

After the two gigs caused such a stir, Mark Willis, the manager of Stuck Mojo, called me and asked, "Do you want to do more with Fozzy?"

"What do you mean?"

"Well, there are record companies that want to sign you guys."

"Sign what? We're a cover band!"

Mark responded, "They know. They also know that you can't really tour. But they still want to sign you."

"Well, what have they heard from us that would make them want to sign us?"

He said, "Nothing. You guys have only done two gigs and I sure as hell wasn't going to send them the video from those, because they were terrible."

I'd never met Willis, but he sure was comfortable giving it to me straight. I liked him already.

"Obviously you hadn't rehearsed or anything," he continued. "But the point is the word is out about you guys, and they've *heard* nothing and *seen* nothing. They just know who's in the band and they want to sign you."

The talk of a record deal had come out of nowhere, but I was stoked since I had two dreams when I was a kid—to be a wrestler and to be a rock star. I'd been playing in bands since I was fourteen years old, a lot longer than I'd been wrestling, and it was surreal to see my other dream coming true.

It was strange that there was a label bidding war going on but we weighed the offers and decided on signing with Megaforce Records. Based out of New Jersey, Megaforce was the first label to sign Metallica and Anthrax to record deals. They were far from their glory days, but the fact that we were going to release an album with the same company that had given James Hetfield and Charlie Benante their starts was good enough for me.

We got a $75,000 advance from Megaforce, and that's when I got a crash course in the music business. When you're a kid, you think that when a band signs a record deal they'll be huge rock stars instantly and be showered with cash. It was the same mindset I had when I first started watching Stampede Wrestling. I assumed that all of the wrestlers were rich and famous because they were on TV. I would watch an opening-match guy like Goldie Rogers and think to myself, "If I can just get to his level,

I'll make a hundred grand a year and have tons of chicks hanging around me."

Goldie was probably making three hundred bucks a week and hanging out with harpies.

The $75,000 they signed us for was more like a loan. You don't have to pay it back if you end up making less, but you won't make a dime more until the record company starts seeing a return on their investment. Plus you also have to pay for the entire recording of the record out of that advance: studio time, producer, engineer, musicians, krell, everything. If a limo picks you up from the airport, your band is paying for it. If you order a hot dog with an exec at lunch, your band is paying for it. If you run out of toilet paper while you're taking a dumpus, your band is paying for it.

After you finish the record, then it's time to try and recoup, and that's when the real work begins. Now, for all of you who think that when a band releases a record they're automatically loaded, think again. So kids, get out your calculators and protractors and let Professor Jericho give you a math lesson.

Let's say your record is released and sells for $10. As the band, you'll get $1 per record sold. While you're getting $1 per record, the record company is getting $5. If you sign for $50,000 and sell 10,000 records, the record company makes fifty grand and the band makes ten grand. The $10,000 you've made gets subtracted from the $50,000 they signed you for, and you still owe them $40,000 even though they've already made $50,000. You have to sell 50,000 albums to "pay back" the contract they signed you for.

Does that make any sense to you? No? Now you know how I feel.

Megaforce was owned by Jonny and Marsha Zazula. Jonny Z made a pretty big name for himself during the '80s and now that he was returning to the music industry, he had decided that Fozzy was going to be the next big thing.

After we had signed the contract he looked us square in the eye and said, "Are you ready to become the next Metallica?"

The next Metallica?? Did he not realize we were a cover band wearing wigs and shit?

Rich and I smiled and nodded. "Uhh, sure."

However, Jonny was adamant that Fozzy was going to become huge by playing covers, so we did what any self-respecting musician would do.

We shut up and took the cash.

Once we saw how motivated Jonny was to push Fozzy, Rich and I decided that we wanted to do something more original with the concept of only playing covers. First, we knew that we couldn't continue as Fozzy Osbourne; the name was just too silly and we didn't know what Ozzy's camp would think of it. So we changed it to the Big City Knights, then to the Originals. But there was another group in the East End called the Originals, so we became Fozzy.

While we weren't crazy about doing a covers record, it was what Jonny Z wanted, and we decided to do the best we could within those parameters. To distinguish Fozzy from the thousands of cover bands in the world, we came up with a twist. Being a huge fan of the Blues Brothers, Spinal Tap, and the Traveling Wilburys, Rich and I decided that all of us would adopt alter egos and play characters within the band.

I became Moongoose McQueen, the most pompous and arrogant lead singer of all time, and Rich morphed into Duke Larue, guitar hero extraordinaire. Our bass player, Dan Dryden, became Shawn Pop. When I asked him why, he said, "Because it's Pawn Shop with the letters reversed," and smiled proudly as if he had just cut the Gordian knot. Our other guitar player was a student of Rich's named Ryan Mallam, who didn't talk much. So we called him the Kidd and decided he had no social skills whatsoever and would remain eternally silent. Frank "Bud" Fontsere, the drummer, became K. K. LaFlamme, and the list was complete.

The backstory we concocted was that Moongoose and the Duke had been swindled by a dodgy record company into moving to Japan to make an album. While they were there, the company went out of business, which left them stranded and destitute, strangers in a strange land.

So they began recording demos that were subsequently sent all over the globe and snatched up by Iron Maiden, Judas Priest, Krokus, et cetera. All of the supposed covers Fozzy were playing were really our own songs that were stolen from us while we were in Japan. Now, after twenty years, Fozzy had returned to the United States to reclaim their glory and their songs, playing them the way they were meant to be played.

We decided to stay in character at all times during interviews. When you were interviewing Fozzy, there was no Chris Jericho, only Moongoose McQueen, and in order to pull this off I took direct inspiration from Andy Kaufman and his Tony Clifton character. Clifton was an abrasive, horrible stand-up comedian who was actually Kaufman in disguise, although he would never admit to it.

Rich and I mimicking the Scorpions on set during the filming of *Unleashed, Uncensored, Unknown* in 2000. No idea why I'm wearing two kimonos.

Jonny Z loved the idea and asked what songs we'd be recording for the record. We told him we were thinking of doing Maiden, Priest, Ozzy, Scorpions, Dio...

"Dio?" he asked, his voice growing stern. "I don't think you should do that. There's a big Dio backlash throughout the United States right now. If you do a Dio song, there could be trouble." What did he mean by a Dio backlash? Was there an angry mob roaming the countryside wielding pitchforks, ready to hang the Holy Diver along with anybody else who had the audacity to play one of his blasphemous songs?

Z sat back in his chair shaking his head and murmuring, "This could really derail the whole thing."

But Dio backlash notwithstanding, Jonny was convinced that the combination of Jericho from the WWE and Rich from Stuck Mojo playing covers under alter egos would be huge. Megaforce kept throwing cash at us and decided that the backstory was so good that we needed to make a short film that would be used as an electronic press kit to promote the band. They gave us $100,000 and told us to show up in Orlando to film for two days. That was it—no script, no ideas, no nothing. So Rich, Willis, and I compiled a bunch of ideas into a bare skeleton of a script so we'd have something to film. The basic premise was that Fozzy had returned from Japan after twenty years to play their triumphant return concert at the Hard Rock Café in Orlando and the entire country was going nuts with anticipation.

We promoted the gig on the local rock station and discussed the trials and tribulations of being stuck in the Orient and the problems we faced as a band. We discussed our first guitar player, Chuck Berry (no relation), who found side work as a sumo wrestler even though he weighed only 145 pounds. Unfortunately, an actual sumo wrestler fell on top of him, crushing his hands forever, leaving us no choice but to fire him.

Then we discussed how Fozzy once got into trouble for using laser lights at a show. The beams were so strong that they blinded people in the crowd. Fozzy avoided a lawsuit by giving all of the injured people seeing-eye dogs. And not just any seeing-eye dogs—these beautiful specimens were so good that people wished they could be blinded so they could have one.

I called in some favors from some of my friends to give their testimonies of how Fozzy changed their lives. Zakk Wylde, Mike Portnoy, Sebastian Bach, and Dee Snider all spoke about the influence of Fozzy.

Zakk claimed that he'd auditioned for the band three times but never made it because his metal wasn't up to snuff. The sting of our rejection led him to crack and heroin addiction. Portnoy talked about how K.K. influenced his drumming and his stick twirling technique. Sebastian said that whenever Fozzy came to town, groupies would welcome us with open arms and open legs.

But the coup de grâce was Dee Snider's performance. I had seen the *Behind the Music* episode about Vanilla Ice, where he was explaining how he didn't steal the bass line for "Ice Ice Baby" from Queen. Ice said, "Queen's goes 'dun dun dun dundundundun.'" Then he hummed the exact same bass line and said with a shit-eating grin, "Mine goes 'dun dun dun dundundundun.' It's not the same thing." Even though it was the exact same thing.

I called Dee and asked him if he'd seen the show. He had and was totally down when I explained that I wanted him to mimic that exact scene when explaining that he didn't steal "Stay Hungry" from Fozzy. He did this great bit in front of the Twin Towers where he said, "The A Tower and the B Tower have similarities, but they are completely different structures. That's the same with our version of 'Stay Hungry.' Their song goes, 'Stay hungry feel the fire,' and my song goes, 'Stay hungry feel the fire.' Just like the Twin Towers are different, so are our versions of 'Stay Hungry.'"

Another one of the stars of the documentary was our pig-faced mascot Arthur. During our very first rehearsal for Fozzy Osbourne, I found a pig mask on the floor of the studio and told Rich that the pig would make a great mascot for us, in the fine tradition of Iron Maiden's Eddie and Dio's Murray. The idea was that Arthur wasn't a guy wearing a mask, but a human being stricken with swinus, a very rare disease that transforms the face of its victims into that of a pig. So we put Arthur in a Boy Scout outfit, gave him a metal hook for a hand, and voilà: instant mascot.

The director of the electronic press kit was Lawrence O'Flavin, whom we quickly renamed Lawrence Awful Haven. His sole claim to fame was making a Volkswagen commercial. Rich and I had specific ideas of what we wanted to do with the film, while Lawrence had his own thoughts. But he was so pompous and arrogant in conveying them that we totally ignored him, blowing off pretty much all of his suggestions. We ended up getting into a lot of disagreements about what was and what wasn't funny, disagreements exacerbated by the fact that we had a much wider sense of humor than he did.

Take the famous Monty Python cheese skit, where an obsessed fromage aficionado names a staggering list of cheeses in one breath: "White Stilton, Danish Blue, Double Gloucester, Cheshire, Dorset Blue Vinney, Brie, Roquefort, Pont l'Évêque," et cetera. Frank knew the entire bit by heart and decided that K.K. had worked in a cheese shop while stranded in Japan and would go off about how much he loved cheese and name them all. Rich and I thought it was hilarious, but O'Flavin wouldn't have it.

"We're not going to do that. It's too esoteric for our demographic."

Too esoteric for our demographic? We *were* the demographic!

After a giant fight the cheese bit stayed, but O'Flavin's pretentiousness and incompetence continued when he set off $10,000 worth of pyro for a scene with no cameras rolling. Les Grossman was not happy and told him to fuck his own face.

Our Spinal Tap homage was turning into the real thing.

When it was all said and done, *Fozzy—Unleashed, Uncensored, Unknown* turned out better than it had any right to. MTV bought the rights to air the movie, and MuchMusic in Canada ran it a few dozen times as well. Zakk loved it and could quote most of it by heart and even turned Ozzy on to it. Sadly, Megaforce decided not to release it on DVD and it just kind of disappeared. A few years later I bought a DVD-making machine and made a thousand copies to sell on my own, not for the money, but for the fans who'd heard about it and had never gotten the chance to see it. I sold it until I was served a cease-and-desist order from Megaforce. If you're a huge Fozzy fan (and who isn't?) and you don't have the DVD, I bet you can find it on eBay—or you can pick one up Sundays between 4 and 6 p.m., when I'm selling them from the back of my trunk on the corner of 53rd and 3rd. See ya then.

CHAPTER 8

Heeeeere's Belding!

WrestleMania is the biggest show of the year for the WWE.

It's the night when every performer vies to steal the show and where careers are made or broken. I would never be a true WWE Superstar until I had been a part of *WrestleMania*, and on April 2, 2000, I finally got my chance. My debut *Mania* match was a Triple Threat vs. Kurt Angle and Chris Benoit, in a Two-Fall match for both the Intercontinental and European titles. Angle had just arrived in the WWE a few months earlier and was getting a huge push by holding both titles. It was decided that Benoit would pin me to win the Intercontinental title in the first fall and I would pin him to win the European Championship in the second, resulting in Angle losing both of his titles without being beaten.

Even though I won a championship, my first *Wrestle-Mania* was not a great experience. The crowd was dead, the match was mediocre, and I was still reeling from the realization that I had been kicked out of the main event.

How did that happen, you ask?

Well, nobody ever officially came out and told me that, but it didn't take Robert Downey Jr. to deduce that something rotten had occurred in Stamford.

Here is the evidence. First, the original poster for the show featured four faces: The Rock, HHH, Big Show, and your fearless scribe.

When it was released I was so excited, I did the WrestleMania Dance (not to be confused with the Nitro Dance).

Here it was, my first *WrestleMania,* and my gorgeous mug was already plastered on the poster! The plan for the main event of *WrestleMania 2000* was a four-way match featuring a McMahon in every corner, each one representing a different wrestler. The problem was that all four of the faces on the original poster were in that match except for me. Then a few weeks before the show, my face was replaced in all of the promo material with Mick Foley's (0 wins vs. Jericho), who was in the main event. So it's not too far off to assume that at some point, I must have been slotted to be in that match, but because I wasn't delivering the goods I was replaced by Mick (0–5 against CJ).

It was a bitter pill to swallow.

In case you haven't figured it out, I'm a weird cat. I need to feel challenged creatively and professionally in order to really deliver in the ring and on camera. Since I felt slighted with my *Mania* match, instead of getting a good night's sleep before the big show, I went to see a Sebastian Bach concert at the House of Blues in L.A. and stayed up drinking until 4:30 in the morning. As I was going back to Anaheim, I passed a giant *WrestleMania* billboard on

Hanging with the Sebastian Bach band (including David Letterman drummer Anton Fig in the sweater) at the House of Blues on Sunset, a scant six hours before the call time for *WrestleMania 2000* in Anaheim. Love my jean shorts.

Sunset featuring the original Jericho-friendly artwork. That made me want to dive even further down a bottle of Crown Royal.

My match was well received by fans and critics, but I didn't care for it at all. I felt the crowd response was lukewarm, and the three of us didn't quite gel. It was a letdown, and for me, my first *WrestleMania* was a *BombaMania*.

After the show there were a bunch of random celebrities hanging around backstage making the scene. Jaleel White, a.k.a. Urkel, was hovering around telling anyone who would listen that his career was on the upswing and he had more work than he could shake a stick at. A very short stick, I assume. Also in attendance was Rob Reiner (who graciously accepted my Fozzy DVD, although I'm sure it met the same fate as the Schwarzenegger storyline I gave to Vince in Baltimore), Robert Sweet from Stryper (who gave me a framed collage of him playing drums, which was ironic since I once waited for hours to get a picture with him when I was seventeen), Wayne Brady, Dennis Miller, Dennis Hopper, Dennis Rodman, Dennis DeYoung, Dennis the Menace, Dennis Stratton, and, most important, DENNIS HASKINS.

Now, if you're asking (a) why there were so many famous people named Dennis backstage at Mania or (b) who in the hell Dennis Haskins is, then keep reading, sport.

Dennis Haskins was the guy who played Mr. Belding, the principal from *Saved by the Bell*. He was also a huge WWE fan, albeit a strange one. Most people would say hi, shake hands, and move along, but Belding followed us around everywhere. In the arena, backstage, catering, crunking, what have you, Belding was there. I felt like Zach Morris trying to cheat in social studies with the amount of attention he was giving me. It seemed like Belding followed the WWE around like a Deadhead. We would show up in Nashville and bingo, there was Belding! I'd walk into the arena in Cleveland and biggity-bam, it was Belding! When I took my seat on a redeye from L.A. to NYC and turned to the passenger next to me, heeeeere's Belding!

"Howya doing Chris?" he said with a nerdy grin.

I stuffed my head into a vomit bag and fell asleep.

*　　*　　*

The night after my *Mania* debacle, I had a match against Eddy Guerrero. I loved Eddy like a brother, but I was praising the heavens above that the finish was Chyna turning on me, costing me the European title, and ending up with him. I was never so happy to lose a title in my life, because it was finally the end of Chyna and Chris Jericho. Overall Chyna was a nice person and she worked hard, but we just didn't get along. But as hard as it was working with Chyna, at least with her I was involved in a storyline. Now, without her by my side, I was dumped back into WWE purgatory. When I showed up in San Jose a month later and was told I was losing to the 450-pound Viscera, I decided it was time to talk to the boss.

One thing about Vince that was so different from WCW boss Eric Bischoff was that he was very accessible. He always made time to speak to his employees and knew the names of everybody on the crew from wrestlers to writers, cameramen to sound guys. All you had to do was knock on Vince's door and if he had time, he would talk.

After our blowout in Tampa, I wasn't as intimidated to talk to him as I was before—the worst thing that could possibly happen already did, and I had survived—so I went into his office and told him my concerns.

"Vince, I've been here for eight months, and besides the feud with Chyna, I haven't really done much. I feel like I'm just spinning my wheels."

He looked directly in my eyes and said, "We need to find a place for you."

He then gave me some cryptic advice. He started talking about Bobo Brazil and what a great babyface he was and how he sold so well. Vince explained that the way a babyface got over was to sell, sell, and sell some more. I felt like Shelley "the Machine" Levine getting lectured by Alec Baldwin, but his point was loud and clear. Then he started talking about how King Kong Bundy's work looked like shit and hurt like hell. It was a subtle message but as Mick (Winless Against Me) Foley had warned, my work was stiff and I needed to lighten up a bit.

He also told me not to get discouraged. "Your time is coming, Chris."

It was a vague statement, but much better than hearing that I wasn't worth the paper my contract was printed on. With his words fresh on my mind, I went to the ring and had what was, in my opinion, one of the best matches Viscera ever had. It wasn't easy, but I worked my ass off to put him over and he did the same for me. I was even able to get him into the Walls of Jericho.

But I was still irritated about being so low on the totem pole, and I decided I was going to talk to Vince again the next week at *Raw* in State College, Pennsylvania.

I couldn't find him all day and had worked myself up into a frenzy by the time I finally ran into Brian Gewirtz.

"Listen, Brian, I'm going to barge into Vince's office and demand that he does something with me right fucking now. I've had enough!"

Brian listened bemusedly and said, "Okay, but before you go in there, let me tell you what we have planned for tonight."

"Whatever, Brian, but don't try and talk me out of it. So what am I doing?"

"You're going to win the heavyweight title from HHH."

My anger blew away like a Buddy Rose diet (obscure,

I know) and suddenly I had a lot more interest in talking to Brian.

He explained the story of the night, a story that had been building for months.

Hunter and Stephanie were together onscreen at that point, and a few months earlier I had done a backstage pretape where I mistook Stephanie for one of the Godfather's hos. It was supposed to be just a one-time thing, but the crowd enjoyed it so much that it became a recurring bit and started a feud between us. I started abusing her verbally on a weekly basis, ending each tirade by calling her a "filthy, dirty, disgusting, brutal, bottom-feeding, trash-bag ho." The fans chanted along with me and it became one of my most popular catchphrases. You gotta love the Attitude Era.

In a lot of ways, my grudge with Steph was the first thing I did that took me to the next level in the eyes of the fans and the company. But it helped her character too, as we had great chemistry as adversaries and played off each other magnificently.

Raw began with me insulting Stephanie, which goaded her into having HHH defend his title against me against his will. The plot thickened when I revealed that I'd hired the APA to be my bodyguards for the night. They chased away Hunter's cronie Shane McMahon, which left me to face the champ mano a mano.

It was my first match against Hunter, and we had gone over things in great detail, since neither one of us quite trusted the other yet and we wanted it to be special. Standing in the Gorilla position as the show began, Hunter told me sternly to take my time and that this was my chance to shine. At that moment all of the animosity that had built up between us over the past nine months disappeared.

It was time to make the doughnuts, and that night we were better than Krispy Kreme.

The match was hard-hitting and went like clockwork. Crisp and in the pocket, it showcased each of us to the best of our abilities. What made the night even more memorable was the raucous crowd. Since my arrival they had seen me lose to women, freaks, geeks, brains, dorks, dweebs, nerds, and Trekkies; now they were ready to see CJ get his due.

HHH had done a spot with referee Earl Hebner a week earlier where he had physically threatened him and Earl said to never put his hands on him again. During the match, Hunter bumped into Earl, and Earl pushed him back. This distracted Hunter long enough for me to nail him with a spin kick, followed by the Lionsault. The crowd worked itself into a frenzy as Hebner delivered what was supposed to be a fast count (it really wasn't), and suddenly for the first time ever, Y2J was the World Champion!

The crowd exploded like Belloq's head.

People were giving high fives and jumping up and down as I grabbed the title and held it over my head in jubilation. It was definitely one of the best moments of my career, made even more special by the first-time-ever standing ovation I received from Vince when I walked through the curtain.

HHH and I deserved every clap in Vince's ovation, as Hunter had made me look like a billion dollars and I had finally lived up to the potential Vince had expected when he signed me.

Most important, I had finally killed the Jericho Curse for good—even though the son of a bitch had more lives than Michael Myers and it took me nine months to do it.

But my victory was only the beginning of the night's story, which continued with me being forced to forfeit the title due to HHH threatening Hebner over the supposed fast count. I felt a little strange doing that, but when I asked Vince about it he said, "You're eventually going to get it back anyway so don't worry about it. That's just the story for tonight."

Stop. Hold on. Stay in control.

Did he just say that I was going to get the title back?

It was the first time I'd heard anything like that from the boss. It was a pretty big statement from Vince and I took it at face value. If he said I would get another chance, then I wasn't going to question giving the title up. But I was still the champion for the next three minutes of commercial break and I was going to enjoy it. I put the title around my waist and looked at myself in the makeup girl's full-length mirror. I allowed myself a mark-out moment as visions of Hogan, Savage, Hart, and Michaels danced around in my head.

I was the World Frickin' Champion!

If aliens from Grimlak attacked Earth right at that moment and blew it up with a gigantic nuclear cannon, I would be the final WWE Champion. That was good enough for me.

It didn't matter that I had to relinquish the title. What did matter was that I proved I could hang at the top and that the fans were with me when I did it. When I got back to the dressing room I had twelve messages on my cell phone from people telling me how happy they were that

I'd won the title. Twenty minutes later, there were twelve more messages on my cell phone telling me how stupid I was to give it back. Fuckin' fascists...

The next night we were in Philadelphia for *Smackdown!*—the first time I'd been back since my ECW days. For the second night in a row I was in the main event, this time against The Rock in a Lumberjack match that I won due to HHH's interference. But even though I beat The Rock, Hunter's music began playing. As far as I'd gotten, I still had a long way to go. But still, for those keeping score (and I am), I had beaten Hunter for the title on Monday and then pinned The Rock in the Lumberjack match on Tuesday. It was a hell of a lot better than losing to Bull Buchanan and Stevie Richards.

Once again it was my night, and after the show ended I stayed in the ring to address the great crowd. It was customary in the Attitude Era for the babyface to give the fans something extra at the end of the night: Austin drank beer, Rocky did improv comedy, Funaki did a jeet kune do demonstration. The crowd seemed like they wanted more, and since I was the last man standing for the evening, I decided to give them a little more Jericho. These were my people and this was my night, dammit!

I picked up the microphone and said in my best Paul Stanley voice, "Did everybody have a good time tonight?"

Twenty thousand Philadelphians roared their approval.

"Well, I did too!"

The crowd cheered wildly for my shameless pandering.

"I've spent a lot of time here over the years, and I can

honestly say that Philadelphia is one of the best fucking crowds in the world…"

The crowd popped even bigger that time.

"And I…"

Wait a minute. What did I just say?

I stopped midsentence as I flipped through my mental Rolodex and asked myself if I had just called Philadelphia one of the best "fucking" crowds in the world. There's no way I let an F-bomb slip in the middle of a WWE ring, was there?

I looked over at Jerry Lawler, and the look on his face told me all I needed to know.

I had just told them they were a great fucking crowd—adults, kids, grandparents, all of them.

To their credit, in another city the crowd would have gasped, children would have run to the door, school-marms would have barfed. But this was Philly, baby!

Swearing here just made me a bigger star.

I walked through the curtain and saw Vince standing there with a big smile on his face, waiting to give me a handshake and congratulate me on my two-day WWE coming-out party.

Even though he was smiling, he had to have heard the F-bomb I dropped on the crowd, right? I had to acknowl-edge it.

"I'm sorry for what I said out there."

The smile wavered on his face and he said, "What do you mean?"

"You didn't hear me say that Philadelphia was the best fucking crowd in the world?"

His smile turned to a look of apprehension. He put his hand down, shook his head, and mumbled that I should keep an eye on my language. Then he walked out of Gorilla, leaving me there with my mouth open and my hand still extended.

Classic Jericho. Even in my finest hour I had still managed to put my foot directly into my mouth. But the taste of my own toe jam didn't change the fact that I had just beaten The Rock and HHH in successive nights. I didn't think I could outdo myself on that one—but I did.

After my *Raw* mitzvah, Vince started relying on me more. I started working in the main events on house shows and getting more important matches on TV. This was never more evident than the night I worked three matches on *Raw* as the top babyface on the show.

We had a PPV in England, and as was the way at the time, we flew out on a Friday night for the show on Saturday and took off directly afterwards, landing in the United States again on Sunday.

But Rocky stayed in the UK to film his first feature film, *The Scorpion King*, and since Austin was out with an injury, I was the top babyface on *Raw* by proxy. Not that it was unwarranted. If you look at the merchandise from 2000 and 2001, the top sellers were Austin, Rock, and Jericho.

The show started with me coming out to insult Vince and Stephanie: "Vince, the fact that you have a big ego is simply a cover for the fact that you have a small penis." After Vince told me to watch my language so as to preserve Stephanie's honor, I retorted with, "The only thing Stephanie knows about honor is jump *on her* and stay *on her*!" (Thanks to Jani Lane for that one.)

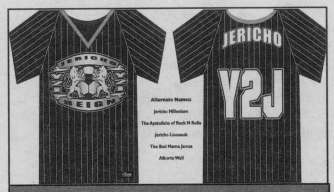

This is a mockup for a Y2J soccer jersey. The name of the fictitious team was the Jericho Reign, but I liked the Bad Mama Jamas. I gave myself that moniker, not realizing that it's slang for a hot chick.

The McMahons were furious, and to exact revenge they booked me in a gauntlet of three matches. First I beat Big Show via count-out, then I beat Kurt Angle with the Walls of Jericho. The third match was against Benoit with HHH as the special referee. The match ended when HHH screwed me, allowing Benoit to win. But I had delivered three good performances and carried the show successfully on my massive back. Vince had given me the ball and I took off with it, runnin' all the way back to Saskatoon.

CHAPTER 9

Moongoose and the Diceman

With the advance Fozzy got from Megaforce, we booked a studio in Atlanta and started recording our first record. I had zero studio experience, and the first song we decided to do was "Riding on the Wind" by Judas Priest.

Nothing like breaking your vocal recording cherry with a Rob Halford song.

Before the very first take, I thought I was a pretty good singer. After listening to said take, I realized I was not. Singing in the studio was the equivalent of warbling in the shower and recording it in Dolby. You could hear every little pop, ping, and bad note emanating from my throat, warts and all. And my voice had more warts than Lemmy at that point.

It took me a while to get into the groove of what I wanted to do and to figure out just how to do it. It's not that I couldn't sing, but I was unpolished and didn't really know what I was doing. One look at Rich's face as he sat behind

In the studio recording the first Fozzy album. I might look like I know what I'm doing, but I don't.

the mixing board told me I wasn't delivering the goods on "Riding on the Wind" the way we both hoped I would. But I improved as the sessions went on, and the last four or five songs we recorded, including Iron Maiden's "The Prisoner," Krokus's "Eat the Rich," and Motley Crue's "Live Wire," turned out really good. We brought in a local musician named Butch Walker to play guitar and sing on Ozzy's "Over the Mountain." A few years later Butch became one of the biggest producers in the country, boasting

Avril Lavigne, Weezer, and Katy Perry on his résumé. We rounded out the album with two originals, "End of Days" and "Feel the Burn," to give the fans an idea of how Fozzy sounded now that we had returned from our innocent exile. When the sessions were done, we ended up with a pretty good first effort that we simply entitled *Fozzy*.

A graphic artist designed our logo and we took photos with a bigwig New York City photographer named Clay Patrick McBride for the cover. We had everything going for us—aside from the fact that we were wearing wigs and playing cover songs.

(Embarrassed Author's Note: We buried "Riding on the Wind" at the end of the record and I still hate listening to it to this day.)

The WWE wanted to get behind us by signing us to their brand-new music division, Smackdown Records. But I didn't want to place the band in the hands of the company. For better or for worse, I had a vision for what I wanted Fozzy to be and I wanted to build it on my own. But the WWE still supported Fozzy as much as they could and decided to do a feature on us for the Saturday morning *Superstars* show.

The piece started with me as Chris Jericho acting like a crazed fanboy, gushing at how excited I was for my favorite band to return to the States. "I'm ecstatic that the best band ever has returned from Japan after all these years to finally reclaim their glory! I'm a huge Moongoose McQueen fan—my look, my act, it's all taken from Moongoose."

Then I did another interview as Moongoose, who said he'd never heard of Jericho but thought he should be sued for ripping off his act.

The way the piece was filmed and edited, it really looked like Moongoose and I were two separate people. After the piece aired, quite a few people were totally confused as to what the hell was going on. Brooklyn Brawler, who'd been working people for fifteen years as a wrestler, asked me, "Did you hear what that Moongoose guy said about you? What a jerk! But that band he plays in is pretty good. I can't believe I've never heard of them before."

I gave him a bewildered look and said, "Come on, Steve! It's me ... I'm Moongoose McQueen!"

He gave me a wan smile and said, "Oh. I thought Fozzy was real."

So did I. So much so that I refused to break character—ever. When I did interviews as Moongoose, I acted like I had no clue who Jericho was. I fell into the Clifton/Kaufman act and wouldn't budge, no matter who tried to make me break character, even Vince McMahon himself.

Fozzy was booked to be the musical guest on *Sunday Night Heat*, a pseudo variety show that aired on MTV on Thursdays—okay, just making sure you're still paying attention.

The idea was that Moongoose and the rest of Fozzy would arrive at the show, act like prima donna rock stars, and finally hit the stage to throw down with a live performance. All of the preparation and scripting was going great until an hour before showtime when the word came down from above that Vince decided he didn't want Moongoose to be Moongoose. Instead, he wanted Moongoose to be Chris Jericho. He didn't like that I was claiming that we were separate people.

But he wanted me to drop the façade onstage and admit that I was really me. I was so committed in what we were doing that I was adamant to not give up the (moon) Goose. I called Vince and told him that I wanted to keep the two characters separate. It's totally preposterous today to think that I was willing to debate my boss over Moongoose McQueen, but I was insistent.

"Vince, Moongoose is just a character I'm playing."

"Why would I allow you to play a character on our show?"

"Well, have you ever heard of Andy Kaufman's Tony Clifton?"

"No, I haven't, and I don't care. Our fans aren't stupid and they'll resent you for trying to fool them with this."

Fooling wrestling fans by playing a character with a storyline and a performance?? Never!! Besides, I was a heel, so wasn't it the idea to make people resent me?

I offered a compromise to Vince: "Well, can I say onstage that Fozzy is Chris Jericho's favorite band? Like in a nudge-nudge, wink-wink kind of way?"

Vince agreed. "Okay, you can do it as long as you insinuate that it's you."

That's what I did and the joke worked.

Unfortunately, the concept of Fozzy wasn't working, and even though we were a pretty smokin' rock and roll band, nobody was buying what we were selling.

Nobody, that is, with the exception of our record company.

Jonny Z and the rest of Megaforce were still treating us like we were Metallica circa 1984. We kept hearing how we were going to break out huge, and some of us started to believe it. After one particularly rousing Jonny Z pep talk, Frank was so excited because he was convinced that after all his years in the music business, he'd finally be headlining arenas with Fozzy. I, on the other hand, woulda been happy headlining a kid's birthday party for a hot dog and a glass of orange juice.

On October 22, 2000, the day the record was released, we went to New York City for a media day. We played a short set at the Virgin Megastore in Times Square to a big crowd and had a successful CD signing afterwards. Then we appeared on a number of radio shows, and everywhere we went I stayed in the Moongoose McQueen character no matter what.

Since part of the backstory was that Fozzy was stuck in the '80s, we dressed accordingly. Leopard-print vests, skintight pants, studded leather wristbands: we looked absolutely ridiculous, but we were committed to the act and had no problem keeping in character. I'd been in show business for ten years, and I knew what kind of dedication was required for success. It didn't bother me at all to walk down the streets of New York City dressed like Vince Neil circa 1983.

Another rule I had was that during the radio interviews I refused to talk about wrestling. If someone asked I'd just say, "I don't know anything about American pro wrestling. But I'll tell you all you need to know about Japanese sumo wrestling." It was like when Will Ferrell went on Conan O'Brien as Robert Goulet, just not as funny or as welcome. I was pissing people off and burning more bridges than Francis Ford Coppola during the making of *Apocalypse Now*.

The last stop on the radio tour was *The Opie and Anthony Show*, hosted by two no-nonsense shock jocks who did not want to play along. They became quite upset that they couldn't get me to admit that I was Chris Jericho.

"Come on! Just tell us you're Chris Jericho! Come on!"

"No, no, no. I'm Moongoose McQueen."

"Okay, Moonjuice or whatever it is you're calling yourself. This is not funny."

I wouldn't budge.

"All right, Moosejuice. What's Lita like? Have you seen her in the shower?"

"Yeah, we've seen Lita Ford in the shower plenty of times. She's pretty hot."

We'd do anything we could do to redirect the conversation back to Fozzy. They finally threw up their hands and gave up, frustrated that they had wasted their time on such a stupid concept. They were about to ask us to leave when the whole appearance was rescued by an unlikely savior: Andrew Dice Clay.

Dice was guest-hosting the show and seemed very confused by what he was witnessing. He had no idea who Fozzy was, who Chris Jericho was, and I'm not quite sure he knew who Opie or Anthony were for that matter. He sat there with a dumbfounded look on his face as I kept saying, "We've been in Japan for twenty years and now we're back to reclaim what's ours. I'm Moongoose McQueen! Enough about this Jericho guy already."

Opie said confrontationally, "Listen, no one cares about Fozzy. We had you in here because we care about the WWE and Chris Jericho."

"Sorry, but I don't know what the WWE is. I'm the singer of Fozzy."

Dice finally piped in. "Listen," he said, "who is this guy? Is he a wrestluh or is he a singuh?"

I said, "Dice, I'm a singer."

"Well, get off his case then . . . he's a singuh."

Suddenly, in one fell cigarette puff, it was now Moongoose and the Diceman vs. Opie and Anthony.

Dice got really into what I was saying and became my hype man. When I mentioned that if you look at our songs chronologically, you could see they were recorded before the other bands released their versions, Dice backed me up by saying, "Listen, he must have a pretty good band if they do all those dance moves. You a good dancuh?"

"Dice, I'm the best dancer," I replied, not exactly sure what he was talking about. It took me a few minutes to realize he had confused the word "chronologically" with the word "choreography."

"I like his aviatuh shades. I like his leopardskin vest. He's talkin' about all the dance moves he can do. I like this guy, give this guy some respect! As a mattuh of fact, I think we should do a show together. You do some of yuh dancin' and singin' and I'll tell some jokes! Hey-ohh, it'll be huge!"

I'm still not sure if Dice was in character, really confused, or really stoned. Maybe all of the above. But it didn't matter, because the two of us took a shit segment and turned it into comedy gold. Any way you slice it (*Asylum*), the combination of Dice and Goose kicked O and A's ass that day and left them in shock.

However I'm still waiting for Dice's call so we can book that show of ours.

The next stop on the promo tour was Toronto, where the band was garnering some interest. The first show we did was a sports talk show called *Off the Record*. It was a panel discussion show, and joining me was an up-and-coming singer named Pink. Once again I stayed completely in character and committed to being a total asshole. She was really nice until I started barraging her with insults.

She had a mild resemblance to Annie Lennox, which prompted me to comment, "Your songs are good, but I liked you better when you were in the Eurythmics."

Pink looked at me, more confused than angry at this point.

"I dig 'Would I Lie to You.' But the rest of your stuff is lame."

"Why is your name Pink if you have blonde hair? Shouldn't you be called Blonde?"

That pissed her off. "Who are you? You think you're some kind of singer?"

"Look who's talking."

She thought I was a total asshole, and she wasn't the only one. I had been on the show before as Jericho and the show's staff was wondering what the hell was wrong with me. To be honest, I don't know the answer either. But I was determined to play this character even though I was dragging my good name through the mud. But what was I accomplishing? Not only was I confusing people, but by acting like a dick, I was driving them away from the band as well.

When I showed up for my next interview on *The Mike Bullard Show*, I was surprised to see the other guest was none other than Pinkie Lennox herself. I sat in the green room in total silence, as she stared daggers out of her eyes, making it a very tense situation. So what? I was still a rock star.

This appearance was different from the others, because the host, Mike Bullard, decided to play along with the gag.

"I remember seeing Fozzy at Massey Hall in 1982.

What a great show! I'm so excited to have you on here tonight!"

There was a smattering of applause as the audience tried to figure out why Chris Jericho was onstage dressed in a leopardskin vest and giant aviator shades, pretending not to be Chris Jericho. The gag was already wearing thin, evidenced by the sales figures for the first week of *Fozzy*'s release. They were lower than Hornswoggle's ballbag.

After Jonny had given us whiplash with his delusions of Metallica grandeur, I was expecting to sell 50,000 copies on the first day. But we didn't even chart in the *Billboard* Top 200.

The problem was that Megaforce was banking on the idea that wrestling fans would flock to Fozzy and buy the CD in droves. I mean, can you blame them? At the time, there were eight million people watching WWE programming every week, and I'll bet that leopardskin vest they figured that even if only 1 percent of those fans bought the record, we'd sell 80,000 copies in a week.

Unfortunately, only .0005 percent of those fans bought the record, and we sold 4,225.

It was a valuable lesson for everybody involved to learn that there's no guarantee that wrestling fans will buy something just because a wrestler is involved.

After the first week's sales figures came in, we could see the difference in Megaforce's attitude almost immediately. Instead of treating us like the next Metallica, they were treating us like the next Odin. Plans for the release of the Fozzy documentary on DVD were canceled, as were plans for release of the record in Europe. Talks of endorsements and appearances on *The Tonight*

Show, Rockline, and *Saturday Night Live* (where we had the idea of using a choir of guest guitar players like Zakk Wylde, Slash, and Eddie Van Halen to back us) were all kiboshed.

The gravy train had run off the rails and we were nothing more than a cover band again.

Allllll aboard . . . hahahahaha.

CHAPTER 10

Vince Loves Apes

*W*restleMania X-Seven was looming and it was decided that I would work with my old friend from WCW, William Regal. Regal was a good worker and a tremendous character actor. He had one of best personas in the company and knew how to garner serious heat no matter what position he was in. Because his character was such a snob, it was easy to make him the butt of a joke, which is why our angle began with me going tee-tee in his tea-tea.

Yeah, you read that right. I pissed in his Earl Grey.

Allow me to explain. Regal was the evil commissioner and was deriving great pleasure from screwing with me. One night in Madison Square Garden, he put me into a handicap match against him and his Japanese minion Tajiri, daring me to find a partner of my own.

"Who would ever want to partner with you?" he said condescendingly. "The Phantom of the Opera?" Then he and Tajiri started laughing maniacally and it was totally preposterous.

Later in the night I stormed into his office looking for justice and found his cup of tea instead.

So I turned my back to the camera and pantomimed pulling out my Piccadilly. Then I took a squirt bottle (pun intended) out of my pocket and squeezed it into the cup, which on TV sounded like I was leaking in his Lipton. When Regal came back into his office and took a sip of the tea, he made comedic history with some of the most ridiculous facial expressions ever made. It made the urine-drinking cop's face in *Dumb and Dumber* seem as funny as a Daniel Day Lewis movie.

The angle continued as I constantly outsmarted Regal with my immense babyface cunning. When a Legends Battle Royal was booked for *WrestleMania*, featuring such household names as Typhoon, Duke "the Dumpster" Droese, and Doink the Clown, Regal was doing an interview and was interrupted and attacked by Doink, who ended up being me in disguise.

I had just applied the intricate clown makeup and was waiting to do my run-in when Shawn Michaels walked past me, gave a double take, and walked back.

Shawn was one of my all-time favorites, and (along with Owen Hart and Ricky Steamboat) was my main inspiration to get into the wrestling business. I came to the WWE with the hope of working with him even though he was only with the company part-time at that point and still battling the demons that were holding him back in his life.

Shawn got in my clown face and gave me a Larry David–esque suspicious stare, and I noticed he was pretty wasted.

"What's going on, Chris?" he said, his eyelids drooping and his speech slurring. "Are you doing the Doink gimmick now?"

"No, I'm just doing it for tonight. I'm ambushing Regal."

"So you're gonna be Doink now?"

"No, no. I'm just doing it for one night as a way to surprise Regal."

"But why do you have to be Doink?" he asked again, slowly swaying back and forth.

"But I'm not Doink, Shawn. It's just for tonight."

"But why would they make you Doink?"

I felt like Abbott and Costello, except instead of Who's on First, the routine was Who's on Drugs, and it wasn't me.

"I'm *not* Doink. It's just an angle for tonight."

Shawn shook his head and waltzed away. "I don't like it, they should never have made you Doink."

He passed out in Vince's office later that night and was fired. Shawn eventually cleaned himself up and came back to the WWE better than ever a few years later. When he did, I finally got the chance to work with him and had one of the best matches of my career.

Wait for it, guys... wait for it.

Regal and I opened the show at *WrestleMania X-Seven*. The match wasn't bad, but I think it could've been so much more. My biggest problem with it was the lack of time we were given. *Mania* took place in the Houston Astrodome, and the walkway to the ring was so long that by the time we got out there we had about seven minutes for the entire match. We did our best but it was rushed and we were off on certain spots. Even though I won, in my mind I was 0–2 in my *Mania* performances.

Later on at the after-show party, Vince complimented me on the match and told me how much he liked it, but I wasn't buying it. I was feeling pretty down on myself and knew I could do better.

Once again, the feud with Stephanie came to the rescue and was taking on a life of its own. The fans were eating it up because there was this great chemistry between the bitchy, spoiled billion-dollar princess and the sharp-tongued rock star who couldn't be outwitted. That was the unique quality about the Y2J character that helped me connect with the fans—I would say things that nobody else could. It didn't make a difference who I was talking to: another wrestler, the boss, or even the boss's daughter.

(Chauvinistic Author's Note: Isn't it ironic—like a free ride when you've already paid—that one female almost killed my career while another one wholly revitalized it?)

I tore poor Steph apart with my insults, and watching my verbal attacks on her is like watching an episode of *All in the Family*—I said things to her that could never be repeated on TV in this day and age.

My entire Stephanie routine was based around the idea that she was a total slut who slept with every man, woman, and hermaphrodite that she came across—who then presumably returned the favor by coming across her.

When it was Stephanie's twenty-fifth birthday I asked her, "How old are you, Steph? Thirty-five, thirty-six? Or is that just how many guys you've been with since last week?"

HHH stood up for his wife, saying, "You can't yell at Stephanie like that, she's a delicate little flower!"

"Stephanie lost her flower a long time ago."

When Stephanie and her lackey Rhyno were in the ring, I explicated what I was going to do at the next PPV. "At *SummerSlam*, I'm going to take care of that smelly, greasy, nasty animal—and I'm gonna get you too, Rhyno!"

Or:

"Standing in the ring you've got the Man-Beast and the Hose-Beast! I'm dealing with the Gore and the Whore."

Well, you get the idea.

It got over huge as the fans delighted in my abuse of the billion-dollar princess, all the while chanting along with my "filthy, dirty, disgusting, brutal, bottom-feeding, trash-bag ho" catchphrase. It was a strange sight, seeing five-year-old kids shouting out "trash-bag ho" at the top of their lungs, but then again I never claimed to be a role model for America's children.

Whenever I went over any of these barbs broadcasting his daughter's supposed promiscuousness with Vince, he would listen with a pensive look on his face and say, "Just make sure after you deliver the insult you take a pause so people can react."

That Vince...ever the businessman.

And ever the fan of apes.

Apes, you say? Well, allow me to elucidate.

Brian called me one evening to go over the standard insult promo on Stephanie that I'd be delivering on *Raw* that Monday. It was business as usual and I didn't think about it again, until he called the next day and said, "We have an issue. We have to figure out a way to add apes into this promo."

What was he talking about?

"Vince loves apes. We're doing a tie-in with the *Planet of the Apes* remake and he wants them on the show. He said, 'If anyone can make it work it's Jericho. He'll figure out what to do with them.'"

Vince's statement was a compliment and a curse. I had developed a rep as a guy who could make anything work, whether it was wearing a referee jersey with HE HATE ME written on the back to promote the XFL or guiding a half-insane Bob Backlund (sans talking dictionary) through a live promo. Now Brian and I had to figure out a way to guide a couple of apes through a segment promoting both their new movie and *SummerSlam*. It was a verbal Rubik's Cube.

Not to be deterred, Brian and I put our heads together and came up with a pretty damn good idea.

The show started and Stephanie came to the ring talking about· *SummerSlam*, until she was promptly interrupted by your noble novelist.

"Stephanie, to you *SummerSlam* is a quickie on a hot August night. You've slept with everybody in this company from the boys in the back, to the cameraman, to the ring crew, to the merchandise sellers, to the lighting guy, to the popcorn vendor in the fifteenth row—congratulations, Lou, you finally did it!"

I spewed the insults out like a Jay-Z rhyme and the fans were going crizzle for my shizzle.

I continued by picking up on a rant she had been on about how her brother Shane always won while she always lost.

"Don't worry, Stephanie, Shane may come out on top, but you always end up on the bottom... and on your knees... on the coffee table... on the kitchen counter."

The crowd licked it up like Vinnie Vincent as I concluded: "Stephanie, since you've slept with everybody on this entire planet, maybe it's time for you to broaden your horizons and sleep with something from another planet—the *Planet of the Apes*, for example."

Ladies and gentlemen, I present to you the worst segue ever.

The apes came ambling down the ramp, with their simian arms and legs swinging to and fro absurdly. They came bearing gifts that included a cake in a box, although at this point a dick in a box would've been better. The bit ended when I adhered to the time-honored tradition in wrestling where anytime a cake is brought into the ring it must end up with someone's face being smashed into it. In this case it was Stephanie's mug that ended up in the icing, leaving her humiliated as the apes lurched around with joy. When I came through the curtain Vince gave me a standing ovation as if I had just delivered a five-star classic at *Wrestlemania*.

An audience of one indeed.

My ape performance once again put me on Vince's good side and suddenly he wanted to use me in every situation. I was sitting in the dressing room in GM Place in Vancouver after my match, cooling down and contemplating a shower. Kid Rock was about to play on *Raw* and I was looking forward to checking him out, as we hadn't seen each other since our all-nighter in Cancun years earlier (story in *A Lion's Tale*, available online now). Back then we were still climbing the ladder to success, and now only a short three years later both of us had made it to the big time.

So I was chillin' like a villain on Thanksgivin' (shameless rapper pandering) when Road Dogg ran into the dressing room at full speed.

"Vince wants you in the Gorilla position right now!"

"Why?"

"You've got to introduce Kid Rock!"

"What? Why?"

"'Cause I was supposed to do it but I'm a heel and Vince just decided he wants you to do it instead! He's on in two minutes! You have to go now!"

I thought he was ribbing me. There's a famous nightmare that a lot of wrestlers have where your music is playing and you don't have your boots or your tights on and you're running around like a lunatic trying to get ready.

This was that nightmare come true. I threw on some pants and sprinted as fast as I could from the dressing room to the stage. As I barreled past Kid Rock and rounded the corner I heard him say, "Don't fuck this up, Chris!"

I took the stairs two at a time and plowed into Gorilla just as a roadie put a mic in my hand.

"What do you want me to say, Vince?"

"Whatever you want, you're the rock star. Just get out there and do it now!"

I ran onstage with the microphone and said in my best David Lee Roth voice, "Ladies and gentlemen, please welcome, straight from Detroit, Michigan, the Early Mornin' Stoned Pimp:

"Kid Rockkkkkkkkkkkkkkkkkkkkkkkkkk!"

My head exploded *Scanners* style.

After I finished being Kid's hype man, his band came out and I was trapped. I couldn't stay on the stage, I couldn't run down to the ring, and I couldn't go back into Gorilla because his band members were filing out and the song was about to start. Plus a bunch of pyro was supposed to go off, but I didn't know where it was coming from and didn't want to get Hetfielded. So I was scrambling around trying to find a place to hide when I noticed a hole between the stage and the back area and jumped into the seven-foot drop. I was safe from the pyro and out of everybody's way, but then realized that I had a whole new problem: there was no way out of the hole. I was too short to pull myself out and I was surrounded by crates and wires, so there was no way to weasel my way out from underneath the stage.

When Kid Rock finished playing "American Badass" and walked offstage to massive applause, I was still stuck in my rock and roll foxhole. Finally a stagehand popped his head over the edge and helped pull me out. As I climbed out of the hole I saw 15,000 people pointing their fingers at me and laughing. I gave them a golf wave and sheepishly walked back through Gorilla.

Vince was shaking his head in bemusement. Court Jester Jericho had struck again.

As much as Vince loved my Kid Rock intro and ape promo, he absolutely hated my all-time favorite Stephanie Insultapalooza.

Raw was in Chicago (which has the loudest fans in the United States by far), and the idea was for The Rock and me to trade insults on Stephanie and her minions Rhyno and Booker T. Stephanie had just gotten a boob job, which was a comedic gold mine, and I started off by showing before-and-after pictures of her on the Tron. Then I hit her with as many mammary jokes as I could.

The theme for the PPV was Drowning Pool's biggest hit, and I said, "Never mind 'Let the Bodies Hit the Floor,' Steph. How about 'Let the Boobies Hit the Floor'!"

"Stephanie, I'm sorry about all this miscommunication. Let me take you to lunch and we'll talk about it. There's a Hooters right down the street."

"Stephanie, you're the breast—I mean the best!"

The crowd was eating it up with a silver spoon and it was one of the best promos of my career. Everything was going great until it was time for Rock to deliver his final line, which was a short rhyme describing Booker and Steph as "a punk-ass sucka and a silver-spoon motherfu—"

At this point Steph was to cut him off before he finished.

But she didn't cut him off in time and The Rock delivered the line as written on live television.

"'Cos you're a punk-ass sucka and a silver-spoon motherfuckaaaaaa!!!"

I figured they would just beep out Rocky's faux pas and that would be the end of it. But when Rock and I came through the curtain buzzing about how great the segment was, the boss's face was bright red and cordlike veins were bulging out of his neck.

"It's not my fault," The Rock said. "She didn't cut me off on time!"

Maybe so, but did he have to actually say *that* word... and with such gusto?

Of course not—but it was the Attitude Era and that was The Rock. Motherfuckaaaa or not, it was a classic bit.

Stephanie kept on taking the abuse like Lindsay Lohan's ankle monitor, but she would always get her retribution by doing something dastardly. She was involved in a relationship with HHH by then (both in the ring and out), and it was only natural that he would stand up for his woman at some point. When he finally did, it led to my best match in the WWE yet.

HHH and I built up our angle, which culminated with a Last Man Standing match at *Fully Loaded*. The PPV was based on the concept of three established headliners working with three up-and-coming superstars. Besides our match, the other two main events were The Rock vs. Chris Benoit and Undertaker vs. Kurt Angle. It was a big chance for all of us and we had earned it.

Stephanie was in HHH's corner, and the fans in Dallas were pumped to see the match. H was on fire as a heel and was at the top of his Game (aren't I clever?), and he showed up prepared to steal the show. HHH is first and foremost a great worker, and he proved that to me forever on that day.

The rules for Last Man Standing are no pinfalls, submissions, or DQs, and it can only end when one of the participants fails to answer a ten-count. This made it easy to get the crowd involved as they cheered and counted along with every tally. We constructed it with so many twists and turns, that the crowd was on the edge of their seats for the duration.

Hunter held my arms as Stephanie tattooed me with a vicious slap to the face. Then he hit me with the Pedigree but I was able to stagger up at eight. I whacked him with a chair and he collapsed in a heap, his face a crimson mask (thanks, Gordon), but was able to answer the count. Then I locked him in the Walls and he tapped out, but it was all for naught as there are no submissions in an LMS. We ended up on the floor and hit each other with the television monitors simultaneously, but both of us made it up at nine. Then the actual finish was going to be me standing on the announce table, preparing to moonsault HHH through the Spanish announce table directly beside it. Hunter would stop me and give me a belly-to-back suplex from one table through another, taking us both out. We would stay down as the referee counted, but HHH would stand up at nine, breaking the count and winning the match.

Sounds great, right? Well, in theory it was, until my old buddy Chyna screwed the pooch and messed it up. Earlier in the night she had a match with Perry Saturn where despite the huge signs at Gorilla saying STAY AWAY FROM THE ANNOUNCE TABLES, they slammed into the table that had been specially constructed to break for our finish and broke it first.

This was a scant twenty minutes before we were supposed to go on, and I was taping up in the trainer's room when I saw our table (and our finish) fall apart.

I told HHH casually, "Chyna and Perry just went through the announce table. We need a new finish."

Such are the trials and tribulations of live TV, folks. You have to go with the flow and roll with the changes, and after we discussed it for about three minutes, I suggested that we could still do the belly-to-back through the table, only start from the barricade right next to it. The problem was we had no idea where I would land. Would I slide right off the table and whack my head on the cement behind it? But it didn't matter as we had run out of options. It was time to remove all the wheel blocks, there's no time to waste. So when it came time for the finish, I rammed HHH onto the table and climbed the barricade to moonsault him. He clocked me from behind and away we went. It was a strange and slightly terrifying feeling because I had no idea where I was going to land and couldn't see where I was anyway. I held my breath and prepared for the worst, but we landed on the table at the same time and it blew apart easily. My head whacked the edge of the table but luckily not the concrete itself. I breathed a sigh of relief as the crowd began chanting, "Holy shit!"—their equivalent of saying, "Nice work, gentlemen, we appreciate the hard work and oh my was that ever impressive."

When HHH got up at nine and a half, answering the count and winning the match, the crowd wasn't happy but they knew they had seen something special. Sure, H had his hand raised, but I had taken him to infinity and beyond and he had barely survived in the process. I had taken the mighty HHH to the absolute limit, and it had light-yeared me into a different galaxy in the eyes of the fans.

Even though I lost the match, I felt I was the real Last Man Standing that night.

CHAPTER 11

Be Froot

After Fozzy's dismal first week of sales, even though Megaforce pretty much gave up on us, we never gave up on ourselves. We continued to play as many shows as we could no matter if there were one, one hundred, or one thousand people in the crowd, doing gigs everywhere from Chattanooga to Atlanta, Macon to Montreal, New York to Norfolk. We mostly headlined, but on the odd occasions when we opened for established bands like Seven Mary Three or Sum 41, we blew them off the stage.

We learned very quickly that between Rich and me, Fozzy had two showbiz vets who had no problem going the extra mile to entertain. We took our music very seriously, but not ourselves, and we began to develop a reputation as a great live band.

One of the reasons for that was even though I was relatively new to being the frontman of a rock and roll band, I wasn't new to the concept of being a party host. I'd always treated wrestling as show business, and part of being a successful wrestler for the past ten years was having the ability to command an audience. I had a knack for involving the audience and setting the tone for everyone to have a good time. The most valuable lesson I learned from all my favorite showmen, from Paul Stanley to Hulk Hogan, was that by making the crowd a part of the show, the gig became an interactive, exciting experience that people would pay to see the next time we came to town.

The WWE opened a first-class nightclub and concert venue in the middle of Times Square called the World. Every time Fozzy played there we had a wild, responsive crowd, which was so important, because whether it's rock and roll or wrestling, the energy from the crowd inspires the performance and vice versa. The boisterous crowds were a great confidence booster for the band, because even though our album wasn't selling like hotcakes, our live shows were tearing down the house.

We had a pretty loose backstage area and anybody who wanted to hang around was welcome. Every time we played the World there was always this guy hanging around who worked in the restaurant as a magician, going from table to table doing tricks for the customers. He had long straight black hair and wore the coolest leather clothes that he made himself.

"I know you like to wear stuff like this, and if you ever need me to make anything for you, here's my card," he told me as he gave me his card with his cell number written on the back. We invited him to eat dinner with us before the show one night. In the middle of the meal, he asked me an odd question.

"Chris, will you please hold up your fork?"

I held it up, and he just stared at it until it started *bend-*

ing in half. It was unbelievable, and he didn't stop until it looked like a 7. I had taken the fork out of the random napkin it was wrapped in, so there was no way it was a gimmick or a plant. It was totally amazing, and to this day I still don't know how he did it.

Even though I'd seen him a few times at our shows, I still wasn't sure what his name was.

"That was incredible, man! What's your name again?"

"It's Criss. Criss Angel."

A mindfreak indeed. Damn, I wish I still had that card.

Months later I saw him at the World and he told me that he was planning on submerging himself in a tank of water for twenty-four hours in the middle of Times Square. I was wrestling at Madison Square Garden that night, so I told him I'd stop by to lend my support. After the gig I went to the World where he had set up shop, stopping to grab a slice of pizza and a strawberry yogurt first. I walked into the lobby and there he was, submerged in a tank of water. He'd been in the drink for over twelve hours at that point, but when he saw me he waved weakly in my direction. His skin was fish-belly white, and with his mane of jet black hair floating around him he looked like a gothic Luke Skywalker floating in the bacta tank.

I was damn proud of him and gave him a thumbs-up as I took a bite of my delicious pepperoni pizza. He stared back at me glassy-eyed and feebly clawed at the glass that separated us. I figured he was delirious at that point but was probably happy to have a friend to cheer him on. I finished the scrumptious slice of 'za and peeled the tinfoil lid off the yogurt, shielding myself from the inevitable storm of tiny strawberry splotches that followed. As I licked them off my fingers, Criss kept staring longingly at me, and even though it was starting to get a little creepy, I gave him the A-OK sign. I took a big spoonful of the delectable dessert, and just as I put it to my lips, a hairy arm slapped on my shoulder and dragged me around the corner.

I looked up as a burly guy with a mustache (Eli Cottonwood represent yo) got in my face.

"What the hell are you doing? You can't stand there in front of Criss eating! He's been in that tank for twelve hours...he's starving in there and you're taunting him!" I sheepishly threw my yogurt in the trash and waved goodbye to my valiant friend whom I'd been torturing for the last ten minutes like a college student in *Hostel*. Criss gawked at me longingly, and even though he was completely submerged with a scuba mask on, I'm pretty sure I saw him drooling.

What Fozzy lacked in original material we made up for with our live show. During our concerts we would tell jokes, bring fans onstage for beer-chugging or stage-diving contests, have them sing the choruses and rock the shit out of some of the best rock and roll songs of all time. After doing enough jumping, running, and head-banging to make the cast of *Celebrity Fit Club* sweat, I would always close the show with the same farewell to the faithful:

"We are Fozzy and We Are Huge Rock Stars!!"

I'd learned from wrestling that to market yourself, you needed a great catchphrase, and we had found ours. We expanded from two guitar players to three and for a short period we boasted the first ever four-guitar lineup when

Andy Sneap, a Grammy-winning (Petty Author's Note: It was a Swedish Grammy so it barely counts.) producer who had worked with Fozzy and Stuck Mojo, joined us whenever he was available.

Sneap became Lord Edgar Bayden Powell, a direct descendant of King Arthur. His stage garb consisted of a full-body chain-mail outfit that made him look like one of the Knights Who Say Ni. Rich liked having him in the band because he was a good friend and a good guitar player. I liked having him in the band because he liked to drink.

Over the years, I had been bestowed with the nickname of Drunkicho, due to a complete personality change whenever I got really loaded. Drunkicho was famous for throwing glasses against the wall, insulting anyone who got in his way, and generally acting like a barmy buffoon no matter the situation. Quite frankly, Drunkicho was an idiot.

After a gig in Charlotte, Sneap and Drunkicho went out on the town and ended up in a diner for a late-night grease meal. Covering the walls were dozens of eight-by-ten photos of various celebrities who had eaten there over the years, and much to my amusement I noticed that one of those eight-by-tens was mine. In my state of intoxication, I decided that because my picture was on the wall, I could do whatever I wanted in that establishment. I hopped up on my table and proclaimed myself the "King of the Diner," and threw my water glass against the wall to christen it. This led to Sneap and me getting into an argument over whether Canadians or Englishmen could drink more. Eventually, I started throwing punches around and preaching from my chair. Sneap tackled me and we rolled

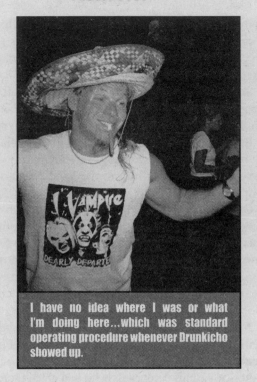

I have no idea where I was or what I'm doing here...which was standard operating procedure whenever Drunkicho showed up.

back and forth under tables and over the other patrons' feet, knocking plates off of tables and laughing like imbeciles. Finally, the owner threatened to call the cops if we didn't stop.

"It's okay," I stammered matter-of-factly as Sneap poured a packet of sugar over my head. "My picture is on the wall!"

"Not anymore," the owner said, and he hurled the frame at my chest.

Sneap and I spent the rest of the night driving around our hotel in circles while honking the horn in time with the radio.

The Duke and Andy Sneap onstage live in 2001. Rich loved playing with Sneap and I loved drinking with him.

The ridiculosity continued after one of our gigs at the World, when one of the bouncers told us about another club he worked at. It was 2:30 a.m. when Sneap, Willis, myself, and Paul Gargano, the editor of *Metal Edge* magazine, stumbled into the biggest gay bar in New York City.

Not that there's anything wrong with that.

So an Englishman, a Canadian, and an American walk into a gay bar and begin to move to the music. It sounds like a bad party joke, I know, but let me assure you that there was nothing bad about the brilliance of the *dance* that followed.

Surrendering to the beat, we let the music take us away on a magical mystery tour and started performing moves so provocative, even Adam Lambert would cover his eyes in embarrassment. I did an old-school electric boogaloo, moonwalking and pirouetting like Baryshnikov on crack. Sneap spun on his back as Gargano held his legs and turned him. The three of us joined hands and did a chorus line kicking routine that would've made the Rockettes jealous—and we had better legs.

We jived when it was time to jive, discoed when it was time to disco, and African anteater ritualed when it was time to African anteater ritual. The three of us were James Brown during the *T.A.M.I. Show*, Michael Jackson during the 1983 AMAs, and Pee-wee Herman during *Pee-wee's Big Adventure* all rolled into one. The crowd formed a circle around us, clapping in unison and hanging on our every move, as haters skulked away realizing they couldn't keep up with our brilliance. We evacuated the dance floor faster than Cascada ever could, and no man (and there were plenty of them there) could match us. We reveled in our ritual of interpretive blood, sweat, and tears until it was time for the grand finale. While Sneap and Gargano stood side by side in a half crouch, I did a running roll and sprang up with both of my feet landing solidly on each of their thighs. At that moment we were golden Gods; a perfect human pyramid basking in the glory of the standing ovation provided by our newfound fans. Then we took a bow and walked the fuck out of their lives forever.

Or something like that.

Sneap and I spent the rest of the night riding the luggage cart into the walls of the Newark Hilton.

The Jericho-Sneap debauchery™ continued a few months later after a gig in Chicago. There were a couple of pretty girls in the audience, which was a rare thing for Fozzy. Most of our fans were guys, and the majority of them could've entered a Joey Ramone look-alike contest and fared quite well. After the show, Sneap and I struck up a conversation with the birds and they invited us to come visit them at the club they worked at. We had no idea what kind of club we were going to meet them at since it was already after 2 a.m., but we followed a map (Archaic Author's Note: These were the days before GPS, kids.) until we eventually found the street the club was on. But the farther we drove, the darker it got. We ended up turning onto what looked like a deserted road, with a burned-out strip mall at the end of it. As we got closer, I saw that the windows of all the stores were painted black except for one that had a little neon sign in the corner that said OPEN.

That was peculiar.

We opened the door, and were greeted by another door. At the end of that small corridor was a small sliding window, like the one on the door leading into the Emerald City of Oz. Sneap knocked, but instead of the Lollipop Guild, a short greasy Danny DeVito–looking guy with a huge mustache slid the window open and said with a growl, "Yeah?"

It wasn't the friendliest of greetings, and even though our Spidey senses were telling us to vacate the premises, we had come too far to turn back now.

"Hi," I announced. "We're looking for Lilly." (Legal Author's Note: Lilly's name has been changed to protect the innocent. Plus I have no idea what Lilly's name actually was, so "Lilly" will have to suffice.) "We met her about an hour ago and she invited us."

Then came the eternal question that every musician from Steve Perry to Joe Perry, Eric Carr to Ringo Starr, and Ryan Ahoff to Paul Baloff has been asked.

"You guys in a band or something?"

When we answered that we most certainly were, Oswald Cobblepot warmed up and muttered, "Come inside."

He opened the door and led us into a makeshift waiting room occupied by three filthy pea green couches. We opted to stand, shifting back and forth on our toes, until Louie DePalma announced that Lilly hadn't arrived yet but was on her way. I wandered over and looked into one of the corner rooms. Inside was a worn-down massage table covered with horrible upholstery seemingly from a 1970s leisure suit. Half-empty bottles of massage oil were assembled on a scratched and worn wooden table, along with stacks of yellowed sheets, skin lotions, containers of baby wipes, an old ster—

My mind zipped back to the containers of baby wipes. I did some basic pervert math and came up with the following equation: Lotion + Baby Wipes = Jack Shack.

It seems our innocent Lilly (and probably her friend) was employed at this fine establishment as a Happy Ending Consultant. If we decided to stick around (and with the funk on the floor that wasn't too hard to do), I could imagine the headline if the cops happened to raid the joint right then:

"Wrestler and Englishman Arrested at Rub N Tug."

We turned tail and ran out of there faster than my first sexual experience.

Now I know what Vincent Benedict meant when he told us to come inside.

* * *

Don't get me wrong, Fozzy did have other female fans beside Ms. Knob Knuckler, including a pack of girls who followed us everywhere. As much as I'd love to tell you they were *Playboy* bunnies or *Maxim* models, they were not. We affectionately referred to them as the Hungry Bunch, and they followed us loyally to every gig, small or big. And these girls were big.

But they were awesome supporters and we treated them as if they looked like porn stars. It was always nice to see them blush when we told them how pretty they looked or how nice their outfits were. They were also the first ones who got behind our attempt to enrich the pop culture vernacular by popularizing the new slang term "froot."

Rich, Bud, and I had long debated the origins of the word "cool," and how it went from being a remark about the weather to the most used slang word in the English language. Someone had to have invented it, and we decided we would try to invent our own version of "cool" with the word "froot." But the difference was, "froot" could mean almost anything, much like the word "aloha."

"Man, this song is froot." Translation: This song sounds awesome.

"That chick is froot." Translation: She's hot.

"Come on, guys, it's time to get froot!" Translation: It's time to get serious, guys!

Despite years of trying, "froot" still hasn't lived up to its worldwide potential, but I'm hoping with the release of this fine book it will get the respect it deserves and finally sweep the nation.

Millions of Team Edward T-shirt-wearing tweeners will use it multiple times daily. "Vampires are froot!"

Movies like *Be Froot*, *Froot Runnings*, and *Froot Hand Luke* will be blockbuster hits.

Famous rappers like LL Froot J will rule the airwaves. *Happy Days* will be released on DVD with new over-dubbed audio featuring the Fonz rocking his new updated catchphrase: "Cunningham, you don't get any chicks because you're just not froot... Ayyyyyyyyyyy!"

Jersey Shore will introduce a new Guido named the Frootuation, who will be obsessed with his daily routine of FTL-Froot, Tan, Laundry.

The whole world, no matter what race, creed, religion, or social status, will be united by froot and world peace will soon follow. Say it loud and proud with me now, friends: Froot! Froot! Froot! Froot!

CHAPTER 12

WTF

Even though we weren't selling millions of records or revitalizing the lingua franca, we were still making headway as a band. Paul Gargano, fresh off his exploits in the New York club scene, liked Fozzy and was a longtime fan of Rich and Stuck Mojo, so he always made sure there were articles on us in *Metal Edge* magazine and eventually gave us a centerfold. Even though the picture was taken right after a sweaty gig and the staple was in the middle of my face, it was still a centerfold, something that thousands of bands will never get.

On the heels of this great publicity and the word of mouth our live show was getting, we were approached to endorse both Dean Markley strings and Peavey amplifiers.

It was a tremendous deal; they gave us free gear and all we had to do was say, "Fozzy uses Dean Markley and Peavey Amps" in the liner notes of our records, and once a year we had to appear at the National Association of Music Merchants convention.

NAMM is a wet dream for rock fans, as every rock star on the planet goes there to repay the companies who give them free stuff, by making appearances and doing auto-graph signings for an entire weekend.

It was an honor to be there, but it was a little ridiculous to be wearing wigs and dressing as knights as we signed autographs next to Jeff Waters, Dave Mustaine, and Eddie Van Halen.

Too much fucking perspective.

Musicians would walk by, staring at the long lines we had for our autograph sessions, wondering who the hell we were or why we were so popular. Some of them even questioned our intentions.

Dimebag Darrell came by to say hi to Rich, since they had gotten to know each other when Stuck Mojo toured with Pantera years before.

"Are you making fun of heavy metal?" Dime asked suspiciously.

When Rich responded that it was quite the opposite and that we were in fact paying tribute, Dime smiled and said, "I figured. I love the album, but I didn't want to have to hate it if you were making fun of metal."

After that, Dime was all smiles and went on to tell Rich that Pantera played *Fozzy* on their tour bus and really dug the way we'd updated and heavied up the classics.

Rich had a great reputation as a guitarist and as a per-former, and after years of internal tension within Stuck Mojo, Fozzy was his chance to have fun playing music again. And fun it was; with our backstory and costumes we were the original Steel Panther, just not as popular.

Later that night, we had a gig in Anaheim that had been advertised as an All Star Jam with Fozzy. Problem was we had no All Stars to jam with.

So the promoter issued an open invite at NAMM,

and throughout the convention, musicians stopped by our signings to see if we were worthy of playing with. Most of them took one look at us and assumed we weren't. If they had stuck around and rocked with us they would've had a blast, but our gimmick was so over the top that you either got it or thought we were idiots.

Most thought we were idiots.

One of the guys who came by was Brad Gillis, who'd replaced Randy Rhoads in Ozzy before playing guitar with Night Ranger. He had no clue what we were, and when he came down to our autograph signing to find out, he just stood there staring at us with a Zoolander Blue Steel face. I could tell he was thinking, "There's no way in hell I'm jamming with these morons."

The same thing happened when Jeff Pilson, the bass player of Dokken, showed up at the gig and asked me, "Hey, is Fozzy here?"

I said, "Yeah, we're Fozzy."

Confused, he said, "Oh, okay . . . are you guys a band?"

When I confirmed that we were indeed a band, I could tell he was thinking, "There's no way in hell I'm jamming with these jackasses."

Jeff nodded his head and said, "Okay, I'll be right back."

Of course he never came back, and at the end of the night after dozens of musicians had been invited to our All Star Jam, exactly zero showed up. None. Zilch. Nada. Fuck-all.

But 10,000 fans (okay, it was fifty) did show up and the gig began. There were a few opening bands, including Iron Horse featuring Ron Keel. Ron's band Keel (what else would it be named) had a few hits in the '80s, including "The Right to Rock" and their cover of Patty Smith's "Because the Night."

Lenny and I had been big fans of Keel in high school, and here he was opening for my band ten years later—a fact that old Ronnie boy didn't look too happy about.

He had forty-five minutes for his set, as there was a strict curfew. So he started playing and playing and playing and soon his forty-five minutes became fifty, then fifty-five. Now, when it comes to concert curfews, if an opening act plays ten minutes long, that takes ten minutes out of the headliner's set, and that's a rock and roll cardinal sin.

Rich was furious at Keel. Years before at a festival, Nick Cave intentionally ran long and cut into Mojo's set. So Rich walked onstage and punched Cave square in the face, ending his performance for the evening. This time, instead of fisticuffs, Rich simply walked onstage and unplugged the power just as Keel was about to launch into his biggest hit, "The Right to Rock."

I was actually looking forward to hearing the song, as were the seven other people who came to see him, but Rich had had enough and gave Keel The Right to Stop. He proceeded to usher him off the stage and that was it. During our whole set I could see Keel in the back of the bar pacing back and forth giving us the stinkeye, like he was planning to mug us after the show. I had three Keel records and thought they were a pretty froot band in 1986, but seeing him stalking around with a boo-boo face just made me feel sorry for him.

Soon after, we figured it was time to do another record, and this time Rich and I wanted to make the album half originals, half covers.

NEXT PHOTO >

Fozzy outside of NAMM 2002. A few hours later we played the Fozzy All Star Jam, in which no All Stars showed up. Note my head-to-toe pleather suit.

Even though the first record hadn't sold very well, Megaforce decided to sign us to a second album mostly due to the fact that Jonny Z had sold the company and was gone.

Recording in the studio was a little easier the second time because I had some studio experience, plus we'd done dozens of gigs since finishing the first album. The covers we chose, including "Freewheel Burning" by Judas Priest and "Where Eagles Dare" by Iron Maiden, pushed my vocals even further, but it was the originals that gave us a glimpse of what Fozzy could do as an original band. Songs like "To Kill a Stranger" and "Crucify Yourself" had a heavy modern sound jam-packed with guitar solos and intricate vocal harmonies. They inspired us to a new creative level, and the days of the wig were coming to an end.

On June 22, 2002, our second album, *Happenstance,* was released and Megaforce decided they wanted us to do a video for the song "With the Fire." We shot the live scenes at a club in Charlotte called Amos' South End, which was where the Jack Black movie *Shallow Hal* was filmed.

The concept for the clip was that I would fall asleep and dream that Fozzy was caught inside a clichéd hip-hop video, complete with low riders, synchronized dance sequences, bling-bling, grills, and midgets. Nothing more hip-hop than midgets, right?

We planned on shooting it in the streets of the 'hood, but on the first day of filming we got hit with a torrential downpour. Classic Fozzy.

Nobody wanted to drive their tricked-out cars in the rain—they were afraid of getting into an accident and messing up their rides. So the cars were out. Then we couldn't set up the equipment at any of our outside locations, so that was also out.

We spent the next three hours trying to find a replacement location, until we found a little covered parking garage next to a supermarket, and after bribing the manager $500 in beans, we had our new set.

A few weeks earlier we had done an open casting call on a local radio station for anyone who wanted to be in a hip-hop video. About forty extras showed up, half of them black and half of them white. I can imagine their shock when they showed up expecting Eminem and got Y2Jay-Z instead.

The video was bizarre and featured Arthur the pigman

chauffeuring us around in a limo; me falling in love with an old lady while brandishing a long sword; Rich sporting a mask and a cape for no apparent reason; and a badass Britney Spears–esque synchronized dance routine. We took the three hottest chicks and Hurricane Helms (who had come to hang for the day), and I choreographed a thirty-second routine comprised of hot-steppin', shoulder twitches, and the Scary Monster ripped off from the "Thriller" video.

Dice would've been so proud of my chronology.

To cap it off, we did a *Soul Train* stroll dance where we all lined up clapping, as each one of us shuffled down the aisle rocking the silliest moves we could think of. It ended up being very entertaining, and if you haven't seen it I suggest you check it out on YouTube. I'll wait.

Go ahead, I'm not going anywhere.

Funny, right? Thought you'd like it. Well, making it wasn't without hitches, let me tell you. After Jonny left Megaforce, our new bosses were Missi Callazzo and her husband Robert John (not the "Sad Eyes" guy). Robert had decided to join us on location as a chaperone for the shoot. We weren't crazy about the guy, as he'd visited the studio while we were making *Happenstance* and given us such useless advice as, "You need to do another chorus in this song," or "This song needs a tempo change here," as if he was Rick Rubin. We had no problems with constructive criticism, but this yutz was talking just to hear himself speak and was annoying and abrasive to boot.

A few days before the shoot, Robert wanted to change the song for the video from "With the Fire" to "Happenstance," because he decided the title track was more commercial. But we had already storyboarded "WTF" and were putting it together accordingly with the beat of the music and the rhythm of the riff and couldn't change gears at that point. After our refusal to switch tunes, Robert became even more difffficult to deal with.

During the shoot he ran around putting pieces of black tape over anything that might be construed as a logo. If someone was wearing a pair of Nikes, he would put a piece of black tape over their logo. If someone was driving a Ford, he would put a piece of black tape over their insignia. If someone was taking a leak, he would put a piece of black tape over their unit.

Every thirty minutes or so Robert would gather us around to give us his "feedback." Whenever he did all I could focus on was the stupid brown leather fisherman's hat he was always wearing.

"Guys, that last shot could've been blah blee bluu…"

[That is the stupidist hat I've ever seen in my life.]

"Furthermore, I think fleezen flobbin flue…"

[That hat is really stupid.]

Needless to say, I hated that damn hat.

Hour after hour, day after day, Robert sported that hat, and it became my white whale. I was Captain Ahab and I wanted to capture that hat. I wanted to torture that hat. I wanted to kill that hat.

I patiently awaited my chance, skulking in the shadows like a voyeur, until finally I received my due diligence. After the rain (Nelson™), the weather turned quite humid and Robert took off the brown leather antichrist to wipe the sweat from his forehead, putting it on the hood of a car. Fate intervened at that exact moment. Someone called Robert into the club, and he turned and rushed inside, *leaving the hat behind.*

This was my chance.

I hurried over to the car and reached to pick it up. But before I could touch it, the demon châpeau flew off the hood, its fangs springing out from underneath the hatband, and latched on to my jugular. I fell to the ground, and started rolling around the parking lot locked in a fight to the death with the blasphemous bonnet. It was with great effort that I finally pried it off and stuffed it into a duffel bag, entrapping it for a thousand years.

As the furious fedora bopped around inside the bag like a puppy caught under a sheet, I was rewarded with the sight of a returning Robert searching for his hat. He searched desperately inside the car, under the car, and on top of the car.

He asked everybody within earshot if they had seen his missing lid.

"My hat! Has anyone seen my hat?"

But no one had. And no one has seen it since.

Long after the video was completed, we got requests from Robert demanding that whoever stole his sou'wester to give it back. It became one of America's great mysteries, on a par with the Kennedy assassination and the existence of Bigfoot. Now the truth can be revealed.

Robert, I stole your hat and threw it the fuck away.

And while I'm at it, the C.I.A. assassinated Kennedy. Can't explain Bigfoot, though.

When the "With the Fire" video was completed, we got the good news that MTV2 had decided to play it in semi-rotation. I was quite proud of the fact that for the first time ever, a WWE Superstar (as they like to call us) was in a band with a video being played on MTV. That's why I was quite confused when the WWE didn't really promote that monumental occasion. Sure they had done a piece on the making of "WTF" for *WWE Confidential* but concluded it by only airing two minutes of the video, and I couldn't understand why they wouldn't show the whole thing. If "WTF" was good enough for MTV, why wasn't it good enough for the WWE? WTF?

But instead of being thankful for the airtime they'd given the band and keeping my mouth shut, I couldn't leave well enough alone and called the producer of *Confidential* to see if they would air the whole video. A few days later, I was in Fort Lauderdale for a PPV and got summoned into Vince's office.

"Here's the deal. You have this video you want to show. We aired a piece of it. What more do you want?"

"Well, I think you should show the whole video the way it was shown on MTV. It's the first time that someone from the WWE has had a video on the channel, and it seems like that would be a big deal." I thought it was a totally valid point.

Vince felt differently and quickly took the wind out of my sails.

"Well, quite frankly, I heard the video sucks."

Well, that was blunt.

"And why did you call the producer of *Confidential* and ask her to air it? We'd already decided not to. If you're going to play that game you have to come to me first, not the people working for me. Listen, Chris, I'm not just trying to teach you wrestling lessons, I'm trying to teach you life lessons here. And going behind my back is not how you do things if you want to get something done."

I didn't understand at the time why Vince was so interested in teaching me life lessons when all I was trying to do was get my video played. But now I think it's because he saw a little bit of himself in me. Just like me, he was a rebel who listened to no one and did whatever it took to get the job done, pissing people off with his stubborness and drive in the process. Therefore he was trying to teach me how to better myself instead of repeatedly getting into trouble by rubbing people the wrong way.

Maybe he was right?

Even if he was, he was certainly wrong about one thing: the "With the Fire" video does not suck. If you don't believe me, Vince, go watch it right now.

I'll wait.

CHAPTER 13

Love at Full Volume

By December 1999, Jessica and I had been together for a year and a half. Things were going great in our relationship and I loved her very much, so I decided it was time to take the plunge and ask her to marry me.

I thought it would be a froot idea to pop the question at the stroke of midnight on January 1, 2000, just as the new millennium began. At the time, the entire planet was nervous about the potential onslaught of the Y2K virus, which could apparently destroy life as we knew it. From what I'd heard there were plenty of similarities between getting married and the end of the world, so I figured my timing was apropos. I didn't believe that Y2K was really going to be the end of the world, but I'd listened to enough Art Bell on late-night radio to be prepared in case something did happen.

I bought multiple boxes of Tang, bottled water, protein bars, protein drinks, and stashed $5,000 in cash at the bottom of a drawer just in case all of the world's power went out and I was left in the dark like Snake Plissken at the end of *Escape from L.A.*

I figured in the wake of the Y2K cataclysm, water

Jess and I strike our best thrash metal pose. Lars and James would be proud.

and cash would be at a premium, and with my foresight and preparation I would rule the world...or at least my neighborhood. But in the end nothing happened and I was left with two dozen boxes of powdered orange crystals. Cocaine for Oompa-Loompas.

When it came time to find the wedding ring, I had no idea where to start. I asked The Rock if he had any ideas, and he mentioned that he'd bought his wife's ring in New York City from the father of one of the WWE office employees. So one night after a Garden show, I went to the jeweler's house to find the perfect ring. I was traveling with Jeff Hardy that weekend, so the two of us perused the selections one by one. I narrowed it down to three final choices, all of them beautiful and unique. I wasn't sure which one to pick so I asked Jeff which one I should choose and the Charismatic Enigma made the final decision on the ring that my wife is wearing right now. Shhhhh...don't tell her.

When I gave Jessica the ring and asked her to marry me at the stroke of midnight, she said yes, and the world didn't end. As a matter of fact, my world was about to get a whole lot better.

I had my bachelor party at Wise Guys, the bar I went to after my first match in Winnipeg. It didn't take long for Drunkicho to surface, and he was a total barbarian. When he drank a shot, he celebrated by smashing the glass against the wall. When a fan was kind enough to order him and his friends a round of drinks, he repaid her by pouring them all over her head...and smashing the glasses against the wall. Not wanting to be left out, he poured the next round all over himself.

All of this ridiculosity was left untouched by the bouncers and bartenders, maybe because the owners felt indebted to me due to my endorsement the year before? Either way they said nothing even when I decided to get behind the bar and pour drinks...and then smashed the bottles against the wall.

Jessica and I decided to have our wedding in July, and while Winnipeg has ridiculously cold winters, it also boasts sweltering hot summers. So our guests were forced to sit outside pouring sweat in the scorching July sun as they waited for the ceremony to begin. However, there was one guest who could have cared less how hot it was and would've waited until she melted for the wedding to begin: my mom.

She had been a quadriplegic for almost ten years, after being injured in a late-night fracas with her then boyfriend. Those of you who have read *A Lion's Tale* know the story of the trials and tribulations my mom and I went through after her accident. She had adjusted to her injury quite well for a few years, until she fell out of her wheelchair in 1997 while riding down the sidewalk in front of her house. She'd been deteriorating mentally and physically ever since.

Her health was one of the main reasons why Jess and I chose to get married that summer, as I wasn't sure how much longer she would have the strength (or desire) to leave her house.

It was the right decision, and on our wedding day all of her pain and hardship from the past decade seemed to drain away. She looked so beautiful and happy in her purple silk dress and it was such a blessing to have her there. It's one of my favorite memories of her.

We wanted to do something different for our wedding, so we ordered a flock of butterflies from Toronto that we planned to release during the ceremony. The idea was to store them in the fridge, which kept them cold and dormant until it was time for them to fly. When you took them out of the fridge a few hours before the wedding, they thawed out, and when released would flutter to the sky to the delight and amazement of your Auntie Joan and Uncle Larry.

But when I took the butterfly envelopes out of the fridge, they were completely silent. I shook them and listened for a rustle, a scratch, a peep, a tremble, a flap (or whatever sound butterfly wings make), but there was nothing. A horrible thought crossed my mind: what if

when the wedding guests opened the envelopes, the butterflies were all dead? Would they be my own personal
"Rime of the Ancient Mariner"? Would I have to wear
them around my neck like an albatross when I said my
vows? In order to avoid certain tragedy, my cousin Chad
wisely advised my groomsmen that if the butterflies were
indeed dead inside of their packets to just toss them in the
air anyway. Luckily, when it came time for the little guys
to do their job, they awoke and fluttered straight up to the
heavens, to the delight and amazement of my Auntie Joan
and Uncle Larry.

The wedding was a huge success and my queen was
the most breathtakingly gorgeous woman in the world in
her beautiful wedding gown(and she still is). I was in love
at full volume and knew that she was the woman I wanted
to spend the rest of my life with.

The flowers were beautiful, the band was incredible,
the food was delicioso, and almost two hundred people
celebrated with us that day. It was one of the best days
of my life and was by far one of the most amazing parties I've ever been to. I highly recommend that everybody
give this wedding thing a try at some point.

I had invited all of my friends in the business, and most
of them showed up, including Edge, Christian, Billy Kid-
man, Disco Inferno, and Cyrus. I invited Vince and he
responded by saying, "Winnipeg. Why would I want to go
to Winnipeg?" The ones who couldn't make it, like Dean
and Eddy, RSVPd to let me know beforehand.

But one friend was quite conspicuous by his absence:
Chris Benoit.

Not only did he not RSVP, but he never mentioned
anything about the wedding at all—beforehand or after-

wards. It hurt my feelings, because even though he was one of my best friends, he didn't have the courtesy to politely decline my invitation or even wish me luck. But it didn't surprise me, as Chris could be quite elusive and hard to figure out at times.

The day after the wedding, Jessica and I were on the cover of *The Winnipeg Sun* with the headline, "Manitoba's Sexiest Man Gets Married!" I'd won that dubious honor a year earlier after topping a poll that saw Burton Cummings, the fifty-three-year-old singer of the Guess Who, finish in second place. Well, I should hope that I'm sexier than any middle-aged man with an afro and a mustache, no matter how good a singer he is.

At the bottom corner of the front page there was a little blurb announcing that Jennifer Aniston and Brad Pitt had also tied the knot the previous day.

It was nice to see that, at least in Winnipeg, my Q rating was bigger than Burton and Brad.

CHAPTER 14

Banned on Broadway

Flashback Heart Attack to 1987

When Iron Maiden came through Winnipeg on their Somewhere On Tour, I found out they were staying on the seventeenth floor of the Westin Hotel. So I snuck into a freight service elevator, like a pimply-faced Jack Bauer, and knocked on random doors until I was rewarded by guitarist Adrian Smith answering one of them. He had a towel wrapped around his head like a turban, with another one wrapped around his waist.

I stood in shock, not believing that one of my rock and roll heroes was actually standing in front of me.

"Uhhhhh, excuse me, Adrian, can I have your autograph, please?"

"Not right now, mate, I just got out of the shower."

He closed the door and I did a primitive version of the Nitro Dance, until the hotel detective (who wasn't outta sight) discovered me and gave me a personal escort out the front door.

Hot Tub Time Machine Fast Forward to 2000

Iron Maiden had just released *Brave New World*, their first album in ten years, with the returning Adrian Smith and singer Bruce Dickinson, who had left the band a decade earlier.

My cousin Chad had the wise idea for the two of us, my other cousin Todd, and my friend Rybo, all of us huge Maiden fans, to take a road trip to see them on their Brave New World Tour in Milwaukee and Chicago. Maiden's PR firm were big fans of the WWE, and with some finagling I was able to procure tickets and backstage passes. We watched the Chicago show from the crowd and briefly met the band backstage but were too intimidated to say

I'm choking Adrian for leaving Iron Maiden in 1989, allowing *Virtual XI* to happen.

much. I mean, this was Iron Fuckin' Maiden, our childhood heroes!

For the next show in Milwaukee we decided to take full advantage of the passes. We wandered backstage and were enjoying Maiden's fine catering when their head of security recognized us from the night before. He brought us back into their inner sanctum and introduced us to Adrian's wife, Nathalie.

"You're Chris Jericho? Wow, my son is a huge wrestling fan, and he would just die if he knew you were here. Would you mind giving him a call to say hi?"

Are you kidding me???

Thirteen years earlier I had interupted Adrian midshower by knocking on his hotel room door, and now his wife was asking me to call his son? Talk about things going full circle!

Nathalie took me to the production office, dialed the phone, and handed it to me. A groggy child's voice answered (it was pretty late in the UK), but I was eager to gain some serious metal points and I went into full babyface mode.

"What's going on, little buddy? It's Chris Jericho here..."

I talked to him for a few minutes, until Adrian himself wandered over to say hi and thanked me for talking to his son. He was so laid-back and friendly that we got along right away. It was surreal having a beer and discussing music, wrestling, and the finer points of Iron Maiden with one of my favorite guitar players of all time. He hooked us up to watch the show from the side of the stage and introduced us to the rest of the band, and I was reminded of the similarity between rock stars and wrestlers. We were both in the entertainment business and we made our living by being on the road. There was a mutual respect between us and I was no longer the sixteen-year old fanboy chasing autographs. I was now at the same level in my world as Maiden were in theirs and had gone from punter to peer.

A few months later, Adrian came to New York to do publicity for his solo project Psycho Motel. I had a show at MSG the same weekend, so Jess and I came in a day early so we could meet up with the Smiths and go see the Broadway play *Jekyll and Hyde*, starring Sebastian Bach.

Sebastian was great and did a tremendous job, and after the play we went to celebrate at a pub across the street that he and his cast members frequented. Gargano was also there, and we were such bad influences on each other that it wasn't long before Drunkicho stumbled in. The night started to unravel with the standard throwing of the shot glasses against the wall and the spitting of alcohol into each other's faces. It got even more out of control when Gargano and Mr. D started squirting condiments all over each other, which the two of them thought was absolutely hilarious. Then Drunkicho (covered in a noxious cocktail of Crown and Ketchup) cornered Adrian, bragging that he wasn't just another garden-variety Maiden fan; he in fact knew every song that Adrian Smith had ever written for the band.

"But I know what songs I've written, Chris," Adrian said in his polite English accent.

"Chris? Who is this Chris?" Drunkicho thought to himself.

"No, you don't understand, Adrian. *I know every song . . .* 'Prisoner,' 'Gangland,' 'Sun and Steel.'"

"Yes. I remember. I..."

" 'Two Minutes to Midnight,' 'Can I Play with Madness,' '22 Acacia Avenue'..."

Adrian was mercifully released from captivity when Sebastian lurched over, blubbering and crying drunkenly about how nice I'd been to his kids when meeting them earlier.

"You were so great to my son. You signed his autograph...snivel...and took the time to talk to him...sob...and I'll never forget that...sniffle...I love you, man."

Then he leaned over and kissed me on the lips.

I'd never been kissed on the lips by a man before. Never mind one who was six foot five with long blond hair.

It wasn't bad.

Before I could kiss him back, Gargano tackled me from behind and we started wrestling on the floor of the pub. After my draw with Sneap in the restaurant in Charlotte, I wasn't about to lose another floor-wrestling match, especially to a lowly writer (wait a minute...). We barreled into a table knocking a big pitcher of beer to the floor, and a million pieces of barley-tinted glass exploded all over the place. That was our cue to leave. Well, that and the manager kicking us out.

He was so angry with our idiocy that he sent a letter to Sebastian (which Gargano printed in *Metal Edge*) that said, "Dear Sebastian, Chris Jericho and his friends are never allowed in this bar again. I don't know what kind of conduct the WWE allows, but I assure you that we do not allow that sort of stupidity here."

Stupidity? I took great offense to that accusation. *Inanity* was more like it.

Either way, I was banned on Broadway.

After we left the pub, Paul, Jessica, her best friend Lisa, and her boyfriend Scott Erickson grabbed a taxi to take us back to the hotel. Erickson was a pitcher for the Baltimore Orioles, whom I met for the first time at our wedding and hadn't liked since. He rubbed me the wrong way with his arrogance and sarcasm right off the bat (see what I did there?). He also had the same horrible hair as Ted Danson in *Cheers*, which led me to dub him Sammy Badweeds.

When we got into the cab, Badweeds got on my nerves again by being his arrogant and obnoxious self.

"Hey man, you're pretty small for a wrestler. You must really get your ass kicked!"

I tried to ignore him, but he could tell from the look on my face that I was getting pissed.

Adrian, me, and Bas were all set for an awesome male bonding photo op in a Broadway pub when Erickson stuck out his arm and ruined the picture. It's no wonder I ended up smacking him in the face a few hours later.

"What are you getting so upset about? It's just fake wrestling! It's not really a sport like baseball!" he said with a smarmy grin. I closed my eyes and tuned him out.

Gargano was in the front seat of the taxicab and the rest of us were sitting in the back. The girls were engaged in conversation, and out of the corner of my eye I saw Badweeds lean in and slap Gargano in the back of his head.

I was the only one who saw him do it, and when Paul turned and said, "Oww! What was that for?!?" Scott turned to me and asked, "Why did you do that, Chris?"

I sneered back, "I didn't hit him! You did!" I couldn't believe that the son of a bitch was trying to frame me! I was Dr. Richard Kimble and Badweeds was the one-armed man.

No matter what I claimed, due to my drunken behavior earlier, it made perfect sense to Jess and Lisa that I would deck Paul from behind. "Chris, you're so drunk, you're hitting your own friend in the back of the head," Jessica said.

"I didn't do it, Jess! I'm innocent! Erickson did it!"

"Now you're trying to blame Scott? Stop being such a jerk and admit that you did it already!"

Weeds sat there grinning like a badly coiffed cheshire cat as his evil plan came to fruition.

I had enough and decided to knock the smirk off his face right then and there. I reached over and took an awkward swing at him in the crowded backseat. Just as I did, the taxi hit a pothole and I ended up grazing Jess in the back of the head with a weak blow.

Sammy burst out laughing at my faux pas and I completely snapped.

"That does it! Pull this car over right now," I screamed at the driver.

I swung open my door and ran around the side of the car to Sammy's half-rolled-down window. I reached through and punched him in the face. Suddenly I was public enemy number one (and I ain't talkin' about Nikki Sixx) to everybody in the taxi.

The evidence was stacked against me, as I had sucker-punched the "innocent man." Even though it hadn't been much of a punch, Erickson sold it better than Shawn Michaels ever could. When we got back to the hotel neither Jessica nor Lisa would talk to me until I apologized to him. I was reminded of my forced apology to Chyna as I mumbled a few words of remorse while Erickson stood there smugly nodding his head. It was torture for me, made worse by the fact that we both knew he had won.

Damn you Badweeds! I'll get you back someday...

The next morning, I woke up with one of the worst hangovers in the history of drunk. I had to go to an autograph signing, and when I slid out of the car in front of a long line of Jerichoholics waiting to meet their hero, I tripped and almost fell down. I started signing covered in an alcoholic sweat, and even though I felt like nauseous prison ass, I scrawled my name on picture after picture as friendly as could be. Finally I put my pen down to greet a cute little guy wearing a Y2J shirt and holding his Jericho doll.

"You're my favorite wrestler, Chris Jericho," he said with an adorable gap-toothed grin.

"Well thank you very much! What's your name, little buddy?"

"Conner," the precious little angel said shyly.

"Awwww. Well hello, Conner. Thanks for being such a big fan! Listen, can you do me a favor and hold on one second, big guy?"

Conner beamed and said, "Okay, Chris Jericho. You're my hero."

I smiled back and got up from the table, giving the crowd a big wave.

I made my way to the bathroom, locked the door behind me, knelt in front of the toilet, and puked my damn guts out.

After a few minutes of bapping and barfing, I splashed some cold water on my face and walked back to the signing table.

Conner was anxiously waiting and couldn't stop grinning as I sat down.

"He's your biggest fan," his mother said proudly as I scribbled my name across his action figure.

"Well, thank you, very much, ma'am. By the way, do you have a mint?"

After my career-making Last Man Standing match with HHH, I had a long feud with Kane, a good worker and one of most intelligent men in the WWE. I always enjoyed wrestling him, and he's still the only coworker with whom I've had an in-depth discussion about Aldous Huxley's (not Iron Maiden's) *Brave New World*. The angle started with me spilling coffee on him backstage and ended three months later with another Last Man Standing match, which I won when I pushed the set (made of dozens of barrels attached together) on top of him, apparently squashing him to death.

Then I moved on to a feud over the Intercontinental title with Benoit. It was always a war working with him, but in a good way. He worked a no-nonsense, raw-boned, strong style that meshed perfectly with mine, and with our similar backgrounds and worldwide experiences, we always had good matches. He was one of my all-time favorite opponents.

The war between the Calgary Kids (see *A Lion's Tale* for an explanation) culminated with a Ladder match at the 2001 *Royal Rumble*. It was a tough assignment, as the high-water mark for Ladder matches was Shawn Michaels and Razor Ramon from *WrestleMania X*, regarded as one of the best matches in WWE history.

So the initial temptation when putting the match together was to try a lot of dangerous stunt spots, but we decided instead to base the match around using the ladder as a weapon and saving all the climbing until the end. We used it as a lance, a battering ram, and a shield, but the best idea came when we were standing in the ring throwing around suggestions. Chris came up with the idea of me bending him over the top of the ladder backwards and applying an upside-down version of the Walls of Jericho. It was brilliant in concept and looked amazing on TV; I have to say it was one of the frootest looking moves I've ever done in my career. I re-created it many times in other Ladder matches, but the first time I did it with Chris was still the best.

After a brutal twenty-minute fight, I finally dumped Benoit to the floor, scaled the ladder, and grabbed the title. The crowd went ballistic as they knew they had seen something special. Watching it back now, I feel that it was just as good as the famous Shawn-Razor Ladder match, and if you see them back to back, you might agree.

It's unfortunate that the match has been buried and technically doesn't exist anymore.

CHAPTER 15

No More Beards

Backstage at *SummerSlam* 1999, I was pleasantly surprised to see Zakk Wylde, Ozzy's guitar player, hanging around. He was in town for a gig with his solo band Black Label Society and was a huge WWE fan. When I say huge, I mean it literally, as Zakk was no run of the mill scrawny rock star. He was well muscled, which combined with his long blond mane of hair made him resemble a rock and roll viking. He had the attitude to match and was a loud, boisterous, and, most important, friendly guy, and we clicked instantly. He also knew his wrestling; more specifically his Ultimate Warrior. The first words out of his mouth when I introduced myself to him were, "Hey, brother, I'm a big fan. But the bottom line is: have you ever met James Hellwig?"

When I told him that I had indeed met Mr. Hellwig, a.k.a. the Warrior, the ice was instantly broken.

I'd worked with Hellwig briefly in WCW, and he was such a character that I had half a dozen stories about him. But it was a quid pro quo (Clarice) conversation, and after every Warrior story, Zakk reciprocated with a tale about his boss.

I told him how Warrior had arranged to make a surprise appearance on *Nitro* by entering the ring through a secret trapdoor. Unfortunately, nobody clued in the rest of the crew and we were bumping on pure steel for the entire show. Zakk listened in wonder like a five-year-old during story time and then told me a tale about the recording of the album *No More Tears*, when he decorated the studio with posters of Jimi Hendrix and Aleister Crowley to inspire him. Ozzy walked into the studio, looked at both posters, and mumbled, "Zakk, I know this guy is Hendrix, but who the fuck is the other one?"

Zakk said bewilderedly, "Ozzy. It's Aleister Crowley...Mr. Crowley? You know, the guy you've been singing about for twelve years?" Ozzy stared at the poster and said, "I've never seen a fucking picture of him before..."

I reciprocated by telling him how Hellwig wouldn't eat dessert, but would instead crush a cookie into a thousand little pieces and simply smell it, which he claimed gave him the same effect as actually eating it.

Zakk then told me how Sharon had imposed a backstage ban on alcohol in an effort to keep Oz on the wagon, so Zakk bought cases of O'Doul's nonalcoholic beer and replaced the beer in each bottle with Heineken. His plan to stay tipsy worked great, until one night he was in the middle of a fifteen-minute guitar solo while Ozzy watched him from the side of the stage and decided to sip on one of the O'Doul's. By the time Zakk finished his solo, Ozzy had drunk three of them and told him, "Zakk, these O'Doul's taste pretty fucking good, man. I almost feel like I've got a fucking buzz on!"

Zakk and I became fast friends. We'd both been in show business since we were teenagers, we both loved the same music, wrestlers, and movies, and shared a goofy sense of humor. We were also quite competitive, and when I noticed he had started growing a beard, I smarmily (great word) mentioned that I could grow a longer one than him.

So we decided to have a beard-growing contest. I grew a goatee so long, that if it wasn't braided or tied into a little bun it resembled Linda Lovelace's bush in *Deep Throat*. I went months without cutting the damn thing in order to win that stupid contest, until finally it became unbearable. I shaved it off, and Zakk was declared the winner. He kept growing his and it currently hangs down to his waist, but for me it's No More Beards.

The comedy continued a few months later when I was in New York City promoting *Happenstance* and I heard Zakk was in town for an Ozzfest gig the next night. I met him at a seedy little pub that had good beer and a great jukebox stocked with the best bands from the '70s like Journey, AC/DC, Foreigner, and Bad Company. My party motto has always been, "It's not where you go, it's who you're with," and Zakk and I proved it by hanging out, drinking beer, and talking music until the bar closed at 4 a.m. Not wanting the night to end, Zakk invited me back to his suite to drink more. So we stumbled out of the pub and wandered down the street to buy more beer, playing car chicken on the way.

Car chicken is when you lie down in the middle of the street and wait until a car comes. Then you stay there as long as possible until rolling out of the way before you get run over. We were in downtown Manhattan and it was like

I tried valiantly to beat Zakk Wylde in our beard-growing contest, but alas, I lost miserably. The weird thing was, Jess actually liked my frenzied facial hair.

Death Race 2000 as the cars swerved and honked trying to avoid the two idiots lying in the middle of the road.

Then we bought a dozen beers and a dozen hard-boiled eggs from a convenience store and walked over to the Waldorf-Astoria, which was quite a contrast from the Jerry's Motel–Hourly Rates Available dive that Megaforce had put me up at. I guess Ozzy was making a little more cash than Fozzy.

Thoughts of sugarplums and strippers danced through my head and I couldn't help but wonder what kind of huge rock star debauchery awaited on the other side of his hotel room door. But as Zakk slid his room key into the slot, he whispered, "You gotta be quiet, brother, my daughter and her friends are inside sleeping."

There would be no snorting cocaine off the voluptuous backsides of exotic dancers that night, my friends, only a quiet march straight into the bathroom. Zakk closed the door and sat on the edge of the bathtub and I squatted on the throne. We said nothing as we drank beer and ate boiled eggs in silence, until finally our eyes met and we burst out in stifled laughter. Here was one of the greatest guitar players of all time and one of the biggest wrestling superstars in the world, hiding in the bathroom and sipping on beer in silence at 5 a.m. so as to not wake the children.

The comedy never ends.

The following year I flew to Ozzfest in San Antonio and was hanging with Zakk backstage on his bus. We'd thrown back a few cocktails and were bored, so we decided to go into the parking lot and play some baseball. Zakk grabbed a glove and a bat from the bus and announced that he'd be up first. So I threw the first pitch and it bounced off the asphalt a few feet in front of him. He started laughing and taunting me.

"Come on, brother! You're throwing like you're a member of the Backstreet Boys!"

I threw another pitch and this one careened wildly into the rapidly expanding crowd that had gathered to watch us play.

"That's fucking terrible, bro! You're gay and your parents know it!"

Murmers of laughter starting emanated from the mob and I started getting angry. I wasn't going to let this dip-shit rock star make fun of me in front of all these people. I focused on my target, assumed the pitcher's position, and in my best Nolan Ryan threw that ball as hard as I could. It careened across the parking lot like Frehley's comet and he swung with all his might—Zakky at bat.

There was a distinct *crack* as the aluminum connected with the leather, and the ball flew above the crowd and over the fence that separated the band parking lot from the fan parking lot.

"It's a home run! A fucking home run," Zakk yelled with glee as he pumped his fists and stomped around. "I beat you, Jeri—"

"ZAAAAKKKKKKKKKKKKKKKK!!!"

He was interrupted by a screech that could've only come from a demon dwelling in the tortured depths of hell itself. When I saw the source of the scream, I realized that my initial assessment wasn't too far off, because storming at us from out of nowhere was Sharon Osbourne.

And she was furious.

"What the fuck are you two idiots doing? You can't be playing baseball in the fucking parking lot! Do you know what kind of a lawsuit we would have if that baseball lands on somebody's head?!? We could lose the whole festival, you stupid twats!"

I'd never been called a twat before.

Sharon shoved her face only inches from Zakk's and scolded him like he was a juvenile delinquent. "Zakk, how can you be so stupid? You should know better!"

Then she turned her death gaze on me.

"And who the fuck are you?"

I wasn't quite sure who the fuck I was and kept staring at the ground, more terrified of her than any other female I'd encountered in my entire life (my wife and mom included). After a few tongue-tied terrifying seconds, I mumbled that I was nobody.

"You most certainly are a nobody, you wanker! Now get back on that bus before I throw you both out of here!"

"Yes, Mrs. Osbourne," we said in unison and scampered back to the safety of the bus with our tails between our legs. Once the door slid shut, we burst out laughing like a couple of kids who had been caught stealing crab-apples from the neighbor's yard.

The word about Fozzy had made its way to Europe and we were offered a slot at the 2002 Bang Your Head Festival in Balingen, Germany. It's hard to understand unless you've been there, but in Europe heavy metal is not just a style of music, it's a way of life: long hair, leather jackets, leather pants all day, every day. It's so popular that during the summer there are dozens of festivals all over the continent featuring bands that are huge in Europe but haven't had a hit in the United States in years. We were still wearing wigs and playing mostly covers, but once again the powers that be figured the concept would go over huge and booked us on a bill that included Slayer, Rob Halford, Nightwish, and Overkill.

The headliners on the night we played were Saxon, a band from England who'd had minor success in the States fifteen years prior. But in Germany they were bigger than ever and 25,000 fans were abuzz because "Saxon is playing *Crusader*, complete with the entire castle stage set!" They said it the same way a movie buff might proclaim, "Spielberg is making another *Jaws* movie!"

When we got to the huge open field that was serving as the concert grounds, we found out that Fozzy was billed third from the top behind Saxon and Nightwish, not bad for a cover band that had only played a handful of gigs—a fact that wasn't lost on some of our fellow musicians.

Gamma Ray, one of the biggest metal bands in Germany, was slotted to play right before us. Their leader was vocalist/guitarist Kai Hansen, who had formed the band after he left Helloween. I'd heard through the grapevine that Kai was furious that they were on before Fozzy, and since I'd met him in Hamburg ten years earlier, I decided to go try and smooth over the situation.

"Hey Kai, I'm Chris Jericho. We met at your house in Hamburg years ago."

His eyes burned through me as if I was Michael Weikath and he said, "I know who you are."

I didn't dig his attitude, but I held my tongue.

"Kai, in my opinion, Fozzy should totally go on before Gamma Ray. If I could change it I would, but I have nothing to do with the order of the bands." I meant every word. "I just want you to know I understand why you're pissed."

Kai continued staring and then gave me an arrogant smirk. He walked away without saying a word. I tried to be nice and he completely blew me off.

Now I wanted revenge. .

I went to our backstage tent and called a band meeting. We weren't sure what kind of reception we'd get from the metal faithful at Bang Your Head, if they would appreciate our homage to the music or crucify us for our costumes. None of us knew for sure but when I told the rest of the band about Hansen's snub we agreed that our mission for the day was to blow Gamma Ray off the stage.

With that mantra in mind, we watched their set from backstage in order to size up the enemy. They were technically proficient and the audience liked them, but it seemed like they were only one step away from simply sitting down onstage during their entire set. They didn't move and they didn't go out of their way to involve the crowd. Big mistake, Gamma Ray—that was Fozzy's forte.

Hansen mmm-bopped his way to the end of the set and now the shit was on. Our intro music played and I sent out our swinus-inflicted mascot Arthur onstage waving a German flag. It was a standard wrestling trick to get a cheap pop from the audience, but it worked. The crowd erupted when he walked onstage, especially since he had spent the day walking around the grounds handing out Arthur buttons. People who had never heard of Fozzy knew who we were now—or at least who Arthur was.

We ran onstage and I stormed up and down the catwalk screaming at the crowd to go crazy. After Gamma Ray had lulled them into a daze minutes earlier, we woke them up instantly.

We played for forty minutes and tore the house down, especially when we did "Balls to the Wall" by the German band Accept. I felt such power in leading 25,000 people to chant like monks (including a guy in the crowd who was actually dressed as a monk), and as strange as we might have seemed with our wigs and costumes in the United States, in Germany we fit right in. The crowd kept chanting, "Fozzy, Fozzy, Fozzy," and their relentless energy helped us blow Gamma Ray out of the water.

Mission accomplished: *Auf wiedersehen*, Kai.

A few weeks later, *Heavy Oder Was*, one of the biggest metal magazines in Germany, backed up our victory by saying, "Gamma Ray could take some tips from Fozzy about how to work a crowd." It was quite gratifying to read that we had gained some respect from the German metal community. It wasn't quite as gratifying to read that *Fozzy* (or *Fotze*) meant "Cunt" in German.

No wonder the crowd wouldn't stop chanting our name.

CHAPTER 16

Twists and Turns

It was May 2001 and I was once again the Intercontinental Champion. The Rock had taken a temporary leave of absence to film *The Scorpion King*, while Austin had won the WWE world title by turning heel at *Wrestle-Mania X-Seven* and began an association with HHH known as the Two-Man Power Trip. The roster lacked top babyfaces to battle them, so it was decided that Benoit and I would get the chance to be the top good guys in the company.

When I arrived at the arena in Oklahoma City for *Raw* I was approached by a new writer named Pete who sported a chipped tooth and an even chippier Irish accent.

"Top of the morning to ya!" (It was the afternoon.) "You're having a match for the Intercontinental title against HHH tonight. And guess what? You're going over!"

His words took me by surprise. I'd never beaten HHH (the State College non-win notwithstanding), and found it interesting that the office was ready to give me the big win.

"Really?" I asked Pete. "So I'm finally going to beat him?"

"No, I'm just kidding! You're not beating him! In fact, you're dropping the title to him tonight." Pete laughed.

I failed to see his humor and sprayed Mace in his eyes.

I snapped out of my daydream and added "Chipping the rest of Irish Pete's teeth with a crowbar" to my bucket list instead.

I lost the championship to HHH, which meant that the Two-Man Power Trip were now in control of both singles titles. Then a few weeks later they won the tag team titles from Undertaker and Kane at *Backlash*, which gave them a complete monopoly on all of the major championships within the company. At the following PPV, *Judgment Day*, Chris and I won a Number One Contenders match to face Austin and Hunter the next night in San Jose. The plan was for us to beat the Two-Man Power Trip for the tag titles and then branch off into two separate feuds for the summer: Benoit vs. HHH for the IC title and Jericho vs. Austin for the world title.

So in San Jose for *Raw*, the four of us spent a few hours with Pat Patterson putting together the match. We wanted it to be the ultimate roller-coaster ride, a match jam-packed with twists and turns that would play with the fans' emotions and lead to the two Chrises standing victorious.

Sometimes the match you plan doesn't work as well as you think it will, and other times it turns out even better than you could have expected and is pure magic. Jericho/Benoit vs. Austin/HHH was one of those matches. It's been called one of the greatest matches in *Raw* history, and with good reason.

First off, the crowd was amazing. They'd been waiting for someone to bring down the Two-Man Power Trip and sensed that Benoit and I were the guys to do it.

As the twists and turns unfolded, the crowd got louder and more voracious. The TMPT got the heat on Benoit until finally Hunter gave him a Pedigree behind the ref's back. I evened the score by dropkicking Hunter from the top rope, which enabled Benoit to make the smoking hot tag. I came storming in and dismantled the two of them, until finally ending up with Austin in the Walls. Hunter ran in from behind to make the save, and that was when disaster struck.

When he planted his foot to nail me, he tore his quad completely off the bone.

People often ask me what happens when somebody gets hurt in the course of the match, and the answer for the most part is—nothing. The first thing any of us thinks about is simply finishing the match and dealing with the consequences later. Hunter followed me to the floor and tore the top off the announce table, where he was going to attempt to Pedigree me as planned. I noticed he was limping gingerly, and when he pulled me onto the table I asked him if he was okay.

"No, my leg is fucked." When one of the boys says he's hurt, you know he must really be hurt, because most of the time he'll just shrug it off. Not this time.

I was supposed to block his Pedigree and turn it into the Walls, which would apply direct pressure onto his injured leg.

"What do you want to do?" I asked, ready to improvise if necessary.

"Put me in the Walls," he said, forever earning my respect. He was in a lot of pain, and even though he knew the submission would hurt him even more, he still wanted to put the match first and go through with it.

That, dear readers, is one tough mofo.

As I slowly turned HHH over on the announce table trying to apply the loosest Walls of Jericho ever, inside the ring Austin hit Benoit with a Stunner. I let go of Hunter's legs as gently as possible, ran to the ring, and pulled the referee out by his leg before he could count to three.

Austin and I fought back and forth until I finally hit him with the Lionsault. As I had him covered, Hunter staggered back into the ring like Jason Voorhees (how he was able to do that I have no idea) and went to bash my brains in with his dreaded sledgehammer. I moved at the last second and he nailed Austin in the stomach. Benoit then tackled Hunter, forcing him to take yet *another* bump, and I pinned Austin for the dramatic 1-2-3. The Calgary Kids were the new WWE Tag Team Champions!!!

The fans rocketed off their chairs and roared like lions. They erupted in a way crowds rarely do anymore, and on that night at that moment those people realized they had just seen something legandary. It's unfortunate that it has been buried forever and technically doesn't exist anymore.

Even though that match was one of the best of my career, the aftermath was one of the worst. After you are lucky enough to have the elusive perfect match, it's tradition to celebrate with your opponents, congratulate each other on your work, go through the minutiae of the performance, and generally just bask in the moment.

Hunter's injury meant that there was none of that after that match. The mood was somber when we learned that he'd be out of action for six to eight months. Everybody was in a state of complete lugubriousness and we never got to properly rejoice in the magical night we'd created.

As a result I'll always have bittersweet memories of that match.

With HHH gone, Austin didn't have a partner against Benoit, and so an unlikely ally stepped in. Vince decided that it would be good heat if Austin teamed with his former nemesis Mr. McMahon, and he was right. It worked out great for me as well, especially when we returned to Calgary for *Raw*.

I opened the show by cutting a promo about how much of a nerd Vince was, flaming him for his outdated pompadour hairstyle and his tacky suits and showing his infamous performance of "Stand Back" from the '80s, where he sang and danced worse than William Hung and Master P combined. The crowd was laughing heartily and hanging on my every word when, in a throwback to my debut appearance at MSG, the mic died.

But this was an older, wiser Jericho, one who had killed the Jericho Curse and eaten it Raw (tastes like chicken), and instead of standing there dumbfounded, I threw the mic into the crowd. I yelled that as rich as Vince was, he still couldn't get me a microphone that worked. Even though the crowd loved my rebel actions, Vince didn't and asked me later why I'd thrown the mic into the crowd.

"Well, I've seen Austin do that before when his mic died."

Vince replied, "Steve Austin can throw dead microphones into the crowd. Chris Jericho should just lay his on the ground and wait for another one."

Stu Hart was at ringside that night, along with various members of his massive family. After the show ended with Benoit putting Austin in the Crippler Crossface submission and me locking Vince in the Walls, we addressed the manic Alberta crowd. I grabbed the mic and said that I had just wrestled my first match in the Saddledome and if it wasn't for the time I spent training in Calgary I never would've made it there. Chris and I continued by thanking Owen Hart and then Stu himself, noting that both of them had made it possible for us to make it in the business. Stu stared straight ahead with a dazed look like he had no idea what was happening as 15,000 Calgarians cheered and chanted his name. But then he slowly stood up and waved at the crowd, showing that he knew exactly what was going on. It was one of the biggest reactions I've ever received, and it was nice to come full circle and thank the Hart family in the city where it had all started for me.

When Stu passed away a few years later, the city of Calgary bought his famous house and decided to tear it down. We had a show in Calgary right after he died and Benoit went to pay his respects to the battleground where he and hundreds of others had trained. At his suggestion, I decided to make one last visit of my own to the house and the dungeon that lurked inside. Armed only with a ten-pound weight plate emblazoned with the name HART that Stu handmade himself (Bret had given it to Chris to give to me), I walked up to the front door and knocked. There was no answer and the door was unlocked as usual, so I opened it and yelled, "Hello?"

There was no reply so I walked inside.

The Hart House was huge and old, made creepier by the fact it was totally empty. It reminded me of the house in *The Texas Chainsaw Massacre*, and as I inched through the kitchen toward the basement, I half expected a homicidal Leatherface to attack me at any second.

I made my way down a set of creaky stairs into the basement and laid my eyes upon the closest thing to a medieval torture chamber I'd ever seen—the infamous Dungeon.

It looked exactly the same as the last time I'd been in its clutches over a decade ago. It still wasn't much more than a dingy ring, eight inches off the ground, jammed into the corner of the tiny basement. But this wasn't your average ring. It was a ring haunted by the ghostly screams of the hundreds of students who'd been tortured and stretched within its storied ropes. In the silence, I could still hear their cries of pain in the distance.

I was spooked and took a quick look around for Leatherface. It had been twelve years since Mr. Hito made me take five hundred back bumps in a row in that very ring, but when I closed my eyes it seemed like it was only yesterday. I stood at the bottom of the stairs, reminiscing about the early days of my career and letting the musty smells of the basement take me away to a time when—CRASH!!

My eyes flew open at the sound of the door slamming against the wall, and standing at the top of the stairs was Leatherface.

"AHHHHH!" I squealed anxiously. How did he find me? What had he done with the rest of the Harts? Was he planning on skinning me alive and wearing my face as an authentic Corazón de León mask?

I stood in terror as Leatherface began stomping down the stairs, shirtless and wearing a pair of tight faded brown dress pants that accuentuated the ample gut hanging over them. It was a ghastly sight, made even more horrific by the human head he held in his hands. I stood at the bottom of the steps like Ichabod Crane as he pulled back his arm and threw the head right at mine. I shrieked and swung at it with my HART plate as it hurtled toward me, but as it flew past I saw that it wasn't a head at all, but rather a balled-up sheet, reeking with the unmistakable odor of urine. I looked up the stairs and saw that Leatherface wasn't Leatherface at all, but in fact Stu's oldest son, Smith.

"Fucking cats pissed in my sheets again," he said and disappeared into the shadows.

I stood frozen for a few moments, my heart double pounding like a Dave Lombardo bass drum, then ran as fast as I could up the stairs (two at a time) and out of the house forever.

CHAPTER 17

Canadian Jesus

After a few weeks, Vince decided that there was no reason for him to team with Austin any longer and added Benoit into our program, making it Jericho vs. Austin vs. Benoit at *King of the Ring* for the world title. I was disappointed that I wouldn't have the chance to prove myself as a legitimate singles opponent for Austin. I also found the match to be a strange dynamic because three-way matches usually work better if it's two heels vs. one good guy. Vince's rationale was the fans would believe Austin had a chance of losing if it was two-on-one, because if it was just me vs. Steve, they might not believe I'd be capable of beating him.

My big push was over before it began...again.

The buildup of the match was even stranger, as Chris and I had no out-of-ring confrontations with Austin and hardly any with each other. There was no drama built into the match regarding whether or not Chris and I would turn on each other or work together. It was a really flat promotion made even more vanilla when a few weeks before the PPV, Austin was put into a mini-feud with Spike Dudley.

You read that right—Spike Dudley. Don't get me wrong, Spike was a hard worker and had a good connection with the fans, but putting him into an angle with the World Champion only weeks before our big match diluted our barely existing storyline even further. Then Vince decided to have us lose the tag titles to the Dudleys the week before the match because he felt that fans would expect one of us to beat Steve if we lost them. It was a solid theory, but I saw the signs (Ace of Base, represent) that Vince for some reason had lost faith in both of us, weeks before the match even took place.

Benoit was also having some serious neck problems after wrestling hard for over fifteen years and it was wearing him down. He told me he was looking forward to a break and was excited to spend the extra time with his family. Chris loved his kids and talked about them constantly and I could tell he was relieved to get off the road for a while.

He was headed for surgery after the three-way, and even though he worked his ass off, the match ended up being mediocre at best and was about as memorable as its buildup.

Even so, it's unfortunate that it has been buried forever and technically doesn't exist anymore.

With all of the prominent matches I'd been having, my profile was bigger than ever. As a result, I was getting more outside opportunities, including being asked to be a presenter at the NHL Awards. I was excited to rub elbows with the players, especially when I found out that one of my all-time heroes, Wayne Gretzky (I'm Canadian, so it's a given, right?), was going to be there.

I came to the ceremony decked out in my Sergio Georgini tuxedo and roamed around with a camera crew while interviewing all of the various celebs in attendance. I had just finished giving Chad Kroeger of Nickelback a Fozzy CD (sell, sell, sell) when a vaguely familiar face approached me and introduced himself. "Hey, you're Chris Jericho, right? How are you doing?"

When I cautiously replied that I was okay, he leaned in and whispered, "Go into that closet and close the door. I'll give you five minutes."

I had no idea what this guy's schtick was, but like I said, he looked kind of familiar.

"Trust me, you'll love it."

What the hell was in that room? The Crystal Skull? The Pick of Destiny? The ghost of Terry Sawchuk?

I walked inside the broom closet and in front of me was a large trunk. I approached it cautiously and opened the lid slowly. I was shocked to see what lay inside.

Gwyneth Paltrow's head.

Actually it was the Stanley Cup, and it was more beautiful than I ever could've imagined. The guy who let me in the closet was Mike Bolt, who'd been transporting and guarding the cup for a decade. Now, for the next five minutes I was allowed to do whatever I wanted with the most coveted trophy in sports!

I briefly considered pulling an American Pie but couldn't find a hole. Then I imagined that the closet was MSG and I had just scored the winning goal of the Stanley Cup Finals—in overtime, no less. I grabbed the cup and lifted it over my head, all the while making crowd noises.

"Hhhhhaaaaaaaaahhhhhaaaaaaaaaaahhhhh!!"

I kissed it and lifted it up and down, still making the noises.

"Hhhhhaaaaaaaaahhhhhaaaaaaaaaaahhhhh!!"

When I told my dad what I'd done, he said he had never touched the Cup. I asked him why and he told me: "Because we lost the Stanley Cup Finals in Game 6 in 1971 against the Bruins. I had my chance and we didn't get the job done, so I don't deserve to touch it."

I respected my dad's sense of honor, but possessed none of it myself, so I kept lifting the Cup up and down over my head before eventually hugging it. I began waltzing with it, and cradling it in my arms like a long-lost lover. I started singing my own little song as I was dancing.

"I love my Cup. I love my Cup. Without you, I'm all screwed up. I love my Cup—"

Lost in the moment, I did a double pirouette straight into Mike Bolt, who was standing in the doorway staring at me.

The silence seemed to last longer than the 1936 Detroit-Montreal game.

"Okay, Chris. Put the Cup down and leave . . . please."

I lowered it to the floor and squeezed past him out the door, sparing one last glance at my long-lost paramour as I left it forever.

Goodbye, Cup. I'll always love you.

After my Cup coitus, I wandered into the banquet hall and surveyed the scene. The attendees of the awards show were milling around, exchanging stories and kibitzing with each other. Here was Jarome Iginla talking to Patrick Roy. There was Scottie Bowman sharing a laugh with Cam Neely. On the dance floor, Moe Mantha was break-dancing with Harold Snepsts. And over in the corner,

Gary Bettman was playing with a brightly colored ball of yarn.

Gordie Howe was signing an autograph, Wayne Gretzky was standing by the bar, Teemu Selänne was—

Stop. Hold on. Stay in control.

Wayne Gretzky was standing by the bar!

My heart jumped into my throat and I immediately forgot about my beloved Cup. It had never treated me right anyway. Besides, just a few feet in front of me was the greatest hockey player of all time. The Canadian Jesus who had been placed on Earth by the Lord above to mystify and amaze us mere mortals, who could only dream to be even 1 percent as talented and as supernatural as the real Great One (sorry, Rock).

I morphed into Ed Grimley and started running in place while doing an odd hop-type thing every few seconds. How would I approach him? Would he like me? What would I say? My track record when meeting famous people wasn't very good; I was famous for delivering the worst opening lines whenever I met somebody that I was a fan of. (Those stories and much more are in *A Lion's Tale*, available at the Dollar Tree.)

Finally, I mustered up all my courage and decided to talk to the G-man while I could. I gave my camera to the WWE rep and asked him to take a picture of me with Wayne when the time was right. I walked up to the bar and sidled up next to the Great One, preparing to deliver my carefully prepared opening line asking him which one of his goals was his favorite.

"Hey!....ummmm....you're Wayne Gretzky, right?"

What?? No, that's not what I wanted to say!! I was at the NHL Awards surrounded by hockey players—of course he was Wayne Gretzky! Who else could he be? AHHHHH!!

Wayne looked at me with a big grin and confirmed the patently obvious.

I stood there in silence, grinning back. Finally, I worked up the courage to continue talking.

"My name is Wayne too," I almost said, before catching myself and saying instead, "Hi Wayne. I wrestle for the WWE and I'm presenting an award tonight. I was wondering if it would it be okay if I took a picture with you?"

Wayne took a sip of his beer and said, "Yeah, no problem. WWE, huh? I knew I recognized you. You're Jeff Jericho, right?"

Boy howdy!! Wayne Gretzky knew my name!!

Well, half of it at least, and that was good enough for me.

"So, wrestling, eh? Wow that's a tough sport, Jeff. I've got a lot of respect for you guys. Do you want a beer?"

Do I want to have a beer with Wayne Gretzky? Does the Pope shit in the woods? I was agog (still a great word) to be shooting the shit with one of my childhood heroes—with his hockey hair, pointy nose, eastern Canadian redneck accent and all. He was super froot and just a regular guy—albeit a regular guy who scored a total 3,239 points in his career.

We talked for about fifteen minutes about hockey, wrestling, and about my old flame, Cup. He explained how it felt to hoist the Cup for real and laughed when I brought up that he had scored more points against my beloved Winnipeg Jets than any other team. Finally I shook his hand and said, "You know, I was so scared to come talk to you, and now I have no idea why. You're one of the friendliest people I've ever met."

"Of course, man, I'm Canadian!"

He gave me his endearing grin and began to leave. Then he turned around and said, "Anytime you're in Phoenix, you've got to come skate with us. Just let me know and I'll set it up. Take care, Jeff."

Skate with the Great One? Yeah right! I'd spontaneously combust and Jeff Jericho would be gone forever.

People often ask me if I prefer being a babyface or a heel. Honestly, it doesn't matter to me. I enjoy both, and as long as people are reacting to what I'm doing, I'm happy. Having said that, it's much easier to make people hate you

It's nice when you meet one of your heroes and he turns out to be even frooter than you could've imagined. The Great One was a perfect example of that. He smelled good, too.

than it is to make them like you. Wrestling is a strange form of entertainment in that even though people know it's show business, they still think there's some reality to it. Sometimes when I meet a fan, they'll tell me that instead of the jerk they were expecting, I'm actually a nice guy. I always point out that Anthony Hopkins doesn't really eat people's livers with some fava beans and a nice Chianti (slurp-slurp-slurp). It's just a part he's playing. It's the same with me: I'm an actor portraying a character.

But once in a while, someone will get so mad with my dastardly doings that they'll attempt vengeance.

I was in Las Vegas teaming with The Undertaker against Austin and The Rock on *Raw* and was on the floor jaw-jacking with Austin before the match started. He was cursing at me and giving me the patented Stone Cold finger, and when I looked away in disgust, he punched me in the side of the head.

I couldn't figure out why he had hit me so hard or how he had gotten to the floor so fast. When I turned my head to ask him what was up, I saw a complete stranger rearing back to hit me again. It wasn't Austin who hit me at all, but a rambunctious fan who had jumped over the guardrail to extract his wrath, and he was about to do it a second time. Before he could land another punch, I popped him in the face on live TV. Thankfully, the camera cut to a shot of Austin's face just as I reared my arm back, saving me from a certain TMZ appearance. The fan hit the ground and before I could pounce on him he was dragged over the barricade by security. As they were manhandling him over the guardrail, I started using his ballbag as a punching bag. I was going all *Rocky II* on his plums when a hand on my shoulder pulled me away.

"Take it easy, kid," Austin said sternly. "You've made your point. Time to calm down."

You know things are spiraling out of control when Steve Austin is the voice of reason.

After the show I jumped straight into a cab to go see George Carlin live at the Mirage. I changed out of my gear along the way and made it to the theater with only minutes to spare. I took my seat at a table next to a darling old couple who had to be in their seventies. They were friendly and we struck up a brief conversation. They told me it was their first time in Vegas and this was their very first show.

"We used to watch George Carlin on *The Tonight Show* all the time," the old lady said. "I think he's so funny!"

Just then the lights went out and George came onstage to big cheers. The old lady was clapping vociferously while whistling and hollering. George surveyed the cheering crowd and delivered his opening line.

"So, when was the last time you heard a good pussy fart?"

Grandma stopped clapping and her face dropped like her breasts without a bra. I glanced at her sheepishly and she stared at me with a look on her face that said, "Why didn't you warn me he was going to say that?" George continued by asking by a show of hands, how many people in the crowd had ever received a blumpkin, and things just got worse from there.

It was the longest ninety minutes of my life.

CHAPTER 18

MC Hammered

On September 11, 2001, I woke up, got out of bed, and dragged a comb across my head. I made my way downstairs and drank a cup, and looking up I noticed I was late. I jumped in the car and started driving out of San Antonio, toward Houston where *Smackdown!* was taping later that night. I had just pulled onto the interstate when I got a call from my dad.

"Terrorists have attacked New York City and blown up the World Trade Center. Fifty thousand people have already been killed!" It was amazing how quickly false facts and figures spread that morning, but the truth was scary enough. I switched on the car radio and listened to the various reports of what was happening. As the horrible story unfolded, I continued driving to Houston, because no matter the situation, I'd been trained that the show must go on.

When I got there, the arena was empty because the show had been canceled. Ultimately, it was decided that all of us would have to stay in Houston until Thursday to do the show. I spent the next two days trying to adhere to some sort of normal routine as the entire country was falling apart and living in fear. Everywhere you looked people were gathered around TVs and radios trying to get information, expecting the end of the free world at any moment.

On September 13, the WWE held the first mass public gathering in the United States after the attack. The mayor of Houston asked us to perform in hopes that the show would take people's minds off the tragedy, which wasn't an easy task as we were all just as scared about what was happening. Our minds weren't exactly put at ease when we were given a briefing by the Houston police and fire departments on what to do if the arena was bombed.

The show went off without a hitch, and after the show Edge, Christian, and I decided to make the 20-hour drive back to Tampa. We finally got back home on Friday and had to fly out for *Raw* in Memphis three days later.

It was surreal walking through the deserted airport a mere six days after the attacks. There was nobody there, as the majority of the country was too scared to fly. Not that I wasn't, but what choice did I have? The show must go on, remember?

I got on the plane, and even though it was early morning, I stayed wide awake during the entire flight, waiting for some motherfucker to storm the cockpit. I envisioned what would've happened had the Taliban tried to hijack a plane carrying the WWE crew. Boxcutters versus the craziest mofos on the planet?

Game over, jihad.

Over the next few weeks, traveling to work got a whole lot more difficult. Pre 9/11 you could check in for a flight thirty minutes before it took off and breeze straight through security without a glance, but after the attacks all that changed. Now you had to check in an hour before and security had increased sevenfold. The airlines and the authorities weren't taking any chances and became very strict with their rules for passenger conduct.

At least most of the time.

I was on a redeye from L.A. to Philly a few months later trying to catch some sleep. I was about to turn off my mind, relax, and float downstream when I heard some mumbling from a few rows behind me. Since I was sitting in first class (I can't go back—I won't) and away from the riffraff, I paid the mumbler no attention. Then the mumbling became a rumbling.

"Hey! I need another drink right now!"

Okay, so here we were only a few months after the worst terrorist attack in U.S. history and there's a belligerent drunk on a plane demanding another drink. It was only a matter of time before the flight attendant took care of this assclown, I thought to myself.

"Gimme another drink, dammit!!"

My good-natured patience was running out as I was tired and hadn't been able to sleep the whole flight. It was almost dawn, with the first faint rays of sunlight peeking through the clouds, and I was getting cranky. I rang my call button and asked the stewardess if there was anything she could do about this moron.

"I'm sorry, sir, but he was cut off already," she said curtly as if I was bothering her.

I couldn't figure out why she was allowing Sir Soused to continue making such a scene. A few of the other passengers had woken up and were giving him side glances.

"This airline is a piece of shit!" he screamed. "This is bullshit!"

He continued complaining, his voice getting louder, and I decided if the stewardess wasn't going to do something about it I would.

I walked over to his seat and got within inches of his face. Then I whispered menacingly in my best Dirty Harry voice, "Sir, I'm trying to sleep and I'm sick of listening to you complain. Shut your mouth and stop yelling right now. Don't make me come back here again."

He looked back at me innocently as if he hadn't said a word. I gave him a wink and felt a tap on my shoulder.

"You need to return to your seat and stop making a scene, *sir*," the attendant said confrontationally.

I was making a scene? How had I become the scene maker?

I sat down, but sleep had escaped me for good on that flight. I was so pissed off that I did nothing but stare out the window for the remainder of the flight, while Three Sheets to the Wind snored underneath his sheet.

We finally landed in Philly in the pouring rain and stopped at the gate waiting to be towed in. MC Hammered awoke from his passout and started up again. "Why the hell are we waiting? I'm fucking late enough as it is!"

We reached the gate and everybody stood up to get off the plane.

"Come on, let's get fucking—"

I cut him off midsentence. "Listen, jackass! There are kids on this plane and you need to watch your language and keep your mouth shut, do you understand?" I warned, as the other passengers nodded in agreement. El Buzzo looked at his feet as I grabbed my bag and walked off the plane. When I passed the attendant, she said, "Sir, you need to settle down."

Settle down? What was with this chick? Did she bang this guy in the bathroom when I wasn't looking?

I got off the plane and headed straight for the men's room to pee and calm down. I was turning over the events of the flight in my head, getting angrier by the second, when a guy in a business suit sidled up next to me, put down his leather briefcase, and unzipped his fly. He glanced at me and muttered a slurred hello.

I couldn't believe it. It was CM Drunk.

What were the chances that (a) this asshole had chosen to take a piss right next to me and (b) he had no idea I was the guy who had gotten in his face and scolded him only minutes earlier? I smiled as he leaned his head against the wall and continued to drain himself. My flow was still going steady as I turned my hips slightly and pointed the stream directly at his briefcase. As I showered his business papers with my golden topping, my morning got a whole lot better. By the time I shook the last few drops into his now soggy suitcase, I was downright happy. His eyes were still closed as I zipped up my fly.

"Have a nice day, sir. Make sure to stay out of the rain. You wouldn't want to get wet!" I said jauntily. He nodded groggily and muttered that he wasn't going to get wet.

His briefcase wasn't so lucky.

CHAPTER 19

Never Trust the Loch Ness Monster

Meanwhile back at the ranch, things had started going down the toilet for WCW. By 2001, the company was completely out of control and losing millions of dollars while the TBS brass were fed up and looking to unload the company. Eric Bischoff put together a group of investors to buy the struggling organization, but just as the deal was about to go down, Jamie Kellner, the new president at TBS, decided he didn't want wrestling on the television schedule anymore. Without a TV deal, the company was pretty much worthless to Eric's group and they were out of the running.

Enter Vince McMahon.

For the paltry price tag of $2.5 million, WCW was sold to the man who had been their blood enemy for the past twenty years. Included in the price were all trademarks and video rights, which gave the WWE complete ownership of every match in WCW history.

The complete bottoming out of WCW proved to me

beyond all doubt that despite the trials and tribulations I'd suffered during my first year in the WWE, I'd made the right decision when I left. Vince took over the contracts of the entire WCW roster in the acquisition. Some he cut, some he sent to the developmental territories, and some he kept. His idea was to start an angle where the entire WCW roster would invade the WWE and try to take over. It was a great idea and a potential license to print money, but there was one problem.

Most of the big-name players from WCW hadn't signed with the WWE. While Hulk Hogan, Bill Goldberg, Ric Flair, Scott Hall, Kevin Nash, Scott Steiner, and Eric Bischoff eventually came to work for Vince, they didn't initially. The first wave of the invasion consisted of such middle of the road stars as Buff Bagwell, Bill DeMott, Chris Kanyon, Mark Jindrak, and Sean O'Haire. All nice guys, but hardly the sort of talent that could lead a credible revolution against The Undertaker, Steve Austin, and The Rock.

Vince's initial idea was to have WCW be its own separate company that existed outside of the WWE's walls and stood on its own. Then at the right time the two promotions would lock horns and battle each other to huge box-office returns. He planned on creating a Saturday night WCW show and had even gone so far as booking the arenas and searching for a new TV deal to broadcast it.

The whole concept fell apart during the last segment of *Raw* from Tacoma, Washington, a WCW title match between Booker T and Buff Bagwell, the two biggest WCW stars who'd signed with the WWE. Unfortunately, they had no idea how to work a proper WWE-style match and the result was horrendous. Ironically, Booker's last feud in WCW was with Lance Storm, and had they wrestled that night things could've turned out differently. But it was decided that Bagwell had bigger star potential than Lance, so he got the match. Big mistake. When Vince saw Booker and Buff stink the joint out, he was convinced that nobody from WCW had any idea what they were doing (sounds familiar, doesn't it?) and made up his mind that the company could never exist as a separate entity. So he took the same concept and made *Raw* and *Smackdown!* two distinctly different shows instead.

So you can thank Buff Bagwell for the brand extension.

The Invasion began in the summer of 2001. In the classic tradition of most wrestling "invasions" (i.e., NWA, UWF, New Japan), instead of milking it for all it was worth, the WWE guys completely dominated the WCW guys and ended what could've been a year-long angle in about four months. After all those years of Bischoff guaranteeing he'd put the WWE out of business, Vince ended WCW as quickly as he could, and who can blame him?

He won the wrestling war for good and got a stranglehold on the entire business as a result. He could now acquire any talent in the world and put together any match he wanted.

Except one.

I had a dream one night that Vince had signed the Loch Ness Monster to a multiyear deal so he could book the Loch Ness Monster vs. Chris Jericho—Live on PPV. I was very concerned about the professionalism of my opponent and was not happy when asked to do the job, especially when Vince explained that the finish would be Nessie swallowing me.

"Vince, you can never trust the Loch Ness Monster! How am I supposed to just let him put me in his mouth and swallow me? I mean, I personally don't have a problem with it, but my character would never do that!"

"I wouldn't ask you to do anything I wouldn't do, pal. I went in his mouth earlier today to test him out and he was fine," Vince said confidently.

I didn't want to tell Vince that I was terrified of the water beast, so I hesitantly agreed—but I wasn't happy about it.

Chris Jericho vs. the Loch Ness Monster took place in a floating ring in the middle of a lake. It was a seesaw match back and forth, and Nessie was getting the upper flipper, so I dove out of the ring and climbed up a bridge. Nessie swam underneath and rammed it with his tail, causing me to tumble into his open mouth, as the ref counted to ten and ruled him the winner by ingestion. When we went to commercial break, Nessie spit me out into the drink and smiled.

"That's how you do it, kid," he said before submerging himself beneath the waves. As I was treading water I looked up and saw Vince smoking a cigar while giving me the thumbs-up.

The next day when I told him about my dream, he looked at me thoughtfully and nodded his head.

"Hmmmm, the Loch Ness Monster, huh? Is he available?"

I officially turned heel on The Rock during the Invasion angle by attacking him at the end of a match where if he lost, WCW would officially take over the WWE. Obviously he didn't lose, but the damage was done and our feud was off and running. I finally had my sustained angle with The Rock and it was a huge chance for me. But there were forces at work, hoping to see me blow it.

A week into the program, agent Gerry Brisco (who had accompanied Jim Ross when he came to Tampa to recruit me years earlier) took me into a corner of the arena to have a private conversation.

"You've got to really step it up, Chris, because there are people on the inside that want to see you fail. They don't believe in you. They're burying you behind your back and telling everyone that you're the shits."

Meet the new boss, same as the old boss.

I thought that the target on my back from when I arrived in the WWE had disappeared, but Gerry's words reminded me that it was still there. As always, I would have to be extra careful and work extra hard if I wanted to keep my head above water in the WWE. But that was no problem for me; I've always liked a good fight.

Speaking of which, I notice you've been looking at me funny for the last few pages, hambone—you wanna go?

Later that night during a match with Kane on *Raw*, I jumped off the apron, landed flat-footed, and felt a flash of pain. I thought I had broken some bones, as it was difficult to put any pressure on my foot or to even stand. I tried to finish the match, and when I grabbed him to turn him over in the Walls, the combination of his long legs and my inability to put any pressure on my foot caused me to lose my balance and fall down. I got back up and tried again but fell down a second time.

I get asked on a weekly basis why I put the Walls on differently from the way I applied the Liontamer and this was the reason why. When I started using the hold in WCW, I would bend my opponent almost in half until he was vertical to the mat by driving my knee into the back of his head. I learned the move in Japan and carried it over to WCW when I was working with guys who were the same size as me or smaller. When I got to the WWE, most of my opponents were simply too tall to apply the move the same way. Big guys like HHH, The Undertaker, Big Show, and Kane just don't bend like that.

So the answer is quite simple. I'm too short to do it properly to the guys who are that much bigger than me.

Not that that mattered now, because due to my wounded foot, I couldn't have bent Kane even if his name was Gumby. But I gritted my teeth and tried it for a third time, ignoring the bolt of pain that shot up my leg when I finally got the hold on. I got the submission, but was totally embarrassed and all I could think of was Brisco's talk with me earlier that day.

"I'm done," I thought to myself. "The guys that are burying me have all the ammo they need now. They're going to laugh me out of this place."

But the reaction I received was quite the opposite. When I got to the *Smackdown!* tapings the next day, Paul Heyman (who had come to the WWE to work as a commentator) had some interesting news.

"Vince was really impressed with you last night. He knew you were hurt but you still did the best you could to finish the match." I was surprised he felt that way. "Vince doesn't expect you to wrestle tonight," Heyman continued. But even though I was in a lot of pain and could hardly walk, sitting out wasn't an option. After all, I was the same guy who had wrestled with a broken arm in Knoxville eight years earlier. (For this story check out *A Lion's Tale*, available in adult bookstores everywhere.)

"It's froot, Paul, I want to work tonight. I'll just tape up my foot."

That night I was in a six-man tag with Rock and me on separate teams. After the match, I further cemented my heel status by beating the crap out of him and mocking him by standing on the second rope and smelling his nonexistent cooking.

By working the match with my injured ankle, I impressed Vince with my tenacity. As a result, he started working with me and giving me more direction on how he wanted me to act in the ring and backstage.

One night I had an interview with Terri Runnels on *Raw*, and right before we went live, Vince handed me an apple.

"While you are doing your interview I want you to start eating the apple. As you're talking, I want you to spit chunks of it in her face."

Confused, I asked, "Why?"

With a gleam in his eye, he said, "Because it's a real asshole thing to do. Really spray it on her! Get it all over her kisser!"

I thought it was a terrible idea, but I did what I was told and spat apple chunks all over poor Terri (who had no idea it was coming) on live TV. It was disgusting, but it worked. People began booing and chanting, "You suck." Afterwards I told Vince that initially I thought the apple was a brutal idea, but in the end it really worked.

"Of course it worked. That's why I told you to do it."

As a matter of fact, it worked so well that years later Vince gave the apple-spitting gimmick to Carlito. But let it stand for the record that I was *the* first apple spitter in the WWE—a Hall of Fame–worthy achievement if I've ever heard one.

Because I was a heel in wrestling, by proxy so was Fozzy. It became froot to boo us whenever we were mentioned in the WWE because of all the dirty deeds I committed on the show. Originally I adhered to the theory that all publicity was good publicity, but in retrospect it might have been a better idea if I had kept church and band separate. The WWE exposure made the fans aware of Fozzy, but also gave them the false impression that we were not to be liked.

We were slated to perform on *Raw* at the Scope in Norfolk to promote *Happenstance*. I was in the middle of a feud with Ric Flair and had attacked and bloodied him earlier in the show. Flair was God in that part of the country, so my actions didn't exactly endear me to the thousands of people in the arena.

As soon as the stagehands began setting up our equipment during commercial break, the crowd began to boo. Bud was standing next to me in Gorilla with a morose look on his face.

"I've been waiting my whole life to play arenas. Now I'm getting booed," he kept saying over and over. Getting jeered was a way of life for me, and normally I considered it a compliment, but not in this case. Vince smiled at me and said, "This is gonna be huge for your record sales." Unfortunately, it wasn't, as *Happenstance* sold less than *Fozzy*. People still weren't sure if we were a legitimate band to be revered or a joke to be booed, and the fact that we were still wearing wigs didn't help either.

When we got our cue, we ran onto the huge stage and

launched into "To Kill a Stranger," a new original song that kicked off the album. Despite our energy and my over-the-top efforts to get the crowd into it, nobody did. I wanted them to hate me, then like me, then hate me. All in the same night. It was like TNA booking.

After we finished playing our first song, I asked the crowd if they wanted to hear more Fozzy and they booed me out of the building. Then Flair came out battered and covered in blood and the crowd erupted into the cheers I'd been pandering for.

Flair was a madman as he tore apart our gear, smashed up the drums, and chased me down the ramp with one of Rich's guitars. He whipped it at me and it bounced off one of the ringposts, smashing it into a dozen pieces. After the show, our bass player Watty got Flair to sign a piece of the broken guitar as a souvenir.

He should have got him to sign a piece of my broken ego while he was at it, 'cos the whole performance was a disaster.

Not only were we panned live, but we didn't fare too much better on TV either. It's hard enough to sound good when you play live on TV because the sound gets compressed into the small TV speakers and sludges it up. To combat this, Rich had spent a lot of time with the WWE soundman to make sure our mix was as perfect as possible during soundcheck. But right before we went on, the Kidd decided that his guitar wasn't loud enough and turned up his amp. Therefore all you could hear during our performance was his guitar. The drums were buried, Rich's solo was nonexistent, and my vocals were dry and raw (of course they were). Worst of all I sang like shit, which didn't help us either.

By the time Flair came onstage, it was a mercy kill, not an interruption.

CHAPTER 20

Rock and Roll Is a Dangerous Game

Because of my day job with the WWE, Fozzy couldn't do any substantial touring, so in order to play as many gigs as possible, we would book gigs directly after WWE shows. It was quite taxing on me physically and mentally, as I would work my match (trying not to scream too much to avoid messing up my voice), then drive straight to the Fozzy concert. Sometimes the crowds would be good. Other times, not so much.

One high point of that tour came when we played Winnipeg. The Peg isn't just a great wrestling town, it's a great rock and roll town too, and the place was packed. I went straight from the matches and changed into my rock clothes along the way. I arrived just as the show started and I could hear the crowd going nuts as soon as I rushed into the backstage area.

I hadn't soundchecked with the band, and as our entrance music hit, I ran across the stage for the first time. I spotted a little balcony at the side and thought

Let me hear you scream!! I cut my hair short the day after this 2004 gig in NYC.

it would be an exciting start to the show if I leaped off the stage and swang from the terrace for a few seconds. What I didn't know was that there was a gap between the stage and the balcony, and as I planted my foot to jump, I plunged into the hole instead. My knee hyperextended and I felt something pop as the tips of my fingers strained to hold on to the balcony.

I'd just wrestled a grueling match and managed not

to get hurt, then tweaked my knee thirty seconds into a Fozzy gig.

Rock and roll is a dangerous game, kids.

That statement became the ghastly truth on February 23, 2003, when we played a show in Albany, New York, at a club called Northern Lights. Even though there was hardly anybody there, we still treated it like we were playing in front of 25,000 at Bang Your Head. We ran around the stage like lunatics, coerced the crowd to sing along, and finally got them to cheer when we set off our usual pyro. We tried to use as much pyro as we could during each show even though it was expensive, because it added a lot to our overall presentation.

That night Rich tried a new device that shot flames from the end of his guitar when he activated a little rocket on the headstock. It was a great gag and the sparse crowd gave us a smattering of applause in appreciation.

However, when he shot off the sparks, they spouted straight up to the ceiling, causing a small wave of fire to briefly fan across the tiles.

"Did you see that?" I asked Rich, laughing. "The roof, the roof, the roof is on fire!" he replied, and we launched into the next song. After the gig we drove to Reading, Pennsylvania, and Rich and I were sharing a room. I was flipping through the TV channels and stopped on CNN when footage of a fire caught my eye. We watched in horror as a grisly report unfolded of how L.A. metal band Great White had just begun their show at a club called the Station in Rhode Island and their opening pyro engulfed the place, killing a hundred people. It was one of the worst fire-related tragedies in U.S. history, and Rich and I were horrified. We'd been laughing to each other only hours earlier when the same thing almost happened to us. We haven't used pyro since.

We had a terrible crowd the next evening in Reading as nobody was interested in seeing a band play the night after the Station tragedy. But the night after that we had a great crowd and show at the legendary Brooklyn venue L'Amour. Everybody from Dream Theater to Metallica had played there, and it was a good morale booster.

Earlier in the day we did an interview for WSOU, a college radio station, which was the third biggest in New York City, and *Happenstance* was number one on their charts. It was the first time we ever had a number one record anywhere and was quite the froot milestone, made even sweeter by the fact that number two was *The Blessed Hellride* by Zakk Wylde's Black Label Society.

The New York area was our best market by far, and we played half a dozen gigs there on the *Happenstance* tour alone. We accepted an invitation to play the March Metal Meltdown at a place called the Cricket Club in Irvington, New Jersey. I was excited because not only were we sharing the bill with such platinum sellers as Anal Cunt and Goatwhore, but also with Raven, one of my favorite bands when I was in high school. Headlining the festival were England's Status Quo and the New Wave of British Heavy Metal All Stars, which included Dennis Stratton, one of the original guitar players of Iron Maiden.

With the caliber of bands on the show, I was expecting a big crowd and a nice venue.

I was wrong. The Cricket Club was one of the biggest shitholes I'd ever played in. This place made some of the dumps I'd worked in Mexico look like the Taj Mahal. It was in the middle of a dark and dirty ghetto, surrounded by a huge chain-link fence lined with barbed wire on the top. It reminded me of something out of *Escape from New York* (You are the Duke! A number one!). It was a firetrap and the first thing I did when we hit the stage was look for the exits to plot my escape in case a Station situation happened. I've done that in every place we've gigged ever since and always will.

We went on right after Raven, and I was too scared to say hi to their singer, John Gallagher. Here I was, one of the biggest wrestling stars in the world, too starstruck to say hi to a guy in a band that had just played to two hundred people. I've never lost that fanboy side of my personality, and that's a good thing.

We played our set and half of the crowd left when we were done, leaving Status Quo (who packed arenas in the UK) to play for less than a hundred people. While I was checking out Quo's set, I spotted Dennis Stratton talking with the promoter in the corner of the room.

I was stoked to see one of the original members of my favorite band, and since I was still kicking myself for not greeting Gallagher, I walked over to say hello. As I approached, Dennis and the promoter stopped talking and gave me the crook eye. I could tell that they had been in the middle of a heated conversation and I stood there awkwardly until Dennis finally asked, "Yeah, can I help you?"

"Hi, Dennis, I'm Chris Jericho and I sing in Fozzy. I wrestle with the WWE too and I just wanted to say hi. I'm a big fan."

"Yeah?" He stared at me intently, obviously annoyed.

"Um, yeah."

Denny kept staring a hole through me as if I was a prowler, so I thought I'd try to take things in a different direction.

"So did you like the show tonight?"

"Move along, ya tosser," he said before turning his back and continuing his argument with the promoter.

I felt like a total idiot and briefly considered knocking his fucking block off, but I didn't think I'd be able to live with myself if I physically assaulted an original member of Iron Maiden, so I just walked away.

It would've been a whole lot different if he was a member of Anal Cunt, let me tell you.

Right before *WrestleMania XIX*, Willis got a call from Howard Stern's people asking us to come on the show. Stern was convinced that every celebrity band was shit and had put together his own group called the Losers to challenge them in a battle of the bands. Each band played one song in front of a panel of judges who then voted to determine the winner.

Previous bands that had suffered the wrath of the Losers included Tina Yothers and Jaded and Corey Feldman and the Truth Movement. But it didn't matter who the Losers faced or how good they were, the judges unanimously voted Stern's group the winner every time.

We thought by doing the show, it would be a great chance to show off what we could do to a whole new audience. The Losers may have been undefeated but they'd never battled the Fozz!

The day before the show, Rich and I decided there was no way we stood any chance of being taken seriously by Stern if we showed up wearing wigs and using fake names. We knew we were good and wanted to take our band to the next level. It was time to drop the gimmick.

So we decided we would debut the new Fozzy on the Stern show. It was like Kiss taking off their makeup on MTV—except nobody could see us because it was radio.

We showed up at Howard's studio at 5 a.m. for rehearsal and soundcheck, then waited in the green room until it was time for us to come on the air. We met Howard before our segment, and I was surprised at how nice he really was. I realized he was just playing a character on his show, like I did on mine, and we hit it off great. But I was surprised at how nervous Howard was. He wouldn't stop pacing back and forth through the studio, snapping at his crew members and chewing on his nails. It was amazing to see the man who invented shock radio being intimidated and unsure of himself in his very own studio.

The battle began and we unleashed "To Kill a Stranger" and sounded good, especially since it was only 7 a.m.—not exactly the best time of day for a singer's voice. Even though it was radio, we still put on a high-energy performance, and during the guitar solo I ran over to Howard, grabbed his curly mop, and banged his head in time with the music. It felt good to be playing without the garish costumes and the wigs—no gimmicks and no bullshit. For the first time since we'd started playing almost three years earlier, we were a BAND.

After we finished, the judges stared at us noncommittally as the Losers began performing Neil Young's "Old Man." I was surprised at how good Howard sounded and how good the Losers were, especially since I figured it was a given that we were going to blow them away.

The judges were all music business snobs, and the first one said, "Well, these guys are too loud. Howard's band was much better."

Too loud? Who was this guy, Huey Lewis in *Back to the Future*? The fix was in.

Losers 1, Fozzy 0.

The second judge said, "Well, Fozzy's song was more contemporary than the Losers' was, so I guess I'll vote for them."

Not exactly a rave review, but for the first time ever the Losers had dropped a vote. Chalk one up for the Fozz!!

Losers 1, Fozzy 1.

It all came down to the third judge's vote. By then my competitive fire had heated up, and I really wanted to win this bitch.

"Well, both bands were really good. But Fozzy, you guys are doing a heavy metal vibe, the devil horn vibe or whatever you want to call it. You ran over to Howard and made him bang his head. It's so old-school and so out of date. Howard's band has got more of the grunge feel. Neil Young is much hipper than metal right now so I'm giving it to the Losers."

My bubble burst and I was pissed. It was 2003. How was grunge hipper than metal? Who cares if I made Howard bang his head? It was a radio battle of the bands. Wasn't it more important who sounded better? I wanted to walk over and give this douche the *Fistful of Metal* treatment right then and there. We had been hornswoggled, and for the second time in my life I had lost a battle of the bands: first with my high school band, Scimitar, now with Fozzy.

But our loss was not in vain as Howard came to talk to us after the show and admitted that we were the better men.

"You guys blew us away and the only reason we won is because it's my show. Consider the Losers officially retired, because I'm not going through that again."

We had lost the battle (of the bands) but won the war. And as long as we did better than Corey Feldman, I was happy.

Our next gig was at the Palladium in Worcester, Massachusetts, and in the weeks leading up to the show I'd done quite a bit of promotion. I was sure that we'd have a good crowd as we'd never played the Boston area and had good record sales there.

I was almost at the venue when I got caught in a traffic jam, but I was pumped to see so many cars heading in the same direction I was. This gig was going to better than I expected! I inched my way to the traffic light, where all the cars were turning left even though the Palladium was to the right. That's when I realized all those cars weren't making their way to see Fozzy, they were on their way to see Good Charlotte, who were playing the arena next door.

The Madden brothers played to 15,000 people that night. Fozzy played to fifty.

But fifty people was fifty people and we were there to rock their fucking socks off. Rich and I had a good rapport onstage that night, bantering back and forth like a couple of stand-up comedians. We sang "Happy Birthday" to one fan and had a beer-chugging contest with another. We did the thrash metal polka, the jelly doughnut chant, and the human mic stand trick. We claimed that the music you hear in porno movies was played by Fozzy, and then launched into a funky jam as I pretended to have doggy style sex, in a move that became known as the Porno Dance.

If you want to see it just ask me, and if I'm feeling frisky, maybe I'll show it to you.

We always made sure that people had fun and worked overtime to get the crowd involved. I considered myself the party host, and each gig was a chance to spread the word and build our following, the same way I did when I was wrestling in western Canadian Quonsets thirteen years earlier.

Building the Fozzy name was a marathon not a sprint, and we were in it for the long run—and I ain't talking about Don Henley.

We did a show in Calgary after a *Raw* that happened to take place during Game 7 of the first round of the 2004 Stanley Cup Playoffs between the Flames and the Vancouver Canucks. The timing was terrible, but we still had a good crowd and we made sure that the game was playing on the giant big screen behind us, so our audience (and me) could watch it during the show. Calgary was holding on to a one-goal lead with ten seconds remaining in the game and the hometown crowd (and me) was going nuts. The last ten seconds played out like the New Year's countdown. We stopped the show and I screamed out, "Okay! Ten seconds until we make it to the next round! Ten, nine, eight, seven..." The crowd was counting down with me and everyone was screaming and yelling victoriously—until Vancouver scored with four seconds left and tied the game.

The place went silent and the party was over.

Nobody knew what to do and I was so pissed off that I walked straight off the stage and into the street. I stood there for a few minutes kicking vagrants and cursing. Then I remembered we were in the middle of a gig and I went back onstage. We didn't want to play during overtime because no one was going to be paying attention, but if we stopped playing entirely, the gig would be ruined. So we launched into AC/DC's "TNT" for the 20 minutes until the game came back on, and sure enough, everyone was ignoring us. So we just kept playing "TNT," turning it into the Phish extended blues jam version. That's show business—you gotta roll with it, baby.

But after only a few minutes of overtime, the Flames scored and won the game. The party restarted instantly and the mighty Fozz were there to lead the way. I was so happy that the Flames had won—and even happier that we could finally stop playing "TNT."

Our next gig was in Giants Stadium—well, it was technically in the parking lot of Giants Stadium, but that's just nitpicking, isn't it?

The New Jersey State Fair took place every year on the grounds of the stadium, and we were booked to play a show for the fairgoers. Earlier in the day we had an autograph signing beside the massive stage and the line was huge. Hundreds of Fozzy fans, wrestling fans, and one Anal Cunt fan stood in line to get our signature and take pictures. It was a beautiful sunny day and we were looking forward to a great gig.

Our dressing room was a trailer behind the stage, and an hour before the show, the parking lot was packed. I put on my stage gear and primped as our tour manager gave me the update.

"We're on in ten minutes, Chris. But it's raining a little."

Nothing wrong with a little rain, it'll just add to the ambience, right? But when I opened the door a gust of wind ripped it out of my hand and I was drenched by a torrential downpour. Raining a little? This was a damn tsunami!

When I got to the stage, our crowd had dwindled down to about twenty-five drenched die-hards standing underneath umbrellas and looking miserable. But the amps were covered in plastic and the fair still wanted us to play. So we had a quick band meeting and decided we wanted to play too. There was a small smattering of applause from the crowd and a big smattering of rain from the clouds as we hit the stage. I always started our shows by running onto the stage and cheerleading to the crowd, whipping them into a frenzy before the first song began. So when the intro tape finished I sprinted out from the wings. The stage was an impressive structure made of stainless steel, and when my feet connected with the smooth surface, it was as slippery as a sheet of ice. I lost control after the first few steps and slid across the stage like Clark Griswold descending down his roof in *Christmas Vacation*.

I careened past Rich, who mouthed, "Oh shit," and continued on past the safety of the microphone stand. I clawed at it like a drowning man trying to grab a root growing out of the bank of a river, but to no avail. I saw the edge of the stage approaching as if in slow motion and was certain I was going to plunge over the edge to my death. (It's irrelevant that the stage was only about eight feet above the parking lot—deal with it, it's my book.)

Then fate took over and tangled up my feet, causing me to take one of the best bumps of my career. I hit the steel hard but the fall stopped my momentum, and in true Indiana Jones fashion I came to a screeching halt just as my feet glided over the lip of the stage.

It was one of the worst/best lead singer entrances of all time.

Due to the slick conditions of the surface we were playing on, we were forced to tone down our usual high-energy set. Any movement at all and I once again faced the danger of flipping off the stage like Shaun White on a half-pipe. So we did our Gamma Ray impersonation and stood there glued to the stage. As we sopped our way through the set, I could count each fan one by one and felt like David St. Hubbins playing a blues/jazz odyssey.

I love festival crowds.

CHAPTER 21

The Undisputed
Champion of the World

In October 2001, I beat Rob Van Dam to become the number one contender for The Rock's WCW title, for a match to take place in St. Louis at the next PPV, *No Mercy*. The WWE and WCW titles were two separate world championships within the same company, the same way that the *Raw* and *Smackdown!* world championships are now. The angle leading up to the match saw The Rock claiming that I had never won *the big one*. He was right—with all of my bragging and bravado, I'd never come through in the clutch. I'd never officially worn the world title around my gorgeous waist.

Rocky and I had great chemistry at this point, and the match at *No Mercy* was one of our best. We worked so well together in keeping the crowd on the edge of their seats with our various false finishes: I kicked out of the Rock Bottom, Rock escaped from the Walls after I had thwarted the People's Elbow. No one knew who was going to win until Stephanie distracted Rock and I gave him a face plant onto a steel chair using my new finisher, the Breakdown. (It was an awkward move and I stopped using it a few months later. It has since been resurrected by The Miz, who doesn't do it half as well as I did.) I watched the ref's hand smack the mat three times and just like that I was the World Champion, and unlike my tainted victory in State College, this one was for real. The irony that I had to leave WCW and come to the WWE in order to become WCW Champion wasn't lost on me.

WWE.com interviewed me after the match and asked me if there was anything I'd like to say as the new World Champion.

"Yeah, I'd like to tell Eric Bischoff to fuck off. And you can print that."

It wasn't the classiest of statements, but I felt such vindication. And I was still angry at Bischoff, as I'd heard after I left WCW that he had told people that Vince wouldn't know what to do with me and I would be a colossal failure in the WWE. Now that I was wearing Bischoff's own title in Vince's company, I wanted to shove it right down his throat. But instead of telling Eric to fuck off, I should've thanked him—after all, if he hadn't let me leave WCW, I never would have ended up as WCW Champion.

I was only the champ for a few weeks when Rock and I had a rematch for the title on *Raw*. The second match was almost as good as the first, despite being hindered by lack of time. We were the last segment on the show, and as we were building up to the finish we were told that we only had three minutes left until *Raw* went drop dead off the air. The only way to make the deadline was to rush through to the finish (which saw Rocky regain the title after surprising me with a rollup) and rush through the aftermath (where I attacked him with a chair to gain revenge). The problem was I panicked when the ref gave me the time cue, and instead of waiting for Rock to set himself up so I could smash him in the back, I pulled a complete rookie mistake and carelessly hit him on the side. He recoiled and held his arm in pain, and I hit him again in the back as the show went off the air.

I was embarrassed at my faux pas, because instead of protecting my opponent like I was taught, I'd carelessly swung the chair with no regard for his well-being. It was like when I threw the cup of tobacco spit in his face. I lost my composure under the pressure and Rock paid the price both times.

I stood over my fallen victim and then milked the boos from the fans as I marched up the ramp. When I walked through the curtain I heard Vince barking, "What's wrong with him, how could he be so careless?" so I made a bee-line toward him. The combination of the embarrassment I felt for what I'd done to The Rock and the anger from hearing Vince talking about me behind my back made me blow my stack.

"Come on, Vince! We were running out of time, what the *fuck* was I supposed to do?"

Everybody in Gorilla fell silent and I realized I'd just sworn at the boss in front of his employees.

Heavens to Murgatroyd! Time to exit stage left…

I hurried out of Gorilla and waited for Rock to come back from the ring. I apologized profusely when he came down the steps, and he was cordial, but I could tell he was pissed, and rightfully so. His arm ended up being okay, but I couldn't sleep that night thinking about what Vince was going to do when I showed up at work the next day.

When I arrived at the arena, I went straight to his office.

"I apologize for lashing out at you, Vince. I'm really mad and embarrassed at myself for what I did. I shouldn't have rushed and hurt Rock and I shouldn't have yelled at you either. It was unprofessional and uncalled for." I could feel that he wasn't really buying my apology, and I was certain I would become the newest member of the Vince McMahon Kiss My Ass club, but luckily I escaped that fate.

Vince, if you're reading this, don't even think about it…

The main event of *Survivor Series* 2001 was the climax of the Invasion angle. Team Alliance, a combination of ECW and WCW consisting of Steve Austin, Kurt Angle, Booker T, Rob Van Dam, and Shane McMahon, faced Team WWE consisting of The Rock, Undertaker, Kane, Big Show, and Chris Jericho, with the winning team gaining control of the company. You could see how much Vince and the rest of the front office felt about the WCW/ECW roster, with 60 percent of the Alliance being made up of WWE Superstars.

In the end, Angle turned on Austin to help Rock and Team WWE win the match, and after thirteen years as a company WCW was finally vanquished forever.

With the Alliance dissolved, something had to be done about the two separate world titles, and Vince made the decision to combine them and crown the first ever Undisputed Champion in the history of the wrestling business.

A tournament was announced for the next PPV, entitled

Armageddon, and the participants in the round-robin format were Austin, Rocky, Angle, and me. While I had no clue who the winner was going to be, I was just honored that Vince considered me elite enough to be in contention for the big prize.

Two weeks before the PPV, I had a match with Austin on a *Raw* from Milwaukee, with the finish being him pinning me clean with a Stunner. Before the match I asked Paul Heyman if it was a smart idea to have Austin beat me on national television with the tournament only a few weeks away.

He responded, "Trust me when I tell you this—just do it. Go out and have the best possible match you can." Paul always gave me the straight scoop and I trusted his judgment, so I agreed and thought nothing more about it.

But I'd been in the business for over a decade and I could feel something was up. There was no reason to have Austin go over on me right before the PPV ... unless ... maybe ... somehow ... I was going to be wrestling him again in the tournament?

The way the brackets were set up, it was Rock and me in the first round, with the winner facing Austin or Kurt in the finals. If Austin and I were going to have a rematch, it would be in the finals for the Undisputed Championship.

But if that was the case, surely somebody would've clued me in by now, right? Wouldn't they?

One week before the PPV, Austin came to me and said, "Congratulations, kid."

"For what?" I responded quizzically.

"You and I are working in the finals of the tournament

and you're going over. Vince is going with you as the Undisputed Champion."

My heart almost puked out straight onto the Memphis Maniax XFL shirt Steve was wearing. Vince was going to make me the champion? I'd been waiting to hear those words since State College, and even though it wasn't Vince who'd said them, I figured that hearing them from the biggest star in the business was close enough.

"So you're going over on me in the last match," Austin said, spitting a stream of tobacco juice into the water bottle in his hand. "I don't want this to be just another match, either. I really want to make you with this match."

Honored and a little bit shocked by what he was telling me, I responded ambivalently, "That's really froot, but I'm sure plans will change between now and the show."

Steve said adamantly, "No. It's not changing. Hasn't Vince talked to you yet?"

When I replied that he hadn't, Steve walked away and said, "Don't worry, kid, he'll be talking to you soon."

About twenty minutes later, Angle and I were talking about the PPV and he told me in no uncertain terms that *he* was winning the Undisputed Championship at *Armageddon.*

The plot thickened once again when Pat Patterson asked me if I'd spoken with Vince.

Playing dumb, I told Pat that I hadn't. He said, "Vince is going to make you the champion. He's going to tell you today for sure." I wasn't getting my hopes up, as Vince changed his mind quite frequently and I was still scarred from *WrestleMania 2000,* when Mick Foley's face (a face that has never beaten my face, might I add) replaced mine on that poster.

As the day wore on, I still didn't talk to Vince. I didn't want to barge into his office and ask if there was anything he wanted to tell me. I figured he'd fill me in when he was ready.

Finally I saw him walking toward me in the hallway with a smile on his face. "This is it," I thought to myself. The architect of the entire wrestling business was about to appoint me as the new chosen one.

"Chris, I want to talk to you about something."

Here it comes—my ticket to immortality.

"I just want to tell you . . . that you have the most effeminate walk I've ever seen. You need to carry yourself in a more manly fashion."

With those words, he burst out in his famous belly laugh and continued walking down the hall.

When I got to the arena in San Diego the day of the PPV, I still didn't think I was going to win the tournament. Most of the time when someone wins the world title for the first time, they have their loved ones in the crowd to share the moment. I didn't bother flying Jess or my dad in for the show, because I was half expecting to have the carpet pulled out from under me and didn't want to look stupid.

I walked into catering and saw Vince talking to The Undertaker. He still hadn't said word one to me about the championship and I assumed he wasn't going to. When I went over to say hello, Vince said sarcastically, "You can tell that the business is going down the toilet when we're going to make *Jericho* the champion."

That was the extent of Vince's big talk with me. Not exactly the vote of confidence I was hoping for, but at least I knew for sure that I was really going to be winning the title.

Vince wandered away, and Undertaker said, "Do it, man. It's your time. Go out there and kick some ass."

It was nice to have someone's blessing, even if it was a dead man's.

I wrestled The Rock in the opening round, and after twenty minutes of the expected Rock-Jericho magic, I pinned him with his own Rock Bottom, when Vince interfered. I was WCW champion for the second time, which was once more than David Arquette.

I was slumped down in the corner after Rock had layeth the smacketh down on my candy ass when the famous sound of smashing glass emanated from the arena speakers. Austin (who had beaten Angle in the first round) stormed down to the ring and the next match began instantly. But before Steve got to the ring, Rocky came back in and gave me the Rock Bottom, just as Angle snuck back in and hit Austin with the Olympic Slam. This left both Steve and me down on the mat as the ref rang the bell to start the match.

This match wasn't as good as the one I had with Rock and wasn't the defining moment of my career that Austin had predicted. The body of the match was hard-hitting and solid, but the finish was a train wreck. It made about as much sense as an episode of *Lost* and boasted almost as large a cast. Ric Flair, Vince McMahon, and Booker T joined Rock and Angle in running in, each one making my win look more like a fluke, which was the last thing I needed. I needed all the booking help I could get to be a credible champion since my name value and status was far below the other three guys'. Instead I beat The Rock using his own finish after interference and then beat Austin by hitting him with the title after Jon and Kate Plus 8 ran in to assist me.

It didn't help that the crowd was quiet during the whole match because they thought there was no chance in hell that I was going to win. But after Booker T hit Steve from behind with the title, I crawled over and pinned him to win the WWE Championship for the first time and became the only Undisputed Champion in the history of the wrestling business. But the fans were nonchalant and didn't buy it even as Vince raised my hand and a blizzard of confetti and streamers drifted down around us.

It was the biggest moment of my career and the San Diego crowd was as silent as a fart in church—or however that saying goes.

But it was still my moment, and I was going drink it in slowly like a baby suckling on J-Woww's teat. It was surreal to raise both titles over my head, and I still couldn't believe I was the champion. I was holding the same championships that Hulk Hogan, Randy Savage, Ric Flair, and Ricky Steamboat had. Since my first match in Ponoka, Alberta, more than eleven years earlier, my goal had been to become the Intercontinental Champion. Now I was the first Undisputed World Champion, the only man in history who could make that claim, and it had only taken me 1,372 matches to do it.

I went through the curtain and looked to Vince for approval. He smiled and gave me a curt nod, but it didn't seem that he was really blown away with my work.

Neither was I.

I found a secluded corner backstage, collapsed on a giant roll of carpet, and reflected on my night. I'd wrestled for thirty-five minutes straight and beaten the two biggest superstars in the world, and even though neither of the matches were bad, they hadn't been the five-star classics I'd been wanting.

I wished I would've wrestled better. I wished the crowd had reacted to my victory more. I wished I had received a better reaction from the boss.

I wished—hell, it was pretty damn froot to be sitting there holding those two titles!

The company had given me the chance to be the man because they appreciated my work rate and believed in my ability to be a moneymaking commodity. Winning the titles was like a pat on the back, a reward for a job well done. I felt like I had just won an Oscar; I was Cuba Gooding Jr. after he nabbed the trophy for *Jerry Maguire*. Unfortunately, my own WWE versions of *Lightning Jack* and *Snow Dogs* were to come soon enough.

I left the sanctity of the carpet room and went back to the dressing room to find everyone gone. Roddy Piper once told me that the one drawback of being in the main events night after night was that when you went back to the dressing room, everyone was gone. After my first PPV main event, I realized how right he was. Nobody had stuck around to celebrate or congratulate me afterwards and I was literally the last one there.

But I hadn't totally been snubbed by my peers. Benoit (who was still out with his neck injury) and Eddy Guerrero (who had been fired by the WWE for his latest relapse) called and told me how happy and proud of me they were. Chris went on and on about how I had won the title not only for myself but for all the wrestlers who had been told they were too small to make it. Rey Mysterio, whom I hadn't talked to since I left WCW, called to congratulate me. Even Dave Penzer, the ring announcer from WCW (whom I had my first big heel moment with when I ripped the tuxedo off his back on *Nitro*), called and said, "You did it, and nobody said you could."

It was nice to hear the groundswell of support from my friends, and even better to know I was Undisputed Champion of the World, bitch!

The WWE World Champion finally drove on to Anaheim and got to his hotel at two minutes to midnight. He was very hungry and was ready for a feast worthy of an Undisputed King!

"What time does room service close, young Squire?" said the King to the check-in clerk.

"I'm sorry, sir, but it closed at 11 p.m. And the bar stopped serving at midnight."

It was 12:02 a.m.

The King wasn't happy and disappeared back into my brain, allowing peasant Jericho to return. Here I was, the Undisputed World Champion of the biggest wrestling company on the planet, and I couldn't get a damn shrimp salad.

The desk clerk gave me the number for Domino's Pizza and I swiped it from his hand rudely, grumbling something about lobster thermidor and couscous. Twenty-nine minutes later (two more minutes and I would've gotten that bad boy for free) the phone in my room rang and the delivery guy told me he was downstairs with my pauper's repast. I told him to just bring it up, but he said, "I'm sorry, sir, but our policy is to not bring pizzas up to the room. You'll have to come down to the lobby to pick it up."

I put on a pair of Zubaz and went downstairs in my bare feet, picked up my pizza (Vengeful Author's Note: Amount of driver's tip that night—37 cents.), and went back to my room. I searched through my pockets for the room key and realized I'd locked myself out. I went back down to the front desk (still in my bare feet) and told the guy I'd locked myself out and needed another keycard.

"Sure, just show me some ID."

"I don't have any ID, it's in my room next to the key. Besides, you just checked me in forty-five minutes ago."

"Well, I can't give you a key without any ID."

"Okay, but I can't give you ID without a key."

We went back and forth in the worst Reeves and Mortimer routine ever, until he finally agreed to allow the security guard to let me into my room, on the caveat that I could describe exactly what was in it.

"Well, there's a suitcase, a toiletry bag, and two championship titles because I'm the frickin' *WWE Undisputed Champion*!"

There were no *Playboy* models, paparazzi, or caviar for the champ that night; only bare feet, fawlty room keys, and a cold Domino's pizza in a deserted hotel lobby. I had achieved the highest accolade in my profession, yet I couldn't even get into my damn room.

That old trickster the Jericho Curse had returned to join me for old time's sake during my first night as the Undisputed World Champion.

But as I was soon to find out, that rat bastard Curse was going to stick around a lot longer than just one night.

CHAPTER 22

Peanut Butter and Chong

Now that I was the champion, I knew I would have to work harder than ever. Pat had told me, "When you make it to the top of the mountain, everybody wants to knock you off." The entire company was watching my every step, waiting for me to stumble in any way, with my biggest critic being Vince himself. I couldn't blame him.

He'd made a big investment in making me the Undisputed Champion, as he needed to make new stars. HHH and Michaels were out, Angle had been the champion multiple times, Rock was spending more and more time in Hollywood, and Austin was already the biggest name in the business. Vince had no other choice but to elevate me.

I was eager to prove my mettle, but the problem was I didn't feel completely at ease being the champion. I wasn't satisfied with my work in the WWE so far, my relationship with Vince wasn't the best, and politically I still had doubters who thought I couldn't cut it on top.

The next night on *Raw* was my coronation ceremony, where Flair (who storyline-wise was the co-owner of the WWE) was going to present me with the two titles. I came to the ring and gave a heartfelt speech, thanking the person who made my championship victories possible—me.

Later that night I had a rematch with Austin inside a steel cage, which consisted of him beating the hell out of me until I was covered in more blood than a fan in the front row of a Gwar concert. He gave me the Stunner and was walking out of the cage when Booker T once again interfered, this time slamming the door on Austin's face and allowing me to escape for the victory. Even though I was the Undisputed Champion, I still hadn't beaten anybody without outside help and my win was greeted with apathy from the sold-out crowd.

Granted, winning with interference was part of being a heel, but the fans weren't buying me as the champion yet.

So far my big title win hadn't made much of a splash with anyone—except airport security.

The first lesson I learned when I trained at Hart Brothers was to always carry your gear with you. You never want to check your bag on the way to a show, in case it got lost. As a result, I had to lug both championship belts through every airport I traveled through. They weighed about twenty-five pounds each and showed up on the TSA X-ray machines every time. Each morning without fail the airport security would ask, "Sir, may we check your bag?"

Then I'd have to stand there and watch as they unzipped my luggage like they were Vincent Vega opening Marsellus Wallace's briefcase.

"Well, what do we have here?" the guard would proclaim as his face brightened with suspicious amusement. "What kind of a champion are you?"

"Wrestling."

"Wrestling, huh? Well, you must be good." Then he would feel compelled to inform his nearest coworker of the treasures just discovered. "Hey, Enos, look at this! We got ourselves a real-life wrestling champion here!!"

Enos (Census Author's Note: 30 percent of all TSA employees are named Enos.) would leave his post looking for penis bombs and check out the merchandise for himself.

"Well, look at that!" Enos would declare as he took the titles out of the bag, inspected them, fondled them, and strapped them around his waist. Wanting to show off to his coworkers Edna, Ethel, and Elias, Enos would strike a few poses until Elvis rushed over from analyzing a bottle of Aquafina and joined him in dress-up time.

"Hey, look at me," Elvis would crow as he snapped the gold around his waist, busting out in a Fabulous Fargo strut followed by a picture-perfect moonwalk.

Now, that may seem amusing to you, fair reader, but imagine dealing with that nonsense four days a week, every week and you can see how the novelty might wear off quickly.

One week into my glorious championship reign, I had a match on *Raw* against Rob Van Dam, and right before we went out we were given an extra five minutes. Normally this was not a big deal, but Rob was still getting comfortable with working the WWE style and I wasn't in the groove either and found it difficult to fill the additional time. The match floundered a little, made worse by the fact that Vince was at ringside commentating. He rarely sat behind the announce table anymore and I wondered if he was out there to evaluate me. Did he want to see my work up close? Was he gauging my crowd reactions? I failed on both accounts if he was, as it wasn't a good match and the crowd was flat throughout.

I was off to a terrible start as champion and everyone knew it, so much so that the next night at *Smackdown!* I starting hearing rumors that Vince was going to have me drop the title. I dismissed them at first, but when three different people informed me Vince was second-guessing his decision, I started to think there might be something to it.

Hearing the gossip really pissed me off. I'd only been the champion for a week, and after working my ass off for eleven years to get it I wasn't going to give up that easily. I decided right then that I was going to go talk to Vince before it was too late.

I found him outside his office and let him have it. I had nothing to lose. If he had already made up his mind to take the title off me, then it didn't matter. But if he was on the fence, maybe I could show him something about me he hadn't seen before. It was time to go hard or go home.

"Listen, Vince, I'm the Undisputed Champion and you gave me this chance for a reason. I'm sure there are some people behind the scenes who aren't too happy with your decision, but I don't care—I'm the champion! This is my time, my chance, and if people don't believe in me, they can go fuck themselves. And you know what, Vince? If you don't believe in me, you can go fuck yourself too!"

There, I'd said it. I had told the great Vince McMahon to go fuck himself. But it was how I truly felt, and I was relieved.

Now I would have to deal with the consequences.

Vince stared at me with an expressionless look. I bowed my head and waited for him to unsheathe the Sword of Damocles and decapitate my mutinous ass.

He continued staring at me with a death gaze, barely moving a muscle.

(Time moving slow ... the minutes seemed like hours ... the final curtain call I see.)

Finally Vince moved, but instead of disemboweling me, his expression changed from that of a stone-cold serial killer to one of a delighted child opening his favorite present at six o'clock on a Christmas morning.

"That's exactly the attitude I want from you! That's what I wanted to hear!" Vince said, his expression mirroring Dr. Emmett Brown's when he discovered the DeLorean could actually travel through time.

"You need to believe you're the champion and act like it at all times! When Bret Hart was the champion, he believed it and nobody could tell him differently. That's what I want from you! I know that you have this passion and believe in yourself, but you haven't shown that to me up until now. You're the first Undisputed Champion in the history of this business, dammit! Now prove to me that you deserve it."

I had just kicked the devil in the nuts and survived to tell the tale.

Minutes later, Pat came over and said, "What did you say to Vince?"

"I told him to go fuck himself," I said in a half daze.

"Really?" Pat said in shock. "Well, whatever you said worked, because he can't stop putting you over! You know what, Jericho, you've got some bigs ball, kid!"

*   *   *

The next PPV was the *Royal Rumble*, where I was booked to face Rocky in the main event for the title. Rock was my favorite opponent and I could finally show off why I was worthy of being World Champion. The idea was for me to retain the title by beating him with a screwjob, which usually meant a low blow, outside interference, or the use of a foreign object. I decided that I'd get as much heat out of it as I could and use all three. So I had the Unamericans (Christian, Lance Storm, and Test) run down to cause a distraction. With the ref preoccupied, I nut-shotted Rock, bashed his head into an exposed turn-buckle, and pinned him with both feet on the ropes. The crowd in Atlanta was furious and booed me like millionaires at an Obama rally. The victory gave me a major credibility boost and was the highlight of my run as the Undisputed Champion.

The PPV also marked the triumphant return of HHH, who finally came back from his quad injury after seven months. He won the *Royal Rumble* and secured a title shot at *WrestleMania X8*, but he wasn't the only familiar face to return to the WWE roster.

At the end of the show, Vince teased that he was bringing the original NWO faction of Kevin Nash, Scott Hall, and Hulk Hogan into the WWE for the first time ever. I wasn't the only one who was surprised or concerned that three of the biggest contributors to the demise of WCW were getting a chance to spread their cancer in the WWE.

There were quite a few members of the roster who remembered what it was like in WCW when the NWO was in power, and they weren't thrilled about their impending arrival. The whole locker room was up in arms, uncertain as to what exactly would happen when they arrived. Would they destroy the locker room with their horrible attitudes? Would they work their dark Jedi mind tricks on Vince like they had Eric? Who could stop them? Who would save us?

There was only one man with the power to combat the NWO. I had to seek out the man who had everybody's respect across the board and the greatest influence within the company. He was the oracle. He was the swami. He was the Fonz.

He was the Deadman.

I expressed my concerns to The Undertaker, who listened intently before giving me his thoughts.

"The one thing that's different here is that Vince is the boss. He's in charge and we all know it. In WCW there were a half dozen bosses, and that made it easy for everyone to get what they wanted. These guys are going to do business and do what they're told, and if they don't, they won't last. I'll make sure of it." With that he waved his hand and disappeared in a cloud of smoke.

The master had spoken.

All shall be well and all manner of things shall be well.

D-Day finally arrived, and after three years of amnesty I found myself in the same company as Scott Hall, Kevin Nash, and Hulk Hogan once again. When they showed up on the first day, they of course were all on their very best behavior, especially Hulk. He shook my hand with a smile and reiterated what he'd said to me at Owen Hart's funeral three years earlier.

"You said you were going to take me with you when you jumped over here."

"I knew you'd find a way to get here on your own," I replied with a bigger smile.

Nash attempted to bust my balls right off the bat by commenting on the bright red color I had dyed in the tips of my hair, inspired by Ozzy's latest coif.

"Nice dye job there, Jericho."

Not missing a beat, I fired back, "Well, some of us dye our hair red when it's blond and some of us dye our hair brown when it's gray." The truth hurt, and Nash's sarcastic smile faded like his hair pigment.

Hall was the last to arrive and was all phony smiles and fake hellos, but I could see his true self waiting to emerge like a shark beneath the surface. It didn't take long for Jaws to attack as only five minutes later he shook Bubba Ray Dudley's hand and murmured in his deep voice, "I love the 3D. What a great finishing move . . . can't wait to kick out of it."

Hall was full of such witticisms and was always saying things like, "It's the wrestling business, not the wrestling friendness," and "It doesn't say anywhere in my contract that I have to be nice to anybody." That was his old WCW attitude, but that shit wasn't going to fly here. The WWE was about making money, not a corporate sandbox where you could drop trou and take a dumpski whenever you felt like it.

Things were different now and I wasn't intimidated by them like I once was. I wasn't the same guy I was in WCW. I was the motherfucking champion now.

But how good of one was still to be determined.

*   *   *

Austin was my opponent at the next PPV, *No Way Out*. Steve and I were pretty much left on our own to think of how to build up the match, and we came up with a few good ideas (including me pummeling him over the head with his own beer cooler) with no input from the boss, which was surprising. But as mediocre as the build was, the match was 316 times worse. Nothing clicked for us at all and my performance was brutal. We'd had decent to good matches in the past, but that night we were like Peanut Butter and Chong. It just didn't work, and I take full responsibility for it because Steve was a proven great worker and I was the damn champion whose job it was to take control and make a match work no matter who I was up against.

I ended up beating Steve after the NWO interfered, and I disappeared as they continued to beat him down for minutes afterwards. I was a complete afterthought and should've been after my dismal performance. Maybe I wasn't good enough to be the top guy in the WWE after all.

The next day, Paul Heyman told me that I would be losing the title to HHH in the main event of *Wrestle-Mania X8* in Toronto. He also told me there were rumblings that certain people were lobbying for Nash to beat me for the title on *Raw* and go on to face HHH at *Wrestle-Mania* instead. But to Vince's credit, he wanted HHH and Jericho, and that's the way it was going down no matter what anybody said.

Unfortunately, Vince also booked Hogan vs. The Rock for the show. It was wrestling's version of Mike Tyson vs. Muhammad Ali and by far the most anticipated match on the card—they were the true main event and everybody knew it.

But the advantage that HHH and I had over Rock and Hogan was the Undisputed Championship. If booked properly, a well-thought-out angle centering around the ultimate prize in the business could compete with the magic of two legends facing each other for the first time.

But it wasn't.

I pitched a lot of ideas, but in my opinion one of them in particular could've made a huge difference in the way our match was perceived. The story would begin after HHH returned at the *Royal Rumble*. He would be in the ring on *Raw* telling the fans how great it was to be back when I would come out to confront him and give him some serious news. In the seven months he was away from the WWE, his wife, Stephanie, was having an affair. I was only telling him about it because I obviously had a huge dislike for Steph and did some serious detective work in order to bust her. In the course of my investigation, I'd found out that she was having an affair with RVD.

Then I'd run hidden camera footage of his wife in bed experiencing unlawful carnal knowledge with a guy with a long brown ponytail grinding on top of her. Trying to gain his trust, I'd attempt to soothe his heartbreak.

"I hate to show you this, but you needed to see the real tramp that you married."

HHH would be steaming with anger and betrayal as he watched the video. The footage would continue until the guy with the ponytail rolled over and we would see that he wasn't actually RVD, he was actually *me*.

As the footage ended, I'd be standing behind him with

his very own sledgehammer and bang the shit out of him, the same way I just had his wife.

I thought Stephanie having an affair with her former worst enemy was the perfect twist to the story. She would justify her actions by saying, "You know how hard it is for a woman to be on the road by herself—she has needs! Needs that can only be satisfied by a champion." I would justify my actions by saying I knew that HHH would be returning to gain revenge for me causing him to tear his quad in the first place. Therefore I needed to gain a psychological edge against him, and what better way to do that than by shtuping his wife?

But my idea was canned due to the mindset that HHH wasn't the kind of babyface who would be stupid enough not to know his wife was cheating on him. The whole plan was scrapped—well, almost all of it.

The last part of my story was that I would be totally pussywhipped by Steph and become a shameless patsy who did whatever I was told no matter how bad she treated me. I thought it would be a great way to get heat if the World Champion was an avatar for Stephanie McMahon. It was the only part of the story that Vince liked, but now the problem was I was pussywhipped without the pussy.

Now I was just whipped—which was apropos, because I became Stephanie's personal Kunta Kinte. She would send me out for groceries, make me sweep the floor, carry her bags, whatever. I wasn't the World Champion anymore so much as Stephanie McMahon's lackey—a fact that was made evident in the *WrestleMania* matchup graphic. It said: "HHH vs Chris Jericho w/Stephanie McMahon," with me in the background behind her shoulder.

The buildup to the match was weak and began with me

Stephanie and I had amazing chemistry, but I was disappointed with our storyline in the buildup to *WrestleMania X8*. The good news? At least I'm in the foreground of this picture.

stealing HHH's first ring robe, a purple velour monstrosity given to him by Killer Kowalski, only for him to get it back later in the show.

When Stephanie and HHH's dog Lucy pooped all over my dressing room in Detroit, I had to clean up the scheisse. Then when she told me to walk Lucy, I accidentally ran the mutt over.

I was the World Champion as played by Lloyd Christmas. Needless to say, it didn't work. Shawn Michaels, Ric Flair, and Bret Hart had been tremendous heel champions who got red-hot heat due to their exploits in the ring and the dirty tactics they used against their opponents. I was an average heel champion who got lukewarm heat due to my exploits of stealing Grimace costumes, cleaning up shit, and running over dogs in the parking lot. With the exception of my *Royal Rumble* match with The Rock, my run as the first Undisputed Champion had been a bust.

But there was a reprieve coming that would prove to the company (and most important to myself) that I did have the attributes to be a great World Champion.

CHAPTER **23**

Whiskey Gargling

Three weeks before *WrestleMania* my salvation arrived in the form of an Asian tour to Japan, Singapore, and Malaysia. I had a good history and a great fan base in Japan, who'd seen me have some of the best matches of my career. I hadn't been there in four years and was hungry to return to show them what I'd learned during my time away. Most important of all, I was booked against The Rock for all three shows and he brought out the best in me. He'd just finished *The Scorpion King* and was killing two birds with one rock by promoting the movie in Asia and touring with the WWE at the same time.

The first show was in Yokohama Arena and had sold 18,000 tickets in sixty minutes. Rock and I were the main event and I was honored to be headlining a sold-out show in my adopted home country in front of some of the best fans in the world.

I was getting prepared for the match when Flair found me in the dressing room.

"This is the real deal over here, Chris. Being the World Champion means more in Japan than it does anywhere else. You know how much these people respect the tradition and the history of this business and the work you have to put in to become champion. They're expecting your best, and I know you're ready to give that to them. Enjoy this night and tear the house down—be the champion that I know you can be."

It was an inspiring pep talk from one of the greatest champions of all time and the last push over the cliff that I needed. I forgot all about dogshit in the dressing room, being pussyless-whipped, and mediocre matches. It was my time to shine.

My music played and as I walked through the curtain the fans jumped to their feet clapping and cheering. I had grown up in front of their eyes, starting in Japan as a twenty-year-old rookie. Now that I was a thirty-one-year-old champion, they had as much pride in me as I did in myself.

I was walking up the ring steps when I saw the Great Muta at ringside. He was one of the biggest stars in the history of Japanese wrestling and had just taken over the reins of All Japan Pro Wrestling. Throughout the evening, many of the other wrestlers had paid him their respects by shaking his hand or giving him the thumbs-up as they walked by. Being a heel and knowing how the Japanese style works, I walked over to Muta and smacked him in the face. He fell off his chair and then tried to jump the rail and attack me as his young boys held him back. All the fans were oohing and ahhing in shock as the ringside photographers snapped as many pictures as they could. Then The Rock's music played and the fracas broke up instantly as the entire arena exploded.

It was the first time that The Rock, the biggest star

in the WWE, had ever appeared in Japan, the most wrestling-crazed country on the planet. The reaction he received was one of the loudest I'd ever heard in my career. It was as if Elvis had joined the Beatles and all of them were wearing Godzilla costumes. The normally polite and reserved Japanese jumped to their feet and chanted, "LOCK-Y, LOCK-Y" in unison with orange-segment smiles on their faces. They had adopted the fairly new American tradition of making their own signs and there were hundreds of them glorifying Rock's name and vilifying mine.

They were ready to be the type of audience they had seen on *Raw*, as opposed to the typical quiet, polite Japanese crowd. There were even boos at the beginning of the show when Shane McMahon used a translator to greet them—they understood English and weren't about to be patronized. The combination of their electric reaction with the special chemistry Rocky and I had spurred us to accomplish exactly what Flair had demanded. We tore that damn house down.

It was as close to a perfect match as I've ever had, a twenty-minute classic featuring the greatest hits of Rock and Jericho. Our "Rock and Roll All Nite" was me thwarting (awesome word) the People's Elbow by putting Rock in the Walls and him subsequently making it to the ropes. We followed with our "Detroit Rock City," which was me kicking out of a well-timed Rock Bottom. We followed up with our "Love Gun" of Rock's Sharpshooter. We were having so much fun that at one point Rock threw me to the floor, grabbed a ringside photographer's camera and snapped some shots of me as I made the stupidest faces I could. Then I turned the tide and took some pictures of my own, with Rocky returning the favor by making even dumber faces.

We rolled back into the ring and continued, and by the time we finished our chain of false finishes, the educated Japanese fans were on the edge of their seats, knowing they had witnessed a classic.

The match ended when I rolled him up and put my feet on the ropes for extra leverage. The fans booed politely at first because they knew they were supposed to, but after the announcements had been made they gave us a standing ovation. They were such an amazing crowd that they deserved an encore. Rock grabbed the mic and started into one of his famous post-match speeches.

"You know, The Rock lost a hard-fought match, but The Rock isn't sad. As a matter of fact, The Rock is very hungry and is excited to go and eat the best *yaku niku* in Tokyo!" The crowd went crazy, hanging on his every word. "After that The Rock is going to have some dessert. He has a sweet tooth and he likes many different desserts, but by far The Rock's favorite is . . . pie."

They all knew where he was going and ate up his words, with chopsticks.

"And The Rock has tasted pie from all over the world—but he has never tried Japanese pie." Thousands of Japanese girls wet their American designer jeans at the thought.

"Now, Chris Jericho, you won your match tonight and I know you must be quite hungry as well. Do you like pie?"

This was my cue to feed Rocky's lines, the same way I fed his moves. "I hate pie. I would never eat pie, especially Japanese pie!"

Rock raised his famous eyebrow. "You don't like pie? What is wrong with you, Jericho?"

"There's nothing wrong with me, I just don't like pie!"

"Well, do you like...strudel?" The Rock inquired.

"As a matter of fact, Rock, I love strudel! Strudel is the tastiest treat in the world and I love stuffing as much of it in my mouth as I can. If I could eat strudel every day, I would!"

Now the fans were catcalling me over my choice of pastries. I put my mic down and whispered to Rocky under my breath, "Call me Okama."

"Call you what...Osama?"

"No...Okama," I said as 18,000 people wondered what kind of horrible trash we were talking to each other.

"What does that mean?"

"It means gay," I whispered under my breath. "Trust me."

Rock gave me a nod, lifted the mic back to his mouth, and asked, "So you like strudel, huh? Does that mean that you're...*okama*?"

The crowd detonated and you would have thought that Buddha himself had waddled into the arena handing out Pocky. They went hamatteru, chanting, "O-kama! O-kama!"

I marched around the ring defiantly with a frown, acting as if I had no idea what they were saying. My line got The Rock more over than he already was, never mind that all the respect I'd accrued during my years in Japan had been deleted in about ten seconds. Despite all of the great matches I had in this country, I'd never live down the night Rocky called me gay in Japanese, a point illustrated by the headline on the front page of *Tokyo Sports* the next day: "The Rock Calls Jericho *Okama*!"

It was worth it.

I mean, how often do you beat one of the biggest stars

in wrestling history, retain the world title, get verbally insulted, have your sexuality questioned, and get Rock Bottomed all in one night?

Later on, I was celebrating a job well done at the Hard Rock Café in Roppongi when I received a call from Muta. He laughingly told me that I "gave him a nice Idaho potato," which is a term for a stiff shot.

"Tonight was very good for business. If you ever want to work for my company, give me a call."

Only in Japan could you sucker-punch the CEO of a company and have him offer you a job.

Taking Flair's words to heart both in the ring and out, I sure as hell acted like an old-school World Champion during that tour. I had three consecutive five-star matches against Rocky in three different countries, combined with three consecutive five-star nights of drinking on about three hours total sleep. I learned that another important duty of a champion was to be the last man standing at the bar—and there were shortcuts to achieve that.

One of my favorites was to buy trays of shots for whoever was out that night. When everyone toasted and drank, I simply tossed every third shot over my shoulder. Or poured it into a nearby flowerpot. Or flicked it onto the floor.

At the end of the night, the ground underneath my feet was wet and sticky from all the alcohol I hadn't drank, but when 6 a.m. rolled around and everybody was plastered, I was still standing—totally loadski, mind you, but still standing.

Hey, I was the champion and I couldn't pass out—I had responsibilities, dammit!

Another of my favorites was to challenge random fans to whiskey-gargling contests. Whenever we went out to a bar, there were always people around who wanted to hang out and be one of the boys. These fans were usually filled with liquid courage and bravado and would always agree to have a Jack Daniel's gargling contest with me.

What the poor fans didn't know was that Curt Hennig taught me how to gargle Jack years earlier, but more important, Flair taught me how *not* to gargle Jack years earlier.

I would let the fan go first and he would dump the shot glass into his open mouth and proceed to gargle it back and forth for a respectable forty-five seconds or so. Now, as I explained in my wildly popular first book, *A Lion's Tale* (available... well, you know the drill), gargling alcohol isn't as easy as it sounds. Imagine swishing yellow Listerine around in your mouth for thirty seconds and then swallowing it. Now multiply that by a hundred and you get a small sense of what I'm talking about.

The fan would painfully swallow the aptly named fire water and look at me expectantly. I would then toss the hooch into my mouth, facing the fan with my left side, and begin to gargle. What the fan couldn't see was me slowly dribbling the sweet amber out of the right side of my mouth, effectively spitting it out. By the time I reached my record-setting three minutes and thirty-nine seconds, I was gargling nothing but fumes, and even that was enough to almost make me bap when I swallowed my saliva. The poor fanboy never knew what hit him or why he was so much drunker than me, but suffice it to say that most of my foes were carried out of the club an inebriated mess. Once again, I had responsibilities, remember?

Another one of those responsibilites was to try and be the most entertaining performer on the show, which wasn't easy when working with The Rock. After another great twenty-minute match in Singapore, we followed up with another twenty minutes of improv comedy. Pat was the agent for the tour and it drove him crazy when we spent so much time in the ring after the match.

"What are you dooooing? You're spending so much time in da fucking ring after da match dat nobody remembers how good da match was!!"

Rock and I respected Pat more than anyone in the company, but we knew this was probably the only time Rocky was going to be wrestling in these countries. The Asian fans wanted to see the most electrifying man in sports entertainment, and that's what they were going to get.

In Singapore, we reviewed *Scorpion King* and plugged its opening in April. We called each other names, got into a mock argument, and then made up. Then I went to shake Rock's hand, he gave me a Rock Bottom, and that was it for me.

Kuala Lumpur was the final night of the tour and we ended things with a bang—literally. After I beat him again, I was walking back to the dressing room when Rock grabbed the mic and informed me that because I'd cheated to win, everyone in the crowd thought I was an asshole. Ten thousand Malaysians smelled what he was cooking and began chanting at the top of their lungs that I was an anus orifice. I was heading back toward the ring, ready to begin our routine for the evening, when I spotted a blue balloon floating in the aisle. I had just seen Tom Hanks in *Castaway* and got an idea. I grabbed the balloon and held it close to me as I stepped between the ropes.

I'm wearing a scarf here in Singapore because it's my theory that if you wear one, you'll NEVER catch a cold. Ever. It really works...try it! (The cut on my forehead is from a Tommy Dreamer kendo stick shot.)

"Everybody in this arena hates me and thinks I'm an asshole, including you, Rock. But there's someone here who still believes in me. Someone who will always be my friend. Someone named Ziggy!"

Then I held my Wilson up in the air like he was the Holy Grail. The place began booing and I found it amazing that I got an inanimate object more over as a heel than half the locker room. Rock did his trademark eyebrow raise as I continued: "Everybody in this country hates me and loves you and it's not fair. But Ziggy here, Ziggy loves me. Ziggy is my only friend and the only thing I need in this toilet of a country! I'm going to hug him and squeeze him and stroke him and never let him go!"

Rock eyed me up and down, pausing as the crowd cheered in anticipation of what he was going to do.

"Ziggy's your only friend?"

"Yes!"

"Well, then Ziggy must be an asshole too." Ten thousand chants of "asshole" began again, this time directed toward my poor Ziggy, who had done nothing to deserve such verbal abuse.

"Ziggy's not an asshole!" I yelled, jumping up and down as the Zigster nodded silently in agreement.

"Well, maybe I was wrong. Can The Rock introduce himself to Ziggy and apologize to him?"

I looked to Ziggy, who gave his approval. "Okay, Rock, but you better be nice to him."

Rocky responded with his trademark dazzling smile. "Of course, Chris, The Rock is always nice!" Rock gently cupped Ziggy in his hands and said, "Well hello, little Ziggy! Let The Rock ask... are you Chris Jericho's friend?"

Ziggy gazed silently at Rock, letting him know that he was indeed my boy.

Rock continued talking to Ziggy as if he were a child. "Well isn't that nice that you're Jericho's pal. But do you know what The Rock thinks of you being Chris Jericho's only friend?"

Ziggy contemplated the question and took the fifth.

"The Rock thinks this..." and he popped my little buddy.

The Rock killed Ziggy.

The crowd went wild, jumping up and down and screaming as if he had just assassinated Pol Pot. I freaked out and threw a tantrum. I collapsed onto my knees, wailing "NOOOOOOOO!" like Captain Kirk in *The Wrath of Khan* after Spock died.

But Ziggy was much frooter than Spock. He was my everything, and I remembered all of the good times we had. The time we double dated in high school. The time we built a birdhouse in the November rain. The time our Flock of Seagulls cover act won a battle of the bands in college. All those hopes and dreams we discussed in our jammies as we huddled together during a cold winter's night.

Rock had taken all of that from me.

I looked up at my nemesis with tears in my eyes, just as The Rock extended his hand in an act of remorse. I dropped Ziggy's carcass like a used blue prophylactic as The Rock told me that I didn't need Ziggy anymore, because he wanted to be my friend. We shook hands and embraced like the newfound brothers we were. Rocky wiped the tears from my eyes and clapped me on the back. I reciprocated, but as I went to walk away he changed his mind and pulled me in for the Rock Bottom.

Instead of executing the picture-perfect rendition of the move we'd been performing nightly, we were so sweaty that my hand slipped out of his. Our timing was off as a result and we awkwardly collapsed in a heap onto the mat. The fans were so primed for the moment that there was an audible groan as everyone in the building knew we had fucked up.

But Rocky never missed a beat.

He popped right back onto his feet, grabbed the mic,

and said, "Wait a second, wait a second, wait a second. Don't you know that this is the part of the show where we're supposed to shake hands, I pull you in, and then give you the Rock Bottom?"

The crowd cheered, delighted that Rock had broken the fourth wall and let them in.

"Yes, I know how it goes, but my hands are really sweaty and I slipped," I retorted apologetically.

Rock looked at me with disgust. "You slipped?"

"Yes, I slipped, and I apologize, Rock. I forgive you for what you did to poor Ziggy and now I ask you to forgive me for my mistake. Can we just be friends again like we were in the old days?"

Rocky pondered my request as the crowd cheered him on. He surveyed the people, looked at his toes, nodded his head, and shook my hand—then pulled me in and gave me a textbook Rock Bottom to the delight of the crowd.

I came through the curtain and received a bollocking from a visibly upset Pat. "That was some of the worst shits I've ever seen in my life!"

I couldn't even deny it because I was still laughing too hard.

CHAPTER 24

A Healthy Scratch

After the show, everybody was excited to blow off some steam and end the tour with a few celebratory drinks. When Pat caught wind of the evening's plans, he vehemently protested. The previous time he'd been an agent on an overseas tour the boys had gotten so drunk the last night, that some of them missed the bus and subsequently their flight home the next morning. He was adamant that we shouldn't go out and party. I took Pat aside and promised him as champion that I would make sure that everyone made it to the bus on time, no matter what. "This is a good crew of guys," I said. "It's not how it used to be back in the old days." Pat reluctantly agreed and the bash was on.

We ended up at a bar that was essentially a big grass hut, and I expected Tugg Speedman to wander out and buy me a mai tai. We went inside and the bar was essentially divided like a snowball dance in high school: boys on one side of the crabgrass club and girls on the other. As we went to get a drink, each of us was instantly flanked by a girl.

Malaysian women are a mixture of Japanese, Filipino,

Indian, and Chinese and are very exotic-looking. They also seemed to be very friendly, and soon it looked like a spring break movie from the '80s, where every guy had an admiring female attached to his hip. I thought it was interesting how quickly it happened and figured the girls must be big fans of the WWE. But after a few words of stilted conversation, I realized that none of them knew our names or where we were from. I started surveying the area, and out of the corner of my eye I saw one of the girls talking on a cell phone. I continued my inspection and noticed a nicely dressed older lady sitting in the back of the room, also on the phone. When the girl hung up her phone, the old lady hung up hers. Another girl dialed a number on her phone and a few seconds later the old lady picked up. Then I saw two burly guys in dark suits sidle up to the old lady and whisper in her ear. The gears in my head started turning as I connected the dots of what was going down. We were in Malaysia. We had instantly been surrounded by a gaggle (fun word) of nubile young ladies, communicating with an older woman flanked by a pair of gorillas in suits.

Hmmmmm. I looked at the guys in the suits, then the old lady, then the girls, then the old lady, then the guys in suits...then it hit me.

The girls were hookers, the old lady was the madam, and the gorillas were the pimps.

We were in some sort of a brothel.

I slapped my hands to my face like the kid from *Home Alone* and screamed, "Ahhhh prostitutes!! Prostitutes!! Run! Run! Run!"

I started smashing drinks and shoving people out of the way like George Costanza at an inflamed children's party, trying to get the boys the hell out of there. A mass stampede to the door ensued, like when the girls revealed themselves as vampires in *From Dusk Till Dawn*—except these girls had revealed themselves to be hookers. We made it out the front door and ran down the street as if we were expecting them to chase after us and drink our blood.

I finally got into bed at 6 a.m., and when the 7 a.m. wake-up call arrived, I closed my eyes to get that crucial one extra minute of sleep. The phone rang again and I hopped out of bed in a panic when I saw that it was now 8 a.m. My heart nipped up when I remembered the bus was supposed to leave at 7:45.

Pat was gonna be pissed!

I woke up, and made the bus in seconds flat—where Pat was standing furiously with his arms crossed. After my grandiose promise to him the night before, the only person late for the bus was me.

A week after the Asian tour, it was time for *Wrestle-Mania*. On the final *Raw* before the big show, I finally got the upper hand on HHH by attacking him with his own sledgehammer and putting him in the Walls on the announce table, the same way I had the night he tore his quad. Vince came to me after the show and said, "How does it feel to finally have some heat?"

The way I'd been booked over the past month, it was amazing I had any at all.

For the week before the show, the entire city of Toronto was abuzz with anticipation. The WWE was on the cover of the *Toronto Sun* for a week straight, I was on the cover

SUNDAY, MARCH 17, 2002
SKYDOME
TORONTO, ONTARIO, CANADA

World Wrestling Federation®

FOR THE UNDISPUTED WORLD WRESTLING FEDERATION CHAMPIONSHIP

CHRIS JERICHO Winnipeg, MB...227 lbs. (CHAMPION)	-VS-	**TRIPLE H** Greenwich, CT...272 lbs. (CHALLENGER)
THE ROCK Miami, FL...275 lbs.	-VS-	**HOLLYWOOD HULK HOGAN** nWo...265 lbs.
STONE COLD STEVE AUSTIN Victoria, TX...252 lbs.	-VS-	**SCOTT HALL** nWo...270 lbs.

NO DISQUALIFICATION MATCH

RIC FLAIR Charlotte, NC...230 lbs.	-VS-	**THE UNDERTAKER** Houston, TX...305 lbs.

FOR THE INTERCONTINENTAL CHAMPIONSHIP

WILLIAM REGAL Blackpool, UK...240 lbs. (CHAMPION)	-VS-	**ROB VAN DAM** Battle Creek, MI...230 lbs. (CHALLENGER)
KANE 326 lbs.	-VS-	**KURT ANGLE** Pittsburgh, PA...237 lbs.

FOUR CORNERS ELIMINATION MATCH FOR THE TAG TEAM CHAMPIONSHIP

BILLY & CHUCK Combined Weight: 529 lbs. (CHAMPIONS)	-VS-	**HARDY BOYZ** Combined Weight: 441 lbs.	-VS-	**A.P.A.** Combined Weight: 567 lbs.	-VS-	**DUDLEY BOYZ** Combined Weight: 556 lbs.

EDGE Toronto, ON...241 lbs.	-VS-	**BOOKER T** Houston, TX...248 lbs.

FOR THE EUROPEAN CHAMPIONSHIP

DIAMOND DALLAS PAGE Jersey Shore...248 lbs. (CHAMPION)	-VS-	**CHRISTIAN** Toronto, ON...225 lbs. (CHALLENGER)

TRIPLE THREAT MATCH FOR THE WOMEN'S CHAMPIONSHIP

JAZZ (CHAMPION)	-VS-	**TRISH STRATUS**	-VS-	**LITA**

TUNE IN AND CATCH THE ACTION!

Mondays	6:00 pm	TSN	RAW™
Sundays	4:00 pm	SPORTSNET	Sunday Night Heat™
Thursdays	4:00 PM	The Score	SMACKDOWN™
Saturdays	6:00 pm	TNN	EXCESS™

Very froot to see my name at the top of the *WrestleMania* card as champion. How many guys can say they were in the final match at a *WrestleMania*? It's also interesting that you can pretty much count on one hand the performers on this show who are still in the WWE today.

of the Canadian *TV Guide* for the second time, and every news channel and talk show had us on as guests.

The biggest of the shows was *Off the Record*, the same program where Moongoose McQueen had batttled Pink years earlier.

In the week leading up to *WrestleMania*, *OTR* had a WWE Superstar as the sole guest each night for the entire thirty minutes. First up was HHH. I was watching the interview, and when host Michael Landsberg asked him what he thought of his opponent for *Mania*, I couldn't believe his response.

"Jericho can be as good as he wants to be but he's missing something. I don't know what that something is, but it's keeping him from being what he could be."

He was basically telling everybody that I wasn't living up to my potential. The first rule I learned about interviews from Bulldog Bob Brown in Calgary was you always put over your opponent. That way if you win, you've really beat somebody. It didn't matter if he thought I was missing something, I was the Undisputed World Champion! I felt that it wasn't the best way to sell the huge match coming up in only a few days, and it annoyed me.

Jericho vs. HHH was technically the main event of *WrestleMania X8*, in that we went on last, but in reality the main event was Hogan vs. The Rock. Their images were on all of the posters, T-shirts, newspapers, and promotional materials, and that's the way it should have been.

I felt that Hogan and Rock would be impossible to follow, but Vince decided that the title match should go on last, which meant we had our work cut out for us.

Hogan and Rock put on an epic match and the fans lapped up everything they did. It wasn't the greatest of matches technically, but with the ridiculous crowd reactions it was one of the best matches of the year. As I watched it I knew we were in trouble. I hoped that maybe my Canadian brethren would save some energy for me and help rescue us, but they didn't.

Before we went to the ring HHH said, "Now it's time to give them something completely different than Hogan and Rock. This is going to be a *wrestling* match."

And that's what we gave them. By no means was it a bad match, but after Hogan and Rock the crowd was mentally done. In the end, HHH pinned me with a Pedigree and we had a new Undisputed World Champion. The crowd reacted, but they were clearly tired and it was kind of an anticlimatic finish to the biggest show of the year.

But no matter the result, the bottom line was I had been in the official main event of *WrestleMania*, and only seventeen other matches in the history of the business could claim that. It was a huge honor, and to commemorate the moment I took the lineup sheet off the wall and kept it as a souvenir.

After the match, I walked through Gorilla and was surprised to see The Undertaker waiting for me.

"Congratulations, Chris. You worked hard tonight and during your whole run as champion and I'm proud of you."

I felt like I was Ralph Malph and the Fonz had just given me a pat on the back. My relationship with Taker had always been respectful, but he certainly didn't have to go out of his way to say that. What made his gesture even more impressive was that he'd made the good ten-minute walk through SkyDome, from the dressing room to Gorilla to give me his compliment, and that meant a lot

The name on the Tron might've said Jericho, but backstage it was Mud. (Photo © Blair Relya)

When I barged into Arnold's dressing room in Baltimore to get a picture with him, his facial expression never changed once. I personally think he was intimidated by my massive guns.

**VANILLA ICE CREAM
and COOKIE WAFER
with CHOCOLATE
COATED BACK**

I've never actually seen a Jericho ice cream bar. Nor have I seen a Jericho bowling ball or a pair of the Jericho designer eyeglasses that also exist.
(Photo © 2010 World Wrestling Entertainment, Inc.)

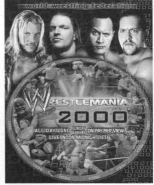

I love this poster. But I hate that my gorgeous face was replaced by the rugged good looks of Mick Foley about a month after it was released. Interesting that the numbers on the right are electric blue and resemble the binary codes I used for my second coming seven years later.
(Photo © World Wrestling Entertainment, Inc.)

Fozzy's first centerfold, published in *Metal Edge* magazine. I wish Gargano would've taken the picture before the show instead of afterward; Sneap and I look particularly disheveled.

My mom and grandma were so excited and happy to be a part of our wedding. This was one of the last times my mom voluntarily left her house.

Me, Adrian, Todd, and Chad (the wise man on the end), during our first meeting in Chicago. Adrian was amazing and even offered us a piece of pizza, a gesture that Todd still raves about to this day.

One of my favorite pictures of all-time. Gargano and I spit alcohol into each other's faces and squirted ketchup over each other's heads, yet our inebriated expressions of pure joy say it all.

The Walls of Jericho on top of the ladder at the 2001 *Royal Rumble* was one of my favorite moves I've ever done in my career, and it was all Chris's idea. The ladder was wobbling under our combined weight, and I was convinced it was going to flip us right over.

At Ozzfest in New Jersey the night after we ate boiled eggs and drank beer in Zakk's hotel bathroom. Here's a fun game to play: Which one of us is more hung over? Maybe Jack Osbourne (in the background) knows.

In Albany, New York, the same night as the Station tragedy in Rhode Island. Rich set off pyro that evening during our gig too. I've formulated fire-escape plans in my head for every show we've done since.

I was the first Undisputed Champion in the history of the wrestling business, an accomplishment I'm very proud of that can never be taken away. I miss that eagle world title.

Rock and I were having so much fun during our 2002 Asian tour that every night we'd grab the ringside photographer's camera and snap pictures of each other. The contest was to see who could make the most ridiculous face. On this night in Malaysia, I definitely won.

This front cover of *Tokyo Sports* talks about the classic match Rock and I had the night before; my incident with Great Muta at ringside; and Rock calling me *okama* ("gay") on the mic in front of 18,000 people. You can see *Okama* written on the bottom of the page, middle line, in dark letters.

The Rock is one of my all-time favorite opponents. Because he's such a great entertainer, people forget how awesome he was as a worker. In my opinion, he's one of the best ever.

When Rock held my arms and told Bruce Willis to do something to me, I prepared for a punch. When he headbutted me in the chest instead, I screamed in pain instinctively. A second later I started laughing when I realized that was all he'd done. Note Rocky's mom, Ata, behind Bruce.

ROTTEN!

WWE show turns into a SICK JOKE

"India is a very very bad place and all Indians are assholes..."
— *WWE Tag team champion Chris Jericho*

Anapam Thapa and Rohit Wadhwaney

INDIRA GANDHI STADIUM: **If at all that was meant to be a joke, it was a very sick one. And that was not the only sick joke either. The entire World Wrestling Entertainment show held at the Indira Gandhi Indoor stadium on Thursday was a big, rotten joke.**

It was so badly organised that the "asshole Indians", who spent a fortune on each ticket to fulfill the dreams of their children, felt cheated.

Vandana Bhargava, a businesswoman, was infuriated. "I spent Rs.3,000 for this ticket. I can't see anything. This is a pathetic show. Everyone is

standing on the chairs. There is no decorum at all. The security should have been much better for such a big event." Bhargava stormed out just 15 minutes after the show began.

A badly organised show it was. The seating arrangement was so bad and freeloaders so many that genuine ticket-holders did not get even a peeking chance at the fake action in the ring. The freeloaders, mostly policemen and their cronies, swarmed the ring like bees and shut out the view. There was nothing that legitimate ticketholders could do, except prattle with their three-or-five-year-olds.

The place was swarming with policemen, but there was no security to talk of. No one to force the front row dudes
>> Turn to Page 2

Talk about a misquote! I didn't say that ALL Indians were assholes, just the ones in the arena that night. Surprisingly, the office didn't say a word to me about this. Maybe they will now.

Shawn Michaels and Marty Jannetty reunited for one night only in Atlanta in 2004, and I was thrilled. I'd always dreamed of being the third Rocker when I was in high school, and sixteen years later my dream came true.

This pic screams "ROCK AND ROLL!" I scoured the shops of London to find the perfect pair of pants to fit the occasion. I only wore 'em once, at the Astoria gig that night. My shirt mysteriously disappeared when Kelly Osbourne and her entourage visited our dressing room after the show.

Australia 2005: This is what happens if you don't wash your hair whilst on a Fozzy tour.

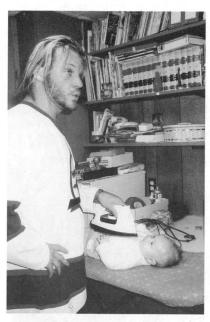

Ash was very wrinkly when he was a baby, but I figured out the solution.

Backstage with Dr. Death at Sai-tama Super Arena, 2005. Even though I was totally hungover and Benoit split me open with a headbutt, our submission match was voted match of the month by *WWE Magazine*. I slept in the training room for most of the day.

Little-known fact: Vince loves babies more than he loves apes. He's also the best boss I've ever had and a big influence on my life. Besides my own dad, there's not a man on the planet I respect more. Maybe someday Ash will work for Vince too.

Backstage in Washington D.C. after my last match in 2005. The four of us were so happy for each other, and it was a magical moment. It was also the last time we were ever together.

Fozzy rocks Canada's Wonderland on the banks of Lake Ontario. My plane was delayed by hurricanes and Rich almost had to sing lead vocals for the gig. But I made it just in time and waltzed straight from the car to the stage like a true prima donna.

Okay, I'll say it: Damn my mom was hot! Sweet Loretta Modern always wore the latest fashions and had the trendiest hair-styles. She also always wanted to be a *Solid Gold* dancer. She would've kicked ass at it too, just like she did doing everything else she tackled in her life.

Telling my dad to take his time and work the crowd as the MSG brethren go nuts with anticipation to see father and son throw hands. The Baby-Faced Assassin won the fight, by the way.

Peter Frampton is a great guy and an awesome storyteller. We talked for an hour earlier that day about his time playing with Ringo Starr and his experiences recording *All Things Must Pass* with George Harrison. Plus he rules cos he's FRAMPTON!

I've been blessed with three happy, healthy children and I thank God for them every day. They love SpongeBob, Scooby Doo and ... Justin Bieber, and for that I curse God every day. There are some punishments coming for sure.

We got hooked up to do promotion for *Opening Night* with the Toronto Argonauts. This ad appeared on the giant Tron about thirty times during the team's 2006 season opener. The owner promised to bring the whole team to the play, but the actual number of Argonauts who showed up was zero.

I would've used this picture (above) of the Hart Brothers Class of 1990 in *A Lion's Tale*, but I didn't know Lance had it. For those of you who've read *ALT*, the middle row is Vic DeWilde, me, Wilf, Lance T, and Deb. The bottom picture is the Storm Academy Class of '07. Fighting Action Guy is over my right shoulder; he quit the camp the next day.

to me. He gave me a boost when I needed it, and I'll never forget that.

Thanks, Take.

But as good as Taker's comments made me feel, Vince's comments brought me right back down to earth again. When I asked him what he thought of the match, he nodded his head noncommitally and said, "It was good."

Vince is easy to read and I could tell he was just giving me some high-class lip service. "Well, I appreciate the opportunity you gave me to be the champion and I hope I get the chance to do it again in the future."

Instead of agreeing with my statement, he just shook my hand and thanked me stoically. I could tell that his mind was elsewhere.

The Jericho as champion experiment was over.

My suspicions that Vince had had enough of the C-man were confirmed the next day when I showed up at *Raw* in Montreal and wasn't booked. I'd been the World Champion for three and a half months, yet wasn't important enough to have any part on the program the day after I lost it. It was a total slap in the face and made me feel like a total failure. To add insult to injury, after I had carried around both titles for the duration of my reign, the day after I lost them HHH was presented with a single brand spanking new Undisputed World Championship belt.

Pissed that I was a healthy scratch, I pitched an idea to Brian where a backstage worker would tell me he was sorry I lost the title and my response would be to furiously beat the shit out of him. Vince liked the idea, and when it came time to film the bit, I apologized to my hapless victim (Trivial Author's Note: The guy was future WWE tag champion Sylvain Grenier.) beforehand for the savage beating he was about to get. I went into a complete zone and took out all of my frustrations on the poor fella, I mean I really beat the shit out of him, so much so that The Undertaker (who happened to be watching) said, "Damn, man! You looked completely crazy the moment that pre-tape began. You weren't acting, were you?"

No, Mr. Deadman, I wasn't.

My banishment from *Raw* was just the beginning. At the next month's PPV, instead of having a rematch with HHH or beginning a new feud, I wasn't booked again. I had to weasel my way onto the show via a promo segment where I spoke my mind about how I was the Undisputed Champion only a short month ago and now I wasn't even able to get a match on the show. Had my championship reign really been that bad? How in the hell did I travel back to 1999? Souped up DeLorean? Magical phone booth? The Guardian of Forever?

No matter the reason, my star was fading.

But Hulk Hogan's was rising.

At *Raw* in Montreal, he came to the ring and got one of biggest pops I've ever heard in my life. He stood in the ring with tears in his eyes as the crowd gave him a standing ovation for ten minutes. It was incredible. As a result of that reaction and others like it everywhere he went, Vince decided to switch the title to him. HHH went from being out of action for seven months, to winning the Undisputed Championship, to losing it three weeks later to a forty-nine-year-old Hulk Hogan.

About a week before Hunter dropped the title, Vince decided he wanted to split the WWE into two separate brands and run them independently. In essence, he was creating his own competition. He booked a draft on *Raw* to decide who would stay and who would go to *Smackdown!* Everybody would find out what show they would end up on that night—except me. I was ineligible to be drafted because I was in a handicap match with Stephanie against HHH, where the winner would become the Undisputed Champion and work on both shows. I knew I wasn't going to be winning the match and the title, but nobody would tell me what show I was going to end up on. When I asked Brian, he told me I would have to wait until they posted the complete draft results on WWE.com after the show. It was the most ridiculous thing ever. And to make matters worse, I had to start driving as soon as I was finished and had no access to a computer, so I was forced to call Lenny in Vancouver to find out where I was going to end up. In essence, I found out my fate at the same time all of you did.

And if you don't remember what show I ended up on, you'll have to go to @iamjericho on twitter.com to find out.

CHAPTER 25

Jelly of the Month Club

In the WWE, you get your PPV checks about three months after the show takes place. It's a strange system where you really don't know what you're going to get until you get it. The number on the check is determined from a combination of the live gate, the PPV buyrate, and your place on the card. I was expecting my *WrestleMania* check in June and was curious to see what I'd get. I'd been in the technical main event of the show, and the second biggest match on the card. I had always heard that when you wrestled in the main event of *WrestleMania*, you made in the high six figures and in some cases even seven.

That's why I was stunned when I opened the envelope and saw a check for five figures. Now, first off, believe me when I say that under normal circumstances a five-figure check is a big chunk of change—but this was *Wrestle-Mania* and I felt that I should have made more. To give you an example of what I'm talking about, I made almost double that for the *Invasion* PPV and I was one part of a ten-man tag. *Mania* buyrates were bigger, the show was held in a stadium, and I was in the championship match that closed the show. Something had to be wrong, and as it stood, I felt like Clark Griswold getting a subscription to the Jelly of the Month Club for his Christmas bonus.

A week later I asked HHH how much he had made for *Mania*. He told me the number and I nodded and excused myself. I walked outside to the back of the arena in Columbia, South Carolina, and blew a fucking gasket.

He'd made almost five times as much as I had.

I was furious and insulted. I would've understood if he'd made a little bit more, as he was the returning baby-face and the bigger star, but *five* times more!?!? I called Shane-O Mac and told him that I was so angry and hurt that I felt like quitting. He told me in no uncertain terms that I needed to talk to Vince about it face-to-face.

I called Vince and left a message telling him I needed to speak to him. The next day, I arrived in Greensboro, North Carolina, and waited in his office with Jim Ross. I told JR how slighted I felt and how I didn't want to work for a company that held me in such little regard. Jim explained to me that he and Vince determined payoffs based on who they thought the fans were paying to see.

"Vince felt that in this match, people were paying to see HHH win the title."

"I have no doubt about that, Jim, and I have no problem with that mindset. But it takes *two* guys to make a match and to sell it to the fans. I don't care that Hunter got a bigger piece of the pie, it's the fact that he got 83 percent of the pie that I have a problem with."

JR nodded in agreement, and shortly afterwards Vince came into the office smiling.

"So what's the problem?"

"The problem is, Vince, I got my check for *WrestleMania*

and I understand how you grade the payoffs, but this is completely insulting. I mean I don't—"

Vince cut me off. "I'll take care of it. JR, cut him another check."

He walked out of the office, leaving JR and me staring at each other.

"Well, that was easy," said the Okie from Muskogee.

A week and a half later, I received a check in the mail that was more than I expected. I'll always admire how quickly Vince dealt with my issue. He heard me out and took care of the problem. End of story.

My return to PPV came the next month in a rematch with HHH in the dreaded Hell in a Cell. Cell matches were famous for featuring at least one big, nasty bump, like when Mick Foley (who has never defeated this sexy beast) was thrown off the top of the cell, or when Shawn Michaels fell off the side through a table. Even Vince fell off the damn thing.

HHH and I decided that we needed to break the chain, both because we wanted to focus on psychology and because neither one of us wanted to take that kind of crazy bump. We also wanted this cell match to be the transition from a spectacle revolving solely around an insane bump to a violent grudge match held within the confines of a barbaric cage. I thought it would be easier to make that transition if we did the finish on the top of the cage, and HHH agreed.

When I got to the arena in Nashville and looked up at the massive structure, it didn't look so intimidating. It didn't seem to be that high and I started having second thoughts about the big bump. I decided that we could break out of the cage, and as HHH was chasing me up the side I would have the Unamericans run down and attack Hunter. Then I would do a majestic cross body from the top of the cage onto the whole pile.

I climbed to the top of the cage to chart my flight plan, but when I looked down I instantly thought, "There is no fucking way I'm jumping off this thing."

I felt like I was on top of Mount Everest glaring down at a gang of ants, and it reminded me of the first time I climbed to the top rope at the Silver Dollar Action Centre (for the full, charming story, check out *A Lion's* blah blah blah), but on a much higher level. So I went back to my original plan of eliminating the big bump from the match.

But we still had to do something spectacular to bridge the gap between old cell and new. We came up with a unique finish where we would fight our way to the top and HHH would hit me with a Pedigree on the roof. We both liked the idea but couldn't figure out a way to get up to the roof. Vince had just seen the *Spider-Man* movie and suggested we shoot webs out of our wrists and swing up there.

We asked Vince not to contribute any more ideas.

Hunter finally pointed out that if a cameraman or referee were to get injured during the match, the ring crew would have to open the cage door to get him out, which would allow us to break on through. Our referee was veteran Tim White, a true pro and most famous for being Andre the Giant's assistant. He agreed that I could knock him off the apron to the cage, which would leave him incapacitated. When help arrived to carry him off the battlefield, HHH and I would brawl outside the cage and begin our ascent. But truth is stranger than fiction, and when I drove him into the side of the cage he separated his shoulder so badly that it never truly healed.

Timmy was as tough as a nihilist's ear and never said a word about the true extent of his injury, as HHH and I brawled out the door. We went through the announce table and Hunter pulled out the same baseball bat wrapped in barbed wire that he had used on Mick Foley (who has . . . okay, okay, I'll shut up now) in the cell match that made him a star. I scaled the cage in fear and when we got to the top he hit me in the head with it so hard the barbed wire got snagged in my hair. I put him in the Walls, which ended up being more than a little terrifying, because the fencing was bending and shaking underneath us. Finally, Hunter Pedigreed me on the top of the cage and pinned me. As I took the bump, I wondered what would happen if the steel beams collapsed and we crashed right through the cage and fell twelve feet to the mat. Thankfully the supports remained attached, as did the barbwire in my hair.

When it was all said and done, it was mission accomplished. We'd had a spectacular match and nobody had taken *the* crazy bump (except Timmy). The whole concept of what a Hell in a Cell match is now changed because of HHH and me, and both of us are proud of that to this day. Vince was pleased too and it seemed like I was back in his good graces again.

So much so that my next angle was with the Hulkster himself.

Even though Hulk had lost the Undisputed title to The Undertaker, he was bigger than ever and to work with him was a thrill professionally and personally. Hulk had been one of my childhood heroes dating back to when I watched him with the AWA in Winnipeg. I was a little intimidated at first, both because of his legendary status and his increasing immobility. It was going to be a little bit of a challenge to have a great match with him given his physical limitations. But I knew I could do it.

To prepare for our first match on *Smackdown!* in Pittsburgh, I watched Hogan's classic *WrestleMania* matches with Randy Savage and the Ultimate Warrior. I came up with a do-rag full of ideas, and to Hulk's credit he went for every one of them.

He had come back to the WWE to work, and he was smart enough to realize that I could make him look as good as he wanted to. And he wanted to look good. The match we had in Pittsburgh and the follow-up in Chicago were two of my all-time favorite matches and (dare I say it) two of the last great matches Hulk had. But I made him work hard. He took a Lionsault and a DDT and gave me a second-rope superplex. The pièce de résistance was when he went for his patented leg drop and I grabbed his legs from the mat and put him into the Walls. I could tell that Hulk enjoyed working with me, and soon I was up against him at every show he was on. He let me put together the entire match and trusted my judgment entirely. He'd get to the arena and ask, "What are we doing tonight, brother?" I would run through my ideas and he'd say, "Sounds goodski, brother." (For some reason he had a penchant for adding a "-ski" at the end of random words the same way my friends and I have since high school.)

He was really impressed with the guys from my generation, who were more interested in having a good match than in trying to get their shit in. He was right, the new generation had a different attitude than the older generation, and before long Hulk was working the same way we were. He wanted to have good matches—not that it was too hard to do that. He was so over with the fans and had them in the palm of his hand at all times, so it was a lot of fun to wrestle him.

I would rate Hogan as one of my all-time favorite opponents.

Working with Hogan was always a blast. I noticed that whenever he hulked up, he would whisper "HulkupHulkupHulkup," under his breath. It was how he got into character, I guess.

He was a master of including the fans and getting them involved in the match every step of the way. One time a kid was holding a sign that said HOGAN IS A JEDI. When I took umbrage to that blasphemy and ripped the sign into pieces, Hogan grabbed me in a full nelson, took me over to the kid, and let him take a free shot. Then he gave the kid a high five and said, "May the Force be with you, brother!"

But Hulk was still Hulk and he had a penchant for exaggeration and self-promotion. Rock was still wrestling sporadically in between movie gigs, and while he was filming *The Scorpion King* he was flown to the shows on a private jet paid for by the movie studio. One week he offered to make a stopover in Tampa on the way to Rochester, New York, to pick up Hulk and me.

Rock always kept quiet about his blossoming film career, but eventually the conversation turned to his ascension in Hollywood as the next breakout star. After a few minutes, Hulk jumped in and started explaining why he never made it as big in acting as Rocky had.

"You've got no competition right now, brother. There's nobody around who can challenge you, brother. When I was breaking into Hollywood, Stallone, Schwarzenegger, Van Damme, Seagal were all really hotski. There was no room for another action hero and I was a victim of the numbers game, brother."

Either that, or maybe *Santa with Muscles* wasn't the right projectski.

Rock and I were quite similar in personality and had become good friends. At that late stage in his WWE career, Rock could pick and choose the shows he wanted to wrestle on. When he found out that the WWE had an upcoming show in Hawaii, he jumped at the opportunity. He spent a lot of his childhood in Hawaii, and his grandfather, High Chief Peter Maivia, was a legend there as a promoter and wrestler. This would be Rocky's first time wrestling on the islands, and it was a big homecoming as he still had a large contingent of family there.

I knew how much it meant to him and was honored and touched when he called me and said, "I handpicked you to be my opponent in Hawaii." Jessica came with me and we were excited because it was our first time in Hawaii. When we came off the plane, we were met by a huge welcoming committee made up of Rock's friends and family, each one of them placing leis around our necks. It was a classy move on Rock's part—he went to the trouble of finding out what flight we were on and arranged everything to make us feel welcome in what he considered to be his homeland. His hospitality continued when we checked into our hotel room and found presents strewn across the bed—a pair of beautiful handmade Hawaiian silk shirts for me and a gorgeous flowing island dress for my wife. Later that night, Rocky took us to a luau complete with fire dancers and I even donned a grass skirt and matching crown and shook my shit to the delight of the crowd. It was a great night and I could see in Rock's eyes how proud he was to be showing off his heritage.

The Blaisdell Arena in Honolulu was a jam-packed sellout of 9,000 people waiting to see one man and one man only. There was a huge chorus of boos as I came to the ring, and a small army of Rock's cousins in traditional island garb again placed leis around my neck and gave

Rocky's cousins adorned us with flowers pre-match in Hawaiian tradition. A few moments later I tore my flowers up and the poor little girls started to cry. Straight up heelin' yo.

me flowers. I feigned happiness for a few moments before throwing the flowers to the ground, tearing the leis off my neck, and ripping them into a thousand pieces. I stomped up and down on the torn petals and screamed, "I don't want these! I'm not Hawaiian and I don't want to be! I'm from the mainland and that means I'm better than you!" The WWE hadn't been to Hawaii in years and the crowd ate up my taunts like a pupu platter.

After my antagonizing antics, the lights went dark and the fans went ballistic.

"If you *smelllll* what The Rock is cooking," boomed the sound system, and it was a wage of mayhem. The cheers were louder than Japan (or anywhere for that matter) as the islanders went bonkers for their hero. It was one of the most magical moments of my career. The Rock entered the ring and bathed in the cheers of his fans and I could see he was ready to deliver. So was I.

We had perfect chemistry at this point; everything we did elicited a tremendous response from the capacity crowd, including Bruce Willis, who was sitting in the first row. Bruce was in Honolulu filming *Hart's War* and came to support Rocky. Halfway through the match, Rock threw me out to the floor and we fought our way over to where Bruce was sitting. He was thin, unshaven, and in the stained wifebeater he was wearing looked more like a concentration camp victim than an A-list movie star. But the crowd buzzed when they were made aware of his presence. I knocked Rocky to the ground and started yelling in Willis's scruffy face.

"*Hudson Hawk* was the shits and you were terrible in *Blind Date*!"

Bruce stared at me bemusedly as Rocky recovered from my crushing blow and pinned my arms behind my back. He told Bruce to hit me while the fans cheered in anticipation. I started apologizing for my harsh critiques and stammered how great I thought he was in *The Bonfire of the Vanities*. He slowly rose up from his seat and turned his head to the crowd for approval. I tensed up my jaw, figuring that he would smack me in the face or at the very least take a Hollywood swing at me. He drew back and with all the force of John McClane . . . headbutted me in the stomach.

Who was he—Bushwacker Luke?

I collapsed to the floor laughing and said, "Come on, Bruce! How do you expect me to sell that?"

After an awesome and very sweaty twenty-two minutes, Rock finally beat me with the Rock Bottom. As he was pinning me, his voice barely audible over the screams of the crowd, he whispered in my ear, "Thank you so much, Chris. That was my favorite match of my career." It was the last time I ever wrestled him and was a perfect end to one of the best rivalries of my career.

Afterwards, Rocky took Jessica and me out for dinner along with my new close personal friend Bruce Willis and his three daughters. Bruce was down-to-earth and really easy to talk to, and we spent most of the night talking about music and our respective bands (did you forget *The Return of Bruno*?). Eventually the conversation turned to Hollywood, and Bruce told Rocky that maybe it was time for him to stop wrestling, because Hollywood wouldn't be happy if he continued and it might limit his opportunities. It wasn't too long before Rock heeded his words and left the WWE for good. It was time for him to move on and I'm proud of him and the great work we did together in wrestling.

When we finished eating Bruce asked me when I was leaving Hawaii. I told him we had an early flight to Anaheim the next morning and he replied, "Oh, that's too bad! I'm taking my daughters and their friends to the big water park in Waikiki tomorrow for a birthday present. If you guys weren't leaving, I'd love to have you come along. I rented out the whole place just for us."

Rented out the whole place? Kind of makes my bitching about the $79.95 I have to pay for a day pass at Adventure Island a moot point, don't it?

CHAPTER 26

Wacky Roll-Up Guy

After my program with Hogan, the plan was for me to work with Edge. But everything changed when Edge suffered an apparent torn rotator cuff and was scheduled to be out for a couple months. To explain his injury, we did a big angle where I trapped his shoulder in the crotch of the steel ring steps and bashed it with a chair. He was carried out on a stretcher, leaving the crowd incredulous at their hero's demise. The good news was we had a ready-made angle as soon as Edge returned, but in the meantime I needed someone to work with.

Enter John Cena.

Cena was a blue-chip prospect whom the WWE had signed out of a wrestling gym in California. He had a great body, a great look, and, most important to me, he had personality. I had seen him do this amazing promo where he would make a statement, then rewind himself as if he was on tape and say it again. He would re-create the exact movements he just made, only backwards. I'd never seen anything like it before and I knew he had something special immediately.

Cena made his debut against Kurt Angle on *Smack-down!* and they tore the house down. I thought I could do the same with him and made the suggestion to Vince to work with John. Vince didn't seem too impressed with Cena at that point, but he agreed and booked the match for the *Vengeance* PPV in Detroit. The finish was me going over, but a few days before the show I called Vince to give him my thoughts.

"I'd really like to put this guy over, Vince. He's unique, he looks great, and he's got a lot of passion. Let's build him up a little."

Who would have thought that this guy would end up being the biggest star of the modern age? At this point, John wore different tights and boots every night bearing the colors of that respective city's sports teams. Shameless pandering at its finest.

Vince expressed that he didn't think it was the right way to go, but I was obstinate.

"I'm telling you, boss, there's something special about this guy. Let me put him over."

I think he got tired of arguing with me and agreed to change the finish. At the PPV Cena pinned me after reversing the Walls of Jericho into a small package and got a small push afterwards. He hadn't started using the AA or the STFU and won most of his matches with various quick pins, so I nicknamed him Wacky Roll-Up Guy. But his push didn't last long, and only a few weeks after his big victory over Jericho, he was back to wrestling in the opening matches.

Cena finally got his big opportunity when he dressed as Vanilla Ice on a Halloween *Smackdown!* and performed a freestyle rap that impressed everybody, so his character took off. He became the Doctor of Thuganomics and went on to become one of the biggest stars in WWE history.

Can I pick 'em or what?

Meanwhile, it turned out Edge didn't need shoulder surgery after all and he returned a few weeks later to save Hogan when I was about to administer the same shoulder-bashing fate I'd given Edge. The returning hero beat the tarski out of me and we were off.

Over the next few weeks, the Edge/Jericho angle was on fire and the writers wanted to build to a *SummerSlam* match of Jericho with Fozzy in his corner vs. Edge with the Osbournes in his corner. I was excited at the prospect of working with Ozzy in any way, shape, or form, but the deal fell through and soon after so did the Edge/Jericho angle.

The reason was Vince felt that *Raw* was lacking in star power, so he decided to send me, HHH, and the Unamericans (Lance Storm, Christian, and Test) back to the flagship show to spice it up. That meant the end of my angle with Edge.

I wasn't happy about the move and the Hulkster wasn't happy about it either. "I can't believe you're leaving me, man. I'm losing my guys."

Of course, Hogan was upset about losing the workers who were making him look good, and he should've been. Match-quality-wise, he was having the best run of his career.

My last night on *Smackdown!* in Indianapolis saw me lose a great cage match to Edge, followed by the Unamericans breaking into the cage and attacking en masse. That brought out Rey Mysterio and Cena to save the day. Rey scaled the cage and did a big dive onto Lance and Test while Edge and Cena threw Christian and me into the fence as the crowd cheered madly. The end of the show saw the four bad guys on the floor yelling and screaming at Edge, Rey, and Cena as Michael Cole proclaimed that "the new era of *Smackdown!* has arrived!"

And I was leaving.

I found Vince backstage and asked him, "Do you like money?"

Vince looked at me quizzically and answered, "Of course I like money."

"Well, you're pissing money down the drain by moving me to *Raw* now," I said defiantly. "This angle with Edge is hot and we could go so much farther with it!"

Vince nodded his head, but it was obvious he disagreed. "I've thought about it, Chris, but I need you on

Raw right now. We can always go back to Jericho and Edge."

It took eight years, but eventually we did. But that's a story for another book.

My first night back on *Raw*, I ambushed Flair from under the ring and brutally beat him down. He had just returned to the WWE and had very little confidence in himself. Ric had been mentally beaten down for so many years in WCW that he had lost faith in who he was and what he could do. Many people would say that Flair is the greatest of all time, but at that time working with Hogan was easier.

Put down your pitchforks and torches, wrestling purists; the honest truth is Flair wasn't himself and was tricky to work with at that stage, while Hogan knew exactly who he was and what to do, brother.

Flair and I worked a program that culminated at *SummerSlam*. Vince wanted me to put him over with a small package, but I disagreed. Why not have me tap out to his famous figure four? He never beat anybody with his signature move, and I think I was the first guy to tap out to it in like fifteen years. Flair vehemently disagreed, and when I asked him why he said, "Why? I don't deserve it. I'm not myself and you know it."

His words really pissed me off. Even though he was going through a bad patch he was still Ric Fucking Flair! I snapped back, "Stop it! You're one of the greatest performers of all time! Start acting like it."

Flair stared at me for about thirty seconds. Then he slowly extended his hand.

"Thank you for saying that."

That night and in the upcoming weeks, Flair slowly got his mojo back. He would've eventually found it anyway, but my words seemed to give him the big kick in the ass he needed. I found out my hunch was correct a few years later when he gave me a copy of his book and he had written inside, "Chris, your friendship and support have always meant a lot to me. Thanks for helping me get my head on straight. Your friend, Ric Flair."

Just goes to show that sometimes even the all-time greats need a little pep talk. Besides, after all the advice he gave me when I was struggling as champion, I was happy to return the favor.

My contract ended in the summer of 2002 and I had every intention of re-signing, but the company had been stalling for months regarding a few extras I wanted added to my deal. But Vince was getting impatient and wanted the contract signed, so one day I arrived at the arena in Sacramento and was summoned into his office.

"Enough of the lawyers and agents, Chris, we've got to get this contract worked out. Where do we stand?"

"We've been working on it for months, Vince, but there's still some holdups."

"Yes, I know there's some issues. Tell me what you want."

I took a deep breath and asked, "Vince, am I one of your top guys?"

"Absolutely you are."

That's all I needed to hear. "Then I want a deal that backs that up."

I told him what I wanted and I couldn't believe the

number that came out of my mouth. I'd come a long way from asking Bischoff for the unthinkable sum of 100 grand six years earlier.

Vince nodded his head and seemed uncomfortable. "If I give that to you right now, will you take it?"

"Of course I will, boss."

He said, "Okay, you got it."

That was it—after six months of haggling, the contract was completed in two minutes.

But it was the last WWE contract I would sign for a long time.

For *Survivor Series* 2002, Vince wanted something big to sell the show. HHH had been petitioning to do WarGames, a match involving two rings and ten wrestlers inside a giant cage. Vince wasn't keen on using the WarGames name or concept, because it was a WCW invention. That's when the Elimination Chamber was born.

The chamber was a vile contraption, essentially a domed steel cage with chain walls and a floor. When it was lowered around the ring, it was the same level as the mat and extended the area four feet around each side. In each corner of the cage was a bulletproof-glass-covered pod where you would wait until it was your turn to enter the fray. You could tell whoever built the chamber had never wrestled a match in their life, as it was awkward, unforgiving, and just plain painful. The rules were that two guys would start, and another performer would enter the ring every five minutes until everyone was eliminated. The winner would be the champion.

The guys in the match were me, Rob Van Dam, Booker T,

Kane, HHH, and Shawn Michaels, and since it was the first time the match had ever taken place there was no precedent for us to follow. We showed up at MSG hours early to try to formulate what exactly we could do within this monstrosity, but after hours of brainstorming we hadn't finalized anything and were still coming up with ideas as the show started. Shawn and HHH were the last two in the chamber and called the finish on the fly; the planning hadn't gotten that far by the time the match began.

The match started with Van Dam and I, then HHH joined in. At one point RVD climbed to the top of the pod, but the roof on the cage didn't allow him to fully stand straight up. He launched himself from a half crouch, and that, combined with HHH being too close, caused his knee to land directly on Hunter's throat. Hunter's larynx was damaged and he could barely talk. He was in immense pain, and when I rolled over to ask him if he was okay, he could only squawk that he wasn't. It was up to me to take charge. I bumped around for Rob and Booker until the clock started ticking down from ten, heralding Shawn's entrance into the match. He had recently returned after being off for almost five years and the crowd was highly anticipating his impending entry. All three of us were down as the clock hit zero. Blue lights flashed and an annoying jingle that sounded like it was from *Who Wants to Be a Millionaire?* tinkled, trumpeting the opening of a new pod.

I was selling on the ropes, keeping one eye on Shawn to my left, when suddenly I was attacked from behind. It scared the shit out of me and I turned around like a dreamer in a *Nightmare* movie. But instead of Freddy Krueger unleashing the fury, it was Kane and he was more maniacal than li'l Frederick ever was. I couldn't figure out why he was kicking the crap out of me and why Shawn was still in his pod, then I figured out what happened: the wrong pod door had opened.

What was this, *Spinal Tap*?

In a controlled environment, where *we* decided which pod opened and our referees were the ones unchaining the doors and opening them, we still managed to get it wrong. None of us in the chamber really knew what to do, because we had spent a few hours on this part of the match. Shawn was supposed to come in and clean house for five minutes until Kane's pod opened and he came in to shut HBK down.

Now we had to call everything on the fly (with HHH still writhing in pain in the corner) and Kane was the one cleaning house—and he was a regular Molly Maid at this point.

Earlier in the day I'd discussed with Kane and Pat if someone could be thrown through the bulletproof glass of the pod. Both had vehemently shut down my idea, saying it was too dangerous and not worth taking the chance of someone getting hurt.

Fast forward to Kane throwing me over the top rope onto the steel platform of the chamber. I staggered up to my feet and said, "Throw me through the pod!"

"Fucking right I'm throwing you through the pod!" he said as if the wrong pod opening had been my fault. All concerns for my well-being blew out the cage opening when the wrong chamber opened.

Kane jerked me up to my feet and chucked me into the Plexiglas at full speed. I hit it as hard as I could and was surprised at how easy I busted through. I landed in a heap inside the pod, and shards of hardened plastic rained down on top of me. Mike Portnoy from Dream Theater was in the front row cheering me on, but I was in such pain I couldn't even lift my head to acknowledge his existence. When I finally did, I was such a bloody mess that Mike's face looked like he'd just had a panic attack.

The glass may have been bulletproof, but it certainly wasn't Jerichoproof. That one hurt.

Shawn's pod eventually opened and he ended up pinning me and HHH with his Sweet Chin Music superkick to win the match and the World Championship. The MSG faithful were genuinely happy to see Shawn win the big one after five years and were cheering their asses off for him, despite the fact he was wearing the ugliest pair of shit brown wrestling tights and sporting the worst bob haircut known to man.

On the other hand, I was currently residing in the purgatory between curtain and Gorilla, going fucking ballistic.

I couldn't believe that at a show as big as *Survivor Series*, in a company as big as the WWE, in a match as big as the chamber, that something like opening the wrong door could happen. It was such a WCW-esque fuckup and I was furious.

But I knew I had to calm down before I said something stupid to Vince or executive producer Kevin Dunn. When I finally walked into Gorilla, after getting control of my temper, Vince and Kevin apologized, but they didn't offer an explanation as to what had happened, and it was obvious they weren't going to. I suppose they didn't owe me one, but as a perfectionist I was pissed that things hadn't gone the way they were supposed to. I still wonder to this day why the wrong door opened.

Gremlins, maybe?

CHAPTER 27

Stealing the Show

Three days later I was standing on the jetway in Frankfurt, Germany, waiting to get back on the plane so I could grab the Discman (these were the prehistoric days before iPods, kiddies) that I'd left in the seat pocket in front of me.

We were on our way to India for a WWE tour and I was already dreading the trip. I'd never been there, but before we left I had to get shots for yellow fever, diphtheria, and malaria, and I was already fearing the worst.

The flight attendant wouldn't let me reboard until everybody deplaned, so I waited as the passengers streamed by. It was a big aircraft and I was getting bored, so I glanced at the guy waiting in a wheelchair beside me. He was a portly fellow with dyed black balding hair and dyed black eyebrows to match. He glanced back and gave me a nod.

"Wow," I thought to myself, "that's Luciano Pavarotti."

I was standing next to the greatest opera singer in the world.

Now that we were aware of each other's existence after

making eye contact, I felt obligated to say something. I decided to open conversation with my best line.

"How's it going eh?"

"Good, good, good," he said in a thick Italian accent, sighing as if the weight of the world was on his shoulders.

"Where are you going?"

"Milan. You?"

"India."

"Oh, India. Nice weather this time of year."

We both nodded and I rocked back and forth on my heels uncomfortably as people flowed by.

"Would you like a piece of gum?" I offered, praying that I'd get back on the plane soon so I could end this awkward conversation with one of the most famous people in the world.

"Oh, no thank you. Sticks to my dental work," he said matter-of-factly.

The last few dregs drifted past and finally I was allowed back on the plane.

"Okay, sir, gotta go get my uh...Discman...so I'll see you later," I stammered, not wanting to be rude.

"Go, go. Safe travels," he remarked as I walked back on the plane.

I went to my seat and quickly grabbed the Discman, hoping that I could get my new close personal friend Luciano Pavarotti to sign it, but when I got back to the jetway he was gone forever. It was one of the stupidest random meetings of my life.

But it was froot to think that I'd just had a conversation with one of the Three Tenors. Now all I have to do to complete the set is meet Placido Domingo and...the other guy.

*   *   *

I flew from Frankfurt to New Delhi, and when we finally landed I was knackered. After ninety minutes of going through customs and getting our bags, the extra rib was a two-hour drive from the airport to the hotel. It was pitch black outside and the steady rumble of the bus helped me to doze off quickly, but I woke up when I felt the bus stop in the middle of the road in the middle of nowhere.

Kane was sitting beside me, and when I asked him what was going on, he said, "There's a cow in the road blocking us and we can't go anywhere until it walks away." The first thing I learned about India is that cows are sacred animals that can pretty much do whatever they want and are not to be disturbed. So we sat in the middle of the road for half an hour until Clarabelle decided to move on.

We reached the outer limits of the city and I saw a conurbation of cardboard-box houses stretching as far as the eye could see. Even stranger was that most of the hovels had satellite dishes beside them. I found out that people could afford satellite TV, but couldn't afford actual homes. It was a way of life to have electricity fed into your cardboard-box abode.

As we continued driving, things got more bizarre.

Four men rode in the back of a pickup truck on the top of a huge pile of manure without a care in the world. A baby dressed in a diaper and nothing else stood by himself on the median in the middle of a busy road. A teenager pulled his sitar out of his pants and took a piss right in front of a grocery store.

The city was in absolute squalor, with people pushing carts of rotten vegetables, scrawny dogs running through the streets, and smelly garbage stacked everywhere. Yet right in the middle of the filth surrounded by a massive chain-link fence was our hotel—a beautiful five-star mansion that looked more like a palace. The difference between the two worlds was astonishing.

I'd decided not to eat any of the food that was provided for us in India, as I'd heard too many horror stories of people getting sick there. For the entire tour, my diet consisted strictly of peanut butter sandwiches and instant Quaker oatmeal (apples and cinnamon) I'd brought with me. All I did during the whole tour was sit in my room eating breakfast three times a day while watching *X-Files* DVDs.

Most of our fans couldn't afford to buy tickets to the events, and the shows were held in half-filled arenas or makeshift venues consisting of the ring set up in a parking lot with plastic chairs and plastic fencing surrounding it. During one of the parking lot shows, RVD pointed to the foliage across the street from the ring and said, "Dude, there's people in the trees."

I thought he was just stoned, but when I followed his finger, he was right. There were a dozen people, entire families, sitting in the thick branches of the tall trees, watching the show with a bird's-eye view of the festivities.

After the show I was introduced to Mr. India, a literal giant of a man with a massive movie-theater-sized chest and arms as big as an elephant's trunk. Through a translator, he told me he was a big fan and was hoping to become a wrestler someday. He was over seven feet tall and I figured he could pretty much do whatever he wanted in wrestling and he did. The guy's name was Dalip Singh, better known as future WWE World Champion the Great Khali.

The next night I was teaming with Christian in an actual

arena in Mumbai, and during my prematch promo the fans started chanting, "Asshole." Taking it all in stride, I said, "I'm not the asshole, you're the assholes! I hate this place!"

The next day, one of our reps gave me a copy of *Today*, New Delhi's paper, and told me to look at the front page. I read the news today oh boy, and the headline said, "Rotten WWE Show Turns into Sick Joke." Underneath, the sub-caption read, "India is a very very bad place and all Indians are assholes." Signed: WWE Tag Team Champion, Chris Jericho.

The story inside was even worse, explaining how the evil confidence men of the WWE had tried to pass off their shoddy product as a real fight when it was obvious that it was show business. I couldn't believe how the reporter had twisted my words to back his theory that we were heinous con artists who had come to India to rip off the paying customers and insult them in the process. The way this guy was talking, I thought I was reading a review of a Toots Mondt show from 1942.

The last show in Bangalore was another parking lot classic where I amused myself by wearing Hurricane's cape and a Halloween mask while brandishing a mudflap for a run in on Kane. But the joke was on me as Kane thought I was an unruly fan and was about to tear my masked head off, until I screamed in a terrified girly-man squeak, "It's me, Glen! It's me!" Realizing that the idiot wearing the Scream mask was really his little buddy Jericho, he guffawed (funny word) and let me go.

During the course of the tour, Lance Storm, Tommy Dreamer, Al Snow, and Booker T all got sick to varying degrees. When we got back to the States, Regal was feeling weak and ended up being diagnosed with some form of heart parasite, which still affects him to this day. I definitely made the right call with my peanut butter and oatmeal.

We flew back from India straight into Charleston, South Carolina, for *Raw*. When I arrived, Brian told me that Vince had challenged him to make him laugh with that week's show, and Brian had obliged. The show was based around Booker T and Goldust stealing Christian's and my clothes out of the locker room, forcing us to spend the rest of the night nakedly searching for our threads.

The story would conclude with us (sporting towels around our waists) onstage in front of the live crowd confronting Booker, who would be in the ring with our stolen bags. As we argued, Goldust would come up from behind and pull the towels off. It all sounded fine and el dandy, except for one thing: Vince wanted us to really be naked underneath our towels.

Yep, I said it. Naked.

I thought Brian was ribbing, but when he assured me he wasn't, I told him, "There's no fucking way I'm standing naked in front of the crowd, and I don't give a shit what Vince says. You can tell him I said that."

Five minutes later I was summoned to the Emperor's palace.

"You cool with everything tonight, pal?" Vince asked when I stormed in.

"Sure...everything except being naked in front of the crowd. There's no way I'm going to do that! I'm a wrestler, not a Chippendales dancer." (If you saw my Zellweger, you would agree.)

"It's not that big of a deal."

"Seriously, Vince? There's going to be kids...little girls...in the audience looking at my horn flapping around. I could get arrested!"

"But we have to make it look real. What do you suggest we do?"

I proposed we wear flesh-colored underwear and pixelate our units, and that's what we did. I'm still not sure if Vince was ribbing me about being naked, but if he was I'm sure he had a good laugh at my reaction!

(Surprisingly, Christian didn't seem to have a problem with being onstage exposing his Reso.)

On top of wanting us to perform the Full Monty, Vince also wanted Booker to discover women's underwear in our gym bags when he went through them. Apparently, he thought it would be funny for his tag team champions to be a pair of nude transvestites. I once again protested and the problem was alleviated when Brian came up with the idea of putting a jar of Ass Cream in our bags instead. Neither one of us were sure exactly what Ass Cream was, but it made us laugh so we went with it.

With all of the controversy settled, Booker, Goldust, Christian, and I put together the match and we were all set to go. I was warming up twenty minutes before the show when Booker was wheeled past me on a stretcher. I did a double take and ran over to ask what was wrong. He could barely answer, but the paramedic told me he was being taken to the hospital for extreme dehydration (they pumped five bags of fluids into his body once he got there).

So at the last minute Booker and Goldust were replaced by the Dudley Boyz. We sat down to put together the twenty-minute opening match that was starting in ten minutes. I was stressed out from the pressure, and as everyone was going over ideas I frantically shouted, "Okay, everybody calm down! We can do this, guys, let's just focus. Come on!!" I looked around the room at the peaceful faces around me.

"We *are* calm, man. Now shut up and let's get this done," Bubba said stoically.

We had a good match, and afterward as Christian and I were taking showers, the Dudleys stole our bags and we spent the rest of the show looking for them. There was some ridiculous comedy involved, my favorite bit coming when I asked a ref if he'd seen our bags. He told me he didn't have time to talk because he was going to the ring for a match.

"You want a match? My face and your ass," I said angrily.

We finally found Bubba and Devon in the ring throwing our clothes into the crowd.

"What's this?" Bubba said as he pulled a jumbo-sized jar out of my bag. "Ass Cream? What is Ass Cream and what exactly do you do with it, might I ask?"

Christian and I were mortified over Bubba's discovery, and as we yelled at him to stop messing with our stuff, Spike Dudley came up behind us and whipped off our towels. We looked at each other and ran around in circles like Keystone Kops, as the digital blurring covered our flesh-colored dong thongs. As I ran off the stage I saw two kids about five feet away laughing heartily at the two buffoons.

I imagine they would've reacted a little bit differently if our exposed Jackie Rogers Jr.s had been flopping in their faces . . .

* * *

Christian and I made a great tag team as we had similar work styles and personalities, along with great comedic chemistry. We teamed all the way up to *WrestleMania XX* until a bet we made with each other to see who could win the hearts of Trish and Lita ended up tearing us apart. The price of the bet? One Canadian loonie.

We were a regular Randolph and Mortimer.

Our first pairing as a team was for the tag team titles in a Tables, Ladders and Chairs match in Las Vegas against the Dudleys, Jeff Hardy and RVD, and Kane and Hurricane. TLC matches are difficult and very dangerous and all of us ended up with some serious bumps and bruises afterwards. Bubba was the worst off though, as after I gave him a bulldog off the top of the ladder he was knocked unconcious and got a concussion to boot. He was lying there looking at me, but it was obvious that there was nobody home. It was his turn to climb the ladder and he was still giving me the thousand-yard stare, so I whispered that he had to get up.

"What do I do?" he asked groggily.

"Climb the ladder!" I hissed.

"How do I do that?" he inquired, as if I had just told him to pull Excalibur out of the stone.

"Just put one foot on the bottom rung and lift the other foot to the next rung. Then just keep doing it!"

Keep in mind that 10,000 people were watching in the arena and millions more were viewing at home, not a one of them realizing I was literally giving Bubba step-by-step directions on how to step up a ladder.

Kane ended up winning the match, but quite frankly

in a TLC match everybody loses in one way or another. Bubba was still completely on dream street afterwards, so much so that he was looking for his mother who had passed away the year before. It was heartbreaking to have to tell him she wasn't there and see the look on his face as he insisted that she was supposed to meet him after the show.

Vince came into the trainer's room to personally thank all of us for the great performance, and I don't mind saying that we deserved it. The match was voted the best in *Raw* history at the *Raw* ten-year anniversary awards show. I accepted the Slammy on behalf of the other seven guys and ended up keeping it. It's in my office right now, so if any of you other guys are reading this and want your turn with it, just let me know.

Since Shawn Michaels returned at *SummerSlam* and won the title at the Elimination Chamber he was a changed man. I'd only met him a few times before and he was always in some state of confusion, à la the Doink debate I'd had with him in Cleveland. With what I'd seen of him, combined with the horrible reputation he'd earned from his behavior in the '90s, I wasn't quite sure what to expect when he came back to the WWE.

But I needn't have worried. He had accepted Christ and his whole attitude had changed. He was happy to be back, and although a little tentative, he was excited to get back in the ring. This was sweet chin music to my ears. As I've mentioned, Shawn was among my biggest inspirations to get into the business, and I was hoping he and I would get the opportunity to work together at some point.

Little did I know he would end up being one of the greatest opponents in my career.

Our first meeting was almost a throwaway segment. I would confront him about being a relic from the past, he would superkick me, and that would be the end of it. But there was a certain electricity when Shawn and I stood nose to nose in the ring and everyone from the fans to the boys to Vince himself felt it.

When Shawn and I walked back through the curtain, Vince approached us and said, "We've got money here."

I agreed, and since it was December, I immediately began thinking *WrestleMania*. But when I approached Shawn about it, he was hesitant.

"I don't know if I'll be around that long," he said, and I really think he meant it. He was a little gun-shy about returning to the ring full-time, as he'd just been out five years with a back injury. But the more he thought about it and the more we talked, he decided that he was ready to return to *WrestleMania* and he wanted to return against me.

I was gob-smacked by his decision. When I first started wrestling, I was essentially a Shawn Michaels clone. I had similar tights, similar canary yellow hair, and did the same highspots as him. But things had changed—I wasn't a clone anymore. It was pro vs. pro and I was looking forward to seeing if I could live up to the standards of a Shawn Michaels big event match.

They didn't call him Mr. WrestleMania for nothing.

We did a three-month storyline that began when Shawn was the first entrant into the *Royal Rumble* and I was to be the second. Except my lackey Christian (yeah, Jay, I said it) came out to my music dressed as me instead and struck my signature pose. As Shawn was paying attention to the stage, I snuck out from under the ring and threw him over the top rope, eliminating him. Later in the match he came back out and returned the favor, and we were off to the races.

Our angle was based around the classic kung-fu movie plot, where the student feels he's better than the teacher and now wants to destroy him. We illustrated how much Shawn had influenced my early career by showing side-by-side photos of the two of us, with me copying Shawn's hair and tights. Then we showed a great split-screen video of Shawn doing a highspot in a match from 1991 on one side and me ripping it off move for move in a match from 1992 on the other.

The angle pretty much wrote itself, and by the time *Mania* came around we were ready to go. We were fifth on the card, and even though it was the first time we ever worked with each other, we had instant chemistry.

We went twenty-seven minutes and it was the best of Jericho vs. the best of Michaels. We constructed an amazing match (with most of my ideas coming a week earlier while shopping for Speedo undertights at Dick's Sporting Goods) filled with so many twists and turns that the crowd in Seattle was on the edge of their seats the whole time. False finish after false finish unfolded until finally Shawn rolled me up with a move I'd seen Owen Hart use fifteen years earlier. Afterwards, the crowd gave us a standing ovation. In the middle of the applause, we shook hands and embraced in a classic *WrestleMania* moment—until I kneed him in the plums. He collapsed and looked up at me with his puppy-dog eyes, asking, "How could you?"

How could I? Well, I wasn't going to let a great match stop me from being a complete dick, now was I?

The general consensus was that our match stole the show which was a huge compliment. Only eighteen other matches in the history of the business could make that claim, and to do so was the goal of every single performer who'd ever been on a *Mania*. Personally winning the Undisputed Championship was an amazing moment, but stealing the show at *WrestleMania XIX* topped it. In a lot of ways it was the greatest night of my career.

I thank Shawn for that, but I also take pride in the fact that he thanks me for the match as well. After *WrestleMania*, HBK was back, and I had helped him get there.

(Quick Author's Aside: When we walked backstage afterwards, we were told that our match had gone too long. Shawn wiped the sweat off his face and said with a smirk, "When you have a match as good as that, you can go as long as you want." Yup, HBK was definitely back.)

CHAPTER 28

The Big Fight

Goldberg was coming to the WWE.

The announcement jackhammered through my stomach the moment I heard it. Rocky had befriended him and had brokered the deal between Vince and Bill to bring him in. Goldberg had been a huge star in WCW and was the prototype of what Vince liked in his superstars: tall, muscular, handsome, and looked like he could tear you apart. Problem was, I don't think Goldberg really wanted to come to the WWE, but Rocky lobbied and convinced him until Bill finally relented.

I wasn't too keen on him coming to the WWE either, since the last time I'd worked with him in WCW was a complete disaster. But I had no choice and decided to make the best of it. On his first day, he came up behind me and slapped me on the back as hard as he could.

"Hey Chris!" he said loudly and sarcastically, like he was Biff and I was McFly. I could tell he was still miffed about how things had gone with us in WCW. I was willing to let the past stay there, but I made a promise to myself that I wasn't going to let this guy throw his weight around in the WWE the way he did in WCW.

Coincidentally, a few minutes later Vince asked me for a strange favor.

"We've got Bill Goldberg coming in and I want you to welcome him and help him out as much as you can."

I don't know if Vince knew about my past with Goldberg—he'd never asked me to help anybody else before. But I told him I'd be happy to do what I could to help him adjust to his new environment. And I intended to do just that.

Until Milwaukee.

It was Goldfinch's first *Raw*, and I worked with HHH vs. Shawn and Booker T. After the match I was pulled aside and informed that Goldsmith had spent the entire match barking to Nash about how I didn't know how to sell properly and how I hadn't wanted to do business with him in WCW.

This pissed me off, because I never had a problem selling for him or anybody else for that matter. I've always done business, and it was business I was trying to do when I wanted to put Bill over properly in WCW. But it was obvious that he still had a chip on his shoulder when it came to me. It made me mad that he had only been with the company for a little over a week and he was already up to his old tricks. It was time to put a stop to it right now.

I marched straight into the dressing room and saw Nash sitting in the corner like a giant praying mantis acting like he owned the place, while Billy Boy sat across from him with a self-indulgent smile on his face. Throwing caution to the wind, I stood in front of him and stared directly into his eyes.

"I heard you were saying some stuff about me during my match. I don't know if you realize it, but things have changed. This isn't WCW. If you have something to say to me, say it to my face."

Goldbug gave a shaky laugh and said, "I didn't say anything about you."

"Bullshit. I know you did."

Something snapped in the Bergermeister and he jumped to his feet. "Oh yeah? What about all that stuff you were saying about me on the Internet?"

Internet? *Internet??* You've got to be kidding me! I didn't spend enough time on the Internet to check out Club Jenna properly, let alone talk shit about Bill Fucking Goldeye.

"What are you talking about?"

A vein in his neck popped out like a worm as he shouted back, "Mike Tenay told me that you said stuff about me on the Internet!"

I looked at him in disbelief and said, "Listen, Bill. It's simple. I could be your best friend in this company or your worst enemy. We're probably going to be working with each other at some point, and I could either make you look like a million bucks or make you look like shit, and you wouldn't know the difference! We're all here to make money and do business together, so just fucking relax!"

"You never wanted to do the job for me in WCW! You're a prima donna!"

"You're totally wrong about th—"

Before I could finish the sentence, Goldfish grunted like a Neanderthal (the vein in his neck now resembling a corpulent slug) and grabbed me by the throat.

Now, let me preface the rest of this story by saying that I'm not the toughest man in the world, nor have I ever claimed to be. However, when someone puts their hand on my throat and begins to squeeze, it's time to throw hands. Am I right? Let's take a vote to make sure: All in favor that a hand on the throat preceded by a prehistoric growl is provocation to fight, say aye.

Okay, we're all in agreement on that, then—except for that one guy in Peoria, and your case is weak.

Once Goldster made his move, I reacted the only way I knew how. I swatted his hand off my throat and gave him a two-handed push to the chest. He rushed forward with his head down and tried to tackle me, like the ex–NFL lineman that he was. I stepped to the side like the world's worst matador and grabbed him in a front facelock. It was the only shoot hold I knew, one that harkened back to my days bouncing at Malarkey's in Calgary. I think I surprised the shit out of him with my lethal hold and was able to power him down to the ground, applying pressure because I knew if I pushed his throat into his chest long enough, he might pass out. I really hoped that he would go to sleep, because I was sure that he was going to fire up and kick the shit out of me. I mean, come on, have you ever seen this guy? He is massive!

I continued to hold my ground and couldn't figure out why he wasn't fighting back. I got a little lazy and released the pressure slightly, and suddenly he rolled on top of me. I was freaking out at this point, convinced that he was going to eat me, but I held on to my patented front face-lock. He started bucking around like a mechanical bull, but surprisingly I was able to use his momentum against him to roll him over again. Yee-haw!! Jericho 2, Goldie 0.

It was like WCW all over again—except this time it was real.

I was getting cocky at this point because he wasn't moving. In the back of my mind, I still had the idea that he was going to morph into a savage animal, throw me off, and draw and quarter me. But he never did. It seemed that the Goldschlager was all smoke and mirrors. Maybe he'd always gotten by on the intimidation factor and had never been tested. Maybe he was being nice and didn't want to fight back because he was the new kid on the block. If that was the case, this muscle-bound Joey McIntyre was getting manhandled.

With adrenaline surging through my veins and my confidence rolling, I thought of the Japanese magazines Funaki had brought into the dressing room earlier in the day containing pictures of Royce Gracie fighting. Gracie's calling card was a front facelock with his legs scissored around his opponent's midsection, and after seeing photos of him doing the hold I decided to give it a try. I egged him on as I crossed my legs around his midsection: "C'mon, Mr. Shooter! Try to get out of this one!" He got to his feet again and we busted through the doors at the back of the dressing room, straight into the hallway filled with surprised fans who got a bonus match that night.

We scuffled back into the dressing room and were finally broken up by Arn Anderson, Terry Taylor, Hurricane, Christian, and Booker T. Nash. Mantis continued to sit in his chair in the corner of the room watching the festivities.

Goldfinger and I were separated, and if you've ever been in a fight that's been broken up by your friends, you can probably relate to what happened next. As Christian and Hurricane were restraining me they were inadvertently setting me up to be murdered at the same time, because when Goldsworthy broke free of the pack they still had my arms pinned to my sides.

"Let go! Let go! He's going to kill me!" I screamed, closing my eyes and preparing to have my face caved in.

They realized what was going on and let me go at the last minute, but it was too late. He broke through and reared his fist back. I tensed up and prepared for him to knock my block off, but—he started pulling my hair instead.

I couldn't believe that the mighty Berggold was tugging at my hair like a five-year-old during play time. What was up with this guy?

I figured if he hadn't knocked me out yet, he was never going to. So I pried his hand out of my hair and pie-faced him as hard as I could. He stumbled back and stared at me in surprise.

I was done with this bitch fight and I screamed, "What the hell is wrong with you, man? You're acting like a goof!"

Goldrush screamed back, "Your mother is a fucking goof!"

Booker T got the most quizzical look on his face as he chewed on the unlit cigar he always seemed to have in his mouth and said, "Hold up! Did you just say his mother is a fucking goof? That's the worst insult I ever heard, man."

We continued jaw-jacking back and forth until we both calmed down. We were separated into our respective corners, and after a few minutes I walked back over to Billbo and said matter-of-factly, "Here's the deal. You can shake my hand right now and we can forget about this. Or we can come to work and do this every single week. I don't give a shit either way. Your call."

GoGoBoy looked me in the eye, stuck out his hand to shake mine, and we called a truce.

I walked back to my chair and saw a text on my phone from Disco Inferno, who had already heard that Goldbone and I had gotten into a fight. It had been ten minutes.

Telephone, telegraph, tell a wrestler.

For the next week, everybody I knew in the business called or pulled me aside to ask me about the BIG FIGHT. I was forced to relay the lion's tale over and over again to everyone from Bruce Pritchard to Jim Ross to Gerry Brisco to the champ himself.

I was surprised when I answered the phone a few days later and heard Ric Flair's distinctive voice.

"Chris, there are guys in this business who want to bring you down, but when you're a great worker, nobody can ever touch that. Don't fall into these traps. Don't let these guys get into your head. You're too good for that, you're too talented. It's beneath you."

Once again, Flair's words put perspective on things. I had just bested Vince's new acquisition and I wasn't sure how everybody would feel about it.

The gossip girls were in full force for this juicy tidbit and I still get asked about it all the time. In a way, I feel bad for Bill, as deep down I know he's got a good heart, but when our international incident happened, it really got him off on the wrong foot with a lot of guys in the dressing room. When the word got out that David had taken down Goliath, I gained admiration while Goldberg gained more resentment than he already had.

But not everybody admired me after the brawl.

A week later in Richmond, Virginia, I got word that Vince wanted to talk to me.

"I've got a bone to pick with you."

"I'm sorry about the fight, boss."

Vince replied, "That's not why I'm upset with you. I'm upset because you didn't tell me about it yourself."

"I didn't think you'd want to hear that I just took down Goldberg."

Vince replied in a stern voice, "Chris, I need to know these things." And then he repeated one of his favorite themes, "I'm not just trying to teach you wrestling lessons, I'm trying to teach you about life. I'm your boss and if something like that happens I should be the first person you call. And if anything like that ever happens again, I want to hear it from you."

His words made sense and I nodded in agreement. But I had to throw one back at him.

"Okay, Vince. Now I have a bone to pick with you. Have you watched my *WrestleMania* match with Shawn yet?"

Vince had worked with Hogan that night and didn't watch any of the matches before his. But he still hadn't seen the whole show and was the only person in the company who hadn't complimented me or Shawn on our show-stealing match on the biggest stage of them all.

"No. I haven't had a chance."

"You should watch it. It was my favorite match ever and I'd like you to see it."

Vince said, "I promise to watch your match."

"And I promise if I ever beat up somebody in your locker room, you'll be the first to know."

After our brawl, Goldberg and I became very cordial with each other, almost friendly. We ended up having a good match at a PPV in Houston (when I walked into Gorilla afterward, I received no reaction, and when Goldberg walked through Vince gave him a standing ovation— grrrrr). Bill even invited me to fly on his private plane a few times. I think he was embarrassed that he got into the fight with me during his very first week of work with the WWE and wanted to show his good side.

I think it still bothers him that his status as a badass (great album title) will always be tarnished by the fact that Chris Jericho took him down. Bret Hart wrote an article in the *Calgary Sun* about how "Jericho used the moves that Stu Hart taught him in the dungeon to stretch Goldberg."

If I died tomorrow, it would probably be my biggest legacy among other wrestlers.

But let's be honest. I'd like to say that in no way shape or form would I want to go through that with Goldberg again. He's a big man and he studies the art of fighting. I'm just a wiry guy from Winnipeg who was sick of being buried and reacted accordingly. I surprised him with my ruthless aggression and he was stuck in a moment that he couldn't get out of and didn't know what to do. I basically held on for dear life and was credited with the win.

Suffice it to say there will never be a rematch.

But for the record the final score is: Jericho 1, Goldberg 0.

CHAPTER 29

A Brutal Shade
of Jaundice

One of the reasons why the Y2J character was so popular was that I was getting time to talk every week on TV. It allowed me to show off my creativity, my sense of humor, and my charisma, all of which helped me connect with the crowd. I was good at it, but I was also very lucky to get that valuable time, because many others didn't. There were tons of performers on the roster who might as well have been mute or had their tongues Oldboy'd, they talked so rarely. How would we find the next Hulk Hogan or Rock if nobody was ever given a chance to talk? With this in mind, I called Brian and told him I wanted to be the host of my own show in the same vein as "Piper's Pit." Except I wanted it to be a strictly improvised segment where every week an up-and-coming star would get a chance to talk and show off their character—or lack thereof.

I wanted to call it "Jericho's Junction," but Brian came up with "The Highlight Reel." It was the perfect moniker, since I'd been recently referring to myself as the Highlight of the Night, so we went with it. Even though my improv concept fell by the wayside, the segment did become a modern day "Piper's Pit," a regular feature that usually led to some sort of angle.

The first episode was in Boston. We assembled a make-shift set, which consisted of a giant carpet painted with my logo, a couple of barstools that I stole from the Players Club in the Fleet Center (send me the bill, guys), and the extravagant, astronomically priced JeriTron 5000. The JeriTron 5000 was nothing more than a 52-inch flat-screen TV, but much like Michael Knight's KITT, it took on a life of its own as my mascot.

Ironically, Goldberg was my first guest. He took me aside beforehand and politely asked me not to verbally bury him during the show. When Scott Steiner appeared, Vince was the one who begged me not to bury him. "Chris, we are hoping for big things from Scotty, so please don't make him look bad out there."

Why did these guys think I was out to bury people? I never had before. It was if I had become the wrestling Bill O'Reilly, a verbal marksman who struck fear into the hearts of marblemouths everywhere.

And there were no mouths more marbly than that of the Big Bad Booty Daddy. At the time he was wearing what basically amounted to a chain-mail kerchief, like a heavy metal Jackie Onassis, and during his appearance on "The Highlight Reel" I asked him, "Who do you think you are? King Arthur?"

Scotty was supposed to reply, "You think I'm King Arthur? How about I come down there and get medieval on your ass?!" But he butchered his retort and instead bellowed out, "You think you're King Arthur? Well, why don't I come down there and kick your medieval ass!"

No, I don't think I'm King Arthur, Scott, you do. You're the one wearing the chain mail.

Steve Austin was having major neck problems and couldn't wrestle anymore, but he was still a big part of the show as the commissioner of *Raw*. We had been tormenting each other weekly until finally a verdict was passed that Austin could never touch me unless I touched him first.

The angle was working great on TV and the decision was made to take it on the road. It was a smart way to take advantage of Steve's immense drawing power, and it gave him the perfect forum and the perfect foil to do his routine—"The Highlight Reel" and Chris Jericho. So every weekend during the summer of 2003, Steve Austin was my guest on "The Highlight Reel." The arena set was much less extravagant than its TV counterpart; made up of two metal folding chairs and—well, that was it. But the fans were ecstatic to see Austin and be a part of his act. This was at the height of his "What?" phase, and we would base the segment on trying to outdo each other with the most references to a region-specific topic. For example, when we were in Green Bay, the routine was based around cheese and went a little something like this:

"We're in Green Bay, Wisconsin."

"What?"

"The home of cheese!"

"What?"

"American cheese!"

"What?"

"Cheddar cheese!"

"What?"

"Gouda cheese!"

I grabbed the mic and, inspired by the spirit of K. K. LaFlamme, went on a run of my own.

"Do you mean White Stilton cheese?"

"What?"

"Double Gloucester cheese?"

"What?"

And so on and so on. We would continue to riff back and forth on cheese to see who could go the longest without breaking stride.

We would do band names in London, hockey teams in Edmonton, or city nicknames in New York:

"Here we are in the Big Apple!"

"What?"

"The city that never sleeps!"

"What?"

"The Windy City!"

"What?"

"Cowtown!"

"What?"

"The City of Lights!"

"What?"

Well, you get the idea. It was completely preposterous, but our rallies provided some tremendous improv training that would prove to be invaluable later in my career.

Afterwards, I would get in Steve's face and taunt him because I knew he couldn't touch me. Austin would tell me, "Fine, I can't touch you, but there's no reason for us to be angry with each other! I'd rather just drink a beer with you, Chris. Do you like drinking beers?"

I wore this outfit to host "The Highlight Reel" every weekend for the entire summer of 2003. By the time fall rolled around, it smelled of glue and stale beer due to Austin dousing me with Steveweisers nightly.

"Of course I like beer, you idiot! Do you have Miller Lite?"

"What?"

"Coors Light?"

"What?"

"Bud Light?

"What?"

"If you want to see Stone Cold Steve Austin drink a beer with Chris Jericho, give me a 'Hell yeah!'" The crowd would yell, "Hell yeah!" enthusiastically. But I wouldn't bite until I had it my way.

"Yeah, I'd like a frosty beverage myself. So if you wanna see Chris Jericho drink a beer with Stone Cold Steve Austin, give me a 'Do-wah-diddy-diddy-dum-diddy-do!'" The crowd would quizically boo my ricock-ulosity as Steve and I would struggle to keep a straight face.

The timekeeper would throw us a couple of beers and we would shake 'em up and toast each other. I'd take a nice sip and then tell Steve, "You know what, Austin, you're not such a bad guy after all. I actually kind of like you," and give him a friendly slap on his back like an old drinking buddy.

Steve would then freeze in his tracks.

The crowd would start to buzz, sensing what was about to happen, since I'd just broken the agreement and touched him. Austin would get that hell-raisin' smile and stare a hole through my back, as I'd be glad-handing to the crowd and acting the damn fool. As soon as I turned around it would be a swift kick to the gut and a Stone Cold Stunner courtesy of the Texas Rattlesnake.

I would gout beer out of my mouth in a sweet amber stream and take a huge overexaggerated bump through the ropes onto the floor. Steve would spend the next ten minutes drinking beer (and pouring it on me) while saluting the crowd with middle fingers. I took one bump a night on the road that whole summer, and besides constantly smelling like Steveweiser, it wasn't a bad way for a grown man to make a living.

In the early 2000s, the WWE was doing PPVs in England twice a year, where the entire crew would fly out from New York on a Friday night and arrive in the UK on Saturday morning. We'd clear customs and go straight to the arena, where we would eat and prepare for the show. The PPV would start at 7 p.m., and as soon as it was over we would head back to the airport and fly back to New York, arriving early Sunday morning. It was a grueling schedule and the quality of the matches was never quite up to snuff as a result. That's why I was so relieved when I found out that I would only be doing a "Highlight Reel" with Austin and Eric Bischoff as my guests for the *Insurrection* PPV in Nottingham.

A few months earlier Vince had made the shocking decision to hire Eric and make him the storyline general manager of *Raw*. I was skeptical, but I have to give Eric credit for having the balls to come to the WWE. With the amount of guys he'd fired or mistreated during his time as the boss of WCW, it was almost like the warden being put in prison with the inmates. But Eric was a consumate professional and slowly began to win over the locker room. I noticed that he was a different person now that he wasn't in charge, and like most of the guys who came from WCW into the WWE, from Big Show to Booker T, to Kevin Nash, to DDP, when taken out of the destructive, cancerous atmosphere of WCW they were actually pretty good guys.

The "Highlight Reel" in Nottingham was the first time

I'd worked with Eric since his big debut, and it was a blast. Eric, Steve, and I knew we could carry our weight on the mic, and we decided to do the whole thing unscripted and improvised—the way I had envisioned the Reel to be in the first place.

Stephanie was producing the segment, and it was really bothering her that we had no specific script to run past her. She kept asking us what our verbiage would be, and finally Steve said, "No offense, Steph, but between the three of us it's safe to say we've made a few dollars over the years doing promos. Just trust us, we'll come up with something." She agreed to give us some space and we had a fantastic segment.

I was on a high as I got on the bus, and I smiled when I saw a fan through the window jumping up and down on the street, mouthing that he was my biggest fan. As we pulled away he began running beside the bus screaming, "Jericho! Jericho!" I was impressed with his foot speed and gave him the thumbs-up as he struggled to keep up with the us. He returned the gesture, smiling from ear to ear at his hero's acknowledgment—and ran straight into a stop sign.

He went down like a ton of bricks and I saw him stagger to his feet holding his face in his hands as the bus left him in the dust. Sorry, mate.

Later that night before we left, I saw Steve and Eric drinking at the airport bar. When Bischoff got on the plane, I asked Steve, "What are you doing drinking beer with Bischoff? Isn't he still the asshole who fired you?" Steve said, "Not at all, he's pretty cool now actually." Years earlier Bischoff had terminated Steve from WCW via FedEx, and I figured if he could let bygones be bygones then it was time for me to do the same.

I wasn't sure why I still held a grudge against him anyway. Things had worked out pretty well for me after I left WCW. Besides, Eric had been nothing but froot to me since he made his debut in the WWE.

I approached him on the plane back to the U.S. and asked if I could talk to him. "Listen, man," I said, "I hope there isn't any heat between us from the WCW days."

He looked genuinely surprised and said, "I don't have any heat with you at all. As a matter of fact, didn't you send me—like a fax or something—thanking me for everything I did for you?"

I told him I did and was happy he got it and even more impressed that he remembered. We had a few beers and that was that. The great Bischoff-Jericho feud was over faster than Spencer Pratt's career.

Over the next few years we had some great conversations, and I found out we had a lot in common. He had overachieved his entire life because of his immense passion and drive just as I had. He might have made some bad decisions as the boss of WCW, but in the end I found him to be a pretty good guy.

Plus he created *Scott Baio Is 45 and Single*, and that alone is enough to earn my praise.

Kevin Nash had to get his hair cut for a role in the *Punisher* movie, and it was decided that I would beat him in a hair vs. hair match. It was the first time we'd ever worked together in any capacity and it was actually a lot of fun. The build for the match was strong, including me nicknaming him Nashhole. (Rocky called me and told me it was the funniest thing he'd seen on *Raw* in months.) Both of us were known for our manes and the fans really had no idea who was going to win, which added to the intrigue. Not adding to it was Nash's decision to dye his hair a brutal shade of jaundice the day before the match. When he showed up at the arena in Grand Rapids, he looked like he was wearing a straw hat. When I asked him why he'd done it, he said, "Well, I thought if I dyed my hair, people would think there's no way I'm going to lose and cut it off."

The problem was, he dyed it such a terrible color there was no way he *couldn't* cut it off.

We had a really good match, one of the best he had during his WWE comeback. We led the crowd through a heap of false finishes before I finally beat him with the dreaded brass knuckles.

Nash enjoyed working with me and wanted to continue doing so, albeit (bitchin' word) in a different way. He discussed the idea of becoming my bodyguard (or slackey, as he put it), similar to what he did with Shawn Michaels in 1993. I wasn't sold on it. I was hungry to regain the World Championship, but it seemed there were no plans to go in that direction. I approached Vince a few times to tell him I was ready to be the top guy again, and he humored me, but I could tell he wasn't into it. He still had a bad taste in his mouth from my first reign. But I was building myself back up and I felt that unless having Nash as my bodyguard was going to lead to another championship reign, it would be better to stay on my own.

My concern was moot, as Vince told me he wasn't considering the bodyguard idea anyway. A few months later, Hall and Nash were gone, with Hogan following soon after, and that was the end of the NWO in the WWE.

Talk about in like a lion and out like a lamb—brother.

CHAPTER 30

AO Jericho

*R*aw was coming to Winnipeg for the first time since I'd joined the company. I was excited to be the conquering hero returning home for my first TV taping since I'd wrestled at the Diamond Club for Tony Condello thirteen years earlier. What made things even more exciting was that Benoit had just won the World Championship in one of the greatest matches of all time against HHH and Shawn at *WrestleMania XX*. (It's unfortunate that it has been buried forever and technically doesn't exist anymore.)

So even though we were both babyfaces, I figured it was a no-brainer that I'd get a title shot in my hometown, so Chris and I could tear the house down. We hadn't wrestled each other since he'd been champion, and I felt we could have a classic with the boisterous Winnipeg fans behind us, but it wasn't to be. It was decided I'd face Randy Orton for the Intercontinental title instead, and even though I lost that match, I added another accolade to my résumé that night.

I became the first and only WWE Musical Chairs Champion.

Yeahhhhh boyeeee.

The special guest GM that night was Eugene, Bischoff's mentally challenged nephew. He booked a batch of curious matches for the show and then decided that he wanted to see a game of musical chairs. He corralled Stacy Keibler (still one of the hottest divas to ever grace the WWE), Tyson Tomko, Tajiri, Jerry Lawler, Jonathan Coachman, and me and told us that whoever won the game of musical chairs would get a championship match that night. When I was announced and sauntered to the ring in a vintage (sorry, Cole) Jets T-shirt, the Peg faithful blew the roof off the old barn (even when Lilian Garcia announced me as from Winnitoba, Manitoba).

It was such a waste that the astounding crowd reaction was squandered on a kid's party game and not a match for the world title. But as I learned in WCW, you make the best of what you're given, and I did.

A cheesy rendition of "Pop Goes the Weasel" began playing and the game was on. Tajiri was quickly eliminated and then spewed his green mist into the Coach's face, which got rid of him. Lawler failed to take a seat in time, as he was too busy staring at Stacy's seat. Flair, (who stole the show during the segment), started stylin' and profilin' around the ring, then pushed Stacy to the ground the next time the Weasel stopped.

Keep in mind that the whole time the crowd was going berserk and chanting "Y2J" at the top of their lungs.

Tomko and I were the sole survivors, and when the music stopped again I pulled the chair out of the way as he sat down. Then I rammed it into his gut and parked myself, becoming the first ever Musical Chairs Champion. The crowd erupted as if Dale Hawerchuk had just scored the game-winning goal to finally get the Jets into the third round of the playoffs.

It was one of the biggest reactions I received during my entire career and it ended up being a tremendous segment. I apologized to Brian afterwards for being against the idea when he first told me about it—proof once again that you just never know what's going to work in this business. It's all in the excellence of the execution.

JR once told me that I was only one of three Grand Slam Champions in the history of the WWE (meaning that I had won every possible title), along with HHH and Shawn Michaels. However, since I'm the first and *only* WWE Musical Chairs Champion, it obviously means that I'm better than those guys, right?

Now I'm anxiously awaiting the first ever WWE Pin the Tail on the Donkey derby.

The Winnipeg faithful weren't just proud of my musical chairs accomplishments, they took great pride in all that I had done. It wasn't too often that a kid from St. James became an international superstar, and now that *Raw* was in town, the city was ready to roll out the red carpet for me. The day of the show I was given the key to the city by Mayor Sam Katz, which I think means that I'm allowed to walk into any house or place of business within the city limits of Winnipeg and make myself at home. Drink a beer, eat some soup, take a dumpski, whatever I want. I'm still waiting for the actual key, though.

After that, Gary Doer, the premier of Manitoba, awarded me with the Order of the Buffalo Hunt, which was the province's highest honor. It was quite the prestigious prize, which had been given to such dignitaries as Mother Teresa, Desmond Tutu, Jimmy Carter, Pope John Paul II, and now Chris Jericho. Which one of these people doesn't belong, huh?

Obviously it's the pope, that son of a bitch.

There was a WWE camera crew filming the presentations for the various syndicated TV shows and the website. When I saw Vince at the building, I suggested that we show some of the ceremony on *Raw*, and he started laughing.

"The Order of the Buffalo Hunt? That's a pretty dumb name. Sounds like something Fred Flintstone would get."

Manitoba premier Gary Doer presents me with the Order of the Buffalo Hunt, along with a tiny bronze buffalo. I'm thinking, "That's all I get?"

Then I informed him of the impressive list of VIPs with whom I shared the award and he begrudgingly agreed to mention it.

A few months later, Vince decided that if a babyface was billed as being from Canada, it would impede his popularity in the United States. Despite the fact that I'd been announced as being from Winnipeg for the past five years and everyone knew I was Canadian, I was suddenly being introduced "from Tampa, Florida."

It drove me nuts, because even though I live in Tampa and it's a nice city, it's not where I grew up. Vince finally compromised and I was introduced "from Manhasset, New York," which is where I was born when my dad was playing for the Rangers. But I am no more a New Yorker than Funaki is a Texan. I didn't understand Vince's logic; I believe you could be billed from Timbuktu and people will still cheer for you if you're good. But he's the boss and they're his rules.

However, just for the record, I'm from Winnipeg. Always have been, always will be. If you wanna discuss further, I'll meet you at the Salisbury House on the corner of Portage and Main and we can head over to Kern-Hill Furniture beside Eaton Place and buy a Hunky Bill perogy maker (that's how the Hunky one spelled it) to feed everyone at the Monterey social.

At *SummerSlam* 2004 in Toronto, I faced Batista and Edge in a three-way match for the Intercontinental Championship. I couldn't seem to break out of the middle of the pack, and it was starting to affect my attitude about the business. Holding the world title was addictive, and like Seinfeld said about air travel, once you fly first class, it's hard to go back to coach. But I was stuck in middle-seat smoking and it was starting to really frustrate me.

Adding to my dilemma was that even though *SummerSlam* turned out okay, I wasn't booked on *Raw* the next day in Kitchener, Ontario. No match, no run-in, no promo, no musical chairs—nothing. It felt like 1999 again when I wasn't booked for the *No Mercy* PPV in Cleveland. I didn't feel that there was enough talent on the roster to where they could afford to leave me off, and it really bothered me.

I instantly went on a manhunt for the boss, and when I found him I got straight to the point.

"Vince, I just heard I wasn't on the show tonight and I was wondering why."

His reaction took me aback. "You're upset you're not on the show? Why don't you grow up? A lot of people aren't on the show!"

I stood there in stunned silence. Grow up? But Vince was incensed and the blitzkrieg continued.

"You know what the problem with you is? You've got a gigantic chip on your shoulder. You think you're an accomplished wrestler, but you're not! You think you know everything and you're getting the reputation of being hard to work with."

Wow, where did all of this come from?

I didn't feel that I was hard to work with, I just had a lot of confidence and the courage to stand up for what I believed in. Chris Kanyon had given me the nickname AO Jericho when we worked together in WCW, which stood for Always Opinionated, and it fit me perfectly.

Being AO was what helped me make it as far as I had, but AO also bit me in the ass at times.

Vince told me to suck it up and stormed away, leaving me baffled. His words really pissed me off, and for the first time since I walked through the doors of the WWE, I began to wonder if I really wanted to be there. I was having serious doubts about my position in the company as it was, and being told to "grow up" by the boss certainly didn't help my disposition. After fourteen years on the job, maybe it was time to take a step back.

Even though the front office of the WWE didn't feel the same way, I began dubbing myself "the Larger than Life Living Legend." I'd been using the nickname for a few months and was getting some good mileage with it, when I got a call from my lawyer, John Taylor. John had been instrumental in getting me out of WCW in '99, and he had since started working for the WWE. I was flabbergasted (kooky word) when he told me the purpose of his call: I was being sued by Larry Zbyszko.

Larry Zbyszko? I hadn't heard his name in years, not since he was the single worst commentator in wrestling history. He would sit at the desk in WCW and talk in the most sarcastic, patronizing voice with the sole purpose of getting himself over, which was the exact opposite of what he was supposed to do. He would bash wrestlers for using high-flying moves and make fun of their costumes or hairstyles or body types or their taste in pistachio brands, whatever he could find to amuse himself. He didn't do it in a froot Jesse Ventura heel-announcer way either, he did it in a smarmy way that downplayed the product. The only time he showed any emotion whatsoever was when he mentioned his golf game.

His biggest claim to fame was a great angle where he turned on his mentor, Bruno Sammartino, and began claiming that he, not Bruno, was the Living Legend. Now a quarter of a century later he was suing me, Vince, and the entire WWE for stealing his nickname, demanding restitution. Whatever his motive, it didn't seem to concern Vince, as when I mentioned the lawsuit to him, he didn't even know about it. Why would he? Larry's claim was lame.

But even so, I still had to waste an entire day of my life giving a deposition in a room full of Zbyszko's lawyers. It was quite outlandish as he had a whole team of them, like this was *Roe v. Jericho.* I had to sit there as his legal beagles asked me if I knew that Larry had received the rights to use the name Living Legend from beating Bruno in a match. I asked them if *they* knew that wrestling was show business and Larry beat Bruno because that's how it was booked. Then they submitted a copy of *Pro Wrestling Illustrated* which had an interview saying I was the true living legend in wrestling.

One of his lawyers said, "These magazines prove that you violated the trademark."

I said, "You do realize that those magazines are semifictional? I wasn't even interviewed for that article!"

The fact that Luscious Lawrence had submitted the fabricated magazines as evidence in the first place, made me want to countersue him for perjury, especially when it came out that he didn't even have a trademark on the epithet. The whole suit was a bigger joke than Larryland, only succeeding in wasting my time and stopping the production of a really froot "Chris Jericho: Living Legend" T-shirt that was mere days away from hitting the stands. It was instead replaced with an awful-looking "Larger than Life" tee that ended up being my worst-selling shirt of all time.

What kind of a name is Zbyszko anyway?

CHAPTER 31

Tonight Fozzy Gay

When the Happenstance tour ended on *The Howard Stern Show* in 2003, it was the official end of the Fozzy gimmick. Rich and I felt that it was time to stand on our own and Happenstance was a great indication of what we could do as an original band. So we dropped the covers, the storyline, the pseudonyms, and the wigs. We debated changing our name to Walls of Jericho, Jericho Siren, Kajagoogootwo, something more "serious," then we started thinking about some of the biggest bands on the planet and how awful their names sound initially. Limp Bizkit, the Red Hot Chili Peppers, Korn, Toad the Wet Sprocket, Hoobastank, the Queens of the Stone Age, Pink Floyd, Kiss, Helloween—and the worst of them all, Def Leppard (just think about that one for a second). All of them are silly if taken literally, but when you hear them over and over again the silliness wears off and they become iconic over time. Rich and I decided that with all of the work and touring we'd done that it would be one step forward and two steps back to start from scratch with a different name. For better or worse, Fozzy was our name and that was that.

We knew we'd have our work cut out for us recording an all-original album. We were under the microscope more than ever, and the only way to combat that was to record the absolute best record possible. Every song had to be good—we couldn't afford to have any filler material whatsoever. With that edict in mind, the Duke put his cock to the grindstone and wrote some of the best songs of his life. He came up with all of the music and the melodies, while I wrote the lyrics with Ed Aborn, our friend and the visual timekeeper of Fozzy. Once we were ready, we set up shop at Treesound Studios in Atlanta, using the same soundboard that was used on the Police's *Synchronicity* and Rush's *Moving Pictures* albums. The studio was huge with a killer ambience and reinforced the idea that we were playing with the big boys now.

We thought it would put Fozzy in a different light if we invited a few of our famous friends to contribute to the record. The first guy I called was Zakk, and not only was he my brother, but a big Rich Ward fan as well. Zakk credits Rich and Stuck Mojo with helping him get back into heavy music after he went through his *Book of Shadows* acoustic period and was happy to help us out by playing an amazing solo on the song "Wanderlust."

Our producer was a friend of Megadeth's guitarist Marty Friedman, who agreed to lay down a solo for "Born of Anger." I'd met Alter Bridge guitarist Mark Tremonti a few years earlier in Tampa when he was touring with Creed and found out he was a Fozzy fan. He'd offered to do a guest solo when we did our next album, but in typical Jericho fashion, I lost his number and never followed up with him. So when I found out that Alter Bridge was also recording their new album at Treesound, I simply walked downstairs to their studio door and knocked. I handed him a tape of our song "The Way I Am" and said, "Will you play on this? Here's your chance!"

Myles Kennedy, Alter Bridge's singer (now with Slash), laid down some backing vocals, and suddenly Fozzy's new record had a whole new slant. Any band that had an album featuring the talents of Wylde, Friedman, Tremonti, and Kennedy had to have some credibility—and we did.

It was froot to know that we were in the same studio with the Alter boys, but Rich and I really flipped when we found out that someone else of status was working there as well. Somebody who was only one of the top ten biggest rock stars in the world—Rico Suave himself, Gerardo.

Actually it was Sir Elton John. He was recording his *Peachtree Road* album in the biggest studio in the complex and we took a quick look around when Elton had a day off. There were fresh-cut flowers everywhere and a ritzy lounge featuring a fully stocked kitchen, stand-up video games, and a full library of books and DVDs. Scoping out the racks of guitars with spools of cords snaking around, along with the corkboards filled with tacked on Post-it notes describing the various time changes and keys of the new songs, made me feel inadequate as a musician. And the coup de grâce, seeing Elton's famous red piano up close and personal, was a rocker's equivalent to a Muslim taking a trip to Mecca.

Rich and I decided that we would make it our mission to meet Sir Elton. We'd been keeping a watchful eye out for him for a few days, to no avail; then one afternoon while listening to one of my takes, we saw a shiny black SUV pull into the parking lot. The door opened and a massive block of humanity sidled out of the driver's seat. He walked around to open the passenger door and out climbed Elton himself—a short pudgy man with chipmunk cheeks, wearing a black tracksuit.

I screamed and ran down the stairs as fast as my little legs could carry me to cut him off at the pass. Treesound was a big studio, mazelike in its setup, and I took a few wrong turns. Finally I burst into the lobby and made a beeline toward the big boy room just as the door was closing. I asked the desk clerk if I could pop my head in and say hi but was told, "Sorry, it's a closed session. No one's allowed to go in."

Closed session? Who did Elton think he was, Sarsippius?

I begged and pleaded but the guy wouldn't budge, so I turned to go back to work.

Suddenly the studio door opened and out walked Elton's gianormous driver. The receptionist had disappeared at this point, so the Kraken turned to me and said in a perfect C3PO English accent, "Excuse me, do you know the address of this studio?"

"No man, I'm just here recording upstairs. Why's that?"

"Oh my. Well, Elton's hairdresser is coming and he needs to know where we are."

"Hairdresser? Is Elton filming something today?"

"No, no. Elton just likes to have his hair done while he's recording."

Sir Elton John had to have his hair styled and looking perfect in order to make an album. How rock and roll is that? I went directly to the bathroom and combed my tresses—it was the least I could do.

We never did meet Elton, but just knowing we were

recording in the same airspace as Captain Fantastic was an incredible feeling. It was a sign that we were about to say goodbye to the yellow brick road of our past and become our own madmen across the water.

Wow, that was pretty bad, wasn't it?

Don't shoot me, I'm only the book writer.

After dealing with all the various record company bullshit from Megaforce and Palm, we still "owed" them money even though our first two records had more than recouped. I'd had enough of record companies ripping us off, so I decided to take matters into my own hands and start my own. So we released our third album, *All That Remains*, in January 2005 on Ash Records.

Another sad truth of the music business is that in order for a band of our size to get airplay in big markets like New York or L.A. we'd have to pay some serious cash. So we decided to concentrate on getting played in secondary (and free) markets like Grand Rapids, Alberquerque, Des Moines. That's what we did, and our song "Enemy" became a sort of hit, getting airplay on over eighty stations across the country.

The next step was to make a video. We filmed the clip for "Enemy" on the top of a government building in San Diego and based it around the concept of a guy with one leg climbing up the stairs to the roof. After struggling to make it to the top, he promptly threw himself over the edge. It was the feel-good story of the spring.

Apparently because "Enemy" featured a one-legged man committing suicide, MTV banned it after one showing on *Headbangers Ball*. Even though being banned

Fozzy, 2005: Delson, The Duke, me, Frank Fontsere, and Mike Martin. We had to get a government permit to film the "Enemy" clip on a rooftop in downtown San Diego. Doesn't the city have better things to do than demand a permit from a rock band shooting a video?

(like the original album cover for *Yesterday and Today*) was very rock and roll, it also made no sense. MTV was also airing the "99 Problems" video by Jay-Z (which depicted him being assassinated) in heavy rotation at the same time. There was machine gun fire and blood spouting all over the place in his video, but a one-legged man falling off a building in our video was too risqué. What's wrong with being sexy?

Despite being banned by MTV (or maybe because of it), we were invited to tour England for the first time. (That "madmen across the water" line doesn't seem like too much of a stretch, now does it?) We didn't know what to expect, but the response was incredible. Most of the shows sold out and the crowd knew all the words to our songs. After all of Fozzy's trials and tribulations, we had found our second home.

It was also the first time we'd traveled together in a tour bus—although in reality it was more of a tour van. It was the size of a small rental car shuttle with make-shift bunks on the side, and there was barely enough room for the five guys in the band and our two crew members. But it was Fozzy's first bus and I loved it.

Although this was my debut tour of the UK with Fozzy, I had been there a dozen times with the WWE. The rush I got from doing the shows was the same for both, but the difference in accommodations was night and day. I went from staying in five-star hotels to sleeping on a thin mattress on a piece of plywood and taking showers at truck stops. But I was paying my dues and making my name as a musician the same way I had in wrestling all those years ago (Harrison represent!).

Fozzy started catching on in England, Ireland, Scotland, and Wales, and we toured the UK five times on the All That Remains—Touring the World and Elsewhere jaunt. We did such good business that we were booked at the Astoria, one of the most prestigious and historic venues in London. The Beatles played there. Metallica played there. Now Fozzy was playing there, and that was pretty fucking froot in my book.

It was a big night for us, so we decided to do something special at the expense of a male version of the Spice Girls called the S Club. If you put Ashley Simpson into a blender with 98 Degrees, sprinkled in a little Miley Cyrus and a whole lot of suck, you might have an idea of what the S Club sounded like.

The Astoria was jam-packed with over a thousand Fozzy Fanatics, with dozens more hanging from the rafters (term used courtesy of the Rock 'n' Roll Express). The show began as the lights went out and a single spotlight shone down on a footstool with a boom box placed upon it. Then our tour manager extraordinaire Toad wandered out on the stage and pressed play. At that moment our sound guy cued the S Club as if they were blaring out of the box. The audience started booing and screaming "This sucks!" until I strolled onstage, baseball bat in hand. The entire crowd understood what was about to happen and the jeers turned to screams of appreciation. I stood beside the boom box and stared at it with disgust, swinging the bat over my shoulder. I slowly raised it over my head and brought it down like the Hammer of the Gods, smashing the shit out of the hapless box and to the delight of the crowd silencing the S Club forever. The rest of the band came charging out and we blazed into "Nameless Faceless," the opening track off *All That Remains*.

There was a lot of press in attendance prepared to drag us over the coals for having the audicity to play original music, but we caught their attention and changed their minds pretty damn quickly. They found out that Fozzy had come to London to chew bubble gum and kick ass— and we were all out of ass.

After the show we had to pack up our gear and leave quickly, as the venue was turning from a concert hall into a trendy discotheque. As the bus pulled away I glanced out at the marquee and burst out in laughter when

I saw the name of the club underneath the name of our band.

TONIGHT:
FOZZY
GAY

You can't make this stuff up....

The marquee says it all.

CHAPTER 32

Rage Raspberry

Ever since Motörhead had recorded HHH's theme song, they appeared on WWE programming from time to time. As a result, I had become acquainted with Lemmy and their guitarist Phil Campbell, and the band's manager, Todd Singerman. They were in the midst of their thirtieth anniversary tour and had a show coming up in L.A. at the Wiltern Theater. Todd had given us a standing offer to open for them, and we thought that the Wiltern would be a great place to finally make it happen. We were second out of four bands on the show, and since we were joining the tour for only one night, I thought I'd make a point of saying hi to the other bands on the bill. I wasn't sure of rock and roll protocol, but in wrestling it was up to the younger guys to introduce themselves to the veterans, so I went and thanked the members of Zeke (and you think Fozzy is a weird name?) and Corrosion of Conformity for letting us play with them. I was met with the same confused reaction Flounder got when he asked the fraternity guys if they were playing cards. I'm sure these guys were thinking to themselves, "Who the fuck is this guy? We didn't let you play with us, Motör-head did."

Motörhead fans are notorious for treating opening bands like a sacrifice. They came specifically to see the loudest band in the world and could not give a shit about anybody else. But we'd never been intimidated by a crowd and charged onstage with our archetypal Fozzy energy. But we were met with total apathy and halfway through our six-song set a tumbleweed blew by and I heard a guy in the balcony shart. Our gig was a massacre of silence (another great album title) as 99 percent of the crowd stood with their arms crossed, doing their time until Fozzy was done. But believe me, the remaining 1 percent of the crowd were *losing their minds.*

I concentrated on the few people who were feeling our set and glanced away to find myself locked in a death stare with a huge biker in the front row who was a dead ringer for Ogre from *Revenge of the Nerds.* He couldn't have looked more unimpressed, and I sensed him telepathically say, "Get off the stage before I bash your fucking brains in."

We were dying a death, so I decided to use an old wrestling trick and call an audible.

During a match when the crowd isn't buying what you're selling, you have to change up what you're doing to get the people interested. Fozzy had planned on playing an all-original set that night but nobody was reacting to our material, so I called the audible to launch into Judas Priest's "Freewheel Burning," a song we had covered on *Happenstance.* Lo and behold, when the crowd heard a tune they knew and loved, they finally started showing signs of life. The 1 percent of the audience who dug what we were doing grew to about 12 percent, and we gladly took it.

But the true sign that we were getting over with the tough crowd was Ogre bobbing his head slightly to the song, as he *uncrossed his arms*. At the end of the set he even gave me a thumbs-up, which compared with his reactions earlier was the equivalent of him throwing his panties onstage.

When our gig was over, I asked Frank how he felt about the performance and he said optimistically, "Well, it wasn't a home run, but it was definitely a double." Rich, however, was a little less diplomatic in his response: "I felt like a black man at a Ku Klux Klan rally."

I began to get the sense that we were being a little hard on ourselves. Maybe we just weren't used to the average Motörhead opening band reception, and when I saw Lemmy backstage, he was very complimentary.

"You guys had a good amount of energy, nice job," he said matter-of-factly in his gravelly English accent. Then he offered me a drink to celebrate the occasion. He poured me a glass of Jack Daniel's and grabbed a fistful of ice cubes with his filthy hand and threw them in the plastic tumbler. I was a little grossed out, as I could only guess why his hand was so dirty and where it might've been, but I figured the straight whiskey would kill any germs.

Besides, how often did one get to have a cocktail with Lemmy?

After a few shots, Lemmy poured me a glass of fine merlot and went to greet the rest of his backstage guests, one of whom was legendary singer Ronnie James Dio. Lemmy introduced me to Dio, who shook my hand and told me he really enjoyed the show and thought I had a good voice. I thanked him and promptly pissed myself. I asked him if we could take a picture, and when I put my arm around him I spilled my wine all over the front of his shirt.

I was totally embarrassed and apologized profusely.

Dio smirked. "It's okay, man, I'm wearing black anyway."

"I'm really sorry, Ronnie, I hope you forgive me. I just don't want you to put a curse on me," I said, smiling.

Dio stared at me and said grimly, "How do you know that I haven't already?"

Then he threw his trademark devil horn gesture in my face and made a spitting sound. I stood motionless, paralyzed with fear that Dio the wizard had just put a hex on me, until he burst out laughing and said he was only kidding.

I promptly pissed myself again.

There were a lot of other celebrities backstage at the Wiltern, including Kerry King from Slayer, Juliette Lewis, Nicolas Cage, and Jenna Jameson (who told me she had a crush on me, whoop whoop).

I was a big fan of Jon Lovitz from his *SNL* days and thought it was pretty froot when he came over and began talking to me. But I was so bored after three minutes of his conversation I wanted to shove bamboo splints up my penis. He kept asking the most frivolous questions possible.

"What do the ropes feel like? Are they made of actual rope?"

I smiled awkwardly. "Yeah, they're made of rope with tape wrapped around it."

"Oh, there's tape wrapped around them...like gaffer's tape? Masking tape? Electrical tape? What kind of tape?"

Before I could reply he continued his onslaught of dullness. "Tell me more about the ropes. What are the ropes made of? Hemp? Twine? And those ref shirts, are they made of cotton or..."

Finally I asked Lovitz if he wanted a drink and never came back. He's probably still in the bowels of the Wiltern, wondering what kind of fiber the ring ropes are made of.

The WWE had brokered a sponsorship deal with an energy drink company to hawk a product called YJ Stinger. They brought me on as their spokesman and the marketing department put together a campaign based around Fozzy. They flew the band out to L.A. and we filmed two commercials based around our song "Don't You Wish You Were Me." But the catch was we had to change the lyrics to something a little more YJ Stinger–friendly.

While my original lyrics went:

*Don't you wish you were me? The king of all you
  see*
Don't you wish you were me? It ain't that easy
*Don't think you'll ever be? everything a man
  should be*
*Don't you wish you were me? Keep dreaming,
  you'll never be me*

—the corporate sellout lyrics went:

Don't you wish you were me? The king of energy
Don't you wish you were me? It ain't that easy

Don't you want sugar-free? Now in rage raspberry
Don't you wish you were me? Catch the buzz and
*   feel the sting*

Rage raspberry? So blatant that even the girls at the Chicken Ranch called us whores.

But we weren't Pearl Jam on a crusade to fight Ticketmaster. We were starving musicians trying to make a living and had no problem selling out—no problem at all.

Riding on the success of our hit single "Enemy" and the national commercial, we decided to do a short run of autumn gigs called the Fall That Remains Tour. We played in nice halls and back-alley clubs, ending up with a gig in a sports bar in Hershey where we couldn't sound-check until the high school reunion that was taking place finished. Afterwards in our dressing room/storage closet, I sternly told the bar manager, "Dammit, I told you the sign on the door should say Fozzy first, High School Reunion second!!" and threw my leather jacket down aloofly on a stack of Heinz ketchup tins.

Some gigs were packed with amazing fans who sang along with every song, genuinely excited to see us, and other shows were worse than anything in the Anvil movie. But one gig in particular stands out as the all-time biggest nightmare in Fozzy history: opening for the Murder Junkies at a skinhead bar in Savannah, Georgia.

Who the hell are the Murder Junkies, might you ask?

Well, dear reader, the Murder Junkies were the backing band for G. G. Allin, an underground punk rock legend who was famous for slicing himself with razor blades, punching his band members in the face, and chasing fans with pieces of his own shit in hand. And the shit didn't fall too far from the Allin, as after G.G. died, his brother Merle continued touring in tribute to his departed sibling.

I had no idea what to expect but I found out quickly when after our intro played, we ran onstage, launching into "Nameless Faceless," and were met by forty mohawk-sporting, swastika-wearing, safety-pin-through-the-nose drunken skinheads. These guys were the real deal, completely 100 percent serious in their Aryan beliefs. When they saw our long hair and heard the pounding metal, they started laughing, playing overexaggerated air guitar, and headbanging goofily. In between songs, they yelled out, "Dokken!" or "Ratt!" They weren't having fun, they were just full-on taking the piss out of our performance.

Normally, I pride myself on being able to entertain any crowd no matter the situation, but not even the mystic powers of Jericho the Voodoo Mon could turn them on this night. They were antagonistic, apathetic, unruly, and confrontational; they made Ogre from the Motörhead gig look like a thirteen-year-old girl at a Jonas Brothers concert.

During "Wanderlust," when I invited a guy with a ring through his lip to sing along, he told me to fuck off. So I eliminated the middleman and tried to lead a *"Fuck"* chant during "Feel the Burn," but not even blatant cursing was going to win this mob over and I was met with total indifference.

We finally lurched our way to the end of the show and began playing "Freewheel Burning," the last of the set. Unfortunately, the song that cracked the Motörhead crowd didn't work for the Junkie faithful, so I decided to go down swinging. During the song's lengthy guitar solo I jumped off the stage and physically tried to get the stone-faced crowd to rock. I figured if they wanted punk I would give them punk and spit attitude into their faces. But my attempt bombed bigger than a Randy Savage rap album. Nobody moved.

I was frustrated and pissed off, so when I saw a guy propped up against the wall smirking at me, I snapped. I got right in his face and snarled, "You better rock!"

He still didn't move.

"You better rock, man! I'm warning you."

He continued staring at me nonchalantly, so I shoved him on the chest as hard as I could. He got a surprised look on his face and began to sway back and forth.

"That's right!" I thought. "I finally got this guy to move!"

Then his swaying turned into teetering, his teetering into tottering, and his tottering turned into a complete Kramer pratfall onto the ground.

That's when I noticed the cast on his leg and the crutch in his hand.

Bollocks.

We got an offer to tour Germany that I insisted on taking despite Rich's reluctance. He felt that Fozzy didn't have a big enough presence in Germany and wouldn't do well, and he was right. We played complete shitholes for sparse crowds of lethargic fans every night.

The second night in Berlin was especially bad. The gig took place in a club that was little more than a big empty room with hardwood flooring like you'd find in a high school gym. The room remained almost empty for the show, I blew out my voice, and halfway through the set somebody threw a roll of toilet paper onstage. Rich glared at me as he wrapped the TP around his neck mid-song, and I could tell by the look on his face that he was furious.

Afterwards he asked, "How did you like that show?"

"It wasn't good."

"Yeah, it was the shits. Not even that roll of toilet paper could wipe that turd up."

Then he proceeded to tear a strip off me. "Listen, you don't know everything. You need to listen to me sometimes. You insisted that we come to Germany, even though I knew it was a bad idea, and I was right. Contrary to popular belief, I've been doing this for a lot of years. I know that you've been on the road for years too, and even though that's wrestling and it's still show business, it's not the music business. So for the good of the band, you need to listen to what I say sometimes and trust me."

He put me in my place and made me realize that I was getting way out of control. Even though in one respect I'm the face of Fozzy, Rich is the conductor of the band and my partner. I'd forgotten that and had been making every decision, some without even consulting him. After that show I took a step back and gave Rich more credit and more respect, and quite frankly, that's the only reason why Fozzy is still around over a decade after we started.

Being in a band is like being married (but to sweaty dudes, not a hot blonde), and you have to compromise and give and take in order to make it work and stay together.

But I'm sorry Rich, the sex is much better with my wife.

We did another successful run in the UK, including another sellout at the Astoria, where a representative from

SPV, our European record label, showed up and asked us, "Why are you guys back here again?" They hadn't done anything as far as supporting the band and they couldn't figure out why we kept selling out our shows. But instead of embracing us and jumping on the Fozzy bandwagon, they left us to fend for ourselves. It worked out better anyway since we were forced to become self-sufficient and make a profit without any tour support from the record company.

One of the ways we were able to do that was by having opening acts buy onto our tours. Because we were selling out most of our shows, less established bands who wanted to make a name for themselves paid us for the right to play with us.

That was another rude awakening to the music business for me. I had always been under the impression that when Metallica opened for Ozzy in 1986, for example, Ozzy had scoured the planet to find a band he liked well enough to take on tour and had handpicked Metallica. In reality, Metallica's record company probably paid Ozzy's organization a good chunk of change for the right to open the shows and be seen by a much larger audience.

We used the money the opening bands paid us to pay all of our road expenses, including a big, luxurious tour bus. It was a double-decker, with a spacious lounge in the back and twenty-four comfortable bunks in the front. This ride was Bruce Dickinson compared to our original Blaze Bayley coach.

The drawback of having the other bands pay our road expenses was that they shared our bus for the duration of the tour. Fozzy has a strict no-smoking, no-drugs policy, which wasn't very rock and roll, but Rich had been through it all during his ten years of touring and didn't want to deal with the debauchery.

Unfortunately, there was no way to enforce a no-pissing policy, and the bathroom stunk so bad after two days of constant urination (Tour Rule #1: no pooping on the bus.) that we had to seal it shut with gaffer's tape to keep the stench at bay. The tape was the idea of our driver Ozzy, who'd earned that nickname because he looked and sounded like—well, Ozzy.

As he sealed the bathroom tomb, he stuttered in his thick English accent, "Gotta watch wha ya eat when ya tour, lads. No leafy greens or coffee."

Apparently not only was Ozzy a bus driver, he was a gastroenterologist as well.

One of our opening bands was called 19th Century and they hailed from Liverpool. When the tour wound its way through their city, their guitar player Paul Hurst offered to take me on a "real" Beatles tour. He knew how much of a Beatles fanatic I am and wanted to get me away from the Magical Mystery Tours of John Lennon's junior high school and George Harrison's favorite chip shop. Hurst's father had been a local musician his whole life and used to hang out with Lennon, and had the pictures to prove it. He even gave me this really froot picture of John sitting on the exact same couch I was sitting on as I looked at it.

Paul took me, our new guitar player Mike Martin, and Fozzy's visual timekeeper Ed Aborn to see such legendary Beatles locations as Strawberry Fields (an orphanage), Penny Lane (a side road that had no street sign as it had been stolen), and the grave of Eleanor Rigby. We went to Paul McCartney's boyhood home and saw the

Ozzy was a great storyteller but a terrible bus driver. We'd often swerve from lane to lane in the middle of the night for no particular reason. (My deformed flashing of the horns is a result of a broken pinky that was never set properly.)

house on Menlove Avenue where John grew up, including the intersection where his mother was hit and killed by a drunken off-duty police officer.

It was a major thrill to see all of these places I knew due to my obsession with my favorite band, especially while I was on tour with my own band.

Tomorrow never knows how froot life can be sometimes.

But the coup de grâce of the "real" Beatles tour was meeting the Hursts' family friend Johnny Hutch. I know that doesn't sound too impressive upon first read, but stay with me, Apple Scruffs. Johnny Hutch was a member of the Beatles for about a minute, when John and Paul tapped him to play a few gigs *after* Pete Best's departure and *before* the arrival of his replacement, Ringo Starr. I couldn't believe my luck when I found a picture of Johnny playing with the Beatles in a magazine for him to sign.

We knocked on his door and I was awash with the anticipation over hearing the certain astonishing tales Hutch must have about his awesome (albeit brief) stint playing with the biggest and most influential band of all time.

Nobody answered the first knock, so Paul tapped his knuckle against the door again.

Suddenly it flew open and an old man with a weathered ruddy face appeared croaking in a sour voice, "What the fook do you want?"

The smile dripped off my face like yellow matter custard.

Paul laughed and said, "Johnny we just came by to see you and have a chat."

"What do you want to talk to me for? I got nuthin' to say."

"Well, Chris here would like to hear about when you played with the Beatles."

"The Beatles? Yeah, I played with the Beatles, and

they were shite! They could hardly play their fookin' instruments. Pretty boys is all they were."

I was taken aback by Johnny's statement. I was so used to hearing everybody say that the Beatles were gods that it was almost blasphemy to hear someone who'd played with them say they sucked.

But when I thought about it, I understood where Johnny was coming from. I've heard of a dozen wrestlers that never quite made it talking the same way about me.

"Jericho is the shits! He can't work—he just got lucky!"

Most of the time they were simply bitter because they never made it, and Johnny was the same way. His band the Big Three was also managed by Brian Epstein, but they didn't hit the big time and Johnny was still resentful about it.

"The Big Three could outplay the Beatles and we could outsing them too! And Ringo...he left Rory Storm completely fooking hanging so he could run off and join the Beatles. He's a right shithouse to have done that!!"

I thought Johnny might have a better disposition if I changed the subject to what he was doing now.

"Are you still playing, Mr. Hutch?"

He responded grumpily, "No, I don't fookin' play anymore. There's no reason for a sixty-five-year-old man to get up on a stage and make a fool of himself."

I walked right into another shithouse when I said innocently, "I saw McCartney live a couple of months ago and he sounded amazing."

That brought back the fire and Johnny turned into a Blue Meanie once again. He stared a hole right through me and said slowly, "Really? Well, the next time you see McCartney, you tell him I said he's a fookin' wanker."

Um, okay. So the next time I talk to Paul McCartney—which will be the first time I talk to him—I'll have to remember to open the conversation by saying, "Hey Paul, nice to meet you. By the way, Johnny Hutch in Liverpool said to tell you you're a fookin' wanker."

We stood there for a few seconds in awkward silence until Ed and I decided it was time to leave the good day sunshine personality of Johny Hutch alone. I figured before I left, I'd try to get him to sign the picture I had. When I opened the magazine and showed him, his face instantly softened.

"Is that you?" I asked.

"Yeah, that's me," he said with a wistful smile. "I know that's me because I remember buying that jacket. They brought jackets like that in from India. I used to hang out by the docks and wait for the ships to come in with those clothes. They always had such great stuff. I loved that jacket."

Suddenly the crotchety old man who hated the Beatles had been replaced by a kid in his early twenties who had his whole life ahead of him.

"Will you sign it for me?"

"Absolutely," he said, delighted. "Would you like a cup of tea?"

I ended up talking with a former member of the Beatles for the next twenty minutes. And he told us some great stories, but I'll save those for Johnny's book should he ever decide to write one.

When I got back to the bus, Ozzy was polishing the hubcaps for some reason and looked up, squinting behind his Coke-bottle lenses.

"So ya went to see the Beatles sights, didya? If you

John, Paul, George, and *Johnny?* It was true for a while, as Hutch was one of only five people to drum for the Beatles. Can you name the other four? Maybe Mike or my scarf know the answer.

want the full experience, you have to take a ferry cross the Mersey, lad!"

Then he started doing a weird little jig as he warbled "Ferry Cross the Mersey" by Gerry and the Pacemakers. I could still hear him cackling to himself as I crawled into my bunk.

CHAPTER 33

Steel Enema

In September 2004 I won the Intercontinental title for the seventh time from Christian in a Ladder match in Portland, Oregon. At only thirty-three years old, I had been IC Champion more than any other performer in WWE history. Not too shabby, especially when you consider that my dream when I started wrestling was to only win it once.

Christian and I had been in a number of Ladder matches, and we wanted to try something different for the finish of this one. We came up with the idea that we'd be fighting for the title atop the ladder, and in the process I would swing the cable the belt was hanging from. In our mind's eye the cable would swing past Christian's head, barely missing him, and then career back and crack him in the back of the noggin when he wasn't looking, toppling him off the ladder.

Sounds good on paper, right?

Unfortunately, when I swung the cable, it missed his head the first time—and zipped straight past him the second time. Then its momentum stopped and the title dangled in midair like a deflated balloon.

We looked at each other for a few seconds before I bull-dogged him off the ladder and climbed back up for the win. So much for creativity, but as W. C. Fields once said, "Never work with animals or children...or cables with titles on the end of them...or ladders for that matter."

He was right, because the botched finish wasn't even the lowlight of the match for me. That came when I fell off the ladder awkwardly and it bit me in the ass—or more specifically went straight up it.

That's right, intrepid readers, I was the proud recipient of a steel enema. I'm not exaggerating, either. I literally felt the ladder's edge penetrating my anal cavity. It was like getting raped by RoboCop.

After the match William Regal walked past me shaking his head. He said that my fall was one of the worst things he'd ever seen and I looked like a wishbone. Yikes—there's a mental image I can live without. My ass hurt so bad I could hardly walk, and I had to sit on one cheek for the next month. When I went to see a doctor I was diagnosed with a cracked coccyx bone, the little tip of cartilage at the end of your tailbone. When I asked him what he could do to help me, he smirked and threw up his hands. "What do you want me to do? Put a cast on it?"

In an effort to stay ahead of the curve, the WWE came up with an interactive PPV called *Taboo Tuesday*. The idea behind the show was that the fans could vote online to decide what matches were on the show. For example, fans would vote for the stipulation in the match between Randy Orton and Ric Flair. The choices were: (a) Steel Cage match; (b) falls count anywhere; or (c) Submission match. It was an interesting concept and totally legitimate: none of the performers (including me) knew how many votes each match was getting until the show actually started. However, while all of the other workers at least knew who their opponent was (just not the stipulation), I had to prepare for an Intercontinental title match against one of eighteen possible contenders. Christian, Batista, Shelton Benjamin, Jonathan Coachman, Chuck Palumbo, Billy Gunn, Rosey, Outback Jack, and seemingly everybody else on the roster who wasn't booked were potential opponents.

With all of the possibilities of who I might be wrestling, I went to Kevin Dunn and asked if he could at least tip me off to who the top three finalists were, but he refused.

"Can you at least give me a clue?"

"Sorry, Chris. I can't do that, it's a secret."

I understood that they wanted to surprise the fans, but did they need to surprise me too? It was my match, dammit!

Not knowing what else to do, I gathered all of the potential contenders in a room and asked each one of them what their finish was and what other moves they liked to do. It was impossible to try to put together a match with each of them, and I knew I'd have to call it all completely in the ring with whoever was the lucky winner. I was actually looking forward to it, as usually most of the matches were put together beforehand with the producers and directors knowing all of the big spots in order to catch them on camera. Common sense said that the guy with the most votes would be either Christian, Benjamin, or Batista. I also thought there was an outside chance that

Coach might get voted in as a joke, and if he was, I told Vince that I would have to beat him in ten seconds.

I went to the ring with absolutely no idea who I'd be facing for the title. Then a drumroll played and the results of the vote were put up on the Tron. Shelton's music played and the crowd got to their feet, excited that he had won the election. Shelton was really getting over at the time and his offense and leaping ability were among the best I'd ever seen.

Incidentally, I hadn't been told the finish beforehand either, and after a few seconds referee Mike Chioda told me that Vince wanted Shelton to go over with his finish. That was fine with me, but I'd never worked with Shelton before and had no idea what his finish even was. I whispered, "Okay, but what's his finish?"

Mike looked at me funny and I could tell he was getting more instructions over the IFB that was jammed in his ear. He finally looked up, his instructions complete, and mumbled, "Tawboww munchex."

I couldn't understand what the hell he said, and I asked him again. "Huh? What's his finish?"

"Beeboo Crawtaints."

"What is it?"

"Steve-O Rufinks."

Chioda had a habit of mumbling instructions while in the ring so fans wouldn't understand what he was saying, but now I couldn't understand him either. At that point I had the most confused scowl on my face, and when I saw myself on the Tron, I wondered if Vince thought I had that look because I was pissed that I had to drop the title. In reality I was just trying to decipher Chioda's mumbo-jumbo. When Shelton climbed into the ring, I told him he was winning the match with his finish. He had to suppress a smile as he heard what Vince wanted, and I hissed at him to stop grinning and tell me his finish already.

"T-bone suplex," he whispered with an exultant look on his face.

The match began and I called the whole thing in the ring, which was a challenge, but it turned out to be one of my favorite performances ever. It was such a rush to be flying by the seat of my spandex live without a net, and I got into a zone. Finally I shot Shelton into the corner, and when he reversed me I jumped straight to the second turn-buckle and leaped back toward him.

I wasn't sure what a T-Bone Suplex was, so I came off with my arms and legs extended like Patrick the starfish. I figured that no matter what it was, he could give it to me if I gave him enough space. Sure enough, he caught me in midair and flipped me over his head for the three-count and the victory.

As I watched the ref raise his arm and hand him the title, I felt a wave of pride wash over me. Despite Vince's words in Kitchener, I did feel like an accomplished wrestler. I'd entered the ring with no finish and no opponent and was able to put together a pretty damn good match on the fly. Backstage all eighteen of my prospective opponents gave me a standing ovation, including Shelton, who was still in shock over his title win. Benoit came up to me, full of his trademark intensity, and said, "That was fucking great. That's wrestling right there. Not too many people could do that. What a piece of art. Congratulations."

It was high praise from the best wrestler in the world and a man I considered to be a mentor and one of my best friends.

CHAPTER 34

Hell of a Hand

My son Ash was born on September 24, 2003. He arrived when Jessica and I decided to induce his birth so I could be home to witness it. I worked on a Monday and flew home to attend my son's birth on a Tuesday, and he was polite enough to wait for his dear old dad to turn up before he made his big entrance into the world.

Being a father is the most magnificent feeling in the world, and it was hard to go on the road to be away from my son, but it was my job and I had to make the sacrifice. However I've always made a point of being there for the important milestones, and I made sure to book off work on the day of his first birthday party.

Ash's bash was on Saturday and I'd fly out to the live event in Springfield, Missouri, early Sunday morning. But a few days before the party, reports began circulating that Tampa was going to be hit by a serious hurricane that might shut the airport down. I took no heed, as nothing was going to make me miss my little guy's first birthday shindig.

I was in the middle of the *Blue's Clues*–themed fiesta

Ash is a ham just like his daddy. Note his shark shirt: he's been obsessed with sea creatures his whole life.

featuring a water slide—bouncy house and seventy-five of our closest friends, when my house phone rang. I heard Howard Finkel's distinctive voice on the machine telling me that because of the storm, the office wanted me to fly out that night. I was watching Ash smear cake all over his face and everything else in his vicinity and ignored the call. I disregarded the next three calls as well, but when the phone rang for the fifth time, I picked up and explained to Howard that I would take my chances on flying out the next morning and that was that.

Except it wasn't.

The next day I woke up to a full-fledged hurricane.

The wind was blowing so hard it looked like the palm

There's nothing more beautiful than a mother and her child.

trees in my front yard were going to snap in two. The rain was coming down in veritable sheets and the airport was indeed closed down. It was decided after much deliberation with the office that I would pick up Stacy Keibler (who had also refused to fly out the night before) and drive to Miami to catch a flight to Kansas City for *Raw* on Monday. Stacy and I drove through the aquatic night, risking our lives to make it to the show, but we got to Miami that night (and Kansas City the next day) safe and sound.

When I arrived at the Kemper Arena (where Owen Hart had fallen to his death years earlier), I was told that

Vince and John Laurinaitis (who had replaced JR as the head of talent relations) wanted to see me in his office.

I walked in and Vince said, "It's been brought to my attention that you missed the show yesterday. I want to know why."

"Johnny already knows the reason why, Vince. It was my son's first birthday party and I wasn't going to miss it."

Vince looked a little thrown off, as if he didn't expect my excuse to be that legit.

"I understand that, Chris, but you still should've made the show. If the airport was closed, you should've rented a private plane."

I could've rented a fleet of private planes, but none of them would've been able to take off due to the little hurricane that was going on.

"I'm going to have to fine you a thousand dollars," Vince said sternly.

Fair enough. I'd missed a show (that I wasn't even in the top two matches of) in exchange for being at my boy's first birthday party. Seemed like a good trade-off and I was willing to accept my penance.

"All right, boss, I'll pay the fine, but you might as well make it two thousand and keep the extra grand for next year, because no matter what I'll be at his second party too."

I was, and I've never missed any of my three children's birthday parties yet.

(Another Quick Author's Aside: I never did get fined for missing the Springfield show. And three weeks later when I got my check, I saw that I'd been paid $1,500 for the gig. I'm not sure what happened, but I suspect Vince respected my resolve and decided to forget about the fine and pay me anyway. Either that or somebody fucked up and I'll get a bill as soon as they read this.)

We went back to Japan in February 2005 and taped *Raw* in Tokyo for the first time ever. The Japanese crowds were unique in that they made minimal noise when watching the matches (their reaction to my match with The Rock three years earlier being a notable exception), which was a direct contrast to the raucous North American crowds the WWE was used to.

But the apparent passiveness of the fans caused great concern to the WWE production team. Both Kevin Dunn and Vince asked me why the fans were so silent, and I responded, "Japanese fans appreciate the actual art form of wrestling—they study the matches instead of just watching them. They pay more attention to the nuances of the performance rather than just scream and yell."

Both said they understood, but the silence was madness to them and they ended up adding canned crowd noise to the show, which in my opinion diminished the novel Tokyo atmosphere.

Because we were taping both shows in Tokyo, it was a rare tour that boasted both the *Raw* and *Smackdown!* rosters. The whole crew had gone out to Roppongi the night before and gotten totally shmammered. I don't remember much about the whole evening, except for the fact that I spent a good portion of it trying to convince The Undertaker to let me kiss him on the lips. There was no way the Fonz was going to allow that to happen, *but* he did let me kiss him on the cheek, so it wasn't a total wash.

I woke up the next day feeling like Mel Gibson's publicist, and when I found out I had Benoit in a Submission match, I threw up. I'm not sure if it was alcohol or dread that caused it—but I'm guessing it was a combination of the two.

Working with Chris was always a battle, but combined with the submission rules and the feeling that my head was going to burst open and spew out a geyser of Crown Royal, you can see I had a frickin' nuclear war on my hands.

We spent the majority of the contest exchanging a plethora of holds, and I almost submitted a few times—to vomit. I eventually tapped out to the Crippler Crossface and we shook hands to the delight of the Japanese fans, impressed with our work and our sportsmanship.

I was just impressed I hadn't shit myself.

Afterwards, the legendary Dr. Death, Steve Williams (who was on tour with All-in Japan), congratulated us on the match and said it was the best he'd seen in years. *WWE Magazine* even voted it the Match of the Month.

Match of the Month? Hell, if they knew how hungover I was, I would've received Match of the Decade.

I've always been of the belief that the story leading to the match is more important than the match itself. It can make the difference between the ultimate battle of good and evil that entices millions to pay money to see it or just two half-naked guys slathered in oil rolling around on a mat in their underwear (I think I saw that once in the movie *Rambone*).

That adage was even more relevant when it came to *WrestleMania*, and I'd always had a hand in crafting interesting stories building to my *Mania* matches. Whether it was the basic story of froot guy vs. stuffed shirt that Regal and I had told, the story of the student trying to destroy the teacher that was the crux of my angle with Shawn, or the returning hero coming to get revenge on the dastardly villain who'd severely wounded him that HHH and I had laid out, my *Mania* stories had always shown great creativity and garnered plenty of interest.

That's why I was so disappointed in 2005 when *WrestleMania XXI* from Los Angeles was looming and I had absolutely nothing planned for the show. I felt like the company had relegated me into the dreaded "Hell of a Hand" category, which meant I could always be counted on to have a good match with anyone but would never be considered a money-drawing main-eventer. It wasn't where I wanted to be, and once again I wondered if it wasn't time get some space and disappear for a while.

But in the meantime, there was no way I was going to head into *Mania* and end up on the DVD-extra dark match battle royal that took place before the show every year.

I called Gewirtz, who as usual was lounging in bed with his harem. He was going through his Jessica phase and couldn't decide if he liked Alba, Biel, or Simpson better. So he had simply chosen all three.

He was sympathetic to my concerns and told me he had an idea that might work. He ordered Biel to fetch his notes so he could explain his proposal of a Hollywood Dream Ladder match, that would include six other performers of prominence who also had nothing going on for *Mania*: RVD, Kane, Benoit, Edge, Christian, and Shelton Benjamin. The concept of the match was that the winner would get his dream of anything he wanted fulfilled, which in turn would lead to RVD winning and bringing back ECW.

It wasn't exactly a World Championship match against The Undertaker, but it was better than nothing. He was in the midst of telling me the details when Simpson grabbed the phone from him and hung up, hungry for more vitamin G.

A few days later, Brian kicked the Jessicas out of his place and resurfaced for air. He told me that Vince thought the Hollywood Dream match was a stupid prize for the winner and wanted something else to be at stake. We kibitzed for a few minutes until I suggested, "Why don't we make the match for a contract that guarantees a title shot the next night on *Raw*?"

Brian took it one step further and proposed that the contract would be valid for one whole year and could be used at any time. Vince approved with his sole modification being that the contract had to be in a briefcase, and the Money in the Bank match was born.

A few days later Vince changed his mind and decided that he would rather have me vs. Edge vs. Benoit in a three-way Submission match, despite the fact that Edge didn't even have a submission. I hated the idea as I thought the concept (and the match) would be a hard sell and that the Money in the Bank was much more exciting and better for all involved. The rest of the guys agreed and we scheduled a meeting with Vince and Stephanie to convince them to stick with the MIB; to their credit they heard us out and agreed.

Everyone was glad they did, because the match was a staggering spectacle that came close to stealing the show. Shelton especially was on fire and tore the house down when he ran up one ladder that had been positioned on a slant next to another and clotheslined me off the top. (Shameless Braggart Author's Note: That was my idea.) I fell to the mat and rolled out of the ring to the floor.

As the normally jaded L.A. crowd chanted, "Holy shit," I looked up to see Adam Sandler and Rob Schneider, sitting in the front row.

Sandler yelled in his *Waterboy* voice, "Get back in there, Jericho! Hoo-hoooo-hoooooo!"

I grimaced and said, "What a way for a grown man to make a living. Loved Cajun Man, by the way."

I crawled back onto the ring apronnn and got kicked in the noggonnn by Christionnn.

The MIB was a huge hit and has been one of the highlights of every *WrestleMania* since. It was such a successful concept that it has since spun-off into its very own PPV.

Awww, our little baby is all grown up.

Shortly after MIB I decided I was going to leave the WWE. Physically I was feeling fine, and after fifteen straight years of wrestling, I'd never been seriously injured (besides breaking my arm in 1994) nor had to take any time off.

But mentally I was burned out.

It was getting harder to leave my wife and my son to go to work and it was getting increasingly more difficult to put together matches. Normally I would go into a quiet corner somewhere and ideas for a match would pop into my head rapidly. Now I'd rack my brain for hours and only the most generic of ideas would come.

My drive and desire weren't there like they used to be either, partially because I'd been painted with the scarlet letter of being a "Hell of a Hand," and further down the card in working with guys like Tomko, Carlito, Muhammad Hassan (remember him??). I once again felt like I'd gone down a rabbit hole and returned to 1999.

If I was working in the '70s territory system, it would've been time to pack up my Caddy and move on to the next company. But now there was nowhere else to go, and even if there was, I wasn't interested in wrestling anymore. I wasn't 100 percent mentally into it, and that's a dangerous place to be. It makes it that much easier to get injured, and more important, it's the source of a bad attitude. I was starting to complain more in the dressing room, and I didn't want to become one of *those* guys.

The WWE had been very good to me and I wasn't going to start grumbling and whining about every little thing, setting a bad example and breeding unrest among the entire roster, especially the younger guys.

Plus, I needed to get away to explore my other opportunities and interests. Fozzy had offers to tour the world, but I had no time to take advantage of them. I also wanted to get a place in L.A. so I could seriously study the art of acting. Most important, I had an awesome wife and a young son whom I wanted to spend more time with.

My contract was coming up in July and Johnny kept asking me about re-signing. I kept stalling and telling him I needed to think about it, but in my heart I already knew that for the first time in my life I didn't want to wrestle anymore.

CHAPTER 35

The Hardest Working Man in Show Business

Our WWE bus pulled up to the hotel in Birmingham, England, and I couldn't wait to hit the sackski. We were in the middle of a UK tour of twelve shows in twelve nights and we'd been driving for hours. It was past midnight and I was surprised how many people were still hanging around drinking in the expansive lobby. As I was waiting to get my bags off the bus, the driver told me that there had been a kickboxing tournament at the arena next door that night and both the boxers and their fans were staying at the hotel.

As we walked through the lobby to the elevators, a drunken fan with a skinjob for a hairdo asked HHH for an autograph. He was being obnoxious, so H ignored him and got on the lift to his room. The punter started yelling, "All you wrestlers are assholes! You're all a bunch of pussies!"

One of our referees, Jack Doan, told him to calm down and the guy popped him in the face and tackled him to the ground. I dropped my bags and ran to Jack's rescue, pulling the guy off by fishhooking his eye socket with my finger. Baldboy's friends rushed over to help him, our guys ran over to stop them, the kickboxers and their hooligan sycophants joined the fray, and suddenly the lobby was a Charlestown Chiefs–Syracuse Bulldogs bench-clearing brawl. But even Ogie Ogilthorpe would've skated away screaming from the beatdown the WWE boys were giving the kickboxers and their fans.

Bodies were being batted around like Hacky Sacks at Woodstock '94, and it wasn't the boxers doing the batting. Viscera, a 400-pound behemoth, was simply sitting on one hooligan, giggling as his victim squirmed and wheezed for breath. Benoit had another guy in the Crossface, laughing outright as the guy screamed like he was in Stu Hart's dungeon. I was wandering around tearing the shirts off of random wankers because I felt like it, which was akin to shooting fish in a barrel. At the end of the brawl, I'd collected five of them as trophies.

Finally the cops came and the boxers and their toadies scattered like the Socs after the Greasers defeated them in the parking lot rumble. The cops were WWE fans, and after asking a few questions, they kicked the remaining dregs out of the hotel, got a few autographs for their "kids," and left us alone.

WWE Superstars 1, Kickboxers nil.

The next night after the show in Manchester, we were getting a little stir crazy so we had a massive party in the hotel. Everybody was running between rooms, singing, telling jokes, drinking barrels of whiskey and washing them down with Guinness. A bunch of us were in Hurricane's room when I decided to throw the TV out the window. I was convinced that I had to because Ozzy and

Keith Moon had done it. Helms tried to talk me out of it but I wouldn't waver.

"Nobody will know whose TV it is. They'll never find out!"

"Actually, they will," Hurricane said matter-of-factly. "When they notice there's no TV in this room, they're probably gonna put two and two together."

Bah humbug! I wanted to throw a TV out the window and nobody was going to stop me! I unplugged the unit and dragged it to the windowsill, propped it up, and got ready to toss the telly.

"I am a Golden God!" I screamed and flung the window open.

It cracked about two inches and then locked on its hinges.

I found out that windows in European hotel rooms never completely open, probably for the purpose of keeping drunken Canadian idiots from throwing their TVs out of them. I stood there for a few more minutes trying to stuff the TV through the miniscule opening, but my big moment was gone. Hurricane's room was empty as my audience had moved on to the next party.

So I took all of his sheets, pillows, towels, every bit of fabric I could find and stuffed them into his closet. I unhooked the shower curtains ring by ring (which were filled with helium, making them very light) and put them into the closet too. Then I pointed the showerhead toward the sink.

The next morning when a still loaded Hurricane woke up on his bare mattress and went to take a shower, he didn't notice the absence of curtain until the freezing cold water hit him directly in the Hurricock.

Wassup wit dat?

*   *   *

Vince approached me in England about re-signing and told me that since there was only one company now, there wasn't much negotiating he could do and started talking about a pay cut. I cut him off and said, "Vince, I'd rather not talk about this right now, let's deal with it when we get back to the States."

The talk of a pay cut was another sign that I needed to disappear for a while. But I didn't want Vince to think my leaving was about money so I didn't even want to hear what his new offer was going to be.

A week later in Wilkes-Barre, Pennsylvania, Vince and I walked around the arena into a storage area and had a one-on-one conversation for forty-five minutes.

"Vince, I need a break from wrestling. I need to step back for a while and I'm not going to re-sign."

Vince nodded and asked, "How long do you need? A month? Three months?"

In my head, I knew it would be at least a year, maybe more, but I didn't want to tell him that. "I'm thinking more like six months. I'm mentally fried, completely burnt out."

Vince said, "Yeah, I feel like that sometimes, but I don't have the option to step back."

I told Vince that I didn't want to be one of those guys who gets bitter toward the business because he's not happy. He agreed and offered me a part-time contract to do PR work during my sabbatical, but I turned it down. I wanted to leave the WWE completely and be free to do the things I wanted to do on my own schedule, with no responsibilities or obligations to the company.

His only request was for me to extend my contract by a month and stay until *SummerSlam*.

I asked Vince if he wanted to do a "loser leaves town" match to explain my exit, and he said it wasn't necessary, that it was cliché. He felt it would be better to just have me disappear with little fanfare.

We talked about old-time wrestling for a while longer and then shook hands. As we got up to leave Vince said, "The door is always open for you, Chris. You're an excellent person and a great performer. When you're ready to come back, let me know and we'll come up with something for you worthy of a talent of your caliber."

It was strange for him to use those words considering he wanted to cut my pay and wasn't using me for shit. But it was nice to hear him say them anyway.

Vince was always open to business ideas that could be profitable to his company, and after years of hearing fans chanting "ECW" (which, as Tommy Dreamer pointed out, always sounded more like "EC-Blah Blu Blah") during WWE shows, he decided to resurrect the brand. Like a wrestling Lazarus, ECW lumbered back to life at the *One Night Stand* PPV in the Hammerstein Ballroom in New York City.

Dreamer, who was booking the show with Paul Heyman, asked me if I would like to be a part of the show in a match with Jerry Lynn or Stevie Richards. I asked if I could work with Lance Storm instead. Lance was an ECW alumnus and he was getting ready to retire. We thought it would be apropos to have Lance's career end against the same opponent it began with: me.

One Night Stand was like being in a time warp. The fans in attendance were reliving their youth like grownups wearing demon makeup to a Kiss reunion concert, and to them it was 1995 all over again. I had predicted that they'd be that way, and when I wore my old Lionheart tights and black leather vest to the ring, the fans knew exactly what I was going for and appreciated the homage.

The crowd went nuts for the show, but it was a different style of wrestling from what Vince was used to. After a particularly violent bout between Mike Awesome and Masato Tanaka featuring multiple broken tables and chair shots, I asked him what he thought.

"I wouldn't want to have a PPV like this every month, but it's definitely very unique."

It was unique enough to be a big success, and soon after Vince fully revived ECW to be his third company brand.

I was in a secret limousine driving to a secret location to have a secret meeting with the secret newest member of *Raw*, who was going to make his secret debut on "The Highlight Reel" in St. Louis that night.

Did I mention it was a secret?

It was no surprise when I found out Mr. X was John Cena (not Ed Langley). Cena's star had skyrocketed over the last few months and it was time to showcase him on the flagship show. But Vince wanted to keep his arrival a surprise until the moment he appeared, hence the cloak-and-dagger routine.

That night when I introduced him as the newest addition to *Raw*, the fans were ecstatic to see him. Cena had become the first (and only) performer in years to break into the mainstream and breathe the same rarefied air as The Rock and Steve Austin. I took great pride in the fact that I had predicted his rise three years earlier.

I recognized that since I was on my way out of the WWE, the best way to go would be in an angle with John. I was currently slotted to face Carlito at *SummerSlam* but I knew I could give Cena (who was the champion) a great match and an excellent platform to really make his mark on *Raw*.

I pitched working with Cena at *SummerSlam* and passing whatever torch I had to him, and Vince agreed. I was happy, as I was finally wrestling for the world title again—even if I had to leave to do so. But the prospect of working for the championship rejuvenated me and gave me the kick in the ass I needed to go out of the WWE the same way I came in—on top.

The Cena-Jericho feud was based on me claiming I was more famous than him. We were both world-renowned wrestlers at the top of our game, as well as being actors and musicians. But the difference was I was constantly bragging about all of my fame and fortune, whereas John was humble and thankful. He started calling me Y2Cheap (which I thought was Y2Lame) due to my constant boasting and self-promoting.

As part of the angle, Vince wanted us to do a battle of the bands. I'd played with Fozzy on *Raw* before, but the concept of the band was different then. Now that the gimmick was over and *All That Remains* had done so well in changing the perception of the band, I didn't want to jeopardize all of that positive momentum by putting us in a situation where we were bound to fail. I was such a hated heel that it wouldn't matter how good we were live, we'd still get booed out of the building. Everyone understood my point and it worked out better anyway as we announced the battle, and after Cena tore the house down with his performance, I claimed the audience was biased and would chastise us no matter how amazing Fozzy was. I withdrew from the contest and walked off the stage to massive boos.

At the time, there were rumors circulating on the Internet that my contract was coming due and I would be finishing up at the end of August. I didn't want people knowing that *SummerSlam* was going to be my last match and assuming I wouldn't be winning the title by proxy. So when I signed the one-month contract extension that Vince had requested, I made sure to have wwe.com announce that I had signed a new deal. Extension or not, after nine years I would no longer be employed by the WWE the day after *SummerSlam*.

But three days before the PPV I got a call from Howard Finkel, telling me he was changing my travel plans, as I was now needed for *Raw* on Monday.

Raw on Monday?

Sunday was my last day on the job and I had already made plans with my family for Monday. I told Howard, "Don't change my travel, because I'm not going to be there."

About ten minutes later Michael Hayes called and reiterated that I was needed for *Raw*.

"I'm not under contract anymore, P.S. *SummerSlam* is my last night."

Hayes responded, "Vince changed his mind, he doesn't want you to leave without doing a final angle."

I had asked Vince if he wanted to do that when we had our talk in Wilkes-Barre three months earlier and he had scoffed at the idea. He'd had plenty of time to change his mind, and now, just three days before the show, he was having his minions call and *tell* me I was supposed to be at *Raw*? If he had had some great epiphany and wanted me to stay an extra day, he should've called me himself.

Ten minutes after that, Johnny called me and said, "Vince wants you to have a Loser Gets Fired match, and have Bischoff fire you."

I was getting hotter that Vince still wasn't calling me, and there was no chance in hell that I was going to *Raw* on Monday until he did. I told Johnny I wasn't going and hung up the phone. Ten minutes after that, Vince finally called. I didn't bother answering, as I was too angry, and when I listened to the message, it was obvious he felt the same way.

"I don't know why you're refusing to come to *Raw* on Monday, but you're making a mistake," he fumed. "Do you have some sort of kayfabe deal in Japan where you can't do any jobs?"

Kayfabe deal in Japan? What was this, 1986?

His message pissed me off even more and I knew that calling him right back would do no good. I took a few minutes to settle my little tea kettle (copyright Nattie Neidhart) until I calmed down enough to call him back.

"So what is this, I hear you're not coming to *Raw* on Monday?"

"Well, Vince, I'm done at *SummerSlam*. You had three months to think about this and now it's too late. I have plans with my family."

"What kind of plans? I need you there."

"Well, if that's the case then you should've called me yourself, Vince. Do you realize how disrespectful it was to have Howard Finkel call me, Hayes, Johnny, all of them basically asking me to do you a favor? Everybody is calling me trying to coax me into doing this. Everyone but you! Why didn't you pick up the phone and call me?"

Vince responded, "You are right about that. I should've called you and I apologize."

That's all I needed to hear.

"Okay Vince, I'll be there on Monday."

Vince appreciated my dedication and said he'd take care of me for the match. He stood by his word, and I was very happy when I got my checks for both *SummerSlam* and *Raw*.

On the Saturday night before *SummerSlam*, Jess and I went to the airport and found that our flight to Washington, D.C., had been canceled. Eddy Guerrero and his wife, Vicki, were booked on the same flight, and the four of us decided to stay at the airport Marriot instead of driving back home. We had a great conversation that night and the next morning they were sitting in front of us on the plane. Throughout the flight Eddy kept turning in his seat excitedly to explain the psalms in the Bible that were really inspiring him. He had gone through a recent resurgence in his faith and was very excited about his new spiritual commitment. We shared a laugh about how we'd been in the same company for years but were hardly ever on the same show. When he was on *Smackdown!* I was on *Raw*, and vice versa, and aside from when he "stole" Chyna and the European Championship from me in 2000, we had never worked a program together in the WWE.

I was happy that our original flight got canceled, as it was great talking to him and spending quality time together.

It was the last time we would get that chance.

Cena and I had a great match at *SummerSlam*. He was much maligned at the time by critics and peers as being a subpar worker, but I didn't agree. "It's bullshit, when people say you can't wrestle," I told him. "You're a really good performer, don't let anyone tell you otherwise. Maybe your style is unorthodox, but it works. Don't limit yourself."

John's style *was* unconventional, but so was a little rattlesnake named Steve Austin, and he ended up being one of the best workers of all time.

We built up the match beautifully with our promos, establishing exactly who was the heel and who was the babyface. But despite our hard work, our match started the tradition of certain fans booing John and cheering for his opponent. Halfway through, dueling chants of "Let's Go, Cena!" and "Let's Go, Jericho!" resonated throughout the crowd.

I was a little miffed at first, because I never liked getting cheered when I was working as a heel. But in retrospect I think the fans were rooting for me because, like me or hate me, they respected all my years of hard work and legitimately wanted to see me win the title.

Alas, it wasn't meant to be, and Cena beat me clean with the FU.

The match was a special one, and when we went through the curtain we got a standing ovation. Benoit, Eddy, and Dean (who had started working as an agent) congratulated me en masse and Jessica snapped a picture. It was amazing to have my three best friends in the business surrounding me and sharing in my triumph. Chris, Eddy, and I had been world champions and Dean was now in Vince's inner circle. We had been through so much together and had risen above all of the bullshit to get to the top of this industry.

The four of us shared a group hug and Eddy gave me a huge smile.

"I'm so proud of you for all you've done, bro. I'm also proud of you for walking away on your own terms. I love you, man."

I gave him a big hug and told him I loved him back.

I never saw him again.

The next night in Hampton, Virginia, I had my last match for twenty-seven months. Despite Cena's reservations about having a rematch after our classic the night before, I think Cena-Jericho II might've been even better. The story was that Bischoff and I were in cahoots, stacking the deck to get the title off Cena and get him out of the WWE at all costs. I agreed that the loser would get fired, figuring there was no way that could ever happen with Eric by my side. Unfortunately for me, Bischoff's interference went awry and cost me the match. But before he could fire me, I went down on my hands and knees and begged for mercy.

"Please, Mr. Bischoff. Please don't fire me...I have a son...I have a family! You can't fire me!"

But Eric stood firm and told a battalion of security to escort me out of the arena. The crowd was taking great pleasure with my misfortune, so I decided to take my exit a step further.

I whispered under my breath to the guards, "Pick me up and carry me out of here."

It took them a few seconds to figure out I was serious, as we hadn't discussed it in rehearsal, but they eventually lifted me up and carried me up the ramp like a Mayan sacrifice.

I had no pride and that's the way I wanted it. As a craven heel, there was no way I was going out with my head held high, riding off into the sunset with my loyal fans chanting my name. I wanted to be forcefully removed, kicking, screaming and crying like a coward. That was the last time I was seen in the WWE for more than two years.

Over the next few days, I had a blast reading Internet feedback from fans who were livid that the WWE would treat me so dishonorably and have me exit in such a demeaning manner. Little did they know that the pathetic exit was all my idea.

John and I received another standing ovation when we walked through the curtain. Ricky Steamboat, who had recently been hired as an agent, said, "There was a rumor going around that you were in a slump, Chris, but you're definitely not in a slump anymore. That was an amazing performance. Congratulations!" Not a bad compliment from one of my heroes.

The rumors were right—I'd been in a mental slump and hadn't been performing at the level I should've been. But I promised myself I would go out on top in working with Cena, and I did. After fifteen years of basing my entire life around wrestling, I could now call it a day with no regrets and move on knowing I was walking away at my peak.

Vince echoed those same thoughts when he called me the next day.

"As good as the *SummerSlam* match was, I daresay that last night's was better. Quite frankly, with all due respect to James Brown, you are the hardest working man in show business."

I wasn't yet—but I was about to be.

CHAPTER 36

Buffet Nazi

Castle Donington is the site of the biggest heavy metal festival in England, most famous for drawing over 100,000 people for the 1988 lineup that featured Iron Maiden, Kiss, Megadeth, David Lee Roth, Guns N' Roses, and Helloween. (Headbanging Author's Note: All six of these bands are in my all-time top fifteen.)

It had since changed its name to Download, and Download wanted Fozzy. Bang Your Head in Germany was a good festival, but Download was the granddaddy of them all. We still weren't getting any support or respect from our record company, or from most of the UK rock press, yet we had still risen to the level of being asked to play Download.

We had to hit a home run on our biggest stage yet.

The 2005 Download lineup was amazing, with Black Sabbath, Slipknot, Slayer, Megadeth, My Chemical Romance, and System of a Down headlining, so we had our work cut out for us.

We were the second band of the day on the second stage of the festival, sandwiched in between Celtic punk band Flogging Molly and Finnish shock metal band Lordi. I wasn't sure what to expect from the crowd, especially after Molly had whipped them into a frenzy. I was imagining pure apathy but was pleasantly surprised when the crowd started chanting "Fozzy!" the second Molly's set finished.

We started the set by barreling into "Nameless Faceless," and I noticed two things right away: the stage was huge and the crowd was massive. There were thousands of people waiting to see Fozzy at only 2:30 in the afternoon, but that was how festivals worked. Fans camped out for days and partied for the entire weekend, checking out as many bands as they could. I was on a mission to grab the attention of the 25,000 rockers in attendance immediately. So I ran across the stage and leaped straight off the edge.

I soared through the air and . . . kept soaring.

And soaring.

And then I stopped in midair with my arms and legs flailing like Wile E. Coyote as time stood still.

Then I dropped.

I hadn't anticipated how high off the ground the stage was and I felt like I was falling a hundred feet. When I finally landed in the photo pit in front of the barricade, I felt my ankles buckle awkwardly, like my bones were bending inward to their breaking point. But instead of fracturing, they snapped back into place like rubber bands.

I was lucky they didn't shatter into pieces, and had the passing mental image of being stuck in the pit writhing in pain with two broken ankles before I even sang the first note. But I hoisted myself back up onstage and made it to the mic just in time to hit my cue.

Fozzy was a machine that day and led the rowdy crowd

through an all-original six song set. We jumped, pogoed, headbanged, led chants, got thousands of people to wave their hands in the air in unison and put on the best show we could. After the last note was played we were rewarded with the sound of 25,000 people chanting our name.

It was an incredible feeling and I was so fired up that I didn't notice the flight of stairs leading off the stage. I had just played the biggest gig of my life and conquered thousands of fans, but none of that mattered when I tripped and fell down the steps.

I skidded and stumbled into the arms of a seven-foot-tall masked monster named Mr. Lordi, who was waiting

This mob of 25,000 at the Download Festival in Donington, England, was the biggest crowd Fozzy ever played for. Fozzy's smallest crowd? Twenty-seven people in Windsor, Ontario.

to go on next. "Watch your step, friend," Mr. Lordi said with a thick Finnish accent. "Don't be such a klutz next time."

Olen idiootti!

Afterwards, we were hanging around the backstage compound watching our bass player Sean Delson take advantage of the free haircut that the festival organizers provided to all bands (a haircut at a rock show?). The stylist spent thirty minutes sculpting his coif into an awful outdated style that could only be called "The Joyce DeWitt."

Strangely the helmet hair kind of fit Delson, as he was a comical guy who referred to things he liked as "Your Dad" and passed the time on the road by replacing the "Driving" in *Driving Miss Daisy* with any form of torture he could think of: "Defiling Miss Daisy," "Eviscerating Miss Daisy," "Cornholing Miss Daisy," "Cleveland Steaming Miss Daisy"—you get the gist.

We were thoroughly enjoying his look of embarrassment at his horrible haircut, pointing our fingers and laughing in his face, when I felt a tap on my shoulder.

I turned and saw Dave Mustaine, the leader of Megadeth and one of the best guitar players of all time. I'd met him a few times over the years, and even though he had a reputation for being surly he was always nice to me.

"You guys sounded great today, Chris, and your lead guitar player really knows what he's doing."

We called our guitar player, Mike Martin, "Sir Shred" and "Mr. Holy Shit" due to the reactions he received after he displayed his guitar wizardry. I knew Mike was a big fan of Mustaine's, so I brought him over to say hi about twenty minutes later.

"Hey Dave, this is Mike Martin, from Fozzy."

Dave's facial expression altered into one of disgust like he had just stepped in a pile of Ulrich shit. He stared at the bearded Mike, sizing him up from head to toe.

"You need to shave. You look like a terrorist," he sneered and sauntered off.

Classic MegaDave.

Download was a huge success for us, and even the previously Fozzy-unfriendly *Kerrang!* magazine called us "the surprise band of the day."

The great reviews opened the doors for us to tour the UK yet again and we crisscrossed the country playing more sold-out shows packed with loyal fans. But in typical Jericho fashion, whenever I got too high on my rock-star horse, something always went down to bring me back to earth.

We were playing in Brighton and there were two pretty girls in the front row. When I strutted past them, I noticed them smiling and giggling at me. It was obvious they were digging my vibe and I decided to sing directly to them. They were sniggering now and I thought how amazing it was that I had the power to make girls swoon with my singing.

When one of them pointed at me I pointed right back and kept crooning. She continued pointing and I noticed she was gesturing towards my lower abdominal area. What was this girl insinuating? Did she want to see my love gun? But the weird thing was, she wasn't pointing sensually or with any modicum of desire; in fact the two of them were outright belly laughing now.

Download, 2005. We're a big stage band, we always have been, and it's where we thrive. Seeing 50,000 hands clapping on my lead is a feeling of pure power that I'll never forget.

Confused, I looked down to see what she was staring at and noticed my fly was wide open.

I guess that's why David Lee Roth wore spandex.

A few nights later I was in the dressing room at the Rios in Bradford talking to Jessica after the show. It had been a good gig, accentuated by the fact that Helloween had just played there a few weeks prior. Fozzy was at Helloween's level in Bradford and that was good enough for me.

I was on the phone for fifteen minutes tops, but when I hung up I realized that everyone was gone. The dressing rooms were in the upstairs of the club, and when I opened the door it was pitch black. I turned on my phone to give me some light and yelled out for someone. Nobody replied. As I walked gingerly down the stairs so as not to fall (Mr. Lordi was not there to catch me this time), the security system went off. Claxon alarms were shrieking so loudly I couldn't hear myself think, and I suspected I'd been locked inside the club.

I shuffled through the empty stage area and saw two huge fireproof silver garage doors pulled down over the exits. The owner of the venue used them to make sure nobody broke in (or out). I was stuck inside with the ear-piercing alarm going off and I started freaking out.

"What if that's not a burglar alarm? What if there's a fire in here? How the hell am I going to get out?"

I tried to text our tour manager Toad that I was locked inside the club, but there was no reception and it took me a few tries to get through.

After the eternity of a few minutes, I heard a rattling against the steel doors. When they rolled up on the hinges, a veritable SWAT team walked in. The police told me to step outside and there were four cop cars with their lights flashing and eight bobbies standing around looking annoyed.

"You know I could arrest you for this," said a stern-faced cop who looked like Simon Pegg with a mustache.

"Arrest me for what, sir?" I replied nervously.

"For being such a plonker!"

Pegg and his cohorts burst out laughing, as Rich ran around the corner and shoved a video camera into my face. I'd been punk'd UK style. I didn't see the humor in it, and if Ashton Kutcher would've jumped out of the shadows with his Von Dutch trucker cap askew, I would've punched him right in the fucking boatrace.

Every day Toad gave us a per diem for dinner. It was in our rider (along with a big bowl of Reese's Pieces with the peanut butter removed) that the promoter had to provide dinner for us on gig nights or we would get ten pounds each and buy whatever we wanted. Most of the time (at Rich's insistence) everyone went for Indian food, except for me and Delson. I couldn't stand the spicy cuisine, and Delson just pocketed the ten pounds to save money and ate fruit backstage. ("These grapes are your dad!")

However, when we showed up at the venue in Portsmouth, I was pleasantly surprised to find out a full-fledged buffet dinner had been arranged for us. The chef had created a wonderful spread of Yorkshire pudding, roast beef with gravy, hash browns, cornbread, and roast chicken. It smelled delicious, and after two weeks of truck stops and fast food, it was a feast fit for a king—or at least Prince Charles.

I walked to the front of the buffet, grabbed a plate, and started serving myself. Suddenly the chef marched out of the kitchen and screamed in a thick limey accent, "Who goes there!?"

I'm not kidding with this, he actually said, "Who goes there?" like he was the fricking Beastmaster.

I stared speechless at this slovenly wart of a man who was the spitting image of the keeper of the Rancor monster and decided that he scared me.

"Odds bodkins! What do you think you're doing?"

As the lead singer of the band who'd sold out the club that night, I deserved more respect, and I wasn't going to let this infidel speak to me this way. I was going to have this fat bastard fired!

I opened my mouth, ready to do my best Donald Trump and said...

"YOU'RE...Ummm.... just getting some food?"

Chef Rancor Keeper looked at me with pure repugnance. "Don't you *ever* touch my catering. Only *I* dish out the food! You tell me what you want and I put it on the plate. No one else. Only me!"

Completely terrified at this point, I sputtered meekly, "Can I please get some roast beef?"

He put the thinnest slice of roast beef I'd ever seen on my plate.

"Please, sir, can I have some more?" I asked pathetically, feeling like Oliver Twist.

"No! There's a limit on roast beef!" said the Buffet Nazi.

I shuffled down the line, like George Costanza buying soup. "Can I have a Yorkshire pudding?" He gave me the smallest one.

"Is there any way I can have another one of those?"

"Only one! Everyone only gets one!"

I nodded at Buffet Nazi, happy that he hadn't beheaded me, and sat down to eat the most delicious meal of the tour. The Yorkshire pudding was delightful and it alone was worth the browbeating I received. I wiped my plate clean and patiently waited until everyone else had eaten. Then I made my move and approached Buffet Nazi timidly.

"Excuse me, sir. Now that everyone else has eaten, may I please have another Yorkshire pudding and another slice of roast beef?"

Buffet Nazi stared at me, deciding if I was worthy of a second helping. Finally Buffet Nazi acquiesced and with a death stare begrudgingly put the food on my plate.

I nodded thanks, and as I left to eat my food Buffet Nazi leaned over the buffet and whispered menacingly, "I'm a big fan."

Fozzy had been approached to do a track for a Judas Priest tribute album and we'd decided on "Metal Gods." I was on my way to Atlanta to lay down the vocals and was at the gate waiting to board the plane when my cell rang. It was Shane McMahon, which was a surprise since I hadn't talked to him for months. But as soon as I heard the somber tone of his voice, my stomach dropped 'cos I knew somebody had died.

"I have some terrible news..."

"What is it?" I asked.

"Eddy Guerrero is dead."

I was hit with a horrible case of déjà vu and felt the same way as I had ten years before when Norman Smiley told me Art Barr had died. My body went numb and I lost all the strength in my legs as I collapsed. I tried to ask Shane what happened, but a stifled squeak was all I could manage.

"I know this is terrible. I know how close you guys were. He was in a hotel in Minneapolis and he wasn't answering his phone, so Chavo and Dean went into his room and found him dead. We don't know the cause."

I buckled into a seat and sat there stunned. Tears welled out of my eyes as I thanked Shane and muttered I'd call him later. I hung up and was about to dial home when Jess called me first. She was in a panic: "Shane just called the house—"

Before she finished the sentence, we both started crying together.

I said, "I don't know what to do. Do I come home or go record this song...?"

But as always the show must go on, and I decided to get on the plane and just keep on keepin' on. I still don't know if it was the right thing to do, but it was a plan, something I could follow that would keep my mind off of what I had just heard. I flew to Atlanta, went into the studio, and sang better than I ever had in my life.

Singing is a lot like acting—the more you relate to the vibe and feel of the song the better you'll do. I was so angry and filled with raw emotion that I nailed the song in two takes and said, "Fuck it. I'm out of here."

We had to cancel the first few shows of a Canadian tour we had booked so I could attend Eddy's funeral. A few days earlier, I'd received a call from "Superstar" Billy Graham, asking me if I would say a few words at the service. I was honored but a little confused as to why Graham was in charge. It wasn't like he and Eddy were the best of friends.

When I got to the funeral home Superstar handed me a rundown sheet, as if it was an episode of *Raw*. "Okay. You'll be up fourth and you have five minutes. Make sure you don't go overtime as we have to make sure that Vince has as much time to talk as he wants."

Five minutes? What was he going to do if I talked longer—go to commercial? It was a funeral, the last chance I'd have to see my friend and share my memories of him with others who loved him like I did. If I wanted to talk for an hour I would, no matter how much "time" I had.

I tried to honor my brother by telling tales of how he and I attempted to be roommates on the road, but we got along like Molson and Jose Cuervo. How we got in a fight at a Minneapolis Denny's and rolled around on the floor (Jericho-Sneap style) under the other patrons' tables. How Eddy pronounced filet mignon "fill-ett migg-non." How we were the best tag team that never was and called ourselves "North and South of the Border" or "Eh and Wey." I had no notes, no cue cards. I just got up and spoke about one of my oldest friends in the business, and tried to get some sort of closure.

After the service I went outside and spotted Benoit. He beelined over and gave me one of the most powerful and moving embraces I've ever experienced; he was clinging to me like a newborn baby to his mother. Then he began to shake.

He was crying uncontrollably with these deep, hitching, heartbreaking wails, and the shoulder of my suit jacket was soon damp from his tears. After a solid minute of this, I started to feel uncomfortable. Finally Chris let go and sobbed that he was furious I wasn't asked to be a pallbearer. "That's what Eddy would have wanted."

Every pallbearer had been given a rose to throw on the casket as it was lowered into the ground, and he murmured adamantly, "I want you to have this rose. You have to throw this rose into his grave. Promise me you'll put this in his grave, Chris."

He stared a thousand miles into my eyes, all the while clutching the flower in his fist.

But he never gave it to me.

At the end of his plea he whispered, "I love you, Chris," and then he shuffled away on zombie legs into the shadows of the funeral home.

After the service, Jess and I went to Eddy's brand-new house he'd just bought in Phoenix. Vicki told me that Eddy was in a lot of physical pain toward the end of his life from all of the various injuries he'd suffered over the years.

She also told me that Eddy was proud of me for being able to walk away from wrestling on my own terms. He was envious and wished he could have done the same thing.

The saddest thing about Eddy's death for me was that so many guys have been eaten up by the business and died because of it. But here was a guy who'd battled his demons, beat them, and was at a good place in his life.

It seemed so unfair that God would take Eddy so young, a man who spread the word of the Bible at every chance, a man who stood out as a Christian in the WWE locker room. He never pointed fingers or preached to anybody, but if you had a question about Jesus he was the guy you would ask. It's beyond my comprehension why God makes the decisions he does, but the world could use more people like Eddy Guerrero.

He wasn't perfect. He wasn't a saint. But he was one of the most genuine, humble, sweetest men I've ever met in my life, and I miss him.

I also think about Eddy every time I go to a restaurant and pay the check. One day we went to eat and the bill came. I left a one-dollar tip on a ten-dollar tab and Eddy looked at me, annoyed.

"You should tip 20 percent no matter what."

"Why?" I asked.

"What's two dollars to you? What's four dollars to you? You're making good money. But to the waitress it could be the difference between paying her electric bill or not. Don't be selfish."

I felt like Mr. Pink talking to Mr. White, so I put another dollar down.

To this day, I tip 20 percent no matter what, and all of you waiters and waitresses that I meet can thank Eddy Guererro for that.

In the coming weeks, the WWE did an angle where Randy Orton in trying to antagonize Rey Mysterio would say things like, "Eddy is in hell." Eddy was a devout Christian, and in my opinion he would've been incensed at the thought of using his eternal soul as the basis for a wrestling angle. I was glad that I wasn't working for the WWE at the time, because I would've needed to speak out against it. I called Benoit and asked him what he thought and he calmly replied, "There's nothing I can do about it."

I could hear in his voice that he was as irate as I was, but he was bottling his feelings up inside. After his out-burst at Eddy's funeral, Chris rarely showed emotion when I spoke to him. He always seemed troubled and distant. Little did I know that his problems ran much deeper than I thought.

CHAPTER 37

Dinkus

I flew to Toronto directly after Eddy's funeral to begin Fozzy's eastern Canadian tour, and my cousin Chad came in from Calgary to hang and get a taste of life on the road like a real rock and roller.

I'd known Chad my whole life and he was very wise. As a matter of fact, it was he who had originally explained the birds and the bees to me.

I was nine and Chad was seven and we were having a deep conversation about life when the subject of how babies were made came up. I told him shrewdly that my mom had explained to me that a daddy's seed was passed into a mommy's tummy while they were kissing. (Thanks a lot for that one, Mom.)

Chad shook his head wisely. "No, that's not how it works. Babies are made by cock and cunt."

I can confirm thirty years later that Chad was indeed correct.

The first gig of the tour was in Ottawa and I was scheduled to do an in-store signing a few hours before the show. Doing in-stores was important because they were an easy way to sell records and create awareness for that evening's gig. I was excited to show off to Chad how big Fozzy was getting, as my previous signings in Winnipeg, Calgary, and Montreal had all drawn over five hundred fans and been huge successes.

We arrived at the Sunrise Mall promptly at 4 p.m. and headed to the record shop. I was a little wary when there was no line outside the store, but I figured that a large mob of fans had queued up inside instead.

I was wrong.

When we walked in there were exactly four people at a card table bearing a handwritten sign that said CHRIS JERICHO OF FOZ ^zY—TODAY AT 4. Whoever wrote the sign had spelled Fozzy with only one Z and had tried to compensate by adding a tiny second z between the letters afterward.

Surveying the wasteland, I said to Chad, "Keep your head down and let's get the hell out of here."

We inched our way to the door hoping to escape before I was recognized, but just as we reached the front a security guard spotted me.

"Hey it's Chris! He's here, everybody! Come on and sit down, Chris! Let's get this party started!"

It was a party all right—if parties sucked.

I sat down to a smattering of applause in front of a wall of *All That Remains* CDs, waiting for Artie Fufkin to show up so I could kick his ass for a man.

Usually at an appearance I would sign my name, shake a hand, and move on to the next person. But due to the lack of humanity in the store, I was writing *War and Peace* on each autograph to kill time. "To Yngwie, Thanks for all your support and I really hope you have a good day and I

think you're cool and fun to talk to and yada yada yada...
your friend, Chris Jericho."

Despite my stalling, I was done signing in six minutes.

I was taking a picture with the five rent-a-cops who had
been hired to protect me from all of my rabid followers, when
I saw the owner of the store looking at me like he wanted to
perform an evisceration. I posed with a morose smile on my
face feeling stupid enough already, when it dawned on me
that there were more security guards in the store than fans.

"It's okay," Chad said, shrugging his shoulders wisely.
"Ottawa isn't a big college town."

The attendance for the gig was almost as bad as the
in-store and I couldn't figure out why. We'd played Canada quite a few times on the Happenstance tour and had
done well, so it didn't make sense that we were bombing so badly this time. The attendance never got better:
Toronto, Hamilton, Montreal—all of them showing that
our appeal was becoming more selective.

But the last night of the tour was in London, Ontario,
and as we drove toward the venue, I could see a huge line
snaking down the block.

"All right," I thought to myself. "This is more like it!
The Fozz finally packs 'em in on the last gig of the tour...
better late than never!"

As we got closer I could see that this was not the
most beautiful of crowds: greasy hair, gaunt faces, tattered clothes streaked with dirt. "Well, they might not
be pretty," I thought, "but we're gonna rock them all the
same." Besides, they sure as hell couldn't be any worse
than the crowd at the Murder Junkies show.

"Gonna have a good crowd tonight, boys!" I yelled
jubilantly.

The van pulled up and I hopped out, waiting for the squeals of delight from my adoring fans. But there were none, and after a few seconds I noticed that the slovenly fans weren't in the line for the Fozzy gig. They were in the line for the soup kitchen next door.

Delson got out of the van and commented drolly, "It certainly is a good crowd... for the clam chowder."

We ventured inside and were assaulted by the stench of stale smoke and sour beer. The carpet was tattered and torn, with the stage being a small platform standing only inches off the ground. We were led up a flight of creaky stairs into a pitch-black hallway with a putrid, filthy dressing room at the end of it. The whole place reminded me of *The Amityville Horror,* and it creeped me out.

The walls had been graffitied with pictures of peepees and weewees, with such pearls of wisdom as "I'll fuck you for a fiver" and "Rub poop all over my pussy" written underneath.

It was disgusting and I didn't even want to put my bag on the floor, never mind change. There were a couple trays of congealed cold cuts and overripe fruit that I wouldn't have touched for all the kids in Octomom's womb.

Standing in the dressing room was giving me the heebie-jeebies (yeah, I said it), so I went into the blackened hall to make my way back downstairs. I was shuffling through the dark blinded, grabbing the wall for guidance, when suddenly a section of it stepped out in front of me. I squealed like Justin Bieber touching his first titty, as the piece of the wall morphed into a human being who'd just lurched out of a room. It turned out that the upstairs not only housed the outhouse of a dressing room, but was a hostel for the patrons of the soup kitchen as well.

Suddenly another vagabond ambled out of their room, then another, and soon I was in Anthrax's video for "Madhouse." I shook free like Marion Ravenwood from the skeletons in the snake chamber and ran downstairs to the safety of the stage.

We've always taken great pride in our live performances, but that night the fine fifteen people of London who showed up to eat soup, play pool, and see Fozzy (in that order) were treated to an eight-song, thirty-five-minute set.

Talk about speed metal.

A few months after the carnage of the Canadian tour, we were invited to headline the Delicious Rox Festival in Kansas City, along with Fear Factory and Drowning Pool. After the less than stellar turnouts of the last few months we needed a morale boost, and D-Rox was just the cure (along with more cowbell), as we were told that the previous year's festival had attracted over 10,000 people.

We flew into KC and started driving to the arena—or so I thought.

After a two-and-a-half-hour haul we pulled into a farmer's field with a makeshift stage assembled on it. It was only a few hours before showtime, and just like the Ottawa in-store there were more security guards than fans gathered around the front of the stage. As Delson would say, it was bleak.

Despite the lack of crowd the show went on as scheduled, and I was sitting in our trailer when there was a knock on the door. It was our soundman telling me that one of our fans had been hit on the head with a bottle thrown by a member of a band called American Head Charge (we'll call him Dinkus). I went and greeted the poor girl, waited for the ambulance and took some pictures, then gave her some Fozzy merch. When I asked if any of the American Head Charge guys had come to apologize to her, she told me no and that infuriated me.

I marched straight to their trailer and barged in the door asking, "Are you guys going to apologize to that girl you hit with that bottle?"

Dinkus was sitting in the corner, a dumpy little guy with tattoos and a bull piercing through his nose. "Oh, we're getting around to it."

Getting around to it? That really pissed me off.

"How about you get around to it right now?"

"I told you we'll get around to it," Dinkus said with an attitude.

I got right in his face like he was the drunk on the red-eye to Philly and growled, "Listen, if you don't go apologize to that girl right now we're gonna have a serious fucking problem. And the first thing I'm doing is ripping out that stupid nose ring."

Suddenly he had a total eclipse of the heart and went and apologized immediately. I haven't heard from Dinkus or his band since.

After the girl was whisked away in the back of an ambulance, the promoter informed me that his festival insurance stated if anybody got hurt and went to the hospital, the rest of the show had to be canceled. "You guys are on next but the cops are on the way. Play as long as you can, but when they get here you're going to have to announce that the show is over."

I thought it was lame that the promoter wanted me

D-Rox, 2006. We called our touring drummer, Eric Sanders (second from right), "Rainman," due to his ridiculous knowledge of metal trivia. It actually got quite annoying, especially when I found out he knew more than me.

to be his harvester of sorrow, but we took the stage and steamrolled through "To Kill a Stranger," "Enemy," and "Eat the Rich." We were soaking in the adulation of 147 fans when out of the horizon came a battalion of cops in full riot gear. They spread out the length of the field until they surrounded the entire (lack of) crowd. The promoter gave me the sign from the side of the stage to make the big announcement, and it was time to become the surrogate heel of the festival. No big deal, I'd been booed a time or two before.

"Sorry, guys, I hate to tell you this, but the show is over. If it was up to me, we'd play for you all night, but it's not. It's up to them." I pointed at the perimeter of police who had assembled themselves around the outskirts. "The festival is finished. Sorry, guys."

"Sorry, guys" was the same thing the promoter said a few minutes later when we asked him to pay us in cash as per our contract. "The crowd wasn't what I hoped, and having to cancel the rest of the festival really hurt me as well. But I'll wire the money to your account first thing Monday morning." Of course when Rich went to the bank first thing Monday morning, the wire hadn't arrived. We're still waiting, and I'm confident we'll get it sometime in the next googol. (Educated Author's Note: Google googol to find out what it means.)

Fozzy's next appearance was much more positive than D-Rox, as we were asked to appear and sign autographs for the troops at Fort Benning in Columbus, Georgia, for their annual "Troops Appreciation Day." The soldiers turned out in full force to meet us and it was a humbling experience. Most of the troops were younger guys who were into both wrestling and heavy metal, and being around them and hearing their stories made me understand how much of an honor it was to do something like this for them and their families. These men and women, some of them mere teenagers, were about to go to war in Iraq, leaving their wives and kids at home for the next eighteen months. (I met babies who still hadn't met their fathers.) I never realized that their call of duty was that long, and being with them helped me appreciate the sacrifice they were making. It was the least I could do to spend a few hours entertaining them. After signing for one particularly charismatic private, I asked, "Hey man, can I wear your helmet?"

"Well, I'm really not supposed to, but okay."

I pressed my luck and asked, "Can I wear your jacket too?"

"I'm really not supposed to do that either, but okay."

I put it on and wandered around pretending to be an army man.

"Look at me!" I said, cupping my junk in my hand. "I'm Private Jericho and I've got my hand on my privates!" Brutal I know, but I never claimed to be Bob Hope.

Everyone was having a chuckle at my expense when suddenly the laughter died and everyone started saluting. I turned around and came face-to-face with a four-star general.

He glared at me with his steely blue eyes, with not a hair out of place in his graying crew cut. He had the vibe of a no-nonsense ass kicker and I would've bet junior's farm that he had a few kills under his belt. I'd never been so intimidated in my life. It was worse than when I went to Vince's house for my secret meeting back in 1998.

"You're a funny guy," he said with a glare, both of us knowing he could rip out my jugular at will. He then barked at his troops, "Are you soldiers having a good time?"

"Yes sir," they replied in unison.

"Are these boys being good to you?"

"Yes sir," they replied in unison.

"Good!" Then General Kickass turned to me and said, "I just wanted to see what all the commotion was about over here. You guys are the most popular act today and I really appreciate you coming to take care of these kids. Some of them might not make it back home alive, but today you're brightening all of their days and I thank you for that. Fozzy is welcome at Fort Benning anytime."

Then he stood at attention, lifted his hand to his forehead, and saluted us.

Wow.

We'd been shit on, pissed on, stepped on, fucked with, and pointed at by lesser men, but now we were being saluted by a four-star general.

Fozz bless America.

CHAPTER 38

Sweet Loretta Modern

One afternoon I received a call from Fozzy's booking agent, the Agency Group, informing me that one of their agents in the literary division, Marc Gerald, was interested in talking to me about publishing my life story. I'd been writing since elementary school and had been thinking of penning my autobiography for years, but the WWE had never approached me to write one. After a quick meeting with Marc, he arranged a conference call with Grand Central Publishing to pitch the idea of a book about the life and times of little ol' me.

I was sitting in a hotel room in L.A. waiting to make the call to the Grand Central offices when I received a call of a different kind. It was Jessica telling me that a doctor in Winnipeg called to say that my mom's condition had deteriorated and she didn't have much longer to live.

The news hit me like a ten-ton hammer, and even though I'd been expecting it for years I had to get home ASAP. When my conference call with Grand Central started, I explained that I had a family emergency and didn't have a lot of time to talk. I pitched my idea as quickly as I could and got off the phone, certain there was no way I was going to be offered a deal. But I hardly cared, my mother was dying.

She had turned sixty in September 2003 and had essentially become a recluse ever since. Her body was physically breaking down, her bones were becoming brittle, she had zero mobility and needed assistance for every meal. It hurt her to chew so her food had to be liquefied, she needed twenty-four-hour home care and did nothing but lie in bed all day watching TV. I rarely spoke to her on the phone because she couldn't raise her voice or open her mouth wide enough to talk.

She was also mentally breaking down, becoming anxious, nervous, and paranoid. When I visited her she'd say things like, "Don't talk too loud, they're listening to me here. I'm sure my room is bugged," or "Don't walk around the bed so quickly. The vibrations really hurt me." It was a nightmare and our relationship was a shadow of what it had once been.

She once told me, "If I start losing my mind, I don't want to be around anymore. If I can't be myself mentally I want you to pull the plug." There wasn't a literal plug to pull, as she wasn't hooked up to a life support machine, but I completely understood what she meant.

The way things were going, I had to do something.

So I asked my dad to start looking for places where she could be taken care of on a twenty-four-hour basis, a place where there would be other people in her situation whom she could talk to and befriend. She hated the idea and didn't want to leave her house, but the problem was she just wasn't able to function there anymore. So I made the decision to move her into a care facility.

A few months later, her health was in a horrible state and her body was simply shutting down after fifteen years of fighting. She was taking a myriad of drugs but after a while they were only prolonging her agony and not helping her feel any better at all.

She got to the point where she told her neighbor Connie (who was like her sister, much closer to her than anyone else, including me) that she was done with the drugs. When Connie said that without the drugs she would die, my mom told her she was ready for whatever happened.

My mom didn't have much control over anything in her life anymore, but she did have power over whether or not she wanted to stick around. She had such drive and stubborness (a trait that I inherited directly from her that I call Iron Will); when she made up her mind about something, there was no deterring her.

Now she had made up her mind that she was ready to move on, and that was the end of it.

I arrived in Winnipeg from L.A. on a Thursday night. The doctor told me that she could be alive for two more days or two more months, it was just a matter of how long it took for her body to shut down. I went into her room and she looked frail and almost deformed. I hadn't seen her for a few months and her body had contorted inward as her bones shrunk. She gazed at me and I could see a flash of recognition in her face, but she didn't say anything. She could still talk but was beyond having a conversation, and as the night went on she started blurting out things that didn't make any sense. She asked me to turn her in her bed, and when I told the orderly on duty he said, "She was just turned ten minutes ago, she's not supposed to be turned again for another two hours."

Five minutes later, she asked me again, "Will you turn me?"

A few minutes later she asked me to turn her again and then asked me what my name was. Then she told me to leave her alone.

It broke my heart.

I knew she wasn't in her right mind, but it still tore me apart to have this woman who had meant everything to me acting like I was a total stranger. I sat by her bed for hours and I'm not sure she even knew I was there.

I asked the doctor for his opinion on her condition. He looked at me gravely and said, "You should say your goodbyes and go. You could be here for a month and she's just going to keep deteriorating. I don't know if you want to put yourself through that."

I didn't know if I wanted to either. I knew my mom needed me, but I'd been there for her constantly for fifteen years and didn't think I could handle her asking me what my name was or telling me to leave her alone anymore.

We had a string of Fozzy shows scheduled in Florida and I thought it might be best to just do them and come back to Winnipeg after. It was almost Christmas and I prayed she would make it long enough for us to spend one more holiday together.

I asked my dad for his advice and he thought it was a good idea to get away, clear my head, and come back. I'd been talking to Benoit daily about the situation also and he had the same suggestion. So I made up my mind to do the gigs, and when I went to see her before I left, her condition had worsened. She asked me if I was the repairman and then told me to leave again. My mom was definitely gone and so was I.

Before I left, I touched her hand and asked her to make

her peace with God. I told her she was going to a place where she was finally going to be free to walk again. I prayed with her, asking God to forgive her for her sins and to accept her soul into his kingdom.

When I was done, she smiled and whispered, "Go." Then she closed her eyes.

My mom had always been a proud woman, a beautiful woman, and I'm sure she didn't want me to see her in this state any longer. She didn't want me to see her die. She had always been fiercely protective of me and this was the last way she could shelter me from the rain and keep me safe.

I knew that she loved me, but the lady lying there now wasn't really her. I walked to the door and saw her sleeping peacefully. I took a mental snapshot because deep down inside I knew I would never see her again.

"I love you, Mommy," I said with tears streaming down my face as I turned and ran through the hall, and out the front door of the hospital as fast as I could until I couldn't run anymore. It was minus-30 outside but the weather didn't feel as cold as my heart. I felt like a coward for running away and I was ashamed for leaving my mom before she died.

But I also felt a strange peace, because in some weird way, I was fulfilling my mom's last wish.

Two nights later, on December 4, 2005, I was driving home from a Fozzy gig in Jacksonville and got the call that Loretta Vivian Irvine had passed away peacefully in Connie's arms.

She was sixty-two years old.

Next up was the lovely task of making the arrangements for my mom's funeral. I'm sure I speak on behalf of everybody who's ever had to deal with this when I say it's a horrible experience. Jess and I met with the funeral director and faced a rash of irrelevant questions about my mom's burial that I had never even thought of before. What kind of headstone? What kind of inscription? What kind of flowers? What kind of plot? What kind of receptacle?

Receptacle? It could've been a coffee can from Ralph's at that point. I wasn't ready for all of this, I was still reeling over the death of my mother! Then, after an hour of having my nose rubbed in her passing, the son of a bitch funeral director asked me how I was going to pay for everything! Geez man, can you at least give me a few fucking days to grieve before you present me with a bill?

Two days before the funeral I tracked down the phone number for my mom's ex-boyfriend Danny, the man responsible for her injury. I had been harboring a deep desire to murder him for fifteen years, and I might've actually done it on the day of her accident if it wasn't for the attentive cop who saw the killer in my eyes and warned me not to. But now that she was gone I wanted Danny to know and invite him to the funeral.

I called him and left a message: "My mom died last week and her last few years were a nightmare. I hope you feel good about yourself. If you have any balls at all and want to face me, you'll come to her funeral."

He never showed.

The service was a beautiful send-off for a beautiful woman.

I arranged for her favorite songs to be played, including "Amazing Grace" by Elvis and "Let it Be" by the Beatles, which I chose because my mom had always supported my obsession with the band and had bought me all of their albums by the time I was ten. I still think of her whenever Sir Paul sings in "Get Back," "Sweet Loretta Modern* thought she was a woman..." For her eulogy I just wanted to tell some funny stories about the woman who raised me.

I talked about the time when I was seven and *Star Wars* had just been released. My friend Scott Shippam took a bunch of kids to see it for his birthday party but didn't invite me. When my mom found out and saw how upset I was, she took me to the same theater to see it and bought me a Luke Skywalker and a Chewbacca action figure to boot.

I told a story about how my mom went away for the weekend when I was in high school and I decided to have a party. It started with a few friends, but in true high school tradition it got out of control quickly. There ended up being 212 people in my house (I know this because I kept a list); all I needed was Wyatt and Gary and it would've been *Weird Science*.

The bash started at noon and ended at midnight when I called the cops on my own party, after I saw a guy I'd never met before eating ice cream in my mom's bed.

"Wanna bite, dude?" he said with a toothy grin.

I shoved the scoop up his chute and chased everyone else out instantly, but the house was a disaster and Kelly LeBrock wasn't there to clean it up. I passed out with my house a DMZ and my mom due home at 6 p.m. sharp the

---

*I just found out as I'm writing this that the lyric is actually "Sweet Loretta Martin." I don't care, it'll always be "Sweet Loretta *Modern*" to me.

next day, and when I awoke at 2 p.m., my work was cut out for me. Luckily, a few of my girlfriends (as in chums of the female persuasion—let the record show I had never even seen a booby at that point) spent the night and offered to help me with the cleanup operation.

The girls and I rubbed and polished for hours (stop it—remember, they were just friends, for gosh sake!), picked up the cigarette butts, the beer bottles, and the assorted trash. We sprayed three cans of Lysol in every nook and cranny to try to mask the smell of smoke and beer. We loaded twelve bags of garbage in the back of one chick's Tercel and off they went. All of our hard work had paid off. The house was immaculate—maybe even cleaner than when my mom had left.

I sat down on the living room sofa with a relieved sigh at 5:55, and at 6 p.m. sharp in walked my mom. She took one look around the living room and said, "Why is that vase moved? Did you have a party?"

My mother was a witch.

"No way, Mom. I just had some people over."

"How many?"

"Maybe ten or twelve?"

"Ten or twelve? That's a party!"

She eventually calmed down, but ten years later when I showed her the list and told her there were actually 212 people there, she blew a gasket and grounded me.

I was twenty-seven years old.

I finished up with a story about the time I was sixteen years old and bought beer with my homemade fake ID. I was walking out of the vendor carrying a two-four just as someone was walking in. Out in the parking lot, I triumphantly raised the case of beer above my head like a trophy, grinning at my friends in the awaiting car. But instead of smiling back, they were frantically motioning for me to get back in the vehicle.

"What's the problem," I solicited to Speewee as I slid into the side seat of his Sirocco.

"Your mom just went into the vendor and your dad is in the car *right next to us*!"

Stealing a glance to the right, I saw my dad calmly reading the paper, completely oblivious to the fact that his sixteen-year-old son (who had just bought a case of beer) was looking right at him.

I felt like Ferris Bueller in the traffic jam and crouched down into the backseat whispering frantically, "Drive... *drive*!!"

Speewee pulled away and ten minutes later we were back at his house drinking a nice cold brown and laughing how we'd pulled off the perfect crime. Suddenly the phone rang.

It was my mom.

"What are you doing?" she demanded. I knew from the sound of her voice that I was busted.

"Just watching movies at Speewee's house."

"You've been there all night?"

Nervously I said, "Yeah."

She clearly wasn't buying it and dropped the bomb. "Then why did I just see you at the vendor?"

"Vendor? Why would I be at the vendor? I'm only sixteen years old, Mom!" I laughed nervously as Speewee reveled in my misery by chugging a beerski right in front of my face.

She knew I was lying. "We were just at the beer store and I'm convinced I saw you. Come home right now."

Get back, Loretta.

As I rushed out of the door I heard Speewee say, "Don't tell her about the beer!"

No shit, Speewee—and what kind of a name was that anyway? Swedish?

As I ran home to face the Dragon Lady, I desperately stuffed a couple pieces of Bubblicious in my mouth to mask the smell of the beer. I got back to my house and walked downstairs, dreading the soon-to-be-coming interrogation.

"So you weren't at the vendor?" my mom said incredulously.

"No."

"Your breath smells like gum. Why is that?"

"Because I was chewing gum."

"You sure you weren't at the vendor?"

My mom was slowly breaking me down with her examination. She was better than the FBI. She was the MBI.

"No! I wasn't at the stupid vendor! Enough already, okay, Mom? Give it up."

"Okay, I believe you. I'll give it up," she said.

What? She believed me? Just like that? I backed up slowly, certain that the hammer was still gonna fall, but it didn't.

She looked at me nonchalantly and motioned for me to leave. "Go back to Speewee's and watch the rest of the movie with your friends. I'm sure they're still there."

Well, well, well. I guess she wasn't a witch after all. The MBI wasn't as clever as she thought.

"All right, Mom." I nodded with great aplomb and began to leave. "I'll see you later," I said with a swagger, pleased that I'd pulled one over on her.

"Yup, see you later. Oh, and by the way, don't forget your fake ID."

My heart dropped into my ballbag as she waved my bogus birth certificate around in her hand.

"You left this on the counter at the vendor. When I told the guy you were my son, he gave it to me to give to you," she said indifferently. "You shouldn't be so forgetful, Chris. Oh, and by the way, you're grounded."

I eventually tunneled my way out of my room six months later.

When I left Winnipeg in 1990 my mom meant everything to me, and that's why I felt a lot of bitterness about her accident and still do. I was forced into a world of total responsibility at nineteen years old, and I wasn't ready for it.

I was just a teenager and still needed my mommy, dammit!

Having to be so strong for her sake hardened me as a person and shaped how I am to this day. I feel like some of my innocence was taken from me, as I couldn't lean on my mother the same way after her injury. I felt that it wasn't fair to burden her with my minor problems when she was fighting for her life almost every day.

I also feel like I was robbed of sharing the joy and excitement that comes with growing up and becoming a man. She was never able to see my first apartment or help me decorate my first house. She wasn't able to cook me spaghetti or carrot muffins or pizza or any of my other favorites (she was an awesome cook) that were her specialty. She was never able to come watch me wrestle in the U.S., or see my band play. But worst of all, she was never able to hold her grandchildren in her arms. That makes me the saddest of all. Ash hardly remembers his granny, and she passed away long before my daughters were born, and that tortures me still.

But she was the bravest, most courageous lady that I have ever met, and for good or for bad I'm just like her. I never would have made it as far as I have in my career or in my life if it hadn't been for my mom. She was the best mother a little guy could ask for, always encouraging me in everything I tried and pushing me to follow my dreams, making me feel good about myself.

She was also a fighter, and I'm exactly the same; her Iron Will lives on in me forever.

Thank you, Mommy, for helping me become the person that I am.

I love you and I miss you every day.

A week after the funeral, I got an email from Danny.

He'd gotten my message about her service and apologized for not having the courage to attend. Then he went on and explained everything that happened on the night of my mom's accident. I'd never heard the real story before, because I'd never had the guts to ask. I was always a little afraid to learn the details of my mom's injury, and instead of inquiring, I chose to let my rage toward Danny fester and poison me for over a decade.

But after reading his letter, he suddenly became human again.

I turned his email around in my mind for a few days, then wrote him back demanding he answer a list of questions about their relationship, before and after that fateful night. He wrote detailed answers to every single one of them and made it very clear that my mom's accident tortured him every day and essentially ruined his life.

That's when I realized he wasn't a demon from hell who had meticulously planned out the crippling of my poor mother. He was just a guy who got into an unfortunate argument with his girlfriend and ended up in the wrong place at the wrong time.

When I wrote him back, I still couldn't bring myself to tell him he was forgiven, but said, "After all these years, I think you owe it to yourself to live your life and not let what happened to my mom torture you anymore." It was time for both of us to let go of the anguish and resentment about what happened and move on with our lives.

When I pressed send and the email disappeared off my computer screen a ten-ton weight disappeared along with it. I was released from the chains that had bound me for so long, and was finally free. I hoped that Danny could feel the same way, but I've always feared he might not feel completely liberated because I never completely absolved him for what happened.

If that's true, I'm gonna do that now.

Danny, I totally and unconditionally forgive you for everything that happened with my mother and I sincerely want you to live the rest of your life in peace. God bless you.

CHAPTER 39

CSI: Sheboygan

One of the reasons I decided to walk away from the WWE was that there were other things I wanted to accomplish in my life. I wanted to spend more time with my family, tour the world with Fozzy, and truly study the art of acting.

I was curious as to what I could do in Hollywood, and while I had no great expectations of becoming the next Rock, I still wanted to learn the intricate details of the craft—how an actor studied, how he performed, how he worked, and how he became great.

I found it interesting that whenever I had meetings with directors or producers in Hollywood, they seemed to view wrestling as the redheaded stepchild of the entertainment world. (PC Author's Note: I personally love all redheaded stepchildren.) It was almost as if they thought wrestlers were bumbling Neanderthals who couldn't string two sentences together.

They usually asked me if I had ever done any acting before, and I would think, "Shit, hambone, I've been playing the part of Chris Jericho for years!"

Working in the WWE was akin to show business boot camp. During the six years I was there, I'd learned a little about every aspect of the entertainment world. I'd done action, comedy, drama, worked backstage and in front of a live audience, hit my marks, took my cues, did my own stunts, danced, sang, juggled, and threw my voice. Hell, I could even be a key grip or best boy if I had to.

I did some research and eventually hooked up with an acting teacher in Los Angeles named Kirk Baltz. Kirk was an accomplished actor who had worked with Kevin Costner in *Dances with Wolves*, Oliver Stone in *Natural Born Killers*, and Quentin Tarantino in *Reservoir Dogs*, a movie where he played his most famous role as Marvin Nash, the cop who gets his ear hacked off by Michael Madsen. There's even a Marvin Nash action figure—complete with removable ear.

Kirk was the real deal, a true Method actor who was very serious about the art of the theater, and he was exactly what I was looking for in a coach.

But when I went to his studio for our first class, I had no idea what I was getting into. I thought we were just going to go over a bunch of lines and do a few scenes together. I was pretty good at playing a character and fully expected to take Kirk by storm with my master thespian abilities.

But instead he sat me on a bench in a darkened room and told me to rotate my shoulders while holding them out beside me in the classic Jericho pose. Then he told me to close my eyes and hum underneath my breath—*ummmmmmmmm*—then insisted I bellow out a deep-throated guttural grunt—*Hah!*

I couldn't figure what this witchy hybrid of yoga and therapy had to do with acting. When I posed the question to Kirk, he explained that it was all part of the "dropping in" process, the crux of Method acting. Dropping in helped you to achieve complete clarity, which in turn helped you delve deep inside yourself to pull out emotions from the experiences of your life.

If your character was supposed to cry, you would drop in and bring back memories of when your dog Joe ran away as a child: the emptiness you felt, the tears that streamed down your face, how you felt your world caving in. Then with those feelings still brewing, you would transpose them into your performance onstage or onscreen. It was a technique that the best actors of all time from De Niro to Pacino to Streep studied and utilized, and even though I felt like I was in a cult at first, the more I practiced the better I got.

Just like wrestling.

When I first trained at the Hart Brothers Camp, they had us lie down in the middle of the ring with our knees up in the air and our hands on our chest. Then we would hit the mat simultaneously with our hands and feet hundreds of times. At first I couldn't understand what that had to do with wrestling, until I figured out that was how you learned to bump, which was the foundation of the art form. Bumping properly was the difference between becoming the next Shawn Michaels or Shawn Stasiak, and learning how to drop in properly was the difference between becoming the next Paul Newman or Paul Shore.

I learned two very important lessons from Kirk, the first being that the words on the printed page meant nothing, it was how you delivered those words that made an actor great.

Kirk explained, "If you know how to harness your emotions and express them properly, you can make someone cry by reading the phone book."

We ran through exercises in his class that helped deliver emotion, not lines. The most draining of them all was called "The Ritual," designed to bring out the rawest emotions from the darkest part of your soul. While my classmates did interpretive dances or conversations to dead relatives, I did something different.

I painted a face on a watermelon and brought it to the front of the class.

"Everyone please say hi to Danny!"

It was a few months before my mom passed away and my hatred of him was at an all-time high as her health declined. The class greeted the melon, smiling and playing along with the joke, oblivious of who Danny was.

"I want you to meet the son of a bitch who paralyzed my mother and ruined my life."

The smiles drained off their faces and I proceeded to tell Danny Melon everything I'd been holding inside since my mom's accident. Then I took a knife and started stabbing him, taking out my murderous anger before bursting into tears.

When I was done, the class was crying too, including Kirk. It was the first time I really understood what true acting was. If I dropped into character and pulled out my real emotions, I could make people believe. I could make them cry. I could make them feel what I was feeling. And I liked it.

The second lesson I learned was the art of making

choices. This was the process that an actor used to decide the quirks and nuances of the character that weren't written in the script. Johnny Depp made the choice to portray Captain Jack Sparrow as a Keith Richards–esque rummy. Heath Ledger made the choice to have the Joker slurp after every sentence. Mike Myers made the choice to make *The Love Guru* unfunny. Making choices was an actor's most valuable tool and something I'd never considered before.

With my newfound knowledge and respect for acting it was time to hit the pavement to find a gig. Auditioning in L.A. was a whole new world, and I found out quickly that my international superstardom from the WWE meant nothing in Hollywood. But I had no problem checking my ego at the door and starting at the bottom; that's where I started in wrestling and in music and I'd done okay with those.

Still it was quite the experience to walk into an audition for *CSI: Sheboygan* and see ten other dudes who looked just like me reciting their one line over and over. Then I'd get called into the room and stand in front of four or five producers (who looked like they had just eaten sour grapes) and deliver my line.

"Hey you, take your damn hands off of her!"

They would say thank you and I'd leave with no feedback, no comments, and no idea how I did.

I auditioned for a remake of *The Rocky Horror Picture Show* for the role of Riff Raff, and had to sing an a cappella version of "Time Warp" in front of the producers. It was brutal. I didn't know the words, the song, or what key it was in. I was asked to leave, and I felt like one of the rejects from the first few weeks of an *American Idol* season.

During another audition, I was in the middle of an impassioned read for the movie *Beer League* when the phone rang and the casting director *took* the call.

"Hold on a second," she said drolly as I stood there like Johnny Drama. Needless to say, I didn't get the part.

When I showed up for an audition for *Cashmere Mafia*, I was puzzled to see a bunch of seedy long-haired biker types standing in line. I took my place at the back and waited, wondering how they were going to get through so many people in the twenty minutes until my turn.

"We're gonna get to film in some pretty exotic locations if we get this," said one particularly disheveled scumbag wearing a do-rag and a Molly Hatchet shirt.

"Exotic locations?" I thought as I fixed my suit. "The show takes place in New York City."

Then a PA showed up with a clipboard, and after asking my name said I wasn't on the list.

"But I have an audition."

"For what?"

"*Cashmere Mafia.*"

He smirked and told me I'd made a mistake and was standing in line for the pirate movie.

So I went over to the proper line, ready to impress and get the part. I'd worked on the scene for a week and felt great about my chances. It was a dramatic part and I'd dropped in by remembering how I felt when Horshack, my pet goldfish, died when I was six.

I was full of emotion as I started my performance. "I can't believe she's dead. Leprosy is a terrible disease, but I never thought it would—"

"Arrrrr be darrrr!"

Wawazat?

I wasn't sure what I'd just heard, but whatever it was, I wasn't going to let it affect my performance.

"I have to come to terms that she's gone forever and—"

"Shiver me timbers!"

What the hell *was* that? I composed myself and continued.

"But I will always love her and—"

"Walk the plank, matey!"

"I need more growling, guys!" yelled another voice through the paper-thin wall. "You're pirates, *give me more pirating!*"

I forged ahead. "She will always be the wind beneath my wings—"

"Yo-ho-ho and a bottle of rum!"

"Is anybody else hearing this!?" I snapped at the moon-faced casting director.

"Well, of course I hear it but if you can't concentrate, maybe you're not ready for this part?"

She was right. I wasn't ready to read with the crew of the *Black Pearl* peg-legging it next door. It didn't matter as my career was on its way down to Davy Jones's locker anyway.

No matter how good or how bad I was, I just couldn't catch a break. Over the next few months I auditioned for parts in *The Oh in Ohio, The Believers, Beer League, Beerfest, Into the Blue, The Dukes of Hazzard, The Devil's Rejects, Knocked Up, Transformers, X-Men 3, The Longest Yard, Wild Hogs, Meet the Spartans, Shoot 'Em Up,*

The Fog, *Gone Baby Gone*, and *Banana Hammock Boys Gone Bad* (actually I did get the part in *Banana Hammock Boys*). That's a combined gross of $1,265,367,185 for the movies I didn't get cast in.

I'm the bizzaro Samuel L. Jackson.

I hadn't booked a job in months and was getting quite discouraged, when a call came in from the Sci-Fi Channel offering me a part in a movie called *Android Apocalypse*. It wasn't exactly *Transformers*, but it was the first offer I'd received and I was thrilled. I was visiting Chad and Speewee in Calgary and had to be on the set in Regina the next day, so the producers arranged for a limo to drive me the five hours so I could make my early call time.

Chad had wisely suggested that the limo company provide me with pillows and blankets so I could sleep during the trip. They set up a makeshift bed on the floorboards of the spacious car, and as soon as we started driving, I dozed off.

A few hours later, the car slowed down and I heard the driver say he needed gas. I looked out the window and saw it was 3 a.m. and we were stopped at a Shell station besieged by a swarm of teenagers. I laid back on the floor and closed my eyes.

Suddenly someone started banging on the windows.

"Hey, it's a VIP! Who's the big shot in the limo?" an obnoxious voice slurred.

I was completely flummoxed that the driver had decided to stop in the middle of a sea of drunken kids and totally pissed that the dipshit wasn't even gassing up the car, but was inside buying a Coke instead. Then the yelling intensified and the door of the limo flew open. A chubby farmboy wearing a Clint Black sweatshirt stuck his head inside the car and said, "Who's in here??"

"Get the fuck out!" I threatened as I untangled myself from underneath the covers. I had taken my shirt off earlier and his eyes widened in amazement as he saw the naked man squriming on the floor.

"Somebody's having sex in there! Everybody come here!"

I kicked Clint out of the car and reached to close the door, but his friends had arrived and were trying to pry it back open. I felt like I was battling with a horde of undead zombies who wanted to eat my flesh instead of a horde of horny farmboys who wanted a glimpse of some. After a few seconds of struggling, they managed to fling open the door and suddenly there were two of them in the car.

"Where's the girl?" asked another bumpkin, this one in a "Wine Me, Dine Me, 69 Me" trucker's cap.

"There is no girl in here, just me, you idiot!"

Wine Me looked at Clint in amazement and said, "He's jacking off!"

They cackled at the fact they'd caught a guy wanking himself on the floor of a limousine.

"I'm not jacking off!" I hollered as the two stooges climbed out of the car.

"Hey, there's some guy in here pulling his pud!"

"I'm not pulling my pud!!" I yelled out the door, slamming it shut and locking it as the dopey driver returned and put his snacks in the car.

"Let's go! Let's get the fuck out of here!" I shouted.

"But I still need gas—"

"Forget the gas, let's get out of here now!!"

As he drove away I saw another wave of pervert

zombies shambling toward the car to get a glimpse of the parking lot peep show.

"I'm not pulling my pud!" I yelled out the open window.

I'd been cast in *Android Apocalypse* in the role of Tee-Dee (who coincidentally was an android), and the first scene of the day involved me and my costar Joseph Lawrence (Whoah!) getting into a firefight with sentinel robots who had been sent to kill us. The scene called for us to run through the canyon shooting our rifles at a red light, which would later become a CGI flying robot. I was given an actual rifle that shot dead rounds and we were coached on how to fire so the shells wouldn't fly out and burn anybody.

I made the choice that Tee-Dee had been hit with shrapnel in a previous battle and walked with a slight limp. To make sure I didn't forget my choice I put a rock in my shoe. I was a veritable De Niro in *Raging Bull*. The problem was the stupid rock made me take a bad step just as I fired my rifle. When the director yelled cut, one of the extras reached in her shirt and pulled a smoking cartridge out from between her boobskis.

"Not a bad shot," I thought to myself.

Android Apocalypse was a great experience and I really turned some Hollywood heads with my three minutes of screen time. Hey, everyone has to start somewhere, right? I mean, Arnold Schwarzenegger's first movie was *Hercules Goes Bananas*, and I know this was better than that one.

Absolutely.

After I wrapped *Android*, I hit the streets once again to take meetings. In Hollywood you don't have meetings, you take them. And where you take them I have no idea. To dinner? To the carnival? To a Chumbawamba concert? I guess only Bronson Pinchot knows for sure.

I had just taken a meeting at Paramount, and when I walked out of the office I saw Matt Dillon a few feet behind me. I was stoked to be in the presence of Dallas Winston himself. Of course I was too froot to say anything, but I gave him a half-smile with a slight nod, and he reciprocated my greeting. We walked down a flight of stairs to the valet parking area, and as Matt approached the attendants, they halted their conversation and began nudging each other, obviously excited to see such a legendary performer. As he reached the bottom of the stairs the three valets were practically jumping up and down they were so excited. Dillon gave the first one his ticket and the guy broke out into a huge grin, not able to contain his excitement any longer.

"Oh my God! I can't believe it! You're my favorite!"

Matt smirked at the valet's enthusiasm.

"I've been waiting for so long to meet you...Mr. Jericho!" the guy said, turning his attention directly to me.

Dally looked completely bewildered as the valet and his two comrades shook my hand and clapped me on the back. "We're big fans, Y2J!"

Dillon gave me a look as if to say, "Who the fuck are you?" I gave him a look as if to say, "Well, I'm the shizznit, aren't I?"

He stared at me for a moment longer, then drove away in his Jaguar. I got into my Taurus, and realized I was the shizznit no longer.

Later that day I took another meeting at New Line Cinema, and when I walked into the execs' office I was surprised to see my old friend Jeff Katz sitting behind the desk. I'd first met Katz when he'd gotten a job as an Internet reporter in WCW at age sixteen. Bischoff had admired his drive and determination and hired him to work in the then fledgling online division. I respected his gumption for getting himself employed by his favorite wrestling company at such a young age. If I'd had the chance when I was sixteen, I would've done the same thing.

In the years since I'd last seen him, he had moved to L.A. and been the driving force behind the *Freddy vs. Jason* movie, simply because it was a showdown he'd always wanted to see. He approached the task of getting the film off the ground the same way he'd got himself hired in WCW—with pure determination. *Freddy vs. Jason* was a huge hit, making $115 million, and a few years later Katz was one of the top young executives in town.

Jeff started introducing me to his friends in Hollywood, including an up-and-coming director named Eli Roth. Eli had just released his first movie, *Cabin Fever*, which had become a surprise box-office hit, and I thought it was great.

We met at a breakfast place in Hollywood and hit it off instantly when we found out we were both obsessed with *American Movie*, a little-known documentary about a scatterbrained small-time filmmaker from Wisconsin. We entertained ourselves by trading quotable quips from the movie, excited to find somebody else who had actually heard of Mark Borchardt. I started to hang out with Eli whenever I was in L.A., and eventually he extended the offer to stay with him whenever I was in town.

Eli and I were kindred spirits, both of us obsessed with

Italian horror movies, Iron Maiden, and everything '80s. The first time I went to his place in the Hollywood Hills, it wasn't surprising that his address was the last house on the left. The first thing I noticed when I went inside was a movie poster for the early-'80s Willie Aames/Scott Baio classic *Zapped*. He got me a cold pumpkin beer, and as I took the first delicious sip, I recognized the weird synth music playing in the background.

"Hey, is that the soundtrack of *Zombie*?"

"Yeah, it is!"

I nodded approvingly. "I don't know what's worse, the fact that you're playing the soundtrack to *Zombie* or the fact that I recognized it."

One night we were discussing the intricacies of *Cannibal Holocaust* when he told me he had an idea for a movie that he wanted to make quickly in between the projects he already had booked. It was called *Hostel* and was about a group of college kids (aren't they always?) in Europe who get kidnapped and sold to the highest bidder to be tortured and killed. He explained the plot in great detail (including the Japanese girl getting her face burned and her eye cut out), and I thought it was a froot concept.

He eventually pitched it, got it greenlit, and *Hostel* ended up earning $80 million worldwide, making Eli one of the hottest directors in Hollywood almost overnight.

Months later after he'd completed filming he invited me to a private test screening for the Lions Gate studio executives. They were literally putting the finishing touches on the print while we watched.

"Could you add some color there? We need some contrast here."

It was incredible to see Eli's vision translated onscreen

almost exactly the same way he'd described it to me initially. I reacted loudly to some of the gory parts and afterwards two of the execs quizzed me about what I liked best about the film and took notes when I gave my answers. So it's quite obvious to me that without my amazing feedback *Hostel* wouldn't have been half the success it was... right?

My time squatting at Eli's place came to an end when I came home one night and found the front door open. I snuck inside and saw Eli working diligently in his office with his back to the entrance. I crept up behind him like Belial and slapped him on the back hard, screaming, "Muahahahahahahahaha!"

He jumped out of the chair in shock and I burst out laughing.

"Ha-ha! Looks like Mr. Horror Man is scared!! Ohhh, you ain't so scary now, are you, *Hostel* boy!"

He didn't invite me back to his house for three months.

CHAPTER 40

The Baby-Faced Assassin

When I was growing up I originally had three dreams: to be a wrestler, a rock star, and a hockey player. As I got older, the hockey dream died when I found out that I just wasn't very good. But I still followed the game meticulously and played for fun in the local rinks whenever I could.

But I never imagined I'd play in the most famous arena in the world until I got a call in December 2000 from the New York Rangers asking me if I wanted to take part in a charity hockey game at Madison Square Garden organized by Christopher Reeve.

A chance to play hockey in MSG? Gee, let me check my skedge...

I was totally keyed up to follow in my father's skate-strides and play in the same battleground where he had become famous, especially since Chris Reeve was involved.

I had been following Chris's progress as a quadraplegic for years, and his advances in the field of spinal cord injury were a real inspiration to me and my mom. His condition was actually worse than hers, as he needed a breathing tube to function, but he had an unbelievably positive attitude and honestly believed he would someday walk again.

He was also highly respected in the entertainment world, and the Superskate became the talk of the town. I found myself shmoozing with such Hollywood A-listers as Cuba Gooding Jr., Michael J. Fox, Kiefer Sutherland, Boomer Esiason, Tim Robbins, and Matthew Modine. I hit it off with David Boreanaz, who gave me his cell number. I complimented Rick Moranis on his work with *SCTV*, but with every mention of Jerry Todd, Skip Bittman, or Linsk Minyk all I got was a simple nod and a mumbled "Thanks." Susan Sarandon was the coach of my team and called me her supermodel. Dammit Janet, I love you.

Brad Roberts, the singer of the Crash Test Dummies and my old guitar teacher from Winnipeg, sang the national anthem. When I skated over to say hi, Brad had no idea who I was and mmm-mmm-ed away midsentence.

But I got a great reaction from the MSG aficionados when my name was announced, and it motivated me to put on a good show. I spent the first half of the game horsing around with Theo Fleury, Bryan Leetch, and Glen Anderson, before dropping my gloves and challenging Denis Leary to a fight. We worked it like a wrestling match as we circled each other milking the crowd for cheers. Then we embraced arm in arm and skated off the ice while stripping off our equipment à la Ned Braden in *Slapshot*.

After the game I was entered in the breakaway portion of the skills contest. I skated down the ice on Rangers goalie Kirk McLean and took the weakest slapshot ever unleashed in the history of the Garden. It fluttered off the ice like a drunken bat and floated end over end directly over the shoulder of McLean. Maybe he wasn't paying attention or was merely mesmerized by my atrocious shot, but it didn't matter. I lost my mind and did a victory lap around the ice, then ran in place like the Baby-Faced Assassin before riding my stick like Tiger Williams.

I had just scored a legitimate goal on the netminder for the New York Rangers in Madison Square Garden.

You can file that one under Most Awesome Experiences of My Life.

At the end of the night, both teams lined up in the center ice and Chris wheeled out to say a few words. "Of all the hockey games I've ever seen...that one was the worst." He worked the crowd like a pro, confident, funny, and appreciative of all of us who had made the night so special. I went and shook Chris's hand, and the first thing I noticed was how big of a man he was sitting in his chair. He instantly reminded me of Droz. I introduced myself, and after a few minutes of chitchat I told him my mom was a quadriplegic and that he was an inspiration to us both.

"You tell her I said not to give up...ever. We'll both walk again someday."

His optimism was contagious, and at that moment I believed he was right.

I was invited back to Superskate the following year, and in keeping with the annual tradition of getting into a fight, I asked Chad Smith, the drummer of the Red Hot Chili Peppers, if he wanted to tussle.

I'd met Chad (who was a dead ringer for Will Ferrell)

earlier in the day and he was friendly, funny, and slightly off his rocker. Who can blame him—he was both a drummer and a goalie. I guess if you hit things or get hit with solid objects for a living, you have the right to be a little bit crazy. If you do both, you must be totally insane.

I told Chad my plan during the second intermission and he was totally into it. I would wait until the play was in his end, and when the puck cleared and the play moved up ice, I'd stay behind and challenge him.

About three minutes into the third, the opportunity arose and it was go time. The both of us threw off our gloves and began to circle each other. The crowd was buzzing at the prospect of Pepper vs. Paragon and we had them right where we wanted them.

"Okay, man, I'll take a swing at you, you duck and throw a swing at me. When I go down you jump on top and start punching."

I took my swing, he moved then pounced on me and started throwing hands. But instead of the show business punches I was expecting he was walloping me in the face for real. There I was in the middle of the MSG ice getting the shit kicked out of me by a rock star. I felt like Rocky Balboa during his exhibition against Thunderlips.

I threw the funky monk off desperately and skated away as fast as I could, but he chased me down and tackled me again with a desecration smile.

If you see me getting high knock me down, indeed.

The next year I agreed to play again on one condition— my dad had to be invited too. His participation was a no-brainer, as Ted Irvine was one of the most popular

Rangers of all time, but I insisted we had to be on opposite teams.

Why did I do that?

Because I wanted to fight him, of course.

I surprised him on Christmas morning with a plane ticket to NYC, and he got tears in his eyes when I explained what it was for. He would be returning to play hockey on the hallowed ice of the Garden for the first time in twenty-five years.

To have him come to MSG to see me work at *Royal Rumble* a few years earlier was froot, but to fly him there to play hockey was incredible. He got a great response when he came out on the ice from the New York fans, who are among the most loyal in the world. Once you play in the Big Apple, you'll be remembered for the rest of your life. I can't tell you how many times people come up to me on the street or in the arena in New York and ask me how "Number 27 Teddy Irvine" is doing.

We lined up on the opposite blue lines for the national anthems (Brad Roberts was nowhere to be found) and I could see my pops had his game face on. He was skating in place with a scowl on his face, and from the distant look in his eye, it seemed like he was having some sort of Vietnamesque flashback to his glory days of 1971. I started having second thoughts about challenging this man (who had once taken down Dave Schultz) to a fight.

We were about four minutes into the game when Teddy whipped down the side of the ice and scored a beautiful goal. After he scored another in the second period, I made my move. I sticked him in the meat in the back of the leg (the part that really hurts) and dared, "Let's go, Irvine!"

His gloves were on the ice before the words left my mouth.

The crowd went nuts, as MC John Davidson (Hockey Historian Author's Note: Davidson is the guy my dad was traded from the Rangers to St. Louis for.) yelled electrically, "Here it is folks, what we've been waiting for… Irvine vs. Irvine!"

He was looping around me like an uncaged animal as I kept telling him, "Wait for it, Dad. Wait for it."

When the cheers reached a crescendo I said, "Now!" and we were off. Using the same spot I did with Chad Smith, I threw a punch, he moved and threw one back. I went down and he jumped on top of me. And for the second year in a row, I was in the middle of the MSG ice getting the shit kicked out of me—except this time the shitkicker was my own father.

As he was slapping me around all I could think of was that he was getting his revenge on me for denting his car when I was sixteen.

To make things worse, not only did I get a beating from dear old Dad, but the son of a bitch (Confused Author's Note: Does that make me the son of a son of a bitch?) won the game MVP as well. He skated away with the trophy and the glory, leaving me in his ice chips.

It was a little embarrassing, for sure, but it was also one of the best times I've ever had with my dad.

The Baby-Faced Assassin 1, Y2J 0.

One of the frootest moments of my life was playing hockey with my dad in Madison Square Garden. Seeing him in action up close and personal made me realize just how damn good a hockey player he was. His speed (even at fifty-eight years old) was amazing.

CHAPTER 41

Yes, and . . .

Paul McCartney had just finished playing "Got to Get You into My Life" and the crowd was going wild. He was performing his first concert in Tampa in three years and I'd flown in Speewee, Rybo, and Chad so we could all see it together. They are as obsessed with the Beatles as I am, and we were all getting schooled on how to put on a show by the biggest rock star in the world.

Sir Paul had the crowd in the palm of his hand and was holding his famous violin bass aloft as a grand piano rose up behind him from an opening in the stage. He kept walking backward as he basked in the roar of the crowd, seemingly oblivious to the opening in the floor. But I had a bird's-eye view of the stage and I could see that he was going to fall right into the pit.

"Look out, Paul!" I yelled in slow motion, as Chad nodded his head wisely.

But my efforts were futile and Paul tumbled over the lip of the stage and landed back first on the piano. Twenty thousand cheers stopped on a dime and the crowd went silent.

A roadie jumped into the gap to help, and I could see Paul was shaken up. But after a minute or so Macca thrust his arm in the air and gave us the thumbs-up sign. Blackbirds began singing and all was well in the world!

He climbed back onto the stage and said drolly, "Well, we've got a slight change in the set. I'm now going to play a song called 'Fixin' a Hole.' "

Even though Paul felt fine, he could've been seriously hurt, and I was certain someone in his crew was going to get fired. Surely a roadie had failed to give Paul his cue or the trapdoor had opened too early by mistake?

It wasn't until months later when I saw him play again in L.A., that I found out what really happened. Paul had once again just finished "Got to Get You into My Life," and as the piano was rising from under the stage, he mentioned the mishap in Tampa.

"I was there!" I yelled, as Kurt Russell and Goldie Hawn turned their heads in annoyance from the row in front of me.

"I forgot that the hole had opened onstage and I fell in because I wasn't paying attention. I was too busy flirting with two birds in the first row."

And in the end the love you make is equal to the falls you take.

The next morning I flew from Tampa to L.A., as I'd been hired by the TV Guide Channel to cohost their red carpet Emmy Awards preshow with Joan and Melissa Rivers. The Rivers ladies had been hosting the show for years, and the producers thought it would be a good idea to add a male presence to the carpet and tapped me to do the job.

When I arrived in L.A. I was whisked away to be

outfitted in a Gucci tuxedo, Prada sunglasses, and Ferragamo shoes, while a hairstylist worked on my hair and a makeup artist powdered me down. Then a limo drove me through a plethora of security checks and searches and dropped me off at the red-carpet area.

There the producers explained my assignment for the evening. The two-hour show would start and Joan would do her introduction, then about ten minutes in she would throw to me and I would interview random celebs on what they were wearing, who they were doing, the typical b.s. It sounded easy enough and was a great opportunity for me to be seen by a different audience and show off my shining personality.

The producer explained, "We've seen your work and we know what you can do. You have great improv skills. If Joan wants to banter with you, just do your thing."

Fair enough; I wasn't afraid of Joan Rivers, and I had even prepared a few jokes to throw at her if she got a little smart.

I was positioned on the edge of the carpet and was told by a gargantuan bouncer that under no circumstances was I allowed to put my foot on the carpet in any way. The show began and I waited for my cue armed with earpiece and microphone.

Ten minutes went by and Joan didn't pitch to me.

Twenty minutes went by and Joan didn't pitch to me.

I asked the producer when she was going to throw to me and he said, "Real soon."

Forty-five minutes went by and she still didn't pitch to me.

I started to think that the fix was in—she hadn't pitched to me because she wasn't going to.

I was furious. I'd left my friends in Tampa and rushed

out to L.A. to stand on the edge of the carpet (in camera range so everyone could see me standing there with my Emmy in my hand) and be completely ignored by a frozen-faced septuagenarian.

What made even less sense was that *TV Guide* had shelled out some decent cash to get me there: first-class air, five-star hotel, and an impressive payoff to do the show. Why had they bothered if they were just going to ignore me?

I was about to lose it when Ricky Gervais waddled past, flashed his shark smile, and said, "Cheer up, mate!" He made me laugh in spite of myself and I decided I might as well enjoy myself since there was nothing I could do at this point anyway. Besides, who knows, maybe I was wrong and Joan was still going to pitch to me at some point. (She didn't.)

A few minutes later my old Superskate sparring partner Denis Leary walked by and I clapped him on the back, happy to see him. He gave me a puzzled smile and continued on his way. Soon after, another Superskate alum, David Boreanaz, strolled by. He'd given me his cell number at the Skate, so I figured *he* would remember me.

"David! Chris Jericho. How's it going?"

"Good, good. Wow, good to see you . . . well, gotta go inside."

I got revenge and deleted his number from my phone.

I spent the next twenty minutes with my foot *directly on the red carpet* (the bouncer would've been so pissed, heehee) until the debacle finally ended. I stormed backstage to ask the producer why they had bothered to hire me just so I could stand on the red carpet like a buffoon. He apologized profusely and explained, "Joan wouldn't pitch to you. We kept telling her to but she wouldn't. I have no idea why."

Right then Rivers toddled backstage and gave me one of the fakest smiles I've ever seen in my life, both physically and metaphorically. "There you ah! I saw you on the carpet and you ah so handsome. I wanted to pitch to you but I was never given the cue!"

I punched her right in her plastic face, collapsing it like a house of collagen cards.

I popped back into reality and fake smiled right back. "Oh, it's okay, Joan. Things happen and I had a great time anyway."

"Are you a wrestlah? Is that what you do?"

"Yes . . . among other things."

Her eyes lit up and she seized her chance. "Well, let me know if you ever want me to appear on your wrestling show. I would be happy to come on and help you out. Now, here's my card—send me a self-addressed, stamped envelope and I'll send you an autographed picture, dahling."

This time I caved in her fabricated fuckface for real.

When I got back to Tampa, everybody was feeling sorry for me.

"You were just standing there and I felt so bad for you," Chad said. "I kept waiting for you to do something, but alas it never happened," he continued wisely.

I'd been embarrassed in front of my cousin again. The last time he was involved in one of my endeavours there were more security guards than fans at my signing in Ottawa. Now he had watched me for two hours standing with my finger up my nose on the red carpet at the Emmys.

For Chad my fame was like Snuffleupagus—it disappeared whenever he was around.

After my stellar appearance as a red-carpet mannequin, I hit another Hollywood dry spell. It was a couple months before I got my next gig, a guest shot on an episode of the sketch comedy show *Mad TV.*

I had a few funny moments, and afterwards head writer Michael Hitchcock invited me to see him perform with the Groundlings, one of the most influential and famous improv groups of all time, that boasted such alumni as Will Ferrell, Paul Reubens, Cheri Oteri, Lisa Kudrow, Amy Poehler, Will Forte, Kristen Wiig, and Phil Hartman.

I was a big fan of Mike's subtle yet hilarious performances in *A Mighty Wind*, *Waiting for Guffman*, and *Best in Show* and was excited to watch him work with the Groundlings. I watched the uproarious show and afterwards Michael introduced me to the director, Mindy Sterling. Mindy had played Frau Farbissina in the *Austin Powers* movies and she and her son were big wrestling fans. She thought my work with the WWE was entertaining and suggested I do a show the next time I was in town.

A few weeks later I made my improv comedy debut with the Groundlings on their Thursday night show "Cookin' with Gas," which was no mean feat. The reason was that becoming an actual member of the Groundlings was like becoming a comedic Scientologist. You had to train and take classes for a year before you could perform on the Sunday night show, which was like the minor leagues. Then if you were good enough on the Sunday night show, all thirty of the full-time Groundlings would cast a vote to decide if you had the skills to become a full-fledged member of the team. The true catch was that there could only be thirty Groundlings at a time, so if you were accepted you would have to wait until someone left before you could join. That meant that some people were stuck on the Sunday show forever.

With years of doing improv with Rocky and Austin under my belt, I did a pretty good job during my first Groundlings performance in the Phil Hartman Theatre in Los Angeles.

For my first sketch, Mindy called my partner and I onstage and asked the audience to name a weird occupation. Someone yelled, "Taxidermist!" and then Mindy asked them to name the worst place for two people to go on a first date and someone else yelled, "An outhouse!" It was then our task to make up a scene where two taxidermists had their first date in an outhouse.

I did well enough that Mindy invited me back, and I began appearing with the Groundlings regularly for the next year. I learned some important lessons along the way, including the first rule of improv, which is, "Don't try to be funny." Never go for the cheap joke.

The second rule is to always use the mantra of "Yes, *and*..." This means that if someone said my hair was black, I would come back with, "Yes, and it's a very blond shade of black that is indicative of my Luxembourgian ancestry."

I learned that improv is a team sport and you have to feed each other and work together to create the best possible show—much like wrestling. The two were also similar in that sometimes you had a great performance and felt like the most entertaining person on the planet, and other times you would bomb terribly and have to bounce back the next time.

But I hit a lot more than I missed, and after a few months Mindy told me she considered me to be an honorary Groundling.

It was indeed an honor, and working with the Groundlings was an invaluable experience. I learned so much about comic timing, thinking on my toes, and committing to a character, techniques that I still use in everything I do to this day.

By the way, do taxidermists still exist nowadays?

CHAPTER 42

Clams Casino

In the summer of 2006 I did a pilot hosting a show called *Ebaum's World* that didn't get picked up. But as they say, when one door closes another one opens, and after the show had been passed on, the *Ebaum* producers called me to see if I wanted to appear on a reality show called *Celebrity Duets*, created by Simon Cowell.

The show paired up celebrities who could sing with pop stars, to perform (what else) duets. Every week there would be a nationwide vote and a celeb would be eliminated. I wasn't sure at first if I wanted to do it, as I was hesitant about the style of music I'd have to sing. I'm a rock singer and wasn't keen on the possibility of singing ska or disco.

But I was assured that each performer would have final say on the song choice, so I agreed. I had to audition first to see if I had the chops, and I went into the studio with Rickey Minor (the leader of the *American Idol* band) and nailed "Enter Sandman" and "Spinning Wheel." I figured by doing Metallica and Blood, Sweat and Tears, Simon and the other producers would get a feel for what my style and range were, and if they didn't like my vibe then no harm done.

Apparently Simon did like my vibe, because I was chosen to be one of eight contestants on the show. *Duets* was on Fox, and was the highest-profile network program I'd ever done, which meant my visibility was bigger than ever. I did interviews with *Entertainment Tonight*, *Extra*, *Inside Edition*, and *Access Hollywood*. I did a photo shoot for *People* magazine (which was my mom's favorite magazine, she woulda been so proud), where they dubbed me the heartthrob of the show. I should hope so, considering the other male contestants were Alfonso Ribeiro, Cheech Marin, Hal Sparks, and Jai Rodriguez.

It was announced that the judges would be Marie Osmond, David Foster, and Little Richard, the band would be the headcutting machine from *American Idol*, and the host would be Wayne Brady, whom I'd known for years after being a guest on his Emmy Award–winning daytime talk show.

Duets was no joke either, as the collection of celebrities chosen were all badass singers. Lucy Lawless and Jai Rodriguez had appeared on Broadway, Hal Sparks, Cheech, and I all had our own bands, and Alfonso had been singing and dancing since he worked with Michael Jackson as a kid.

I was really looking forward to seeing how I matched up with the others vocally—until I found out that my first duet partner was country singer Lee Ann Womack. Country? I'd never sung a country song in my life. It would be like Paul Stanley singing reggae.

"Buffalo-oh-oh-whoa Tholdier..."

I also found out that the promise of having the final say

For some reason the producers liked this cast photo where I wasn't looking at the camera. I was probably too busy worrying about singing country, while Alfonso Ribeiro was probably thinking about coitus.

on song selections wasn't the case, as I was given the Willie Nelson tune "Mendocino County Line." Not only did I have to sing a country song, but I had to sing a Willie Nelson country song. Willie Nelson could hardly sing a Willie Nelson country song. My chances of winning seemed worse than his tax history.

I felt better when I found out that Peter Frampton was going to be my other partner, but my heart dropped again when I was given "Signed, Sealed, Delivered," a Stevie Wonder tune that Frampton covered.

Willie Nelson and Stevie Wonder? Were the rights to Steve Perry and Michael Jackson songs not available? I felt even more snubbed when I found out that Hal Sparks's partners were Sebastian Bach and Dee Snider, and I'm sure I don't even have to explain why.

Maybe the producers were trying to be cute in pairing the wrestler with the country singer? Or maybe they thought I was the worst singer in the contest and wanted me off quickly.

It didn't matter, as I was willing to give it a try and rehearsed my ass off trying to make the song work, but when it came to showtime I sucked. My pitch was off, my tone was bad, and every time I got close enough to Lee Ann to sing deep into her eyes, she recoiled like I had just taken a big bite of shit. In a way I had.

After bombing worse than a Jesse James appearance on Oprah, I tried to regroup for a show-stopping performance with Frampton. I was better vocally, but still off my game, and I delivered another heaping helping of clams casino.

I tried to make up for my mediocre vocals by running around the studio, trampling over the judges' desk, and performing a David Lee Roth split-legged jump off the drum riser, but alas I just ended up looking like a speed freak in a sparkly purple jacket.

The judges were actually quite kind and didn't tear me apart, but instead gave me comments like, "Good for you. It's nice to see you trying new things and having fun up there" (Marie); "You had great energy even if the vocals weren't perfect" (Foster); and "Ohhh, honey, I just felt my big toe rise up inside my shoe!" (Little Richard).

Good golly!

But at the end of the show I was the first one voted off by the producers and the judges. The fact that the fan voting didn't start until the second week of the show was another shady deal that made no sense to me.

Either way, I took the elimination like a man, vowing to return to TV on the next season of *Celebrity Bad White-Boy Dancing*, and shuffled off the stage doing a horrible robot.

Despite my blasé demeanor on the outside, I was humiliated on the inside. I mean, here I was the singer in a very good rock and roll band and I'd been the first one eliminated on a nationally televised singing show. I was going to have to eat some serious crow with a dish of humble pie on the side.

But after hiding in my dressing room for a few minutes, I came to terms with the fact that at least I'd tried. I've always said there's nothing wrong with trying something and failing.

As a matter of fact, I'd based my whole career on that statement.

After licking my wounds I poked my head out of the dressing room and saw a pissed-off Peter Frampton. "There's no way you should've been the first one eliminated. You did a great job. You can come sing with me at one of my shows anytime!"

I gave him a genuine hug in appreciation for his words. If my performance was good enough for Peter Frampton, then it was good enough for me!

Then I saw one of the judges in the hall, who told me, "You weren't the one we chose to be eliminated. We wanted to get rid of one of the ladies, but the producers didn't want five guys and two girls so you were the next in line."

Even if it was just lip service, it was still good for my bruised ego to hear that I wasn't the worst.

Although I was the first one booted off the show, the *Duets* experience wasn't a total bomb. Because when I returned for the finale, I got a chance to rub vocals with some of the best singers of all time.

I sang the blues with Little Richard as he warmed up for his performance. Just the two of us. He sang a verse, then I took one, and he nodded approvingly at my vibe. It was a remarkable experience to sing with the man who invented rock and roll vocals and had influenced everyone from Elvis to the Beatles. Now if I ever meet Paul McCartney I have something else to tell him besides Johnny Hutch's message that he's a fooking wanker.

After jamming with Little Richard, I spent an hour talking with Gladys Knight, who was flirting with me and calling me her Big Teddy Bear. If I was twenty years older I would've pipped her right there.

Then I went to craft services to get a drink and saw Smokey Robinson leaning against the wall sucking on lemons.

Lemons?

Could that be the secret to his legendary vocal talent? Did the citrus sooth his voice? Did the lemony nectar coat his throat and give him more power?

This was my chance to unlock the clandestine reasons for Smokey's success.

"Excuse me, Mr. Robinson," I inquired. "I see you're sucking on lemons. Do they help your voice?"

Smokey looked at me with his ice chip blue eyes.

"No man, I just like lemons."

After getting Smokey's advice that nothing helps your

voice more than drinking water and getting a good night's sleep, I was called to rehearsal for the finale's showstopping number. The eight of us were going to sing a medley of '50s songs, beginning with "Rock Around the Clock" and ending with Little Richard joining us for "Tutti Frutti." It was really frooti to get the chance to sing with Richard again, but other than that I was ready to wash my hands of this huge chunk of television fromage.

I was waiting by the side of the stage for my cue when Alfonso Ribeiro sidled up beside me.

"You like sex?" he asked matter-of-factly.

"Um. I guess," I answered.

"Yeah, me too. Mmmmmm...I musta banged over a thousand chicks," he said, dreamily.

Whether it was true or not, the thought of Carlton laying pipe made me uncomfortable—and nauseated.

Alfonso ended up winning *Celebrity Duets* and received the grand prize of nothing. The show was canceled soon after, and even though I'm glad I did it, I'm still bothered that I was the first one kicked off. I know I could've done better with the right songs, but that's the way it is sometimes.

The only saving grace was that the week after I was eliminated, the ratings for *Celebrity Duets* fell 50 percent and got worse from there.

Suck on those lemons, Simon.

CHAPTER **43**

Hill Street Blues

A few months after my mistimed haunting of Eli Roth, he forgave me and invited me to a party celebrating both his thirty-fourth birthday and the DVD release of *Hostel*. It was a great Hollywood bash, except for when I told Jack Black I was a huge Tenacious D fan and he glared at me as if I'd just eaten Kyle Gass and walked away. I didn't mind; CJ had been big-leagued by far bigger stars than JB.

I spent the night hanging out with the Roth family and drinking a few Crowns, nothing too crazy. The party was wrapping up and as I was getting ready to split, a fan asked me to have a shot with him.

"Come on, Chris! I watch you every Monday night! [I hadn't been on *Raw* in eight months.] I paid seventy-five dollars for this tequila shot and I want you to drink it with me!"

Never one to turn down a free drinkski, I tipped it back, thanked the guy (in retrospect I should've slapped him), and hopped in my car to drive back to my apartment in Burbank.

I'd just moved to California and still wasn't exactly

At Eli's birthday party in Hollywood. After discussing how awesome his Cannibal Holocaust T-shirt was, I drank a shot of top-shelf tequila and left. Thirty minutes later I was arrested and spent the night in an L.A. jail.

sure where I was going. I was driving down the 101 and made a right onto Universal Drive, but then swerved back onto the freeway when I realized I'd turned off too early. Right then I got a text from Eli's brother Gabe asking me if I'd made it home okay, and I began texting him back.

When I swerved again on the empty freeway due to my

driving and texting (Oprah is right . . . that's a no-no, kids), a pair of flashing red cherries appeared in my rearview mirror. My heart skipped like Sheffield and I pulled over on Lankershim (about five minutes from my place), as the officer slowly approached my car.

After looking at my license and registration, he asked me if I'd been drinking. I told him I'd had a few drinks. That's all he needed to hear and asked me to step out of the car.

"You were swerving all over the place and driving really slow. Plus your eyes are bloodshot. Are you sure you haven't had more than a few drinks?"

Of course I hadn't!

Or had I?

I sure had all the excuses in the world for my shoddy driving. I was going slow because I was lost. I was swerving because I made a wrong turn. I've always had a problem with my eyes being red and have to carry a small bottle of Bausch and Lomb Opcon-A (cheap plug) at all times so my eyes don't look like Snoop Dogg's in a smokehouse.

But the bottom line was I *had* been drinking all night, even though I didn't feel drunk.

Famous last (call) words.

The cop asked me to take a bunch of field sobriety tests. I stood on one foot and counted to ten while touching my nose. I had to recite the alphabet, forwards and backwards—who the hell can say their ABCs backwards even when they're sober?? Then I wavered a little while walking a straight line with my eyes closed, and that was the final straw.

"Sir, can you please step into the car."

Now I was getting scared.

I slid into the backseat, and the cop asked me to take a breathalyzer. When I blew a 0.088 (which was over the legal limit of .08), it was bye-bye, baby, bye-bye, that was all she wrote.

"Mr. Irvine, you're over the legal limit and I'm going to have to take you to jail."

Wow. I was going to jail. I'd never heard that one before.

He took my fingerprints, then handcuffed me. The clock on the dash said 3:15 a.m.

As the cop arrested me he told me not to worry; I wouldn't be at the station for too long as I'd be able to bail myself out once I got processed.

I was trying to stay calm, so I struck up a conversation with the popo to attempt to gain a few brownie points. When I mentioned that I didn't feel drunk, the cop said that most people drive over the legal limit an average of eighty times before they ever get caught.

Eighty times, huh? Well, the odds had finally caught up to me, as there'd been plenty of other times I should've been busted for drunk driving. But this time I'd blown over the limit and was legally drunk, no excuses, no sympathy, no escape; and now I had to face the consequences.

I just thanked God I hadn't hurt anybody.

I arrived at county at 3:30 a.m. and had to blow again. My blood alcohol count now read 0.089, and because it had risen (stupid $75 tequila), I was escorted straight into processing, and bingo—I was officially a ward of the state.

To make things worse, I was being held prisoner at the Hill Street station in downtown L.A., one of the roughest precincts in town. To say I had the damn Hill Street Blues was an understatement and there was no Daniel J. Travanti there to rescue me.

They let me out of the handcuffs and I had to fill out a bunch of forms (in triplicate) before they took my mug shot and fingerprinted me again. Then I was given a small plastic bag holding a bologna sandwich and a juice box that proudly proclaimed on the side: CONTAINS 0% REAL JUICE.

I was escorted to an expansive holding area populated with my fellow undesirables in one corner and a bank of pay phones in the other. There was a portly officer with a mustache (why does every cop have to have a mustache?) sitting behind a barred window, and I asked him what I had to do to bail myself out.

"Bail yourself out? Ha! You can't bail yourself out. Who told you that?"

"The officer who arrested me. He seemed like a nice guy and he told me I could bail myself out."

"Well, you can't bail yourself out under any circumstances. Not to mention that you're so mildly over the limit, I wouldn't have brought you into the station to begin with. I just would've made you park your car and walk home. Guess your cop buddy wasn't such a nice guy after all."

With my hopes of bailing myself out dashed, I asked the officer how I could get out.

"Call a bail bondsman."

"Do you have the number of one?"

"Nope. Can't give you that information. If you don't know of any, call your lawyer to get the number."

Who in the hell memorizes his lawyer's phone number, let alone a bail bondsman's? The only numbers I knew by heart were my house phone and Jessica's cell, and there was no way I was going to call either of those.

"Well, if you have nobody to call, you need to go sit in the holding cell until we call your name. Shouldn't be more than four or five hours."

Four or five hours?? The clock on the wall said 4:30 a.m.

So I skulked into the cell. The other occupants didn't seem too happy to see me, and it was obvious why. I was surrounded by a crew of East L.A. Chicano gangbangers, all of them sporting wifebeaters, baggy jeans, tan work boots, mesh do-rags, and tears tattooed under their eyes. I'm talking serious mothertruckers here, folks.

I was in the cell for thirty seconds when one of the vatos with biceps bigger than Snookie's hair, sized me up and asked, "Hey homes, are you Chris Jericho?" After a few seconds the rest of them joined in and suddenly I was a very popular jailbird.

"Yo, Jericho, let's have a wrestling match," another one said. "Can you really fight, vato, or are you just a fake?"

This tête-à-tête with my newfound friends was not going well. If something went down I thought I could probably take one of them, maybe even two, but there was no way I'd be able to fight them all. I wasn't Jean-Claude Van Jericho.

I decided to take a powder and leave the cell before things got too en serio, and I could hear them laughing as I powerwalked through the cage door, still clutching the plastic Baggie in my hand.

I was trying not to show it but I was scared shitless and they could smell it. I'd never been arrested in my entire life, let alone spent a night in jail. All I could think was, "I'm not supposed to be in here."

I flinched when a voice boomed over the speaker system, "Get back in the cell!"

I glanced back and saw Señor Musculo giving me the stinkeye, so I decided to take my chances with the cops again.

"Get back in that cell now!!" the voice said as I hurried back to the gated window. I peered through the bars and a young cop peered back. Thankfully this one didn't have a mustache and kind of looked like Bob Saget.

"Sir, I can't go back into the cell. Those guys recognize me and I think things might get rough."

"Why would they recognize you?"

I told Saget I was a wrestler. He asked which one, and when I told him he smirked and motioned back to the holding area. "There's a lot of people who obviously shouldn't be in here, and you're one of them. But you are here, so get back into that cell until your name is called."

I headed back to the cell praying to God that I wouldn't be seriously beaten (or killed) by Los Lobos. I had just reached the door as Señor Musculo made room for me to sit beside him, when the loudspeaker boomed again.

"Chris Irvine to the front."

I rushed back to the window and saw a group of cops gathered around a computer.

"We found your website," Saget said. "You better come with us."

I practically jumped into his arms with relief when he opened the door. My fame had paid off and I was free! My joy was short-lived, however, as Saget slapped the cuffs back on and led me through a long, dank hall before depositing me into an eight-by-eight room by myself.

"All right, Chris Jericho, you're gonna stay in here until you hear your name called. Shouldn't be more than four or five hours. Try and get some sleep."

What was the deal with this four or five hours statement? It was apparent I wasn't going anywhere for a while, so I took inventory of the closet that was my new home.

Stainless steel toilet with no seat—check. Stainless steel bench—check. Roll of piss-stained toilet paper—check. Smell of piss in the air—double check. Freezing cold—triple check. Yeah, I was going to be able to sleep like a baby in this place. My only regret was that I hadn't given the cop my Hilton Diamond number so I could get my points.

I lay down on the cold steel, using the pee-stained toilet roll as a pillow, and felt the first fingers of panic inside my stomach.

I hadn't called Jessica before I went to bed as usual and I knew she would be awake as it was past 8 a.m. in Tampa. She was four months pregnant and I felt worse for her than I did for myself. She would be worrying, wondering where her husband was, not knowing he was in a putrid jail cell in downtown Los Angeles after being arrested for drunken driving.

I always took some kind of warped pride in the fact that I could drink a lot. I was proud of my Winnipeg upbringing and how I'd been weaned with a beer in my hand. Partying was fun! Getting wasted was froot!

I didn't feel too damn froot right now. As a matter of fact I felt like a pathetic thirty-five-year-old loser. I also felt really cold, because it was about 60 degrees in the damn cell. I closed my eyes with my mind racing and lay on that steel bench for hours. It was after 8 a.m. when another cop finally opened the door and told me to follow him. I'd been in jail for almost five hours and at this point was stone cold sober and ready to go home. But I wasn't finished yet.

The cop led me down another dingy hallway and up a dark flight of stairs before dumping me in yet another cell. Was this ever going to end?

Before he closed the door, the cop asked, "You're in a cell by yourself—a K-100. Why's that? Are you a homosexual?"

"No."

"Are you violent?"

"No."

"Are you suicidal?"

"I'm about to be when my wife finds out."

"Sit tight. You should be out in—"

"Four or five hours?" I said with a wan smile.

The cop nodded as he slammed the door. There were no bars here, only a window made of three-inch-thick Plexiglas. But my new cell was the fucking Waldorf-Astoria compared to the last one: the toilet had a seat, there was a small sink in the corner, and most important there was a phone on the wall.

Thinking back to every police show I'd ever seen that didn't feature Stewart Copeland, the officers always spoke about a prisoner's right to one phone call. I hadn't been offered one phone call, and come to think of it, I hadn't been read the Miranda rights when I was first arrested either. Andy Sipowicz was full of shit! But I wasn't ready to call home just yet.

I decided to get my thoughts together and kill time by looking out the window of my cell. I saw inmates shackled together marching down the hallway in their orange jumpsuits. I saw an old black prisoner with white hair and a white beard swabbing the floor.

Would that be me someday? Perhaps that guy had started out with a DUI too and just never got out? Then I saw another prisoner across the hallway staring out of his window aimlessly as well. Ah, a fellow convict passing the time observing the world around him just like me, all the while singing, "Nobody knows the trouble I've seen..."

The jailbird broke into a snaggle-toothed grin and mouthed, "I'm going to fucking kill you..."

I darted away from the window and concentrated on eating my bologna sandwich on white and gulping down my fruit drink containing 0% REAL JUICE. If you've ever eaten a piece of cork and washed it down with cardboard-flavored Gatorade, you'll have an idea of what my breakfast tasted like.

It was time to face Hurricane Jessica. I picked up the phone and took a deep breath.

I dialed my home number and when she picked up an operator said, "You have received a collect call from the L.A. County Jail from Chris..."

"You've got to be kidding me...," I heard her say.

To get into the details of the verbal thrashing my wife gave me that morning is moot. Suffice it to say she made her displeasure regarding my current situation exceedingly clear. Then she said she'd call my manager, Barry Bloom, to see if he could get me out of there. My fate was in her capable hands, and I felt a little better (for now) that she was on the case. I knew she would bake me a cake with a file in it to get me out if she had to.

After another hour, the loudspeaker eventually boomed, "Will prisoner Chris Irvine please identify himself."

My spirits soared! I was getting out! I banged on

the glass for what seemed like twenty minutes until an annoyed-looking guard (with mustache of course) opened the door.

"Officer, I'm Chris Irvine! The loudspeaker told me to identify myself!"

"Well, good for you. Do you want a fucking medal?" he queried, and slammed the door shut.

I was crestfallen and collapsed on the floor trying not to cry. I eventually picked myself back up and glanced through the window across the hallway.

"I'm gonna fucking kill you," Snaggletooth mouthed again.

"I'm gonna fucking kill you first," I mouthed back, and I meant it.

Snaggletooth's grin vanished and he disappeared into the bowels of his cell.

The clock struck noon and I was taken to another holding cell. But there was one last glitch before I was released, when I was told the smudged fingerprints the cop took from me on the street didn't match the ones I'd taken at the station. The front desk officer was confused and wouldn't discharge me without confirmation.

He surveyed the assorted group of convicts, who were just as anxious to get the hell out of jail as I was. "Are any of you guys wrestling fans?"

They looked at each other nervously, afraid to answer one way or another, in case it was a trick question designed to put them back in the hoosegow.

All the crooks sat silent until one redheaded Richie

Cunningham–looking cat squeaked, "I am. He's Chris Jericho, right?"

Indeed I was, and I was ready to get out of the big house. After the positive identification I was given back my belongings like Joliet Jake (sans one soiled prophylactic) and the electronic door to freedom swung open. The clock on the wall said 1:30 p.m.; I'd been in jail for over ten hours and was ready to explode. How anyone can serve one week, one year, or one decade behind bars is beyond me.

My court date was six weeks later and I was charged with wet reckless driving (not quite a DUI, but close enough), lost my California license for six months, had to attend ten AA meetings, and was fined over ten grand. I deserved everything that I got, and considering I could've killed myself or somebody else, it was a small price to pay and a lesson well learned.

The moral of this story is simple, dear readers: Don't drink and drive.

Oh, and the other moral is: Don't drink juice boxes containing 0% REAL JUICE.

CHAPTER 44

Miracle Babies

I woke up at 5:30 in the morning to the most terrifying text of my life.

JESS CELL: "I'm going into labor right now!"

How could that be? She was only twenty-seven weeks pregnant! Even worse, I was in Toronto, only a short 1,097 miles away from Tampa.

I was rehearsing for the opening night of *Opening Night*, a play I was starring in written by Canadian playwright Norm Foster. I'd been offered the lead role of Jack Tisdale, a forty-five-year-old varnish salesman who was taking his estranged wife to a play for their anniversary.

The production was being put on by Bird Entertainment, a fledgling Ontario theater company who were looking to boost their profile by casting me as the lead. It was a perfect fit as I'd wanted to do theater for years, and I jumped at the chance to be a part of the wacky Peter Sellers/Ricky Gervais–style farce.

I'd been flying back and forth from Tampa for six weeks rehearsing and promoting the show, and all of the hard work was paying off. All four of the shows had sold to 90 percent capacity and the city was abuzz waiting to see Chris Jericho's stage debut.

I made some great choices for Jack, including growing a mustache, padding my stomach with a pillow, greasing

My choices for Jack Tisdale included a mustache, glasses, and a pillow stuffed in my shirt. The best accolade I received for my performance was from a fan in the front row who whispered to his friend after I'd been onstage for ten minutes, "Where the hell is Jericho?"

my hair back, and wearing glasses, all of which made me look nothing like the WWE Superstar I was known as. It was the first time that I'd been able to really apply the acting techniques Kirk taught me, and they were working. I spent hours learning my lines and rehearsing with the amazing cast and really dropped into the character of Jack in the process.

I went to bed after our final rehearsal knowing I had one more day to relax and work on the final nuances of the character and the play.

Or so I thought.

When I got Jess's text, I quickly called the hospital. I found out she was already in the delivery room about to give birth to our twin daughters thirteen weeks prematurely, which was a potential disaster.

The little monkeys had already tried to sneak out four weeks earlier, and Jess had been on bed rest ever since. It had been a difficult pregnancy, much harder than her experience with Ash, mostly because this time there were two babies inside of her. Both of us had thought there was only one until we went for our four-month ultrasound to find out the sex (yes, please) of our child. Jess had a hunch she might be carrying twins since she was huge and they ran in her family, but the nurse said there was no way. But when she rechecked the blurry image on the screen, she digressed and said, "Well, what do you know. Congratulations, Mr. and Mrs. Irvine, you're having a girl...and another girl!"

I fell off my chair.

Let me say that if there are any nurses reading this tome and they someday have the honor of telling an expectant father that his wife is having twins after four months of thinking there was just one baby please tell him to sit down or hold tight to the wall or down a straight shot of Grey Goose because that's quite the surprise to hear.

Okay, thanks for that. I'm going to take a breath now.

Panicking over the fact that my wife was giving birth to my twins at that very moment, I booked the next flight to Tampa and flew home. I rushed to the hospital and there in an incubator in the newborn intensive care unit were my daughters Cheyenne and Sierra. They weighed two pounds seven ounces and two pounds five ounces respectively and were the size of large ferrets.

I started freaking out inside, but tried to remain as calm as possible for Jess's sake. I took the doctor aside and he told me as plain as day that he'd seen much smaller babies and chances were good that everything was going to work out. I believed him, but it was hard to comprehend that as tiny as they were they would be okay.

I sat with my little girls all day and night as they clung to life. Then the next morning I got back on a plane and flew back to Toronto to do the play. The old adage says that the show must go on, but I don't know what the hell I was thinking. I was leaving my traumatized wife and my two premature babies in the NICU to fly to another country to perform a comedy. Thankfully my dad had flown to Tampa for a visit and was there for our family, but it should have been me who was there. With the luxury of hindsight I see that now as clear as day. But just as I had done with my mom's passing, I ran away from the possibility of tragedy and left everything in God's hands. I don't know why I left my family when they needed me, and I'm not proud of it.

Thankfully God was listening, because he kept my babies and my wife safe while I was away.

The play was a huge success, but it didn't matter because my heart and mind were back with my family in Tampa and all I could think about was getting back to take care of them.

When I got home four days later, I spent the next ten weeks in the NICU. Even though there were a few ups and downs along the way, because of the healing powers of the Lord (and a little help from modern medicine), our miracle babies were released from the hospital with a clean bill of health only two and a half months later.

Ash was so excited to meet his sisters, as he wasn't allowed in the NICU and had never seen them. He was (and still is) obsessed with sea creatures, and when we brought them home he was quite disappointed to find out that his siblings were human beings, not sharks.

I'm thankful to say that now my daughters Cheyenne and Sierra are healthy, happy, beautiful little girls (not fish) and a true testament to the strength of prayer and the power of God.

Thank you, Lord . . . I owe you one. Or should I say two.

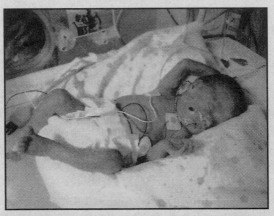

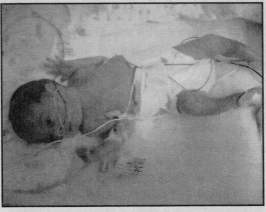

My little angels Cheyenne and Sierra were born at two pounds seven ounces and two pounds five ounces, respectively. They were so tiny that their diapers were the size of small napkins, and I could fit them both down the front of my shirt at the same time.

CHAPTER 45

The Howard Hughes of Rock and Roll

Eddie Trunk is the most trusted and recognized hard rock DJ in the country and I'd gotten to know him over the years through Fozzy and the WWE. Whenever I was in New York I'd guest on his show in what we called the Metal Summit and discuss useless metal minutiae with whoever else happened to be in town, whether it be Mike Portnoy, Mike Piazza, or Zakk.

One week I was guesting along with Sebastian Bach and Scott Ian and we were debating whether Iron Maiden was better than Judas Priest. I was in the middle of a well-thought-out dissertation on why Maiden was better, when I was interrupted (as usual) by Sebastian.

"Holy shit! I just got a text from Axl Fuckin' Rose," he said in his high-pitched stoner voice. Axl was in town rehearsing for an upcoming Guns N' Roses tour and Bas hadn't heard from him in years—until now.

Axl was quite reclusive and didn't do many interviews, so it was quite the coup when Bas called him and put him on the radio by holding the phone up to the mic. The audio was horrible, and when Eddie suggested that Axl call in, he surprised all of us by actually doing it. Eddie made small talk for a few minutes and finished the call by inviting Axl to join us in the studio after rehearsal, and that was it.

About half an hour later we were having a serious debate over what was Raven's best album (*All for One*) when an intern ran into the studio completely out of breath, like he was going to announce the British were coming.

"He's here."

"Who's here?"

"Axl Rose! He's coming up the elevator now."

The conversation halted and the four of us looked at each other with disbelief.

"Besides Mick Jagger or Paul McCartney, the biggest rock star in the world is coming in this studio right now," I said to Scott.

At that moment the door opened and in walked—some random older lady.

She said nothing to no one and looked around the room suspiciously. She gave us all a quick glance and left the room. I found out later that her name was Beta, Axl's personal advisor, who was apparently checking if the vibes in the room were good enough for him to enter.

They must have been, because a few moments later the door opened and in walked W. Axl Rose.

You've never seen four loudmouths shut up so quickly, and suddenly after two hours of nonstop jabbering none of us had anything to say. Except Bas, who kept proclaiming over and over again, "This is the Howard Hughes of rock and roll, man!"

Axl was in good shape and looked pretty froot with

his cornrow hair and trim goatee. He sat down at the console and his charisma and presence were off the charts. Eddie asked a couple of generic questions, but the rest of us were still tongue-tied, not wanting to say anything to instigate any display of the legendary Axl Rose temper.

The interview was sterile, almost boring, and I could see that Axl was losing interest. That's when I decided to jump in and break the ice.

"Hey Axl, I'm Chris Jericho. I'd like to ask you a question that every guest on the Eddie Trunk show has to answer. Who's better—Priest or Maiden?"

Axl's vibe changed instantly and suddenly he was into the interview. I don't think he'd been asked that question before.

"I like Priest better, but the first Iron Maiden record is my favorite out of all of them."

From that point forward it was no longer Axl and four idiots, it was five music fans shooting the breeze. He opened up and told some great stories about his love of W.A.S.P., his issues with Vince Neil, and his experiences with David Lee Roth. We listened intently as he told a great story about how he and Jack Russell from Great White were doing cocaine with a Cuban drug dealer. After Axl and Jack snorted up everything they had, the Cuban revealed that he had another eight-ball, but wouldn't share it. Jack caught a fly while the dealer was in the bathroom, and when he returned pulled it out of his pocket. Jack fawned over it and convinced the Cuban that it was a rare African tsetse fly that when snorted would produce a wicked high. So the Cuban traded the eight-ball for the dead housefly and Jack and Axl disappeared into the night.

After an hour of mindless chatter, I felt comfortable enough—and drunk enough—to call Axl out. "Hey Axl,

I have a bone to pick with you!" The studio went silent and Trunk gave me a look that said, "Jericho if you blow this, I'm going to kill you!"

But I was undeterred. "Axl, when Guns were opening for Iron Maiden in 1988 in Winnipeg, I asked you for your autograph outside in the parking lot and you told me you would be right back. Well, you never came back and I want to know why."

"That's it?" Axl said with relief. "I thought you were going to tell me I had sex with your girlfriend…or your mother."

(Your mother's a fuckin' goof.)

Eddie's show was supposed to end at 2 a.m., but the program director realized how much of a coup it was to have Axl Rose live on the radio (he was the Howard Hughes of rock and roll after all) and told Eddie to keep him on for as long as he could. We finally wrapped up the show at 4 a.m. and made our way over to the Bungalow, a trendy NYC hotspot that despite the late hour was wall-to-wall packed. Hanging out with Axl Rose has its benefits, and we were escorted to a huge VIP section, even bigger than the one Lindsay Lohan occupied beside us.

After a few hours of Patrón and Grey Goose (alas, no Nightrain) I stumbled over to Axl, who threw his arm around me and smiled his mischievous grin.

"You know what?" he said. "I had a really good time with you guys tonight. It's pretty rare that I get to talk about music and just be a fan without having to worry about all the bullshit. Thanks for hanging out with me."

Thanks for hanging out with you? Thanks for hanging out with me, spacebrain!

And by the way Axl, I thought *Chinese Democracy* was genius.

CHAPTER 46

Benoit

In the two years I stayed away from wrestling, I literally stayed away. I didn't watch the shows or read the Internet for results. I became a casual fan who paid slight attention to what was going on, and that was about it. I got a few phone calls from Brian Gewirtz asking if I'd do a one-shot deal here and there, most notably as John Cena's surprise guest tag team partner for a *Raw* at the Meadowlands in New Jersey, but I politely declined. You're either in or you're out, and if you're not in then you must be out (Hurricane™) and I didn't want to be one of those guys who would show up every once in a while. But slowly I started to feel the wrestling fire kindling inside me again, and I can attribute that to two factors.

The first was that I had just finished writing my book (the critically acclaimed *A Lion's Tale* in case you've forgotten), and the experience of reliving my entire career in such detail made me realize how fortunate I'd been to live my dream and have so many tremendous adventures along the way. The book also made me remember that I was pretty damn good at what I did, and I started thinking what it would be like to return.

As a result, I started doing autograph signings to get a feel for what the fans were thinking and whether they wanted me to come back. While I enjoyed doing them it was also a little depressing. The final straw was when I did a signing in Long Island that was about as well attended as the one Randy the Ram did with the guy with the colostomy bag. Looking around at all the old-timers clinging on to the business, hoping for one last break, really got to me.

What was I doing here? I was thirty-six years old, not fifty-six, and if I was going to be doing something involving wrestling, it should be in the big leagues.

The second and most important factor was when I watched Cena and Michaels wrestle for a full hour on *Raw*. It was an amazing performance that showcased the true art of the business; a business that I'd once been a part of and wanted to be a part of again.

The match excited, intrigued, and quite frankly annoyed me. After having great matches with both guys in the past, I was jealous that I wasn't involved, and watching it made me antsy.

After it was over I knew it was time to come back. It was time for Chris Jericho to return to the WWE.

But there was another factor that cemented my decision to come back. If Cena and Michaels had just showcased the best of wrestling, the man whom I considered to be my best friend in the business was about to showcase the worst—almost destroying the entire industry in the process.

I hadn't seen Chris Benoit since the day of Eddy's

funeral. He had been devastated, and even though we promised we would keep in better touch, that became increasingly more difficult, due to the fact that Chris would simply drop off the grid for weeks at a time. I called him the Loch Ness Monster because he would surface for a short period, then submerge himself again shortly afterwards and be impossible to find. Sometimes I'd miss his call and get back to him literally minutes later, but he wouldn't answer and I wouldn't hear from him again for weeks.

But as hard as he was to get on the phone, he would always return emails and texts. So that became our main mode of communication to keep in touch, stay up to date, and send each other pictures of our kids. Chris was always interested in how my children were doing and asked about them frequently. He loved kids, especially his own, and would write about them all the time.

It seemed strange that he would rather write long emails than pick up the phone and talk, but that was Chris—always a little strange. He wore a long black leather overcoat even in the summer. He constantly chewed on coffee straws, with an extra cocked behind his ear waiting to be gnawed and a fresh supply in his pocket. He was very intense during conversations, to the point of being angry.

"How are you doing, Chris?"

"GOOD . . . YOU?" he would reply, straight-faced with a steely glare.

Chris also didn't share the same sense of humor with too many other people and never laughed at the obvious. Once when we were on a long drive with Chavo Guerrero, I popped in a cassette (remember those?) of a famous

Canadian comedy radio show called *Brocket 99*, which was a broadcast of a fictitious Indian reservation radio station. Growing up with Canadian Indians and near reservations, I found the routine hilarious. Benoit was from the prairies as well, so I thought he might get a kick out of it too. I was wrong, and instead of doubling over with laughter like me, he remained stone-faced during the whole show.

His lack of reaction made me question my own sense of humor.

"Do you not find this funny? If you don't like it I'll turn it off."

He responded stoically, "No, keep playing it. I think it's hilarious. I'm howling inside."

I let it play, but he still didn't laugh. Not a giggle, not a chuckle, not a tee-hee—never went "Ha." Yet when somebody threw up or fell down the stairs, he would belly-laugh out loud for hours on end.

We spent the rest of the drive in silence, and when we arrived at the hotel someone was throwing a party a few doors down from us. Chris grabbed a garbage can filled with trash from the hall and dumped in a bunch of ice. Then he pulled down his pants and filled the rest of it with 100 percent Canadian wolverine piss. He propped the can against the door at an angle and knocked furiously. We ran down the hall like three teenagers and I heard the cries of disgust when the partiers opened the door. We snuck into our room, trying to be quiet but failing miserably due to Chris's giggling, and called the revelers.

When they answered Chris said in a creepy little-kid voice, "You don't know how to party," and hung up laughing uncontrollably.

*   *   *

In February 2007, I decided to take Ash up to Edmonton
so he could play with his cousins in the snow. My cousin
Todd (Chad's judicious brother) lived in Sherwood Park,
the same suburb in which Benoit used to live and two of
his children still did. I hadn't seen him in over a year, so
I sent him a text before we left notifying him I was going
to be there on the off chance he would be too. He texted
back instantly saying that by sheer coincidence he was
also in Sherwood Park until Saturday. Ash and I got in
Friday afternoon and we agreed to meet as soon as we
landed. I called him when I arrived at 2 p.m., but he didn't
answer so I told him to call me when he could. I didn't
hear anything from him, so I texted him again at 5 and at
7, but still nothing.

I was getting annoyed because it was near Ash's bed-
time and Chris was going to miss out on seeing him. I
was leafing through the *Edmonton Sun* waiting for his
call and saw his picture advertising an appearance he was
making at an indoor lacrosse game that night. I figured he
would call me after the game, but he never did, so I went
to bed.

I awoke at 3:30 a.m. by the beep of my cell phone
informing me I had a text.

"Hey Chris, just got back from my appearance, sorry I
missed you. Hope to see you soon."

Who gets back from a personal appearance at 3:30 in
the morning?

His actions really annoyed me. I hadn't seen him in so
long and here we were by pure luck in the same town, yet
he still couldn't make the effort to see me and my son for

a measly twenty minutes? How lame was that? I considered Chris to be a brother, but it wasn't always easy to be his friend. You had to take the good with the bad when it came to his friendship.

As strange as he was, I still trusted him more than anybody in the business, and a few months after watching Cena-Michaels on *Raw* I texted him to get his advice on a comeback.

He replied, "The business fucking misses you, the fans fucking miss you, the locker room fucking misses you, I fucking miss you...I think you should come back."

I told him that the time off had been good but I was ready to return.

He responded quickly, "I can't wait to help you get into shape for your return!"

A few days later Chris sent me another text that said, "Hey Chris, it's been awhile, I just wanted to say hi. Call me when you can." I asked him when I should call since he was always so difficult to get on the phone and he replied, "Haha. You know me too well! Daniel goes to bed at eight, so call me any time after that."

I called him every night at 8:30 for a week and of course he didn't answer. I tried a few more times until he finally called me back on a Friday afternoon. I was playing with Ash so I didn't answer. He left a stoic message saying, "Hey Chris, just looking to talk with you. Hope all is well. Call me back. Bye."

In retrospect, I really wonder what it was he wanted to talk about.

*   *   *

That night I watched the Brian Pillman DVD that the WWE had just released. Chris knew Pillman quite well, and when it was done I texted him, "Hey man, I just watched Pillman's DVD, it's amazing how many of us have died young. It's so sad. I'll give you a call tomorrow." He didn't respond.

On Saturday I was booked to do an autograph signing on an indie show in Evansville, Indiana. When I landed I returned Chris's call and there was no answer. Coincidentally, a few hours later I got the news that local Calgary wrestler Biff Wellington had passed away. Chris knew Biff quite well from Stampede Wrestling when they were both starting out, and I thought he needed to hear the news. I sent Chris another text: "I don't know if you heard but Biff Wellington passed away today." He didn't reply yet again.

On Sunday I had another signing at a small indie show in a roller skating rink in Martinsburg, West Virginia, and I was embarrassed to be there. I felt even worse when I saw Bobby Eaton, one of the great workers in the '80s who was now wrestling for small shows like this one. It was an honest living and there was nothing wrong with it, but the difference was he had no other options and I did. I was ready to return to the WWE, and signing pictures in a skating rink was not where I needed to be.

Still, it was good to see Bobby and we had a great conversation. Halfway through I asked him if he had spoken to Benoit lately and he said he hadn't for a while. When Eaton went to the ring for his match I thought about texting Chris to tell him I'd just seen Bobby but I didn't, too self-conscious to let him know what I was doing.

Chris wouldn't have cared, but I felt he would've been

disappointed in me for lowering my standards so much. Even though I hadn't seen him for so long he still had that kind of influence over me. I didn't want him to feel that I had let him down.

After the signing, I got back to my hotel and went online to read about the day's events. I was surprised to see that Chris had no-showed that night's *Vengeance* PPV in Houston. It was very unlike him to no-show an event, especially a PPV. I thought maybe he was having some kind of family problems and didn't want to bother him, so I decided against sending him another text.

I flew home on Monday and went to the gym with Ash, leaving him in the play area as I worked out. Right before I started training, I got a message from Brian Gerwirtz asking me to call him. "I have some funny news for you, something you'd be interested in hearing. Get back to me when you can."

I finished my workout an hour later, and after loading Ash into the back of my Expedition, I called Brian back. When he answered, the tone of his voice had changed drastically. The jauntiness he had displayed in his message only an hour earlier had disappeared and been replaced with panic.

I was overwhelmed by an awful sense of dread.

"Hey man, I got your voicemail, what's up?"

Brian could barely squeeze his next words out. "Oh, this is terrible. This is the worst news. I don't know how to tell you this, Chris."

Not understanding what the hell he was talking about, I asked him what the problem was.

"I don't want to tell you this. This is horrible and I don't know what to say."

I started guessing what could be so bad that he couldn't bear to tell me. The first thing that popped into my head was that Vince was going to go live on *Raw* and totally bury me. I'd just begun early negotiations for my return to the WWE and maybe for some reason I had pissed him off and he didn't want me back. Was he going to go on the air and call me a piece of shit that would never work for his company again?

Midway through my thought, Brian dropped the hammer.

"Chris is dead."

Chris is dead? Chris who? Chris Masters? Chris the Trainer? Chris the Writer?

"Chris who?"

"Chris Benoit," Brian said, his voice cracking.

The world froze as I processed what I had just been told. Chris Benoit was dead.

Did I know a Chris Benoit? The name sounded vaguely familiar; like someone from high school maybe? Someone I played rec hockey with?

The car behind me honked alerting me that the red light had turned green, snapping me out of my daze and bringing me back to reality.

"What do you mean, Brian?"

"He's dead, Chris. I'm sorry."

I let out an anguished groan and I could see my face contorted into a grotesque grimace in the rear-view mirror as I swerved down the road at a snail's pace.

"What happened? What happened?" I was a broken record, but it was all I could say.

"Nobody knows what happened, but he's dead. They're all dead."

They're all dead? What was he talking about?

"What do you mean, they're all dead? Who's all dead?"

"Nancy and Daniel. They're dead too."

Those words pushed me over the edge and I had to pull over.

"Brian, I have to call you back," I muttered as I started sobbing uncontrollably. I lost control of my faculties like Benoit had at Eddy's funeral. I was moaning and my breath hitching as I tried to compose myself.

Ash, all of three years old, commented innocently from his car seat, "Daddy, you cry funny."

I wiped my eyes and put on my brave face for my son's sake, but I was tearing apart inside. I couldn't stop thinking about what had happened to Chris and his entire family. How could they all be dead? Carbon monoxide poisoning? Food poisoning? Had someone murdered them? But despite all of the possible scenarios that were running through my head, I knew in my heart that something much worse had happened.

My gut feeling was Chris had killed them.

I chased the horrible thought out of my head and finally made it home. I wasn't interested in talking to anybody; not even Jessica or especially John Laurinaitis, who kept calling my house until Jess told him that I wasn't up to speaking to anyone.

Ironically, *Raw* that night had originally been slotted to feature a "funeral" for Mr. McMahon, who'd been "blown up" in a limo accident a few weeks earlier. The office told everybody to dress in black mourning clothes and the set was all decked out with flowers, with a choir, a priest, and a coffin set up in the middle of the ring.

There were going to be special guests eulogizing Vince, one of them being Bruce Campbell, Ash from the

Evil Dead trilogy and the inspiration for my son's name. Knowing I was a big fan, Campbell's appearance was the funny news that Brian had originally called me about.

So when Vince called a talent meeting to inform everyone that Chris had died, the whole roster was already dressed for a full-service memorial.

The plans for the *Raw* interment were canceled and replaced by a Chris Benoit tribute show, a compilation of his greatest WWE matches (which might be the last time they'll ever be aired on TV), along with heartfelt comments from his peers. Amid the kind words and valiant portrayals of Chris was a serious, more ambiguous comment from William Regal that chilled my blood. He said that Chris wasn't quite the person everyone thought he was and there might be more to his death than meets the eye. I could tell that Regal suspected the worst, just like I did.

I watched the show drinking Crown Royal straight from the bottle, barely paying attention when they aired our *Royal Rumble* Ladder match, which I consider to be one of my best matches ever. During the match Jim Ross mentioned, "Chris Jericho has been reached at his home in Tampa and is despondent over the news of his good friend's death."

I watched the rest of the show in silence, trying to wrap my head around the fact that I would never see my good friend again.

I spoke to Dean Malenko after the show to try and make some sense out of what happened. He brought up that there was going to be another tribute show on *Smackdown!*

and asked if I would like to fly to Texas to participate. I'd already missed Eddy's tribute show and was seriously contemplating going to this one, when rumors started circulating on the Internet about what had really happened to the Benoits.

I decided I didn't want to go to *Smackdown!* until I found out more information, as I was becoming more and more convinced that something very bad had happened.

I spent the next few hours scouring the Internet for information: wrestling websites, news websites, fan forums, anywhere I could find details. Not that they were hard to find, as it seemed like every ten minutes something new was revealed.

Within a few hours of the tribute show the truth came out: Chris Benoit had murdered his wife and son and then killed himself.

When I got the confirmation, I called Vince. It was the first time we'd spoken in almost two years, and I didn't waste his time with small talk or petty greetings. I was too distraught for that.

"Vince, it's Jericho. What the hell is going on?"

"I don't know, Chris. It seems that Benoit wasn't the man we thought he was. He fooled us all."

Chris had the reputation of being one of the most straightforward, salt-of-the-earth, what-you-see-is-what-you-get type guys in the business. People trusted him, went to him for advice, and respected his opinions. I know I did. How could he commit such blasphemy?

"Vince, if this is true and he killed his family, who can we ever trust again?"

He couldn't answer me.

*   *   *

I've said it before but I'll say it again—Chris loved his children. He talked about them constantly with a gleam in his eye and I know it devastated him when he got divorced from his first wife and moved away from his oldest two kids. He rearranged his schedule on a monthly basis so he could fly to Edmonton and spend as much time as possible with them.

"Don't ever get divorced," he told me. "It's too hard on your kids and it's not worth it. The only true form of unconditional love is your love for your kids and I'm sorry for what I put them through."

It was this unconditional love that made it so difficult for me to comprehend how he could've done what he did. Everyone in a relationship knows the pure anger that you can feel for your significant other at certain times, and I could understand how a fight could spiral out of control. Everyone knows how it feels to be totally depressed and how one might consider the easy way out of taking their own life.

But who can ever envision killing their own child?

It still gives me chills and horrifies me to even think about it. How could he do it? Was he possessed? Insane? Was it a horrible accident or a premeditated plan? Would we ever really know?

I went back on the Internet to research every possible theory I could contemplate, to try to explain or rationalize what he had done. Chris was a coffee addict, so I looked up the side effects of excessive caffeine intake and found that under extreme circumstances high doses of the drug could cause delusions, psychosis, and even violent behavior. That had to be it, right? It was the caffeine.

Other reports began leaking out that Daniel, his eight-year-old son, had fragile X syndrome. I researched the disease, and its symptoms kind of described Daniel (or I convinced my broken soul that they did). Maybe Chris got in a terrible fight with Nancy, and after the unthinkable happened, he thought that nobody would ever be able to take care of Daniel due to his condition and took his life as some sort of mercy killing? That had to be it, right? It was the fragile X.

It turned out Daniel didn't have fragile X, but at the time it made sense because I was grasping at straws.

What can I say about this picture? It breaks my heart to see it. I remember how much fun Daniel, Ryosuke (Funaki), and Ash had that day backstage at *WrestleMania XXI* in Los Angeles. They were running around all over the place and just being kids. May God bless his innocent soul.

I spent most of the night on the floor in Ash's room, watching him sleep, listening to him breathe, wanting to be close to him. I sat in the dark surfing the Net, researching every detail and texting others who were close to Chris. I talked to his riding partners, Travis Tomko and Chavo Guererro. I spoke to Regal and Dave Penzer, his neighbors in Peachtree City, Georgia. Two things became evident after talking to all of them.

Nobody could explain or understand what had happened, but everyone agreed: (1) Chris was a dark, troubled individual who was bottling up some very serious issues; and (2) he rarely expressed what he was really feeling inside.

I think that's part of why he was such an amazing performer. He took out all his aggression and insecurities on his opponents in the ring and during his workouts. He became an unemotional machine whose sole release was to have the best match and the most muscular body.

But what had caused him to go off the deep end? Why did he snap and commit such a wicked atrocity? Was it steroids? No chance—this heinous act stemmed from something much deeper than roid rage. This wasn't some gassed-up gronk punching someone in the face after being cut off on a side street. This was a disturbed individual dealing with severe mental problems.

Was it pills or alcohol? Side effects of multiple concussions? Personally, I think it was a combination of a number of things that caused him to snap—a deadly cocktail of steroids, painkillers, and caffeine abuse, combined with depression, paranoia, repeated blows to the head, and the fact that he kept his emotions and feelings locked up inside. That had to be it, right? It was a combination of all of these things.

Another factor that could have sent him over the edge was the staggering number of personal losses he had suffered over the last few years. On September 22, 2004, the day that The Big Bossman Ray Traylor passed away, Chris called me crying.

"I can't take it anymore, Chris. I can't take any more of my friends dying," he sobbed. "It's not supposed to be like this! I can't handle any more of my friends leaving me!"

Between the deaths of Bossman and other close friends like Owen Hart, Brian Pillman, and Davey Boy Smith, Chris had suffered so many losses in just a few short years that he had reached the end of his rope.

But it only got worse when he lost three of his absolute best friends in the course of three months. Eddy died in November 2005, followed by his close confidant Johnny Grunge in January 2006. Then his trainer from Japan, Black Cat Victor Mar, passed away a month later. Chris was never the same after that.

In life, best friends Eddy and Chris couldn't be more parallel.

They both grew up loving wrestling and learned their trade around the world before ending up as two of the best performers in the history of the business. They were regarded as great people, great fathers, and locker room leaders who had the respect of their peers.

But in death, best friends Eddy and Chris couldn't be more different.

Eddy died a hero, a reformed drug addict with the heart of a champion who was taken from us too early. Whenever Eddy's name is mentioned, people smile fondly and remember how great a person he was and nothing else.

But his legacy will live on forever as a revered hero who loved his family. His classic matches have been glorified by the WWE to be watched for years to come, and his name is lionized within the industry, never to be forgotten.

Then there was the other side of the coin.

Benoit died a murderer, a psychotic madman who killed his wife and seven-year-old son before cowardly killing himself. Whenever Chris's name is mentioned, people get silent and remember the atrocities he committed during the last day of his life and nothing else. His legacy will live on forever as that of a demented monster who executed his family. His classic matches have been buried by the WWE, never to be seen again, and his name is taboo within the industry, never to be spoken.

The triple homicide was being talked about worldwide and people wanted answers as to how something like this could happen. The media was on a witch hunt for anything Benoit and everything wrestling. The government joined in soon after, arranging inquests and investigations into the entire industry, trying to shut it down.

Soon every has-been, never-was, and wanna-be wrestler looking for some sort of face time was put on national TV as an authority on the business. Touted as "experts," these charlatans were encouraged to give their inside opinions on things they knew nothing about. I watched them come out of the woodwork, the majority of them more concerned with putting themselves over than discussing what had really happened.

One after another they paraded past my screen: Marc Mero, Brian Christopher, Ultimate Warrior, Chyna, Billy

Graham, Jacques Rougeau, Debra Marshall, each one of them more inane and irrelevant than the last.

Bill O'Reilly and Geraldo jumped on the anti-wrestling bandwagon, spewing whatever kind of bullshit that came to mind, while their producers did no research whatsoever. The majority of people watching who knew nothing about the business just assumed that what they were hearing about steroids, drug use, and inhumane conditions from a collection of bitter, vindictive hustlers was the truth.

I was mad as hell and wasn't going to take it anymore.

After declining half a dozen interview requests, I decided it was time to break my silence. Time to explain to the unwashed masses who Chris Benoit really was. I felt that I owed it to him and his remaining children to explain that there was another side to this man.

They knew him as a psycho killer and a sinister fiend. I knew him as a good father, a good husband, a big brother, a mentor, a confidant, and most important one of my best friends. I needed to tell people that.

I needed assurance, so I called my dad, who told me I should do it for Chris. "You owe it to him to tell the world what kind of a person he really was."

Then I called Vince to ask for his opinion. Whether I was ever going to work for him again or not, I needed to hear his advice as a boss and a friend.

"I think it's a good idea, Chris, and you're the perfect guy to do it. You're smart and well-spoken and you know Benoit and this business very well."

With both of their blessings I agreed to do only three shows: Nancy Grace, Greta Van Susteren, and Larry King. I only wanted to do the biggest programs with hosts who didn't have an agenda. I had no problem being asked the hard questions, but I didn't want to deal with hosts who would put me behind the eight-ball and try to crucify me right from the start.

I also refused to do any shows where other wrestlers were appearing. I wasn't there to debate anybody, I was there to tell my side of the story. I wasn't interested in getting into an argument with a jaded former employee of the WWE who had some kind of vendetta against the McMahons or the business.

The shows went well and I think I did a good job of painting a different picture of Chris, by demonstrating that not all wrestlers were yelling, screaming buffoons. I explained with pathos and gravity that he was a loving father and a tremendous positive influence on everyone he met within the business. I told both Grace and King that I trusted Chris so completely I would've left my own children with him without any reservations. I did the best I could to add a little humanity to the monster and prove that he did have friends who loved and believed in him.

After the tragedy I spoke to Chris's father a few times and he encouraged me to call Chris's other son, David. I'd known David since he was four years old and always got a kick out of how much he loved wrestling. Chris and I enjoyed watching him get completely immersed in a match, dutifully cheering the good guys and booing the bad guys. I felt that I owed him a call, and after a few days I finally got up the nerve to phone him. Before he answered, I thought, "What do you say to a fourteen-year-old kid whose father had just murdered his half brother and stepmother and then killed himself?"

When David picked up the phone, it was obvious he was still in shock. He didn't have much to say and I did the majority of the talking. I asked him how and what he was doing, but his answers were one-word and stoic.

I eventually broached the subject of his father, telling him, "I just wanted you to know that no matter what happened at the end of his life, for the majority of it your dad was a good man. Please don't let this horrible tragedy dictate the rest of your life. You could let this take you down a very dark path. You have to rise above it."

I was trying my hardest to be comforting, but my words felt hollow. I sounded just like the cop who talked me out of killing Danny after my mom's accident seventeen years earlier, and I wonder if that guy felt as much of an asshole as I did right then.

When I was finished David responded with one question.

"Can I still go to the wrestling matches?"

It completely broke my heart to think that David's whole life was his father and wrestling and in one night he lost them both. Quite honestly, that's the reason that I'll never be able to forgive Chris for what he did. As horrible as it was that he killed Daniel, it's even worse that he forced David and his daughter, Megan, to deal with his unexplained crimes for the rest of their lives.

Benoit never defended anything he did and lived with a real "don't ask, don't tell" mindset. Whenever I asked him a question that he didn't want to answer he would always say, "Ask me no questions and I'll tell you no lies." That was him. He felt that he didn't need to explain himself to anyone for the choices he made. But it's a shame he felt the same way towards the two children he left behind.

Here it is years later and still nobody knows what exactly happened on June 23, 2007. If you're looking for more details of that unspeakable night (or day), you need to read another book, because they're irrelevant to my story and you're not going to find them here.

What is relevant is that I'll always remember the man who was my biggest influence in wrestling and who I strived to be like. I'll always love the kind, funny, excitable, supportive, levelheaded, polite, and humble man whom I trusted more than anyone I've ever met in this business. But I'll always despise the man who murdered his family and ruined his entire legacy in the last days of his life.

Only God knows why Chris did what he did. My pastor Chris Bonham told me, "If someone is possessed by a demon God doesn't judge them or hold them accountable for the horrible acts they commit." I hope that's true, because a Chris Benoit possessed by evil spirits causing him to commit such hideous acts makes about as much sense as any of the other theories I've heard, and that's the one I'm going with. Nothing else can explain how such a pure-hearted person could do what he did.

Like everything else in life, as soon as the next tragedy occurred (a mineshaft collapsed in Virginia) the media forgot about Chris Benoit, and the government inquests into the wrestling business quickly went away. Not long after that, the WWE erased Chris Benoit from their memory forever, and I don't blame them—he almost brought the entire company down.

But I'll never be able to erase Chris Benoit from my memory, and his actions still haunt me every single day.

CHAPTER 47

The Paul Is Dead
of Wrestling

Before Chris died, I was gung-ho (Anthrax) to return to the WWE. After writing *A Lion's Tale* (which debuted at number 22 on the *New York Times* best-seller list) and seeing Cena and Michaels tear it up, I knew it was time. But after the maelstrom of emotions I went through after Benoit's passing, I started to second-guess whether it was worth it. Since I had left the WWE only twenty-five months earlier, Eddy Guerrero and Chris Benoit, two of my best friends in the business, had died; Mike Lozanski, one of my oldest friends in the business, had died; Jerry Palko, the man who had taken me into his family when I first moved to Okotoks to train with the Hart Brothers, had died; my mother had died; my grandmother had died; even my dog Blaze had died. All of those losses had changed me. I wasn't the same person as when I left, and I didn't know if I wanted to return after all.

But by defending the industry on the talk shows and becoming its unofficial spokesman, I realized who I was.

I was a professional wrestler and always had been.

Much like a bullying big brother who protects his little brother in the schoolyard, I could say derogatory things about wrestling if I wanted to, but there was no way I was going to let anybody else bag on it. I wasn't going to allow people to verbally trash the business and demean the sacrifices that me and my peers made to entertain millions of people all across the world. The WWE once again needed a savior to bring the business back to where it was before the tragedy.

Another reason I wanted to return was because I felt I was the last of a literally dying breed. I had been a part of a small group of performers who had learned the art of the business in different countries around the world, and almost all of us were gone.

Owen, Davey, Pillman, Chris, and Eddy were dead. All the luchadores were back in Mexico with the exception of Rey. Lance, Dean, and Ultimo Dragon had retired, and to the average fan so had Chris Jericho.

Except I hadn't retired and I never claimed to. I just needed a break to recharge my batteries so I could come back better than ever, and I was ready to do that. It was my duty.

Dixie Carter, the president of TNA Wrestling, had been calling me ever since I left the WWE. She made it quite clear that her rival company was interested in bringing me in and wanted to have (take) a meeting with me at my leisure. I had no intention of working anywhere but the WWE, but I figured it couldn't hurt to have a meeting. It also wouldn't hurt to use TNA's interest to give me a bit of leverage with Vince.

So I agreed to meet Dixie and her right-hand man, Jeff Jarrett, for lunch in Tampa. We had a good meeting, but it didn't dissuade me from going back to the WWE even though I was excited for them and their organization. After all, the better TNA did, the better it was for the whole business. For the first time since Vince bought WCW, he had some competition.

Barry Bloom and I had been negotiating with the WWE for weeks and couldn't come to an agreement. I had a certain dollar figure in mind that I wanted in order to come back, and they were hesitant to give it to me. So after my meeting with Dixie, I had Chad type up an email asking if Chris Jericho was going to TNA since he had just seen him eating lunch with Jeff Jarrett and Dixie Carter in Tampa. He signed it Ralph Molina (the drummer of Neil Young's Crazy Horse), and wisely sent it off to a few prominent wrestling websites.

The news spread quickly, and suddenly the magic number was soon agreed upon. That meant everything to me, as it proved that Vince saw me as a major player, something I hadn't felt for the last few years I worked for him.

Two weeks later I signed my contract, and for the first time in twenty-six months I was once again an employee of the WWE. All thanks to the assist from Ralph Molina.

I wanted to make my return to the WWE as unique and impactful as my debut was eight years earlier. I didn't want to repeat the countdown clock again, so I was looking for something a little more cryptic. Then the idea struck to use the phrase "Second Coming," while incorporating the black-and-green binary codes I'd seen while watching *The Matrix* a few nights earlier.

I flew to WWE headquarters in Stamford to meet with Vince and Brian and pitch them my concept. My idea was a four-week run of vignettes that would begin with the binary codes filling the screen with computer-generated 2s. In the second week all but one of the 2s would disappear. Then in the third week the 2 would grow to the size of the screen and morph into the words "2econd Coming." I would show up on the fourth week and make my grand return. Vince listened to my ideas, nodded, and agreed to the concept in about two minutes. His only caveat was that he wanted the vignettes to run for more than four weeks.

"The longer, the better," he said, and then he talked about old-time wrestling and Bobo Brazil for the next half hour.

I met with Stephanie, Kevin Dunn, and Adam Penucci (who had created the graphics to my original countdown clock) to discuss the details of the vignettes. We decided to change the color from green to blue (to avoid any comparisons with DX) and Adam came up with a slogan of "Save_Us.222" to be buried in the middle of a jumbled jungle of blue-and-white computer graphics. Adam then created the first teaser, which was going to run the following Monday night on *Raw*.

It was time to party like it was 1999.

I wanted to be in the best shape of my life for my return, so for the first time I enlisted the services of a personal trainer in Tampa, Chris Gonzales, who tortured my body until he got the results we both desired. I also thought it would be a smart move to work off some of the ring rust I'd accrued over the last two years by going back to Calgary to train right where it all started. The Hart Brothers Camp was long gone, but it had been replaced by an even more esteemed school run by my oldest friend in the business and first ever opponent, Lance T. Storm. He was the best trainer I knew and the only guy I trusted to help me get back into ring shape.

I flew to Calgary to attend the Storm Wrestling Academy, and what an impressive facility it was. The academy was housed in an expansive warehouse decorated with giant hanging banners advertising various PPVs, which Lance had acquired while working for the WWE as a trainer a few years prior. He'd installed a world-class ring and a nice lounge in the front of the building with a DVD player where students could study classic matches. This place blew the pink bowling alley where Lance and I trained out of the water!

Moments after I arrived I sat down on a plush couch and changed into my training gear of a white tank top, black spandex New Japan shorts, and Trace knee pads.

Then it was time to put on my boots. As dusty as they were when I had taken them off the shelf at my house, they had seemed to magically reboot themselves (real groaner). It was as if they had gotten newer since I'd rescued them from the darkness of the closet, like they were a footwear version of Christine.

I laced them up and they felt clunkier than a pair of Paul Stanley Starchild boots, but after a few steps they began to feel like a part of me again. Then I made my way to the ring to re-acquaint myself with my old battleground. I had grown up within these ropes, and now that I was an older man it was time to try my luck with the surly wizard yet again.

I climbed inside and hit the cables a few times. They were a little tighter than I remembered, a little less forgiving, but after a few crisscrosses they seemed to loosen up a bit. It was like riding a bike—if a bike bounced back and forth within a twelve foot-radius. Then I thought about taking a bump, but it had been such a long time and I was a little tentative. What would it feel like? How would my body react? Would it hurt?

After my warm-up, Lance invited his students into the ring and started his drills. I watched in silence, giving tips when I could and getting the feel of being back in a ring again.

And the feeling was good.

Being around these kids who had given up everything to follow their dreams reminded me of a certain canary-yellow-haired kid who had done the same thing seventeen years earlier. Their enthusiasm for the business fanned the flames of my renewed passion and inspired me to get off my ass and start bumping.

One student who had named himself Fighting Action Guy (you figure it out) was having problems learning how to take a fast-snapping back bump, and I decided I would step in and show him how it was done. Lance shot me off the ropes and I hit them with authority, running like a juggernaught straight into his elbow. I threw myself back as fast as I could and took my first bump since the Attitude Adjustment from Cena two years earlier.

It almost killed me.

My body threatened to shatter into a million pieces

like a frozen T-1000 and my head wanted to explode like a thirteen-year-old's wet dream. I lay on the mat, not wanting to let the young boys know that the mighty Chris Jericho had almost taken a dumpski in his spandex. Thankfully the next bump wasn't quite as bad (I just peed myself), and the one after that felt almost normal. Then after the class ended, Lance and I wrestled a ten-minute match with Lance calling, and I felt my (stuck) mojo begin to return.

Lance helped me regain my confidence in 2007 the same way he helped me find it in 1990, and I can't thank him enough for both.

One of the things that was missing from my first run in the WWE was an explosive finish that I could hit from out of nowhere, à la the Stone Cold Stunner or the RKO. The Walls was a submission move and the Lionsault took too long to set up. I needed something new.

After some intense thought I came up with a move I'd never seen, a bulldog into a DDT-type maneuver that I wanted to call the Boomstick (a homage to Bruce Campbell in *Army of Darkness*). Less than a week later, I almost had an aneurism when I saw WWE Diva Candice Michelle use my new move as her finisher on *Raw*. Even worse, she named it the "Candy Wrapper."

What does that even mean?

Back to the drawing board . . .

A few weeks later I was watching a DVD from an independent company called *Ring of Honor*. A Japanese wrestler named Marufuji hit this move in the middle of the match where he jumped into the air and grabbed the back of his opponent's head, driving it into his knees. I jumped out of my chair thinking, "Secret Squirrel! That is the frootest move I have ever seen and I shall now steal it for my new finish!"

I showed it to Lance while we were training and he thought it was perfect.

"What are you going to call it?" he asked.

"The Boomstick!" I replied enthusiastically.

"Boomstick?" Lance deadpanned disgustedly. "That name sucks."

It was 1990 all over again.

Somewhere in a parallel universe where Lance Storm does not exist, there is a famous wrestler named Jack Action who defeats his opponent every night with the dreaded Boomstick.

The following Monday the first "Save Us" vignette played and the speculation started immediately about who it was referring to. My phone blew up with calls and texts asking if it had anything to do with me. Cena texted me right after it aired and said that if the vignette was indeed signaling my comeback, he would fly to the ring on the head of a dragon to wrestle me when I returned.

The trailer was an amazing fifteen-second riddle that said nothing of note, but was enough to get everyone talking. Some fans thought that I was behind the teaser, but nobody really knew for sure. They searched for clues, watching it repeatedly on YouTube and analyzing it frame by frame.

I became the "Paul Is Dead" of wrestling—people were finding Jericho clues in the computer scramble that didn't exist. One fan claimed to have seen the date 10-27-03 in the alphabet soup, which was the date I won the Intercontinental Championship for the seventh time. Another found numbers representing a Bible verse relating to the Walls of Jericho, and yet another fan was convinced the word "Jericho" was being played backwards in the audio mix of the vignette. None of those things were programmed intentionally and Adam Penucci and I knew we were onto something good.

For the next few weeks we crammed the teasers with red-herring clues that made people think that the messages were heralding the return of Shawn Michaels or the debut of a rumored new Hart family stable. We placed legit Bible verse numbers and phrases within them, like "Save Us," "The Second Coming Is Upon Us," and "Can You Break the Code?"

After six weeks Vince decided he wanted to hold off my return even longer to make it as impactful as possible. I was getting paid, so it didn't bother me even though fans had pretty much figured out that I was the one behind the bits and were chanting my name at shows.

When Cena tore his pectoral muscle and wasn't able to wrestle Randy Orton at *No Mercy* in Chicago, Vince had to announce a replacement on the PPV. He got in the ring and told the fans, "I always give you people what you want, and I'm going to give that to you tonight."

The arena exploded with "Y2J" chants that were so loud they threw old Vincenzo off his game, forcing him to acknowledge them.

He looked like someone had just pissed on his toupee as he said, "Well, I'm not going to give you *that*."

To fuel the speculation, I started posting misleading items on my website to make people guess if my return was ever going to take place. If *Raw* was taking place in

Philadelphia, I would say I was taping VH1's *I Love the 60s* in New York City. I wanted to keep the cat in the bag for as long as I could, even though at that point my return was a worse-kept secret than Clay Aikens's sexuality.

In the three weeks leading up to my return, the clues became more advanced; instead of "Save_Us.222," the phrase now became "Save_Us.X29." Despite all the clues the fans had found, this X29 code was the one that gave them the most problems. It was a pattern that was deciphered like this: if you added one letter to each of the characters you would get X + 1 = Y and 9 + 1 = 10. The tenth letter of the alphabet is J. Therefore, "Save_Us.Y2J."

Wow. After typing that, maybe it is more complicated than I thought. No wonder nobody figured it out. I feel like a real 9-D-17-J!

Finally, to erase any confusion and eliminate any further doubts on when my return would be, the last vignette simply said, "Next week the Second Coming arrives."

In the two years since I'd left the WWE, I had changed my look considerably. The Y2J that had captured the fans' imagination was a wildly dressed rock star with multiple earrings and chest-length blond hair—hair that was now cut short. I was wondering how people would react to this new-look Jericho, as I knew how I felt when James Hetfield and Bruce Dickinson cut their hair. It threw me off, and even though nothing had changed about their music (*Load* notwithstanding in James's case), I didn't relate to them or like them as much. I felt a disconnect toward them and I wondered if my fans would feel the same way about me as a result of my new 'do.

I also wanted to come back with a whole new look wardrobe-wise. I saw Sting on the cover of *Rolling Stone* (Dr. Hook like a maafaaakaa!), wearing a wifebeater/vest combination that I thought looked really froot. But being Chris Jericho, I couldn't wear just any vest, so I found a tuxedo shop that specialized in flashy ones and ordered a dozen of them in different colors. I bought a pair of black skintight jeans and black boots to match, and voilà!

The new-look Jericho was complete.

My return was going to take place on the November 19, 2007, edition of *Raw* from Fort Lauderdale, and I was so nervous that I drove down from Tampa the night before. I wrote a lengthy promo about how I was going to save the WWE just as I had done the first time around in 1999 and spent the better part of the night working on it. I'd contacted Zakk, to record an updated version of my "Break Down the Walls" theme song for my return, but Kevin Dunn didn't care for it and wasn't convinced he wanted to use it for my first night in. (He never did use it and I'm one of the only people who's ever heard it. It's on my iPod right now.)

There were so many details to go over, but Brian and I had decided that we would protect the secret of my return for as long as possible and keep me from showing up at the arena until after the show started, the same way Cena had when he made his secret debut on *Raw* over two years earlier.

The storyline for my return was that Randy Orton, the World Champion, had organized his own ceremony where he would demand that the torch of the WWE be literally passed on to him. Brian and I had come up with the idea of having an Olympic runner come all the way from Miami to Fort Lauderdale carrying the flame of the WWE. He would run straight into the arena, but I would get involved before he could pass the torch over to Randy. Then I'd attack the champ and hit him with my new finisher, which I had named the Codebreaker (with Lance's approval, of course).

I spent the day driving around the arena listening to the Doors, memorizing my promo, and trying to quell my nervous energy. I was fiddling with my tie, as I'd decided as part of my new image that I would wear a suit to work every day. A few years earlier the WWE had implemented a dress code that I fought tooth and nail. I was a rock star, dammit! I didn't dress in business casual clothes! But I had matured during my time away from the company and figured that wearing a suit wasn't so bad. Vince dressed in a suit every day, and if it was good enough for him, it was good enough for me. So I became the dress codebreaker. Good one, eh?

(Ironic Author's Note: It wasn't until I arrived at the arena that I found out they had abolished the dress code a month earlier. I was back to wearing my rock-star clothes within weeks.)

I needed to find a mall though, because earlier in the day as I was getting pimped out in my fancy new Hugo Boss suit I realized that I forgot my Prada dress shoes at home. Therefore I needed to buy a new pair of shoes, but there was no rush since I wasn't needed at the arena until after *Raw* started at 9 p.m., right?

As if on cue I got a call from Brian telling me I was needed at the arena immediately, because Vince wanted to explain what he wanted me to do that evening in person.

Doh! All I had to wear with my fancy new suit was a pair of cowboy boots, and I couldn't walk into the venue wearing those.

Who was I, JBL?

I found a T.J. Maxx on the way to the building and hurriedly bought a pair of cheap dress shoes for $29.99, polishing kit included. So I walked into the arena for my first day of work wearing a thousand-dollar suit and thirty-dollar shoes.

When I arrived, Vince gave me a big hug and complimented me on my sharp new threads. Luckily he didn't look at my feet.

Vince wanted to know what I was going to say that night, so I recited my perfectly written, well-crafted promo for him. He listened intently and promptly cut it in half.

"We don't want to hear too much from you tonight. Less is more."

Well the audience sure as hell wanted to hear from me, as "Y2J" chants filled the arena during the entire show. Throughout the course of the program, cutaways of the torch runner progressing toward the arena aired. Just as he was about to arrive, Orton went to the ring and began cutting a promo heralding the runner's entrance.

The sprinter made his way off the highway, across the parking lot, through the backstage entrance, and to Randy's bliss was about to run up the flight of steps that would bring him into the arena. Suddenly a dark figure stepped out of the shadows and leveled the poor son of a bitch with a vicious clothesline. The audience was taken by surprise and shrieked in shock at the force of the blow—I mean this guy really took the poor runner's head off. The camera panned up from the motionless carcass to reveal a sparkly vested form with his arms held out by his side in a familiar Jesus Christ pose.

I'd been worried about how the crowd would react for my return, but my worries were for naught. The roar of the fans ignited me and I instantly transformed into Chris Jericho.

It had been a while and I missed the crazy bastard.

Becoming Jericho again was like putting on a favorite pair of jeans that I thought I had lost—a little tight at first, but within minutes it felt like I never took them off.

Orton reacted and there was fear in his viperlike eyes, as the alphanumeric "Save_Us.X29" appeared on the Tron and the X started spinning like a Vegas slot machine before finally settling on Y.

Save_Us.Y29

The crowd buzzed like a fistful of bees, knowing exactly where this was going, as the 9 began spinning into a 10 and then morphed into a J.

Save_Us.Y2J

The wait was over. For the audience and for me.

It had been a long hard road that led me to the WWE the first time, and it had been just as long and hard a road that led me back.

I walked up the stairs to the Gorilla position as the countdown began...

Acknowledgments

I'd like to first thank God and Jesus Christ for allowing me to write another one of these bad boys! Jesus Rocks!

If I included everyone's name who has been an influence or an ally to me over the last three years in these thank-you's, the list would take up the entire book and have to be printed microscopically, probably giving everyone who read it cataracts. Besides, nobody except for the people whose names are on the list really care about thank-you lists anyways. So, here's a froot thumbs-up to all of my family, friends, confidants, band members and business associates who have believed in me!

However, I would like to personally thank Jessica, Ash, Cheyenne, Sierra Irvine, Ted Irvine, Joan Irvine, Chad Holowatuk, Todd Holowatuk, and Dave Spivak for being the best family a guy could have!

I'd also like to thank Pete Fornatale, Ben Greenberg, Bob Castillo, Tanisha Christie, and Flamur Tonuzi for helping me to create another killer book!

Finally, I'd like to thank the following auteurs for taking some of the photos used in this book: Jessica Irvine,

Ed Aborn, Ian Nicol, Michael Lacey, Bruno Lauer, Paul Gargano, Ryan Ahoff, The Rock, Chris Jericho, Speewee, Henry Di Rocco, Brian Bird, Glen Butler, John Howarth, and Dan Winters.

CJ

Bonus Acknowledgments

There are all kinds of different co-writing setups. In the case of my collaboration with Chris, *co-writing* isn't even the right word. Our dynamic is more like that of producer and recording artist: I'm involved from the start, I brainstorm, I organize, I help select material, I edit. But the writing is all his. Chris, it's been a pure pleasure working with you.

Another note: We know what Vince McMahon's wrestling company was called in 1999 but for simplicity's sake, we're calling it the WWE throughout.

I would like to thank my friend Ron Epstein for his assistance in putting this book together. And thanks to Rich Bienstock for his musical knowledge.

It's been great working with Benjamin Greenberg and Bob Castillo and all the folks at Grand Central Publishing.

And to my wife, Susan Van Metre, I'd just like to say you are the best.

PTF

VISIT US ONLINE AT

WWW.HACHETTEBOOKGROUP.COM

FEATURES:

OPENBOOK BROWSE AND
SEARCH EXCERPTS

•

AUDIOBOOK EXCERPTS AND PODCASTS

•

AUTHOR ARTICLES AND INTERVIEWS

•

BESTSELLER AND PUBLISHING
GROUP NEWS

•

SIGN UP FOR E-NEWSLETTERS

•

AUTHOR APPEARANCES AND TOUR
INFORMATION

•

SOCIAL MEDIA FEEDS AND WIDGETS

•

DOWNLOAD FREE APPS